"Police
PATROL
Operations "

Mark R. Miller

COPPERHOUSE PUBLISHING COMPANY

901-5 Tahoe Blvd.
Incline Village, Nevada 89451
(702) 833-3131

Your Partner in Education
with
"QUALITY BOOKS AT FAIR PRICES"

Police
PATROL
Operations

2 3 4 5 6 7 8 9 10

Library of Congress Catalog Number 95-67382
ISBN 0-942728-59-9 Paper Text Edition

Printed in the United States of America.

DEDICATION

To Judith Ann, my best friend.

TABLE OF CONTENTS

CHAPTER 7
VEHICLE OPERATIONS 167

CHAPTER 13

COURTROOM PROCEDURES 363

PREFACE

Police Patrol Operations was written to satisfy the material requirements of courses dealing with the modern patrol function and techniques in both college coursework and academy training.

What makes *Police Patrol Operations* different from other books in this field is the way the information is presented. By using the first person style of writing, I've endeavored to draw the reader into the role of a modern day patrol officer. With the insight afforded me as a current patrol officer in a mid-sized agency, you will gain a practical insight into the function of patrol along with the ancillary support services provided by the department and community-at-large.

At the beginning of each chapter you'll find stories of some of the "routine" situations you'll encounter out in the field. Some are funny, others are sad—but all are real. The point of their inclusion is to reinforce the idea that anything can and will happen during the course of your career and you must remain alert to the possibility of the improbable.

Missing from this book is the sterile view of patrol that breaks down the function to little more than theory and concept. At the conclusion of reading this book you will have gained a working knowledge of patrol—the good, the bad, and the ugly. You'll be lead through the material from the standpoint of the author as the FTO (Field Training Officer) and you as the rookie. Theories and concepts are supplemented with real-world experience so as to produce an excellent understanding of the patrol function and a more well-rounded appreciation for the total environment within which a modern patrol officer must function.

Mark R. Miller

ACKNOWLEDGEMENTS

No book is ever written in a vacuum, and every author has many debts owed to others. First and foremost, I'd like to thank my wife Judith without whose help, constant support, and ability to keep my children Joshua and Katie away from my computer, this book would never have been completed.

I would also like to thank Derald Hunt, my developmental editor, for tracking me down and making me write this book. His knowledge and constant guidance proved essential.

This book would have been impossible without the support of Chief Thomas Mahoney and the assistance of the officers of the South Pasadena Police Department. All of you have my sincere thanks for your help and encouragement with this project.

A special thanks goes to Lieutenant Bill Gitmed of the Cathedral City Police Department, my friend and former Field Training Officer, who taught me more than he will ever know about community policing and what it means to be a police officer.

Thanks to all the thousands of people that I have talked to, assisted, arrested, cited, fought with, chased, or otherwise contacted in my career. Each and every one has been a learning experience and is reflected in this book.

I would also like to thank those involved in the critical review of the manuscript. Dr. Dan Dale, Albert Lugo, and Vince Leone provided great help in organizing and focusing my thoughts.

Also, thank you for the support from the following agencies:

Sacramento Police Department

Houston Police Department

Costa Mesa Police Department

Pasadena Police Department

Broward County Sheriff's Department

St. Paul Police Department

THE
PATROL FUNCTION
average time utilization

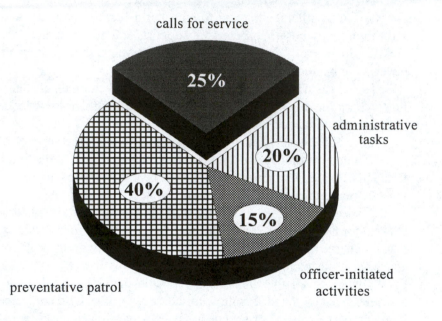

calls for service

25%

administrative
tasks

20%

40%

15%

preventative patrol

officer-initiated
activities

*The latest issue of the "Jobs Rated Almanac"
rates the job of president of the United States at
241 out of 250. Jobs rated slightly lower included
roofer and meter-reader, while jobs rated slightly
better included boiler-maker and police officer.
Worst scores for the presidency were in the
categories of outlook, job stress, and security.*

INTRODUCTION

LEARNING GOALS: After studying this chapter the student will be able to:

- Define the basic function and purpose of police patrol.

- Describe a law enforcement *mission statement*, and explain its purpose.

- Discuss the legal and Constitutional basis for all police powers.

- List the historical "milestones" that were important in the development of modern law enforcement.

- Explain how typical public perceptions of the police are shaped and changed.

- Describe the basis of police resources allocation and deployment in the typical community.

- Analyze factors which must be considered in determining the quality of patrol services appropriate for the community.

THE POLICE: WHO ARE THEY?

In its broadest sense, the term *police* refers to *any* branch of government charged with the preservation of public order and tranquility, the promotion of public health, safety and morals, and the prevention, detection, and punishment of crimes. The members of our law enforcement agencies wear many titles — police officer, peace officer, deputy sheriff, state trooper, deputy marshal, highway patrolman, constable, inspector, and federal agent are but a few of the more common ones.

Mission Statement

Almost every law enforcement agency has a *mission statement* which outlines the goals and purpose of the organization. Some mission statements are brief and clearly defined. Others are couched in flowery idealism and politically correct buzzwords. A few go on for pages in great detail about every conceivable function of the agency. These mission or goal statements typically include the agency's stated policies in the prevention of criminal and delinquent behavior and the repression and investigation of crime.

Ultimately, no matter how lengthy or confusing a mission statement may be, they all mean exactly the same thing which is: *"Our goal is to protect the lives and property of the people we serve."* That is the core value—the fundamental ideal—of police patrol. Many patrol cars have the motto *"To Protect and Serve"* painted on the doors. Basically, that is the job of a patrol officer.

THE BASIS OF POLICE POWER

In the United States the Constitution is the "supreme law of the land." No law enacted by a legislative body or decision made by a court can stand if it is in conflict with the Constitution. The Bill of Rights, which are the first 10 amendments, are also part of the Constitution. They were adopted as part of the Constitution in 1791. We have since added additional amendments for a current total of 26.

Many of the first 10 amendments to the Constitution are important to you as a patrol officer. Of specific importance is the First Amendment right to free speech; the Sixth Amendment right to trial by a jury of our peers and the right to counsel; and the Fifth Amendment right against self-incrimination. But by far the greatest impact on police officers comes from the Fourth Amendment which deals with the issuance of warrants, the concept of probable cause, and the right of citizens to be free from unreasonable searches and seizures. Most state constitutions echo and often expand on these same fundamental rights.

As a patrol officer, your basic police powers are conferred on you by the state in which you are employed. States delegate that power to counties and cities via the 10th Amendment to the Constitution. This amendment enables states, and other local governments, to establish a department of police and to adopt such laws and regulations as tend to prevent the commission of crime. They may also adopt laws designed to promote public safety, morals, health, and prosperity by preserving public order and preventing conflict of rights in the conduct of business.

"To protect and serve" — the bottom line of police work.

Police Power Limitations

Your police powers are subject to the limitations of the federal and state constitutions and are strictly subject to "due process" (right to a public hearing) requirements.

> *Police power* is the exercise of the sovereign right of any government to promote order, safety, health, morals, and the general welfare within constitutional limits. Misuse of police power often constitutes a violation of another persons federal civil rights. If you go beyond the scope of your powers, you may well find yourself unemployed and on the wrong side of a civil rights lawsuit.

Statutory and Case Law

Most of the powers law enforcement officers use are not spelled out in the Constitution, but they are defined by statutory law and case law. *Statutes* are the actual laws which appear in various codes such as the Penal Code, Vehicle Code, Health and Safety Code, and the Welfare and Institutions code, to name a few. For example, the state of California has 26 separate codes covering topics from veteran's affairs to harbors and navigation. Some of these codes occupy more than a dozen volumes. As if these thousands and thousands of laws weren't enough, *case law* actually represents the majority of the laws under which patrol officers operate.

Case law represents actual cases that have gone to trial and been decided in the state and federal courts. They are records of how the courts *interpreted* the application of statutory law to specific circumstances based on the Constitution. As an example, everyone has heard of the so-called *Miranda Rights*. These rights weren't originally codified in law, but came about as a result of case law interpreting the Fifth Amendment which states that a person "shall not be compelled in any criminal case to be a witness against himself."

In 1966, the United States Supreme Court decided that police officers had a specific duty to warn persons suspected in a crime about their specific Constitutional rights whenever they were *in custody* and *about to be interrogated*. That ruling has affected every law enforcement officer in the United States in every arrest since that time. Case law is simply a matter of court opinion, and it is an opinion that could be reversed or modified by the court at any time.

EARLY POLICE PATROL IN THE UNITED STATES

Since the United States was populated primarily by European colonists, early policing efforts were modeled after Sir Robert Peel's Metropolitan Police. The Metropolitan Police Force created in London was highly disciplined, wore uniforms and carried billy clubs. It is still considered by many to be the foundation for modern policing.

Night watches, constables, port patrols and watchmen were established fixtures in the early 1600s throughout the colonies. The first organized police service was established in Philadelphia in 1833, while a formal "modern" police force was established (based on the British model) in New York in 1844. Similar law enforcement agencies were established in nearly every major city by the time of the Civil War.

Outside of the major population centers, law enforcement took on different appearances. Throughout the southern United States, the dominant form of law enforcement was the county sheriff and his deputies. This system was well-suited for the needs of a widespread, rural, plantation and farm-based population. Unfortunately, the position of sheriff became highly political and was often totally subservient to the desires of politicians and the wealthy. The elected office of sheriff is still often a hotly contested and highly political position. Sheriff's departments remain the primary providers of law enforcement services in much of the South today.

The Early West

In the West and along the frontiers, law enforcement was far less formalized. Towns sprung up overnight and died almost as rapidly. The population was highly transient and well-armed, and life itself was uncertain and filled with many dangers. Military units concerned themselves with operations against the native Americans and avoided involvement in civilian law activities unless specifically requested.

Western lawmen, often appointed and hired directly by town councils as "marshals" or "sheriffs," served primarily to protect the lives and property of the those who hired them. While many of the frontier officers were brave men of tremendous integrity, many other lawmen were mercenary in spirit. Often the latter enjoyed only brief careers in a succession of towns. Their methods and ethics were virtually indistinguishable from the outlaws.

The gunfight in the streets at high noon rarely ever happened. Most of those stories were the result of fictional accounts in newspapers and penny novels, the popular entertainment of the day. Most accurate accounts of peace officers going after outlaws indicate that they brought overwhelming assistance with them in the form of *posses*. Sometimes they were assisted by federal marshals, railroad police, or private police agencies such as Pinkerton's. Often these posses had little objection to dispatching a murderer by ambush or by lynching rather than worry about the issues of due process, legal niceties, and the transportation of a dangerous prisoner back to the nearest available magistrate.

Interestingly, many newspaper accounts from that era have been preserved and show that those famous frontier officers such as Wyatt Earp and Bat Masterson performed many of the same tasks as do officers today. They also had to deal with some of the same bureaucratic problems and political entanglements. They argued with city councils over pay, the cost of guns and bullets, squabbled over the cost of prisoner's meals, and argued over feed and care for their horses. Amazingly, the situation is much the same today.

Our romanticized notion of western lawmen has them constantly chasing murderers, robbers and horse thieves. In fact, these officers spent the majority of their time mediating business disputes, handling marital squabbles, keeping the streets clear of stray dogs, and locking up local drunks. That's what they were hired for, and those were the demands of the community they served. These men were indeed "peace officers," practicing *community policing* and responding directly to the needs, desires, and concerns of the populations they served.

A Rise in Professionalism

The next hundred years brought about numerous fundamental changes in law enforcement that altered the character of police work and the officers themselves. Following the Spanish-American War, World War I, World War II, the Korean War and the Vietnam War, waves of veterans entered the ranks of police service. The military units in which they had served offered greater training and professional standards of conduct with each conflict. Also, veterans benefits for education brought ever greater levels of education into law enforcement. Police work, which was once an underpaid, low-esteem job, did an "about face" and rapidly became staffed by disciplined, highly-trained combat experienced veterans. August Vollmer, O.W. Wilson and W. H. Parker, just to name a few, were instrumental in upgrading the professionalism of police work and training.

This "new breed" of men and women brought higher standards of behavior and dedication to police agencies. They also brought new expectations of performance and integrity. Many police agencies were restructured along more military lines thus forming a more strict chain of command consisting of successively higher ranks from patrol officer to chief. Intermediate ranks included: corporal, sergeant, lieutenant, captain, major, and colonel (or commander). The civil service concept came into being in many states, eliminating the political appointment of officers. This move helped distance police agencies from the direct control of politicians.

New Technology and Increased Education

Technology made incredible advances during this same time period. Bicycles, automobiles, telephone, mobile radio, portable radios, radar and computers all had tremendous impacts on the ability of police officers to respond to and successfully investigate crimes.

True to the military model that was a common heritage, this new breed of police officer liked structure, discipline, policies, general orders and comprehensive training. In response to demand, federal programs, and the explosive growth of community colleges in the early 1960s, criminal justice programs developed across the nation. Bachelor and master's degree programs were developed at the university level.

Houston Police Department Training Academy

New standards of education were backed up by new standards of training. The Federal Bureau of Investigation played a major role in establishing goals, guidelines, curriculum, standards, and regional training academies for police officers. In the period immediately after World War II, a police officer's entire training might consist of a few days of patrol with a senior officer, after which he was considered "trained." Today, the men and women entering law enforcement must successfully complete rigorous six-month academies and year-long field training programs offering comprehensive training to meet the specific goals of modern police patrol operations.

Organizations such as the International Association of Chiefs of Police (IACP) have helped in the development of standardized model programs, policies, tactics, and training. State commissions such as the California's Peace Officer Standards and Training Commission (POST) create and enforce requirements and standards for the selection and training of police officers. POST also offers successive levels of professional certification recognizing basic, intermediate, and advanced training. By law, and under public demand and scrutiny, law enforcement agencies everywhere are reaching higher standards of performance and professionalism.

MODERN POLICE PATROL

Most law enforcement professionals agree that the patrol officer is the most important, essential, and fundamental person in any law enforcement agency. *Patrol* is simply the concept of a person traveling around a defined jurisdiction, observing the situation and maintaining the safety and security of people and property. It is a universal concept carried out by virtually every nation and government throughout the world.

Patrol officers are on the front lines of law enforcement and carry out its primary functions. Almost every police activity stems from the work done by patrol officers, and every other division or bureau within a police department is dependent on patrol for their existence. Patrol officers take the initial reports that create the paper flow requiring a records bureau. Patrol officers make the initial investigations that supply the basis for the operation of detective bureaus. The employment of patrol officers is what creates the need for police management activities such as personnel and payroll, the deployment of officers to the field creates the need for supervision, and supplying and equipping patrol officers creates the need for support positions in the police administration like captain and chief.

No matter where you go, most patrol officers are obvious because they work in distinctive uniforms. Their mode of transportation be it a patrol car, motorcycle, horse, boat, bike or helicopter is distinctively marked and equipped.

Police Agency Organization

The vast majority of police and sheriff's departments in the United States are very small — generally less than 10 officers. Often the chief or sheriff works the street on patrol as well. In the typical small department, there are no specialized divisions such as juvenile, traffic, or detectives. The two or three patrol officers on duty at any given time are required to handle any situation that arises, with assistance from other agencies possibly many hours away. As a result, patrol officers in smaller jurisdictions tend to be highly trained *generalists*.

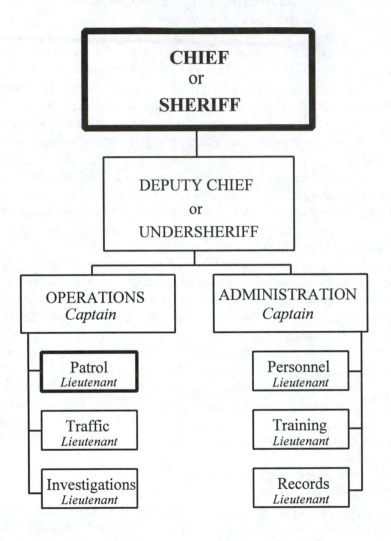

Typical agency organizational chart.

Larger law enforcement agencies often have an incredible variety of specialists available to assist the patrol officer. When a murder occurs, homicide detectives, crime scene specialists, evidence technicians, photographers, and press information officers all descend on the scene. Still, it is you, as a patrol officer, who is first on the scene dealing with suspects and victims, containing witnesses and preserving the crime scene so the specialists can do their work. In an agency loaded with specialists, patrol officers become highly skilled patrol *specialists*.

Similarly, there are specialized law enforcement agencies, but each one still centers on the *patrol* function. In major cities and states you may serve, for example, in the Harbor Patrol, Highway Patrol, Park Police, School Police, or Transit Police. Each agency simply specializes in a unique area or type of patrol they perform.

Regardless of where you work or how your agency operates, to the general public it is the *patrol officer* who represents law enforcement and the presence of the government. When citizens are hurt or in need of assistance, they're looking for a uniformed patrol officer to come to their aid.

THE BACKDROP OF PATROL

If you talk to just about any group of cops, they'll most likely tell you that patrol is the most important thing we do, but typically is the part of the department that receives the least attention. It's the classic case of the tail wagging the dog where patrol is treated like an orphan child in many agencies. In those agencies, it is assumed that the goal of every patrol officer is to get out of patrol, graduating to specialized assignments such as detectives, traffic, SWAT, K-9's, or the bomb squad. Those assignments get extra pay, premium hours, take-home cars, and extra prestige. There is an assumption that you have to "pay your dues" in patrol before you could possibly be qualified to work in any other specialized area. I'm not at all sure that assumption is valid.

In many agencies, patrol is considered to be a dumping ground, and there is an assumption that those officers who spend their entire career in patrol must be lazy, unmotivated, or cause disciplinary problems. Detectives who screw up are often "punished" by being returned to patrol duty. Those in specialized assignments seem to get all the glory, tend to form snobbish cliques within the department, and generally look down their nose at the troops in patrol.

In such agencies, patrol is often the last division in line to receive its share of resources. Patrol gets new cars only after the detectives get theirs. They're the last division to be computerized, the last to receive new radios, the last to get a copier or camera. When the department has people resign or retire, patrol officers are immediately promoted to fill vacancies in detectives, but vacancies in patrol may take forever to fill.

As a patrol officer you'll be doing the most difficult and demanding job in all of law enforcement. Specialization is easy by comparison to the vast knowledge and wide range of skills required of patrol officers. Every day will challenge your knowledge and skills, and your ability to adapt and flexibly apply the training, knowledge and common sense you possess. That makes patrol the hardest job to learn, supervise, and evaluate.

A patrol officer has one of the most dangerous jobs in the police department. With the exception of those serving on high-risk teams, like narcotics or bomb squads, many of the specialized positions in law enforcement are much safer than patrol. Patrol officers are right there on the front line, breaking up fights and making arrests. More patrol officers die in the line of duty in any given year than any other assignment in police work. A successful career in police patrol is a major accomplishment, seldom achieved without a combination of skills, intelligence, courage and, sometimes, just plain luck.

Patrol officers are also on the front lines of civil rights and are at the greatest risk of being sued and generating citizen complaints. Since they are the first ones on the scene, victims' and witnesses' emotions are often running high. Those emotions may alter their perceptions and affect their reactions. In their anger, fear, and frustration, they often unfairly blame those initial response patrol officers for their difficulties. By comparison, by the time the specialists in a department arrive, things have usually calmed down allowing for rational thoughts and rational acts.

Regardless of where you work or how your agency operates, to the general public it is you, the patrol officer, who represents law enforcement and the presence of government. When a citizen is hurt or in need of assistance, he is looking for a uniformed patrol officer to come to his aid. That's you.

PUBLIC PERCEPTIONS: PATROL IN THE MEDIA

Society's perceptions of the police, and the patrol function in general, have been shaped and influenced far more by the media than by reality. Hollywood has always been fascinated by the role of law enforcement in society. This has included silent comedies such as the *Keystone Cops,* elaborate morality plays such as *High Noon*, starring Gary Cooper, and the creation of cop cult heroes such as "Dirty Harry" Callahan and, now, even *Robocop*.

Movies are not the only source of this illusion. Books, magazines and television are all important factors in the public's perception of patrol. Novels featuring some aspect of law enforcement represent a huge segment of the fiction market. The world read about the role and activities of patrol officers through the writings of Dallas Barnes, P.D. James, Joseph Wambaugh and a host of others. From "reality based" books such as *The New Centurions* and *The Choirboys*, people took a jaded view of patrol officers, seeing them as human, fallible, corruptible, and all too mortal.

Probably the greatest impact of all has been television, both in fiction and in fact. Consider the mixed and confusing image of officers presented to the public by programs such as: *Dragnet, Adam-12, Hill Street Blues, Sirens,* and *21 Jump Street*. Is it any wonder that the public has an unrealistic view and expectation of their police?

More recently, the camcorder revolution brought the public a little closer to the truth with so-called "reality" shows. These include programs such as *American Detective, Cops, Real Stories of the Highway Patrol, Rescue 9-1-1, Code-3, Cops*, and *Top Cops*, to name a few. These programs showed a new view of law enforcement — gritty, violent, and frightening. How "real" they are is highly debatable. Some are re-created, using the actual officers and victims when possible. A few of these shows include segments filmed live when it happened. Of course, all such shows are heavily edited to remove the 95 percent that constitutes routine police patrol. Obviously, they concentrate on the tiny percentage of activity that is highly entertaining. Such shows really offer the public only a tiny glimpse of reality and serve only to, again, distort public perception.

To many people, "seeing is believing." They may always believe that the Rodney King videotape proves that excessive force was used. Visual images provide powerful perceptions. Such perceptions are interpreted through our eyes and minds. They are very subjective in nature and are easily altered by a lifetime of experience. It is unfortunate that for many people, the Rodney King videotape will define their view of *all* patrol officers for many years to come.

THE QUALITY OF PATROL SERVICES

Once law enforcement resources have been allocated, someone in authority has to make the decision as to what level and quality of service the public expects, will accept, and can be provided. What response times does the community expect and demand? Will the department spend its resources only on responding to violent crimes, or will they fully investigate every burglary, petty theft, and lost bicycle? Will they devote resources to rounding up truants, towing abandoned autos, locating runaway juveniles, and regulating the use of skateboards? Will officers respond to loud radios and barking dogs? Will the department provide the community with crossing guards, impound stray dogs, and assist persons locked out of their cars? Or do the limited resources of your community require a far lower level and quality of service?

Compare the level of service quality you expect from the police in your city. In major metropolitan areas, the police may be occupied full time simply responding to emergency calls. They generally will not respond to routine calls for service such as non-injury traffic accidents or domestic disturbances. Residential burglary reports are often taken over the phone, and calls for service are often backed up for hours.

Conversely, in many smaller jurisdictions, the police always respond to routine calls for service. They respond to every call within a few minutes, and often provide "courtesy services" such as "lock-outs," escorting local business persons to the bank, vacation house checks, or assisting the elderly or disabled. While the investigation of "petty" crimes in major cities may be quite cursory, the quality of the investigation may be much higher elsewhere.

For example, in a rural county in California, the theft of some stop signs was investigated by calling a crime scene investigator out to the scene, fingerprinting the sign poles, and taking plaster tire tracks in the area. Clearly the citizens of this county are receiving a different level of service than the citizens of a major city where such effort would be reserved for homicides. Obviously, the cost to those taxpayers for the same level of service might be unacceptable.

Consider how much it would cost to sustain a law enforcement effort equal to that in preparation for the Los Angeles riots on a daily basis. To be sure, the citizens would be much safer from crime, but how would the huge presence of police and National Guard troops throughout the city affect the quality of life? How would the quality of life be affected by the huge tax burden? Which is worse — the crime or the cure?

DISCUSSION QUESTIONS

1. Identify all of the law enforcement agencies that have jurisdiction within your community. Who is the primary provider of patrol services?

2. What is the *mission statement* of the law enforcement agency patrolling your community? How effective do you feel this statement is in meeting the needs of your community?

3. As presently interpreted, do you think the Fourth Amendment severely limits the powers of the police? What changes do you think might be appropriate?

4. Of all the television portrayals of police officers, which show do you think is or was the most accurate in its portrayal of patrol officers? What was your favorite show, and why? Which show do you think did the most harm, and most good, to the image of police officers?

5. Did you see the Rodney King videotape? How did what you saw affect your opinion of the LAPD? How did it affect your opinion of police officers in general?

6. What is the ratio of police officers *per capita* in your community? Do you think there should be more or fewer police? Is your jurisdiction spending too much money or not enough on law enforcement services?

7. Based on the quality and level of patrol services in any jurisdictions you are familiar with, which agency would you want to work for and why?

David Nereau, 25, resigned his position as a sheriff's deputy in West Palm Beach, FL, after he was accused by several female motorists of improper policing. It seems that Nereau would stop female motorists and demand to see their breasts, claiming to be after a woman with a distinctive breast tattoo who had just robbed a bank.

2

ETHICS IN LAW ENFORCEMENT

LEARNING GOALS: After studying this chapter, the student will be able to:

- Explain the importance of ethics, values, and principles.

- Discuss the critical importance of the *Law Enforcement Code of Ethics*.

- Apply the *Code of Ethics* to realistic situations in police patrol.

- Discuss the ethical use of deadly force by police officers.

- Describe the public's perception of police ethics.

- Analyze civil litigation in relation to police misconduct.

DEFINITION AND DIMENSIONS OF ETHICS

Ethics, values, principles, morals, integrity — such words and terms have become "buzzwords" within contemporary culture. They have become almost meaningless words that are casually thrown about by beleaguered politicians and flamboyant talk-show hosts. While the words may have lost meaning in our society, they have certainly not lost their importance. America still strives to hold society to "moral values."

The United States senate has an "Ethics Committee," the American Bar Association has "Canons of Judicial Ethics" and a "Code of Professional Responsibility," doctors throughout the world swear to the "Hippocratic Oath," and young men swear to the "Boy Scout Oath." Almost every profession, trade, corporation and organization has a specialized moral code defining the "ethical behavior" required of its members.

Despite these solemn and public oaths, the news is full of compromised senators, disgraced ministers, disbarred attorneys, and doctors stripped of their licenses. One of the most popular television shows in history, the venerable *Sixty Minutes,* has continued to fascinate America by its almost weekly focus on unethical and immoral behavior. Our lack of ethics is scandalous, everybody talks about it, yet very few people understand the concept of ethics or its application to their own lives.

In law enforcement you will be expected to maintain some of the highest ethical standards in our society. Patrol officers are highly visible members of our community and are constantly being watched by citizens and the media. They are rarely forgiven for any ethical shortcomings or breach of public trust.

THE LAW ENFORCEMENT CODE OF ETHICS

Law enforcement also has a ***Code of Ethics***, a solemn oath adopted by the International Association of Chiefs of Police; a code most law enforcement academies require each cadet to memorize; a code that many states have adopted and require each cadet to swear to prior to their graduation. That same code is posted in almost every police station in the United States, sometimes very publicly in lobbies and hallways but, unfortunately, sometimes almost hidden and forgotten.

Can you see yourself proudly wearing this uniform?

Despite our commitment to the *Law Enforcement Code of Ethics,* the media is full of stories of corrupt and discredited police officers who are often filmed at their trials or on their way to jail. We see police officers accused of excessive force, corruption, stealing money from drug dealers, burglary and even murder. Obviously, to those officers, the *Code of Ethics* means very little. Simply swearing to a code doesn't mean you understand it, and understanding a code doesn't mean you have made a commitment to uphold these ethics.

Unless you are willing to do both, to understand and commit to this code of behavior, ***stop reading now!*** Just close this book, sell it back to the campus bookstore, and find a career with more compatible ethical standards. The concepts we'll talk about in this chapter are the most important concepts in this entire book, and the concepts of ethical police behavior are the most valuable concepts you will encounter in your career and throughout your personal life as well.

Ethics, values, principles, morals, integrity — these are the cornerstones of law enforcement and police patrol, the strong foundations that will carry your career to retirement. I have seen rookie officers fired in a heartbeat because they lacked these elements, and I have seen chiefs of police resign in disgrace for the same reason. These concepts are essential to your survival — to the survival of your career, your life, and your very soul. ***Learn everything you can about them! Understand them to the best of your ability!*** By doing so, you will learn and understand more about yourself, you will comprehend the expectations of your community, and you will embrace the concept that ethics *must* remain in the forefront throughout your law enforcement career.

First, a few extremely simplified (and, therefore, debatable) definitions:

CODE: Any system of rules or principles. *The Law Enforcement Code of Ethics* is a basic system of ethical rules for police officers. Where I use the word "code" in the rest of this chapter, I will be referring to the *Law Enforcement Code of Ethics.*

ETHICS: The principles of conduct dealing with what is right and wrong, and with moral duty and obligation. The rules in the *Code of Ethics* describe the moral duties and obligations of police officers.

INTEGRITY: Closely related to honesty, integrity is the firm and incorruptible adherence to a code of moral values. To truly follow the *Law Enforcement Code of Ethics* requires not only firmness but great inner strength and character.

MORALS: The judgments we make relating to societal principles of right and wrong behavior. The duties of a police officer under the *Code of Ethics* deal primarily with principles (or rules) about what is "right" and what is "wrong."

OATH: A formal and solemn commitment, usually asking God and others to witness that you sincerely intend to do what you say, and promising that what you say is the absolute truth. When a police officer swears to the *Law Enforcement Code of Ethics*, he promises that he intends to follow and obey these rules and asks God and others to witness and hold him accountable to that promise.

PRINCIPLES: A rule or code of conduct. *The Code of Ethics* are the basic rules that every police officer must follow and a system of rules that must control your behavior both on-duty and off-duty.

VALUES: A principle or quality that is intrinsically desirable. These are the priorities that an individual gives to the elements in his life and career based on his ethics, morality, and integrity.

The definitions I've given above are highly simplified and specifically tailored for applications to this chapter. Scholars and philosophers have been trying (and failing) to come up with adequate definitions of these terms for most of recorded history, so don't worry if you or your professors don't entirely agree with me on the definitions. In fact, I encourage you to discuss these at length until you can arrive at definitions with which you feel most comfortable. To help you in applying these definitions, consider the following:

Statement of Professional Values
from the California Highway Patrol (CHP) approved in October 1989:

We, as members of the California Highway Patrol, are responsible for protecting lives and property. We serve with professional pride and want the citizens of the State of California to share in this pride. The law enforcement profession is difficult and demands dedication far beyond most other professions. For that reason, we ascribe to the following personal traits and values to be the foundation of our commitment to public service, safety, and security.

INTEGRITY is the cornerstone of our profession. It is being honest, open, and fair in the performance of our duties. It is being responsible for our actions, willing to admit mistakes, and ensuring that our behavior is above reproach; thereby fostering confidence, mutual respect, and trust.

PROFESSIONALISM is the premise upon which we perform our duties. It is having a defined sense of commitment, perspective, and direction in serving the public. It is striving for perfection, quality, and excellence in our commitment to public service. It is being accountable for our actions.

LOYALTY is our commitment to the people of this State. It is ensuring we fulfill the trust and confidence placed upon us by the citizenry of California. It is our commitment to the Department; its mission, principles, and philosophies. It is our commitment to each other and the fostering of an unbiased, nonjudgemental work environment.

PRIDE is the attitude we display towards our chosen profession. It is striving to achieve in the face of adversity. It is the manner of our dress and the way we announce our association with the Department. It is the way we perform our duties with devotion and dedication.

RESPECT is a value reflected in our dealings with the public. It is our commitment to professional, quality law enforcement; one in which the citizens of California can be proud. It is an attitude we display toward the public and each other; and one we expect in return.

DEDICATION is our unwavering commitment to public service. It is our devotion to the mission of the Department and our oath of office. It is serving the public despite self-sacrifice; it is our commitment to lay down our lives rather than swerve from the path of duty.

COURAGE is our commitment to the above principles. It is our devotion to the premise of public service and protection; to equality and justice. It is maintaining our conduct both on and off duty above reproach, facing adversity without hesitation, and committing our lives to the safety of others.

I find the California Highway Patrol's *Statement of Professional Values* to be an interesting analysis of law enforcement qualities as well as an interesting contrast to the *Law Enforcement Code of Ethics*. The CHP's statement does not mention ethics or morality. Certainly many of the items reflect moral values and are based on ethical premises, but they don't come right out and call them ethics.

Similarly, the CHP's code is lacking in absolutes. While the term "unwavering commitment" appears, there are few absolute terms such as "ever," "always," or "never." The values are presented as desirable goals, rather than clear, unequivocal mandates. That is a very different approach than the black and white absolutes presented in the *Law Enforcement Code of Ethics*.

What follows is the *Law Enforcement Code of Ethics* as adopted by the International Association of Chiefs of Police. You should consider this your *complete* system of rules to guide you through a career in law enforcement. You may want to read them aloud for better comprehension. Read these rules carefully and thoughtfully, do your best to understand them and apply them, and be prepared to make a lifelong commitment to them.

This code has some pretty words and noble concepts, but those words and concepts are absolutely meaningless unless you can apply them to the reality of police patrol operations in the streets of your jurisdiction. These words are absolutely worthless without personal integrity and commitment. Are you ready to make that deep, life-long commitment? Do you really understand what this *Code of Ethics* means?

Take a look at this *Code*, and you find it is full of absolutes (words like "never" and "always"). The *Code of Ethics* is very short, and as a result lacks detail. This lack of detail makes it subject to a variety of interpretations. As a result, it was supplemented by the *Code of Professional Conduct and Responsibility for Peace Officers*, (commonly called the *Canons of Ethics*) which define and set forth, in much greater detail, exactly what the ethical standards are for law enforcement.

Law Enforcement Code of Ethics

As a Law Enforcement Officer, my fundamental duty is to serve mankind; to safeguard lives and property; to protect the weak against oppression or intimidation, and the peaceful against violence or disorder; and to respect the Constitutional rights of all men to liberty, equality and justice.

I will keep my private life unsullied as an example for all; maintain courageous calm in the face of danger, scorn or ridicule; develop self-restraint; and be constantly mindful of the welfare of others. Honest in thought and deed in both my personal and official life, I will be exemplary in obeying the laws of the land and the regulations of my department. Whatever I see or hear of a confidential nature or that is confided to me in my official capacity will be kept ever secret unless revelation is necessary in the performance of my duty.

I will never act officiously or permit personal feelings, prejudices, animosities, or friendships to influence my decisions. With no compromise for crime and with relentless prosecution of criminals, I will enforce the law courteously and appropriately without fear or favor, malice or ill will, never employing unnecessary force or violence and never accepting gratuities.

I recognize the badge of my office as a symbol of public faith, and I accept it as a public trust to be held so long as I am true to the ethics of the police service. I will constantly strive to achieve these objectives and ideals, dedicating myself before God to my chosen profession — law enforcement.

CODE OF PROFESSIONAL CONDUCT AND RESPONSIBILITY FOR PEACE OFFICERS

I. PREAMBLE

WHEREAS, peace officers are vested with a public trust which requires that they consistently demonstrate the highest degree of integrity and good moral character; and

WHEREAS, the need to maintain high standards of moral character, integrity, knowledge, and trust requires the establishment of a Code of Professional Conduct and Responsibility for Peace Officers as a matter of highest significance to the health, welfare, and safety of the citizens of this state; and

WHEREAS, the establishment of a Code of Professional Conduct and Responsibility for Peace Officers, which includes Canons of Ethics and minimum standards, requires the granting of authority to enforce these standards of professional conduct through disciplinary action as necessary for the protection of the health, welfare, and safety of the public;

BE IT RESOLVED that the need to maintain high standards of moral character, integrity, knowledge, and trust require that peace officers establish and conform to a Code of Professional Conduct and Responsibility for Peace Officers.

II. GENERAL STATEMENT

Peace Officers are granted a public trust which requires that they consistently demonstrate the highest degree of integrity. To be worthy of this public trust, and to ensure that their professional conduct is above reproach, members of the peace officer profession must not only conform to a *Code of Ethics* but must also abide by these Canons of Ethics and Ethical Standards which constitute this Code of Professional Conduct and Responsibility as a means of internal regulation.

The essence of a profession requires that, in addition to prescribing a desired level of performance, it must establish minimum standards of ethical conduct with prescribed rules for internal discipline to ensure compliance. Accordingly, this Code of Professional Conduct and Responsibility is established for the peace officer profession.

Nothing in the Code of Professional Conduct and Responsibility for Peace Officers is intended to supersede any provision of law relating to the duties and obligations of peace officers or the consequences of a violation thereof. Whereas these rules specify certain conduct as unprofessional, this is not to be interpreted as approval of conduct not specifically mentioned.

Nothing in this Code is intended to limit the authority of an agency to adopt and enforce rules and regulation that are more stringent or comprehensive than those that are contained in this Code of Professional Conduct and Responsibility for Peace Officers.

III. DEFINITIONS

The Code of Professional Conduct and Responsibility for Peace Officers is comprised of nine Canons of Ethics, with explanatory statements in the form of Ethical Standards, Examples of Disciplinary Rules and Enforcement Procedures are included as an addendum for individual agency consideration. Following are definitions of these terms, as used in the context of the code.

A. "PEACE OFFICER" means a regular employed and full-time sheriff, undersheriff, or deputy sheriff of a county; a chief of police, or any police officer of a city or any chief of police or police officer of a district authorized by law to maintain a police department, or any other person within the state who is defined as a peace officer.

B. "CANONS" are statements which express in general terms standards of professional conduct expected of peace officers in their relationship with the public, the criminal justice system, and the peace officer profession. They embody the general concepts from which the Ethical Standards and the Disciplinary Rules are derived.

C. "ETHICAL STANDARDS" are statements that represent the objectives toward which every peace officer shall strive. They constitute principles that can be relied upon by the peace officer for guidance in specific situations.

D. "DISCIPLINARY RULES" specify an unacceptable level of conduct for all peace officers, regardless of their rank or the nature of their assignment. Any peace officer who violates any agency rule that applies to these canons and standards is guilty of unprofessional conduct, and is subject to disciplinary action. Violation of disciplinary rules requires appropriate adjudication and disciplinary action ranging from oral reprimand to termination and/or criminal prosecution or other administrative action sanctioned by law, as dictated by the individual case.

E. "ENFORCEMENT PROCEDURES" are the fundamental rights of an accused officer which are applicable to a disciplinary investigation or proceeding against the officer.

F. "ADMINISTRATIVE INVESTIGATION" is an investigation conducted to determine whether an officer has violated any provision of this code, or an agency rule or regulation; or whether an officer is impaired or unfit to perform the duties and responsibilities of a peace officer.

G. "FORMAL DISCIPLINE" refers to the final adjudication of administrative or disciplinary charges. Formal discipline shall be deemed final only after an officer has exhausted or waived all legal remedies available and actual discipline has been invoked.

IV. CANONS OF ETHICS

CANON ONE

PEACE OFFICERS SHALL UPHOLD THE CONSTITUTION OF THE UNITED STATES, THE STATE CONSTITUTION, AND ALL LAWS ENACTED OR ESTABLISHED PURSUANT TO LEGALLY CONSTITUTED AUTHORITY.

STANDARD 1.1 Peace officers shall recognize that the primary responsibility of their profession and of the individual officer is the protection of the people within the jurisdiction of the United States through upholding of their laws, the most important of which are the Constitution of the United States and the State Constitutions and laws derived therefrom.

STANDARD 1.2 Peace officers shall be aware of the extent and the limitations of their authority in the enforcement of the law.

STANDARD 1.3 Peace officers shall diligently study principles and new enactments of the laws they enforce.

STANDARD 1.4 Peace officers shall be responsible for keeping abreast of current case law as applied to their duties.

STANDARD 1.5 Peace officers shall endeavor to uphold the spirit of the law, as opposed to enforcing merely the letter of the law.

STANDARD 1.6 Peace officers shall respect and uphold the dignity, human rights, and Constitutional rights of all persons.

CANON TWO

PEACE OFFICERS SHALL BE AWARE OF AND SHALL USE PROPER AND ETHICAL PROCEDURES IN DISCHARGING OFFICIAL DUTIES AND RESPONSIBILITIES.

STANDARD 2.1 Peace officers shall be aware of their lawful authority to use that force reasonably necessary in securing compliance with their lawful enforcement duties.

STANDARD 2.2 Peace officers shall truthfully, completely, and impartially report, testify, and present evidence in all matters of an official nature.

STANDARD 2.3 Peace officers shall follow legal practices in such areas as interrogation, arrest or detention, searches, seizures, use of informants, and collection and preservation of evidence.

STANDARD 2.4 Peace officers shall follow the principles of integrity, fairness, and impartiality in connection with duties.

CANON THREE

PEACE OFFICERS SHALL REGARD THE DISCHARGE OF THEIR DUTIES AS A PUBLIC TRUST AND SHALL RECOGNIZE THEIR RESPONSIBILITIES TO THE PEOPLE WHOM THEY ARE SWORN TO PROTECT AND SERVE.

STANDARD 3.1 Peace officers, during their tour or duty, shall diligently devote their time and attention to the effective and professional performance of their responsibilities.

STANDARD 3.2 Peace officers shall ensure that they are prepared for the effective and efficient undertaking of their assignment.

STANDARD 3.3 Peace officers shall safely and efficiently use equipment and material available to them.

STANDARD 3.4 Peace officers shall be prepared to and shall respond effectively to the demands of their office.

STANDARD 3.5 Peace officers, with due regard for compassion, shall maintain an objective and impartial attitude in official contacts.

STANDARD 3.6 Peace officers shall not allow their personal convictions, beliefs, prejudices, or biases to interfere unreasonably with their official acts or decisions.

STANDARD 3.7 Peace officers shall recognize that their allegiance is first to the people, then to their profession and the government entity or agency that employs them.

CANON FOUR

PEACE OFFICERS WILL SO CONDUCT THEIR PUBLIC AND PRIVATE LIFE THAT THEY EXEMPLIFY THE HIGH STANDARDS OF INTEGRITY, TRUST, AND MORALITY DEMANDED OF A MEMBER OF THE PEACE OFFICER PROFESSION.

STANDARD 4.1 Peace officers shall refrain from consuming intoxicating beverages to the extent that it results in impairment which brings discredit upon the profession or their employing agency, or renders them unfit for their next tour of duty.

STANDARD 4.2 Peace officers shall not consume intoxicating beverages while on duty, except to the degree permitted in the performance of official duties, and under no circumstances while in uniform.

STANDARD 4.3 Peace officers shall not use any narcotics, hallucinogens, or any other controlled substance except when legally prescribed. When such controlled substances are prescribed, officers shall notify their superior officer prior to reporting for duty.

STANDARD 4.4 Peace officers shall maintain a level of conduct in their personal and business affairs in keeping with the high standards of the peace officer profession. Officers shall not participate in any incident involving moral turpitude.

STANDARD 4.5 Peace officers shall not undertake financial obligations which they know or reasonably should know they will be unable to meet and shall pay all just debts when due.

STANDARD 4.6 Peace officers shall not engage in illegal political activities.

STANDARD 4.7 Peace officers shall not permit or authorize for personal gain the use of their name or photograph and official title identifying them as peace officers in connection with testimonials or advertisements for any commodity, commercial enterprise, or commercial service which is not the product of the officer involved.

STANDARD 4.8 Peace officers shall not engage in any activity which would create a conflict of interest or would be in violation of any law.

STANDARD 4.9 Peace officers shall at all times conduct themselves in a manner which does to discredit the peace officer profession or their employing agency.

STANDARD 4.10 Peace officers shall not be disrespectful in their official dealings with the public, fellow officers, superiors and subordinates.

STANDARD 4.11 Peace officers shall be courteous and respectful in their official dealings with the public, fellow officers, superiors and subordinates.

STANDARD 4.12 Peace officers shall not engage in any strike, work obstruction or abstention, in whole or in part, from the full, faithful and proper performance of their assigned duties and responsibilities, except as authorized by law.

STANDARD 4.13 Peace officers shall maintain a neutral position with regard to the merits of any labor dispute, political protest, or other public demonstration, while acting in an official capacity.

CANON FIVE

PEACE OFFICERS SHALL RECOGNIZE THAT OUR SOCIETY HOLDS THE FREEDOM OF THE INDIVIDUAL AS A PARAMOUNT PRECEPT WHICH SHALL NOT BE INFRINGED UPON WITHOUT JUST, LEGAL AND NECESSARY CAUSE.

STANDARD 5.1 Peace officers shall not restrict the freedom of individuals, whether by detention or arrest, except to the extent necessary to legally and reasonably apply the law.

STANDARD 5.2 Peace officers shall recognize the rights of individuals to be free from capricious or arbitrary acts which deny or abridge their fundamental rights as guaranteed by law.

STANDARD 5.3 Peace officers shall not use their official position to detain any individual, or to restrict the freedom of any individual, except in the manner and means permitted or prescribed by law.

CANON SIX

PEACE OFFICERS SHALL ASSIST IN MAINTAINING THE INTEGRITY AND COMPETENCE OF THE PEACE OFFICER PROFESSION.

STANDARD 6.1 Peace officers shall recognize that every person in our society is entitled to professional, effective, and efficient law enforcement services.

STANDARD 6.2 Peace officers shall perform their duties in such a manner as to discourage double standards.

STANDARD 6.3 Peace officers shall conduct themselves so as to set exemplary standards of performance for all law enforcement personnel.

STANDARD 6.4 Peace officers shall maintain the integrity of their profession through complete disclosure of those who violate any of these rules of conduct, violate any law, or who conduct themselves in a manner which tends to discredit the profession.

STANDARD 6.5 Peace officers shall have responsibility for reporting to proper authorities any known information which would serve to disqualify candidates from transferring within or entering the profession.

STANDARD 6.6 Peace officers shall be responsible for maintaining a level of education and training that will keep them abreast of current techniques, concepts, laws, and requirements of the profession.

STANDARD 6.7 Chief executive peace officers shall accept the responsibility of utilizing all available resources and the authority of their office to maintain the integrity of their agency and the competency of their officers. These Canons and Ethical Standards shall apply to all legally defined peace officers regardless of rank.

STANDARD 6.8 Peace officers shall assume a leadership role in furthering their profession by encouraging and assisting in the education and training of other members of the profession.

CANON SEVEN

PEACE OFFICERS SHALL COOPERATE WITH OTHER OFFICIALS AND ORGANIZATIONS WHO ARE USING LEGAL AND ETHICAL MEANS TO ACHIEVE THE GOALS AND OBJECTIVES OF THE PEACE OFFICER PROFESSION.

STANDARD 7.1 Peace officers, within legal and agency guidelines, shall share with personnel both within and outside their agency, appropriate information that will facilitate the achievement of criminal justice goals or objectives.

STANDARD 7.2 Peace officers, whether requested through appropriate channels or called upon individually, shall render needed assistance to any other officer in the proper performance of their duty.

STANDARD 7.3 Peace officers shall , within legal and agency guidelines, endeavor to communicate to the people of their community the goals and objectives of the profession, and keep them apprised of conditions which threaten the maintenance of an ordered society.

CANON EIGHT

PEACE OFFICERS SHALL NOT COMPROMISE THEIR INTEGRITY, NOR THAT OF THEIR AGENCY OR PROFESSION, BY ACCEPTING, GIVING OR SOLICITING ANY GRATUITY.

STANDARD 8.1 Peace officers shall refuse to offer, give, or receive gifts, favors or gratuities, either large or small, which can reasonably be interpreted as capable of influencing official acts or judgments. This standard is not intended to isolate peace officers from normal social practices, or relatives, where appropriate.

STANDARD 8.2 Peace officers shall not consider the badge of office as a license designed to provide them with special favor or consideration.

CANON NINE

PEACE OFFICERS SHALL OBSERVE THE CONFIDENTI-
ALITY OF INFORMATION AVAILABLE TO THEM THROUGH
ANY SOURCE, AS IT RELATES TO THE PEACE OFFICER
PROFESSION.

STANDARD 9.1   Peace officers shall be aware of and shall
meticulously observe all legal restrictions on the release and dissemina-
tion of information.

STANDARD 9.2   Peace officers shall treat as confidential the
official business of their employing agency, and shall release or
disseminate such information solely in an authorized manner.

STANDARD 9.3   Peace officers shall treat as confidential that
information confided to them personally.   They shall disclose such
information as required in the proper performance of their duties.

STANDARD 9.4 Peace officers shall neither disclose nor use for
their personal interest any confidential information acquired by them in
the course of their official duties.

STANDARD 9.5   Peace officers shall treat as confidential all
matters relating to investigations, internal affairs, and personnel.

THE CODE OF ETHICS IN THE REAL WORLD

Once a police officer graduates from the academy, a rookie
officer is generally handed over to the loving care of a Field Training
Officer (FTO). Often the first thing a rookie hears is, "Kid, you can
just forget everything you learned in the academy. I'm going to teach
you how *real* police work is done." From that point on, you will learn
about the job of policing by observing how your FTO does things and
by doing those things yourself under his observation and guidance.
Undoubtedly you will see him do things you've been taught to never,
ever do. Suddenly, you find yourself in a deadly crossfire between the
Code of Ethics and your FTO's procedures.

Be prepared for a major reality shock. There are unethical FTO's,
some who are themselves involved in unethical behavior, and some
who may try to involve you in the same activities. Court cases involving
fired officers describe some of the horrors that rookies have encountered (i.e., drinking on duty, sexual acts, brutality or bribery).
Oftentimes a minor situation will be offered to a rookie to see if he takes

the bait, if he can be trusted, if he can keep his mouth shut, and if he's willing to compromise and violate the *Code of Ethics*.

There are many possible responses: you can go along with the activity; you can ignore the activity and not participate; you can try to escape from the situation, seeking a transfer that removes you from the

Absolutely, positively no excuses for drinking alcohol on duty.

moral dilemma; you can leave police work altogether; or you can tell your FTO how you feel about his activity, and you can report his activity to your superiors. The pressure on you will be to give loyalty to your fellow officers, loyalty to the secret you all will share. You will be told that your duty is to protect your fellow officers, after all, wouldn't they give their very lives to protect you? As a result, you may be an outcast, hounded and harassed into resigning. Ultimately, you may have to choose between this particular job (not your career, but your employment with this one agency) and your integrity. When you consider the absolute mandates of the *Law Enforcement Code of Ethics*, you have only one choice. You must remain loyal to yourself.

As you go through your police career, you will learn police ethics, and you will learn how to apply them. You alone must set your standards, deciding how to address the moral choices that confront you, deciding which values to adopt, and determining the course of your career.

GRATUITIES

The *Code of Ethics* is absolute about gratuities ("and never accepting gratuities."), while the *Code of Professional Conduct and Responsibility for Peace Officers* is a bit more lenient ("Peace officers shall refuse to offer, give, or receive gifts, favors or gratuities, either large or small, which can be reasonably interpreted as capable of influencing official acts or judgments. This standard is not intended to isolate officers from normal social practices, or relatives, where appropriate.")

The subject of accepting gratuities is one of the toughest dilemmas for patrol officers. Many people in your community genuinely like you and want to demonstrate their support. Other persons genuinely want to manipulate you and may use gratuities to achieve these means. Obviously, there is a difference between gratuities, gifts, social practices and common courtesy. On a hot summer day when you are in the home of a victim who politely offers you a glass of lemonade, there is no harm at all in politely accepting it. That's common courtesy.

There's a clear difference between a citizen's demonstrating their concern for etiquette and your comfort by offering you a glass of lemonade and offering you a gratuity. In my city we enjoy a great deal of citizen support, and it is not uncommon for grateful citizens to bring by a cake or some cookies, or sometimes even a turkey on a Thanksgiving evening when they know all the restaurants are closed. We've had citizens who donated gym equipment to the police association, local businesses who donated vehicles to the department, and corporations who donated equipment and supplies to operate D.A.R.E. programs. Those are clear indications of a successful partnership between citizens and their police, and accepting support for police programs is certainly consistent with the *Code of Ethics*.

Those aren't gratuities, they're gifts. They are given out of gratitude, with the intention of benefiting police service to the community, rather than simply benefiting an individual officer or influencing the department. A big difference exists when an officer goes to a local doughnut shop, intending to get a cup of coffee, and is offered the item for free. Other authors have referred to it as the "slippery slope," or the "tarnished badge," but the concept of gradually eroding one's ethics is the same.

There's an old bar joke in which a woman agrees to sleep with a man in exchange for a million dollars. The man then asks her if she will sleep with him for one dollar. "What do you think I am, a prostitute?" she demands. He replies, "We've established that already, now we're just negotiating the price."

You face the same dilemma once you accept that first free cup of coffee. Where do you draw the line? If you accept a free cup of coffee, then is coffee *and* a doughnut okay? Do you distinguish between a plain old fashion doughnut and a filled eclair? How would you feel about a free hamburger? If a hamburger is okay with you, how about a nice filet mignon steak? How would you feel about steak and lobster followed by a little cheesecake, and maybe some espresso? After all, isn't a meal just a meal? How about a new suit, a television set, a car, a new house, or a million dollars? After all, a gratuity is just a gratuity, regardless of its value.

All of the above are simply varying degrees of accepting a gratuity. With a million dollars, you are clearly violating the *Code of Ethics* if you accept. If you think it's all right to accept a free cup of coffee, you've already made an ethical compromise. You've already accepted the label of prostitute, and are going to spend the rest of your career negotiating "the price."

Refusing to accept a gratuity from a well-intentioned citizen may require great diplomacy on your part. He may not understand why you **cannot** accept what he views as an offer of support and friendship, and you want to continue to build an environment of mutual trust and partnership with the citizens of your community. You may have to be firm and polite and should certainly thank the business owner for his offer, but you have to tell him that you **cannot** accept, and you ought to tell him the reason why. Tell him how important the *Code of Ethics* is to you, but also tell him how much you appreciate his support of law enforcement. Tell him that you hope he will continue to support the police in other ways. If all these explanations fail, it may mean you just have to leave your payment for the meal (or whatever) on the counter and go on your way.

THE ETHICAL USE OF DEADLY FORCE

The use of force in police work has changed dramatically in the last few decades. Once there was a "fleeing felon" rule, which simply meant that if you ran from the police you would be shot. Officers did not hesitate to use force of any kind against those who they felt deserved it, or when they thought the use of force would help them in solving a crime.

Typically, a police officer is legally allowed to use deadly force in three basic situations:

1) To protect his life, when his own life is in danger. Clearly, every police officer has the right to self-defense.

2) To protect the life of another. Given the mandates of the *Law Enforcement Code of Ethics*, every police officer has not only the right, but the duty to protect the lives of the citizens of his community.

3) To prevent the commission of a violent felony, or prevent the escape of a violent felon after all other means have been exhausted. In violent felonies and the escape of violent felons, a grave danger exists for the community. In those cases, a police officer may use deadly force in order to eliminate that grave danger.

It is vitally important that every police officer know the Penal Code's limitations on the use of deadly force and his department's policy in detail. Nevertheless, the mere legal reasoning to shoot someone does not give you the moral or ethical right to do so.

The ethics of force in America have changed dramatically. In the early 1960s, federal law came into being to protect civil rights. There was community outrage over police shooting, and explosive growth in lawsuits against the police that created an entire new industry for attorneys and literally bankrupted several cities. The attitudes and behaviors of police officers have changed, in part due to a different generation of police officers coming into the field and, in part, due to restrictive new laws and department policies. Whatever the reasons, police shootings in nearly every major city have shown dramatic declines.

POLICE MISCONDUCT LITIGATION

Prior to the Rodney King incident, lawsuits against police agencies throughout the nation were declining in number, and the awards that juries were giving to clients were generally becoming smaller and smaller. Now, juries everywhere can visualize that infamous tape in their heads, and a whole new industry has risen in the legal profession. In Los Angeles, an organization called *Police Watch* (formerly called the *Police Misconduct Lawyer Referral Service*) boasts a membership of more than one hundred attorneys. Some of these attorneys specialize in nothing but police brutality cases, and even list "1-800" hotline phone numbers. Attorneys in each new police misconduct case try to present their clients before the media like the next Rodney King because they know that there is "big money" at stake (King's initial suit requested $54 million, since that time a settlement in the $4 million range has been made).

The vast majority of cases against police officers never reach a jury. In fact, many cities simply settle any case, regardless of the merits, when it appears that fighting the case would cost more than settling the case. The real money is in attorney's fees, which can amount to thousands of dollars as long as the person bringing the suit wins. The attorney's fees may be many times higher than the jury award. In one case the plaintiff received $1, the attorney over $26,000, plus costs. Cases taken on contingency can bring the attorney 40 percent or more of the judgment, and many attorneys specializing in police brutality are now millionaires.

Increasingly, punitive damages are being brought not just against the agency employing the officer, but against the individual officer himself. Just remember that there is no right way to do the wrong thing. If you use excessive force, if you violate your ethics, you will pay a price in the loss of your integrity, and you may well be sued for your job, your liberty, and everything you own.

DISCUSSION QUESTIONS

1. Rank the following professions in order with the professions you trust most at the top and least at the bottom: attorney, college professor, fast-food cook, gas station attendant, nun, physician, police officer, politician, television news anchor, used-car salesman. Explain why you ranked police officer where you did.

2. Do you think the use of God's name within the *Code of Ethics* adds or detracts from police professionalism?

3. Do you think a "code of silence" exists among police officers? If you do, is it contrary to the *Code of Ethics*?

4. A recent crime trend has been that of juvenile murderers, children as young as 12 recruited by gangs specifically to shoot rivals. Traditionally, police officers have not used deadly force against juveniles. Should they?

5. Make a list of the ten character qualities you think are most important in a police officer. Rank them in order of importance, and justify how you ranked them.

6. A large chain of doughnut shops in the San Francisco area serves officers coffee in cups specially printed with "Complimentary

coffee for police officers." Do you think that is an ethical position for the corporation to take?

7. Think about the videotape of the Rodney King arrest. Do you feel the officers involved acted consistently with the *Law Enforcement Code of Ethics*? Why?

8. The *Law Enforcement Code of Ethics* requires a police officer's private life to be "unsullied, an example to all." Who is an example for you, and why?

Marlene Lenick had had enough, and told her husband so. There was a brief war of the remote controls as he tuned to the Eagles-Cowboys game and she clicked back to the news, and then the shots rang out.

After warning husband Michael she'd "had enough of that football," Marlene fired two rounds from her .38 special, one grazing his abdomen and one punching through his shoulder blade to exit his neck. Michael passed out, and she then went back to watching the news. When Michael came to, he had to call an ambulance himself. Police said the Sewall's Point, FL., couple had been drinking.

PREPARING FOR DUTY

LEARNING GOALS: After studying this chapter the student will be able to:

- Relate mental attitude to police patrol.

- Describe the proper relationship between a Field Training Officer and his trainee.

- List the basic equipment carried by patrol officers.

- Select proper patrol equipment.

- Describe the purpose of a patrol briefing.

- Identify the purpose of inspecting the patrol car prior to driving it, and describe the proper method of inspection.

- Discuss the fundamental concept of police patrol.

THE RIGHT ATTITUDE FOR PATROL

Your first day on police patrol could be the most important day of your career. I still remember my first day on patrol. It was an exciting and confusing day; I recall my partner and I chasing a stolen truck around the city. I didn't know the streets, I didn't know the codes, I couldn't understand the radio, and suddenly my partner was telling me to put handcuffs on an absolute mountain of a man walking down the sidewalk and I really didn't even know how my partner figured it was the perpetrator. I remember the suspect's name to this day.

Your first day on patrol may be quite different, but I'm sure it will be equally memorable. One cadet who graduated from my academy class had a busy day and promptly resigned at the end of his first shift. Another officer was shot and killed his first (and last) week. Your survival depends largely on how well you prepare yourself.

The most important thing to bring with you on your first day is the right mental attitude. You need to come to work with a *commitment* to professionalism and the *Law Enforcement Code of Ethics*. You need to demonstrate your interest in the community itself, show your enthusiasm, show a career orientation, and consistently prove your overall support of the agency's values and mission. You must be prepared to receive and accept criticism (you'll receive plenty in your first days) with a mature attitude, be prepared to always accept personal responsibility for your actions, and be ready to show your eagerness to address and correct any personal deficiencies.

YOUR PARTNER — THE FIELD TRAINING OFFICER

On your first day of patrol you will generally find yourself assigned to your partner, a *Field Training Officer (FTO)* — in some departments, this is simply an experienced officer assigned to show you the ropes and direct your on-the-job training (OJT). The definition of "experienced" varies greatly from agency to agency and could mean anything from a few years to a few decades. Typically this is an informal process which lacks the structure required to ensure comprehensive training, since this method depends primarily on the random occurrence of calls in the field to teach you how to become a veteran patrol officer. This often leaves many holes in your training and creates a tremendous burden on you to make yourself proficient in your duties.

Hopefully, you will be lucky enough to have a specially trained instructor who will take you through a formal, systematic, professional training program with clearly defined lessons and goals. Structured programs with specific learning goals are now the norm in most agencies.

Hopefully, your FTO is going to be a highly motivated officer that really wants the job and takes it seriously. Most FTOs have gone through a selection process, competing with other officers. Often FTO's are required to meet some sort of minimum qualifications of education, training and experience. Ideally, your FTO should be a highly ethical person, have good interpersonal skills, be extremely knowledgeable about police patrol, be skilled in the use of teaching techniques, and be the type of dedicated officer who takes his duties very seriously. In essence, the FTO should model the type of officer you aspire to become.

Whenever I am assigned a new officer to train, I am very much aware of the heavy responsibilities that assignment brings. Throughout every stage of training, I have to keep the trainee alive and prevent him from being injured. I also have to protect him from traffic, criminals, and ethical compromise and, at the same time, protect the public from the trainee's errors and ignorance. I proceed on the assumption that the officer I am training will stay with my agency for the rest of my career and that I will have to depend on that officer to get the job done as a partner, as a back-up, and as a subordinate. I recognize that the community is depending on me to supply them with a proficient, competent police officer. I realize that my own life may depend on how well each rookie officer is trained, and I have learned to take my job very seriously. Sometimes, that responsibility requires almost brutal frankness on an evaluation and, on rare occasions, I have had to recommend that a trainee be terminated.

The Evaluation Process

Generally, the FTO is responsible for completing a regular evaluation on each of his trainees. Evaluations may simply consist of a memo detailing outstanding or unusual activity during the evaluation period. Sometimes it will be a comprehensive examination of every imaginable functional area. Some agencies require daily evaluations, others require weekly or monthly evaluations. When properly and conscientiously completed, these evaluations will serve as a lesson plan for the areas in which you need to improve.

Evaluations also serve as documentation of both the FTO's and the trainee's achievements and deficiencies. If the trainee consistently fails to meet the agency's minimum performance standards, the evaluations will serve as the basis for termination. Once you successfully complete your field training, these same evaluations may be called into court years later to prove exactly how well you were trained and how well you performed. Your career success and future promotions may be deeply effected by these evaluations for years to come.

The Goals of the Field Training Program

You and your FTO share two immediate goals. The first goal is to provide law enforcement patrol services to your assigned area of your community. People's lives depend on your ability to protect them and to provide for all of their law enforcement needs. They deserve the best you can give.

The second goal you share is to continue making steady progress through your training program. You and your FTO have the joint responsibility of providing your agency with a fully trained, fully capable, community-oriented police officer within the allotted period of training time.

Despite the horror stories you may have heard of rookie officers who were terminated during training, the purpose of field training is not to get you fired. You've already reached a point where your agency has a substantial investment of time and money in your career. They have invested in your recruitment, preliminary screening, training, background investigation, medical and psychiatric evaluations, and, perhaps, a polygraph examination. If they have paid your way through the academy, your agency may already have an investment in you approaching $100,000. They aren't about to waste that investment, so the training program has to be designed for achievement, to help you perform at your very best. To be successfully trained as a patrol officer, both you and your FTO have to understand, believe in, and support a totally professional approach to police training.

The Importance of a Professional Attitude

You and your FTO will be partners: riding together, working together, eating together, and risking your lives together. You will have to treat him with respect and rely on his knowledge, training, experience, and judgment on a daily basis. Your initial training will be heavily oriented toward observing your FTO, emphasizing officer safety and basic patrol responsibilities. You and your FTO may even develop a real friendship, but you must always maintain a professional and respectful attitude that will create a productive learning environment. Coming fresh out of the academy, you will probably have some new techniques that you can share with your FTO, but avoid coming across as a "know-it-all," and recognize that he may require you to do things in a different manner than your academy staff. You must have the right attitude, giving a 100 percent effort each and every day. Make sure your agency gets every bit of what they paid for, and never compromise your job or your ethics.

Police Humor

Having the right attitude includes remembering your place in the social order of the organization. You won't be instantly accepted simply because you wear the same uniform and badge. Despite your own opinion, you may not be God's gift to law enforcement. The other officers on your watch have probably worked together as a team for years. Their relationship has been founded on mutual trust and the dependence on each other for their lives. You will be fully accepted by them only after you have demonstrated your ability to pull your own weight and perform police work at their level.

Most police officers have a great sense of humor (although sometimes a bit bizarre). You will observe police officers playing jokes and seeming to have a lot of fun. You'll see a lot of humor in the irreverent way they deal with themselves, their partners, and often with their supervisors. Remember your place! Treat the other officers and their supervisors with proper respect at all times, and demonstrate your support for your superiors and their positions. There is a very thin line between the typical station-house humor and outright insubordination, and it's a bit early in your career to find yourself on the wrong side of that line.

The Survival Attitude

Last of all, but most important, you *must* have the right attitude about officer survival. Death would definitely interfere with your career plans and limit any future advancement. It would be a great waste of time and effort on your part, and on behalf of your agency, if you got yourself killed. You have to be totally committed to coming home every night and equally committed to making sure your partner comes home as well. You need to have a survival mentality, knowing that whatever you face, whatever happens to you, no matter what you see or do, no matter how badly you are hurt or injured, **you will survive!**

BASIC PATROL EQUIPMENT

Being properly equipped for patrol starts with you. We've talked about your mental attitude, now let's talk about your physical attitude. In order to be an effective police officer, you have to be physically fit and have a good physical appearance. I'm not going to offer you any specific physical fitness regimens, diet plans, or methods to stop smoking; **you** have to find a program that works to keep you physically fit. More police officers die of heart disease, high blood pressure, and cancer than all the criminal assaults combined. If you are too fat to run or too weak to protect yourself, *you* need to make radical changes in your life if you want to remain a police officer and stay alive.

It sounds so stupid, and so basic, but your physical appearance is also vitally important to your success in the job. If others find your physical appearance objectionable, you will be that much less effective as a police officer and less likely to pass your training period. Proper physical appearance means coming to work freshly bathed and groomed with neat, well-trimmed hair, clean fingernails, etc. It means using deodorant and mouthwash, watching your weight, and leaving both your snuff can and your favorite dangling earrings at home. It means dressing for success when you walk in the door of your station and looking just as squared away in your off-duty civilian dress as in your uniform. Know your department's dress standards and follow them exactly.

The Basic Police Uniform

In most agencies, you will appear in uniform for patrol duty. Uniforms vary widely depending on your agency, geographic area, and assignment. Any type of dress may be specified — from a formal tunic with gold braid and brass buttons to an informal uniform utilizing a golf shirt and bike pants. Whatever your uniform, it should express your pride in your chosen profession. Your uniform should be clean, pressed, lint-free, and worn in a neat and orderly manner. Your shoes and leather gear should be clean and spit-polished to mirror-like perfection. Your badge should be sparkling and worn with pride.

Once you have been issued a weapon and other equipment, they should reflect that same meticulous care. As an FTO, I always made a point of carefully inspecting my trainee's weapons, ammunition, baton and handcuffs. It always amazed me to find handguns polluted with dirt and lead, ammo boxes and magazines packed with lint, threads hanging from the leather gear, dirty and rusted handcuffs, and other poorly maintained equipment. Think of the impression these things made on my first day with a trainee. What a way to start a career!

Basic Patrol Footwear

Shoes are another important piece of your equipment. You will be surprised at the amount of walking you will do as a patrol officer, even when assigned to a car. One study estimated that the average police officer walks six miles per day, and that has always seemed pretty consistent with my experience. Given the unpredictable nature of police work, it's certainly possible you may be standing for 10 or 12 hours. With this in mind, you need to take care of your feet and wear comfortable, practical shoes. Agency regulations vary widely, so check on your department's rules before you spend any money.

My advice is to select something that looks professional, offers your feet the protection you need, and still provides you with the greatest possible comfort when worn for long periods of time. When in doubt, conform to the norm. Look at what your FTO and other officers are wearing, and pick something similar.

The Ballistic Vest

You should be wearing a ballistic vest under your uniform, either issued by your department or purchased on your own. These are sometimes erroneously called "bullet-proof" vests, but "bullet resistant" is a more accurate term. The standard ballistic armor issued by most departments will stop a majority of commonly encountered handgun rounds, most shotgun rounds, and some rifle rounds. Vests are available in a variety of "threat levels" and need to be the appropriate level for your assignment.

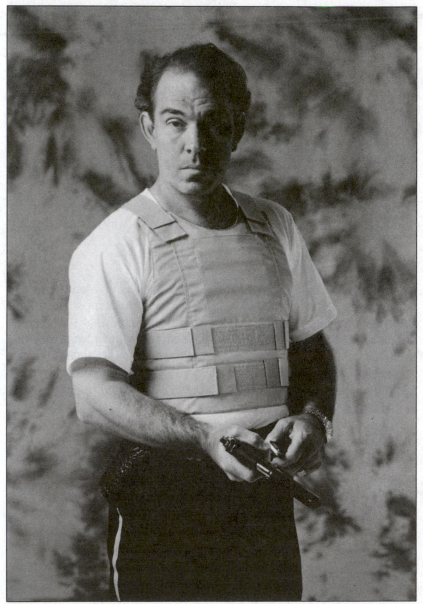

Ballistic vest — Courtesy of Second Chance Body Armor, Inc.

The Sam Brown Belt

Your "Sam Brown" belt (they also sell "Sally Browns" tailored for female officers) is the wide gun belt you wear around your waist and serves as the support system for your gun, baton, portable radio, handcuffs, and other equipment. This equipment will weigh between 15 and 20 pounds. It will feel like 50 pounds after a long shift (think about what a handicap this weight represents in a foot pursuit).

The belt is held in place at your waist either by Velcro™ hook and pile fasteners or by a number of "keepers" (small straps that hold the Sam Brown in place around your trouser belt). Initially, your Sam Brown will be rather stiff and uncomfortable, but it gets softer and more pliable after a couple of years use. This is both a blessing and a curse, because as the leather becomes more comfortable and soft, its lack of rigidity means it will offer less structural support to your equipment, increase difficulty in using certain types of holsters, lower security, and increase difficulty in retaining all of your equipment in a foot-pursuit or a fight.

Your Duty Weapon and Holster

The most important piece of equipment on your Sam Brown is your "duty weapon," retained securely in its holster. Most agencies either provide or require you to purchase a medium to large frame handgun, generally in a caliber between .38 and .45, in either a revolver or a semi-automatic configuration from a reputable manufacturer.

Regardless of the weapon you carry, it is vitally important that you carry only an approved weapon, and then only at approved times, in an approved manner, loaded with the approved ammunition. Know your state law and your particular agency's rules, policies, and regulations, and make sure you operate in strict compliance with them at all times.

It's been repeatedly proven that under stress you will react based on the way you were trained. That makes it important for you to take every opportunity to train with your weapon and related equipment. Pulling your weapon, getting on target, firing when necessary and total firearms safety should all become instinctive and second nature. This kind of familiarity and appropriate reactions are only achieved by training, training, and more training.

Shown above are the basic police uniform and support equipment.

Your holster is just as important as your weapon. Without a good holster, you will never have the opportunity to draw your weapon under stress. Your holster must fit you correctly, be designed to fit your specific handgun and fit your particular body in order to make your draw as easy and natural as possible.

Your holster should be made of the highest quality materials and should attach firmly (usually with a tensioning screw) to your Sam Brown. This firm attachment ensures that the gun is "indexed," meaning that the grip stays constantly in the same relative position so your gun hand can naturally find the grip every time you draw.

The ability of your holster to retain and protect your weapon is critically important. Your holster has to retain your gun when you are running, going over walls, or rolling around on the ground in a fight; otherwise you may be providing a suspect with your own murder weapon. You can test your holster by jumping up and down vigorously with the weapon in place — if you lose it, get yourself another holster.

Your safety requires that you always keep your eyes on a suspect, so you must be completely familiar with the process so you can draw your weapon and then re-holster and secure it without ever looking at the gun itself. Practice is essential.

Your Back-Up Weapon

If your department policies allow, you should also carry a ***back-up weapon*** (a second handgun within easy reach in case you lose your primary handgun or it malfunctions). Most officer survival experts consider a back-up gun to be an indispensable and critical piece of equipment. Generally these guns must meet similar requirements to your duty weapon. Small-frame .38 revolvers and .380 or 9mm semi-automatic pistols seem to be most common choice. Good sense tells you that your back-up must be concealed from view, yet easily accessible in emergencies.

Your choice of weapon should be a handgun as similar in configuration and function to your duty weapon as possible. That way the gun is loaded, operated, and fired in an identical manner as your duty weapon, thus training is much easier and more likely to pay off under stress.

Your Reloading System

Also of prime importance is the need to have a means of reloading your weapon once you have fired all your rounds. In the days of the Old West, everyone carried extra ammunition in open loops of leather on their gun belts. Incredible as it may sound, over 100 years later some officers are still carrying their extra ammunition in the same manner, in open loops on their belts.

The modern law enforcement standard is two or more magazines for semi-autos or two or more "speed-loaders" for revolvers. These are generally carried on the front of the belt on the side opposite from the weapon. Your extra ammunition should be the same department-approved loads that you carry in your duty weapon. The ammunition should be well secured with a snap or other closure, and again, practice is essential for the swift and smooth reloading of your handgun under pressure. The standard you should strive for is to be able to reload without ever looking away from your target. Practice this one in a dark room and you'll get the idea of how difficult this can be, yet how essential it is that you master this skill.

Non-Lethal Weapons

In addition to your duty weapon, you will probably carry one or more secondary weapons such as a baton (or "night-stick"), other impact weapons such as a sap or billy, and some form of chemical agent such as tear-gas or pepper spray.

Patrol officers usually carry their batons on their "weak" side, the side opposite from their handgun. Batons are striking and jabbing weapons used to disable or gain the compliance of suspects by causing non-lethal pain and injury, primarily to the abdomen, joints and limbs. They are considered to be deadly weapons, since death can very easily result from their use. Batons are available in a variety of lengths, materials, and configurations. Straight batons (generally 26-inches long) are often made of hickory, but are also marketed in aluminum and plastic. The side-handle "PR-24" 24-inch baton is the contemporary standard for many departments in the last decade, while others carry a variety of extendible or collapsible "tactical" batons. Some are outfitted with leather thongs, rubber grips, integral flashlights or tear gas canisters.

A modern version of the Nunchuks, an ancient martial arts weapon, are the latest popular innovation for law enforcement. Consisting of two 18-inch handles connected by a short cable. These have proven very effective in specific situations for crowd control by using pain compliance holds and are carried by some officers instead of batons. For officers working in limited spaces (particularly in correctional institutions), small saps are a popular impact weapon, generally carried in a special pocket in the trousers. Be certain such weapons are specifically authorized by law and your department. Otherwise, your mere possession of such weapons may be a felony.

Chemical Agents

In many agencies, you will also carry an aerosol can with a chemical agent such as CN Tear Gas or OC Pepper Spray. Both types of agents have their relative strong points. CN tear gas tends to contaminate a much larger area, and thus can be useful for clearing non-inhabited areas such as storm drains where a suspect might be hiding. OC spray can be directed at a much smaller target, thus eliminating incidental widespread contamination of the area and other officers. OC spray has the added advantage of working equally well on suspects and vicious dogs.

Handcuffs and Other Restraints

You will also carry handcuffs, and since it seems likely that you might have to arrest more than one person at a time, carrying two pairs of handcuffs seems prudent (carrying two pairs also balances out your back when sitting and seems to be more comfortable).

Handcuffs are available in a wide variety of configurations and finishes including special high-security handcuffs with special keys. Select good quality cuffs from a reputable manufacturer that are strongly made and capable of being "double locked." I carry two types of cuffs on my belt: a standard pair, and an oversized pair joined with a hinge instead of a chain. I have found this second pair works well on violent suspects.

You need to have additional restraints handy in case you end up detaining many people. I carry two extra pairs of standard handcuffs in my "pursuit box," along with half-a-dozen "flex-cuff" plastic restraints. I've seen officers carry plastic restraints tucked in their belts or into their hats as well.

As with your duty weapon, the way you carry your handcuffs is very important. They need to be "indexed" in the same place, so during a fight or scuffle with a suspect you can reach back and find them without looking. They have to be properly secured in some kind of pouch or holder, and you must train with them so you always know how to draw them and apply them with virtually no thought on your part. You should also be mindful that suspects are well aware that a standard key fits most handcuffs. I've encountered a number of criminals who thoughtfully carried their own keys and lock-picks with them.

Along with your handcuffs, many officers carry a "hobble" (a strap or cord with a loop and a snap) that can be used to restrain a violent suspect's feet. The hobble loops around the suspect's ankles and is then generally snapped to the handcuffs, drawing the feet up under the suspect's buttocks. This can cause some suspects to asphyxiate, particularly very heavy suspects. So great care must be taken in using a hobble. Hobbled suspects must be closely monitored at all times.

Your Portable Radio

If you're relatively thin, you'll find that your Sam Brown is rapidly filling up with equipment, but you'll have to find room for a portable radio as well. Your agency may refer to them as "portables," "extenders" (a special type of radio that slaves off of the patrol car's radio), "rovers," "handi-talkies," or sometimes just "H-T's." They come in all sorts of sizes and configurations and range in cost from about $800 to $2,500 per radio. In the past, many officers have simply carried their portable radios in a back pocket, but this tends to rapidly result in lost or broken radios.

The ideal carrying position seems to be centered on the weak side, so that you can still grab the radio and yell for help while you have a suspect held at gunpoint. Microphones extending from the radio and clipping to a uniform pocket or epaulet have become very popular. They make it possible to talk on the radio without looking or removing the radio from the belt pouch but have the disadvantage of significantly lowering range (one study estimated as much as 80 percent of UHF radio signals were absorbed by the body when used in this manner).

Whatever radio and carrier you use, you should be totally familiar with the controls and practice emergency techniques.

Your Flashlight

Whether you work day or night, you will need a good flashlight. Up until a few years ago, my department was still issuing officers cheap little 2-cell plastic flashlights, and there was a mountain of "D-Cell" batteries stored in the watch commander's office (oddly enough, the mountain always seemed to get a little smaller around Christmas time). My FTO told me to buy a rechargeable halogen light, and I've owned one or more ever since.

The Write Stuff

As a final part of your basic patrol equipment, you will need something to write on and some department approved writing implements. Our department provides us with little notepads that fit in our uniform pockets, preprinted with the *Miranda Warning* on the cover, but some officers seem to favor a basketweave leather notebook stuffed in a rear pocket.

Writing instruments will vary according to the user's preference, but I've always favored a cheap but durable plastic pen (about twenty-nine cents each when you buy them by the dozen) and a standard #2 wooden pencil.

BEFORE YOUR PATROL SHIFT

Now that you are familiar with officer's equipment you need to know when and how to report to work. As a general rule, there are no stupid questions, only rookies foolish enough *not to ask* questions.

You need to know a great deal of basic information. If you're assigned to a large city with a number of precincts or districts, where do you report for work on your first day? When does your shift start? When are you expected to report in? Where do you park? What uniform do they expect you to wear (some departments require a long-sleeve "Class A" uniform for your entire probationary period.) Where is the locker room, and which locker is yours? Where is the restroom? Where is the Chief's office? Where are the pre-shift briefings held? Where are you expected to stand or sit? (Hint: rookies generally have a reserved spot right up in front of everyone else). How are lunches handled? Do most officers buy their meals out in the field or bring a brown bag from home? If you have the opportunity, don't hesitate to contact your FTO at work before reporting for your first shift. It's a lot better to show up and ask a few questions than to show up for work unprepared for your shift.

You'll need to learn many things about the station itself. At this point, don't worry about procedures, your FTO will teach you. Worry about being able to find your way around. You should know all of the basic information: where your watch commander or sergeant works, where dispatch is located, where the armory is (for storing weapons and equipment), where the evidence is stored, where officers are expected to write their reports, where officers are allowed to take a break or have lunch, where prisoners are booked, where the patrol cars are parked and where to find the gas pumps. You need to know where to find reference materials such as policy manuals and legal codes, where to find computer terminals and what access you have, and where the detectives work in case you need to contact them. You'll want to locate important information such as crime bulletins, pin maps that show crime patterns in your district or beat, wanted posters, announcements from your employer, and the station log which shows activity from previous shifts.

Getting Information Before Briefing

Get into the habit of studying the above materials prior to every shift. You'll gain an idea of the problems and the people you'll be dealing with during your shift. What kind of arrests are being made? Who is being arrested? Read the actual names. If you're really a "community oriented" patrol officer, you'll see those same names time and time again. Take a close look at the faces on the wanted posters. Where are crimes being reported? What's being stolen, and where? Who are the victims? Are there any special requests for extra patrol or inspectional services? You may want to write down specific information you think you might need for the upcoming shift (i.e., the plates of stolen or felony vehicles, specific addressees, and/or names).

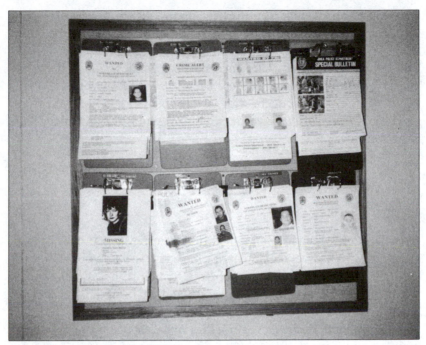

Typical crime bulletin board.

Your Collective Bargaining Unit

Chances are you will also have to deal with your bargaining unit on your first day. Whether it's called a union, a benevolent association, or a police association, some organization probably acts as a collective bargaining agent to negotiate your pay, benefits, and working conditions in the form of a contract or "memorandum of understanding." In some agencies, the same organization will represent everyone from the lowest clerk to the chief. In others, there will be separate unions for non-sworn personnel, police officers, supervisors, and management. You will be asked to join the appropriate organization (although in some states with a "right to work" law you are not *required* to join, but you'll have to pay dues to this organization regardless).

In addition to representing you at the bargaining table, the union will provide you with a variety of benefits. Typical benefits will include: life insurance, health insurance, disability insurance, widows and orphans benefits, scholarships, legal defense, assistance with job grievances, and membership in credit unions. Again, you need to know specific information about what benefits are provided and the costs.

These associations also organize social events for police officers and their families (i.e., Christmas parties, picnics, and golf tournaments.) If you participate in these events, you'll find yourself drawn closer to the other officers with which you work. Once you're off probation, give serious consideration to running for an office in the organization.

THE BRIEFING

Different agencies call it by different terms — roll-call, line-up, or briefing. Whatever they call it, it's the way you start your shift every day. Generally, all the personnel from that shift, or "watch," come together in one place. The supervisors can then brief those assembled on new information, laws, policies and procedures; give each officer his assignment; designate patrol cars and responsibilities; conduct training and inspect officers and their equipment.

On your first day you should be introduced to those assembled. You're likely to see a wide variety of personalities. This may also be the first time you actually meet your FTO or your sergeant. In some agencies it could be the first and only time you meet some of your senior staff, so make the most of it.

Be prepared to be the focus of some of that police officer humor as well. In one agency I know, the rookie officers are required to stand through the entire briefing, while the veteran officers all get to sit. In another agency, the new rookie was actually locked out of the briefing room. No matter what happens to you, just stay professional and do your job and expect some type of humor at your expense. Believe it or not, this type of initiating humor is what starts the process of you becoming accepted as a peer.

Listen carefully to what the sergeant or other briefing officer tells you, with particular emphasis on your beat and assignment. In a small town, there may be no specific beat responsibilities, but larger cities are divided into precincts, districts, divisions, beats, and reporting districts. In a rural agency you may be patrolling hundreds of square miles, in a large city you may spend your entire shift on one block.

Usually, you'll have an assignment sheet, an "Officer's Log," "Daily Field Report"(e.g., DFR) or some other means of documenting all of your assignment information, your activities for the day, and the statistics you produce. At the top of the sheet there will be places to record your names and I.D. numbers, your assignment, unit designation, the date and the shift you're working. Fill in all the blanks, and don't be afraid to ask your FTO for help.

Part of the briefing may include an inspection in which all the officers line-up for close scrutiny by the supervisor. We've already discussed, at length, what standards are expected, and you can expect your supervisor and FTO to be exceptionally critical of you on your first day. They want you to be sharp and to look sharp if you're going to be a member of their department.

After the Briefing

Once you're dismissed from the briefing you'll need to check out any equipment needed (departments often issue radios, flashlights, and shotguns at the start of each shift) and get it out to your assigned patrol car. You'll find that you'll start acquiring a lot of equipment such as jackets, hats, helmets, gloves, keys, code books, binoculars, ammunition, tape-recorders, cameras, clipboards, citation books, report forms, first aid kits, CPR masks, etc. Although much of this equipment is useful, you'll find officers generally refer to this baggage as their "junk" or "trash."

It's absolutely amazing how much gear you can end up carrying on patrol. You will want to organize it in some fashion that makes it convenient to carry and locate. Unless you have the luxury of being assigned your own personal patrol car (yes, there are several agencies that do exactly that), you'll want to organize and carry your gear in a "pursuit case" (a big tub that hangs over the seat back), a "posse box" (a giant briefcase with a clipboard on top), or SWAT bag (a big utility bag with lots of little pockets on the outside). Here again, this is a great topic to discuss with your FTO *before* your first day. Be prepared!

The Patrol Vehicle Inspection

Once you've found your assigned patrol vehicle and loaded your gear inside, you should thoroughly inspect the vehicle. This serves two important functions. First and foremost, it documents the condition of the car, so you and your partner won't get blamed for any new dents and scratches that weren't yours. (Report any new damage to your supervisor immediately.) Most departments keep log books for each vehicle — use them. Secondly, it ensures your personal safety. Patrol cars get used hard, treated roughly, and driven for a lot of miles. You can't prevent every mechanical malfunction (I've literally had wheels fall off and an engine drop out of my car onto the street while on patrol), but you can avoid obviously unsafe conditions that could make a pursuit or just plain patrol a lot more dangerous.

Start with the inside of the car. Put the pursuit case in the rear seat (secured with a shoulder harness to keep it from flying around in case of an accident). Check under the back seat for any contraband, drugs or weapons hidden by the previous shift's prisoners. Clean out any trash left by previous officers (which hopefully doesn't happen often). Be sure to conduct a thorough check. FTO's frequently leave simulated bundles of dynamite and baggies full of oregano under the back seat as a check on a trainee's thoroughness.

Sit behind the wheel, check the gas gauge (our units are supposed to be left full at the end of every shift), start the engine, turn on the radios, check the safety belt, and then check the function of every piece of equipment (i.e., brakes, horn, siren, wipers, heater, etc.). Check the shotgun release, make sure the shotgun is safe and properly loaded, turn on every light in the car and then conduct a "walk around" inspection.

On the walk around, circle the entire car checking each body panel for damage (I've seen officers try to hide scratches in white paint with typing correction fluid and color in scratches in black paint with marking pen, so you need to look carefully). Check each tire for sufficient tread and inflation. (A visual inspection only gets tires that are obviously low, you need to check it with a gauge. This is imperative due to pursuit driving and the strain that it places on tires.) Look at every individual light to make sure that it illuminates, flashes, blinks or swivels correctly. Open the trunk to make sure you have a spare tire, flares, cones and a fire extinguisher. Also make sure that you don't have anything you don't need (I've found everything from dead animals to television sets left behind in patrol car trunks). Your agency might have additional equipment like blankets, first aid kits, tire chains and tear gas kits.

Last of all, check under the hood to make sure you have oil, transmission fluid, coolant, and nothing obviously wrong with the belts, hoses or cables. The department doesn't expect you to be a mechanic, but they also don't expect you to be stupid. Think how dumb you would feel if your engine seized in pursuit due to a lack of oil or an underinflated tire rolled off the rim under hard cornering. You don't need a college degree to check a dipstick, but you do need a deep commitment to your personal safety and to professionalism if you plan on making these same safety checks every single day. Take the time to do it right, each and every day.

Safety Belts and Survival

Part of doing things right is to put on your safety belt. I've heard every excuse in the world for not wearing a safety belt. Officers complain that it hangs up on their badge and other equipment, they need to be able to bail out of the car rapidly, that they could be trapped in the car and burned to death, and that they would rather be thrown clear in an accident.

Yes, a shoulder harness does snag on your badge and other equipment, but that is easy for mature adults to deal with by simply training yourself to push it out of the way as you arrive at the scene of a call. You are far more likely, as a police officer, to be killed in an auto accident than killed by a bullet. Traffic accidents are an occupational hazard. The facts are clear — safety belts and shoulder harnesses save lives and may save *your* life. Stop making excuses, and start wearing your safety belt your first day and every day.

The final thing you need before driving out on your first day of patrol is your FTO, who has hopefully been supervising and guiding you through your entire inspection, perhaps with an admiring audience of other officers. Generally, on this first day you won't be driving, so enjoy being a passenger and start working on your patrol skills.

DISCUSSION QUESTIONS

1. Should a community have any say in the weapons and ammunition carried by their police officers?

2. Can you name the mayor and city council of your own city? Can you name your county Board of Supervisors? Discuss why not.

3. Explain an FTO's typical responsibilities.

4. Would you be willing to spend your own money on equipment for your use in patrol when limited equipment is provided? When outdated equipment is provided? Why or why not?

5. Would you be willing to join a collective bargaining unit? Explain.

Lemon Grove may be stuck in the middle of the San Diego metro-slurb, but in many ways it reflects small-town values and attitudes. Maybe you can openly victimize somebody at Fifth and Broadway and nobody will come to your rescue, but as Luis Vasquez recently learned, "don't mug no ladies in sleepy Lemon Grove."

Vasquez ripped two gold chains from a woman's neck on a recent Friday afternoon and didn't hit the afterburner for his escape until he noticed- uh-oh - several citizens closing on him like heat-seeking missiles.

"Unfortunately for him," said Sheriff's Sgt. Bill Hogue, "About half the town went in pursuit." Four men began chasing Vasquez on foot, they were joined along the way by a camper truck driven by a couple of senior citizens, another pickup carrying a crew of construction workers and a couple in a Monte Carlo sedan.

The chase went on for several blocks, with the vehicles cutting off Vasquez's routes of retreat until, exhausted, he had made almost a complete circle back to the scene of the crime, where deputies grabbed him. Officers reported that Vasquez seemed glad to see them. Apparently he was more than a little concerned with his fate if the citizens caught up with him.

Good. If they don't fear the "criminal justice system," let them fear us!

BASIC CONCEPTS OF PATROL

LEARNING GOALS: After studying this chapter the student will be able to:

- Explain how we define "community policing."

- List common factors in community policing programs.

- Give examples of successful community policing programs that really work.

- List resources, training and skills required to implement community policing programs.

- Explain why business people support community policing programs.

- Describe how to make a police station an effective part of community policing.

- Classify the advantages and disadvantages to community policing.

- Relate an officer's personal life to his effectiveness on patrol.

- Explain how patrol patterns are determined.

- Identify selective enforcement.

COMMUNITY POLICING: AN ORIENTATION

Just when I thought law enforcement was getting this concept of "community policing" down, I started seeing a series of articles dealing with revolutionary new concepts called *Total Service Quality* (or "TSQ" which apparently means doing good police work), and *Problem Oriented Policing* (e.g., "POP"). Don't confuse this with "NOP," which is *Neighborhood Oriented Policing*. NOP is generally credited to the Houston P.D., and is entirely different than POP according to the authors. In NOP, officers deal with assigned neighborhoods and address their problems, while in POP, officers deal with assigned problems within neighborhoods.) This is obviously a different approach than *Community Oriented Policing* (e.g.,"COP") and completely different than the old concept of *selective enforcement* which we'll talk about later on in this chapter.

I'm poking a little fun at the authors and proponents of these concepts to make a valid point. Each of these programs deals with the transfer of power, specifically the power to direct and influence the way in which police and patrol services are delivered to individual communities. POP gives more power to the individual police officer, leaving him the freedom to work with the people in his patrol area to best direct his efforts. NOP and COP give more power to the neighborhoods and communities to give their direct input and desires as to where police efforts should be directed.

Revolutionary concepts? It *is* revolutionary to old style traditional police departments whose administrators have been totally in control of that power for decades. They've lost sight of the fact that the people who really know what they need are those closest to the problem — the average citizen on the street working hand in hand with the cop on the beat. Maybe we should call it *Beat Oriented Policing* (e.g., "BOP"). You can call it "COP," "POP," "NOP" or "BOP"; it's simply a common sense approach to directing patrol services based on a partnership between the police and the community.

If you want to be effective as a patrol officer, you have to learn your community inside and out. You have to know its geography, its history, its cultures, its business community, and the organizations that drive it. You have to know the people of your community, both the good, the bad, and the 99 percent that will never get your attention but deserve to be the focus of all your efforts.

COP means getting to know the people on your beat.

Your Law Enforcement Agency

First, know who runs your department. You need to understand your department's organizational chart, learning the rank structure, the divisions, and the separations of responsibility. You'll probably fall under the "Patrol" or "Operations" division. You should know the name of your chief of police, division head (often a captain, commander or similar rank) and watch commander. You should know about the other major city departments, how they are administered and who the department heads report to. Is your chief responsible to a police commission, the mayor, or a city manager? Do you know the names of the mayor, city council, city clerk and other elected representatives? Learn them!

Your Local Government

By understanding your own organization, you can understand why it is essential for you to work well with other member of your city government. Each department in a city — be it streets, parks and recreation, the city library, or the fire department is headed by a chief administrator equal in rank, in the mayor and city council's eyes, to the chief of police and sheriff. Each department competes for a piece of the municipal budget. When the city decides to buy a dozen patrol cars, it may mean sacrificing the purchase of a new fire engine or giving up programs and personnel at the library. Each department in the city provides important and desirable services to the citizens of the community. There's no room for interdepartmental rivalries and bad feelings among fellow employees, and you should show proper respect to other department heads and supervisors.

The Geography of Your Patrol Area

As you and your FTO tour your assigned beat, you need to learn your jurisdiction's geography. That's a lot more than just learning the street names (although you will certainly want to learn those by heart). Also you'll need to know your operational boundaries, the city limits, shared intersections, boundary markings, signs and major landmarks.

You don't always have to walk a beat.

You should learn what jurisdictions neighbor and overlap into your city and what other federal, state, regional, county, or local agencies share your jurisdiction. You should learn what resources they can offer you as well, who has canines, helicopters, SWAT teams or other items immediately available, and who to turn to for incidents involving school buses, aircraft, interstate commercial trucks, trains, or transit buses.

Natural features and physical barriers in your city are also necessary to learn. My city has hills and valleys, freeways and major streets, winding trails and nature preserves, railroad right-of-ways and flood control channels. Each of these can become a major factor in response to calls and the ability to provide the highest level of service to the community.

Knowing the Streets

You need to learn the street names in your city. You learn the street names by working with them, by constantly reviewing maps, and by looking at the name on every street sign at every corner without fail. You can't help anybody if you can't find your way to your assigned calls, and if you don't look at all the street signs you pass, you're going to find yourself playing one of the FTO's favorite games: *"Name That Street."*

The way the game works is: The FTO is behind the wheel on a quiet night and waits until you're deep in concentration with your head down. Then he suddenly jams on the brakes and demands to know exactly where you are. If you can't answer, you win a quick jog back to the nearest street corner to tell your FTO what street you're on. As a bonus, he will usually require you to tell him over the radio, so everyone else on the frequency can share in your new-found knowledge.

Along with the names of the streets, you should learn the logical pattern behind the street layouts. What divides north and south streets and east and west streets? Does the numbering system start at a particular central intersection and progress outward from there? On which side of the street do you find odd and even addresses? Within this context, what are the boundaries of your assigned beat? Which are the dividing streets, and who has responsibility for overlapping calls?

You need to know what is located on those streets. Where are the banks, the bars, the gas stations, the parks, the liquor stores, the markets, the schools and the hospitals? Which of these businesses operate at unusual hours, or necessarily handle large amounts of cash? Are there areas where citizens are particularly vulnerable like senior citizen centers, playgrounds, and ATM machines, or inaccessible areas such as underground parking lots? Where do gang members live, socialize, or just hang out? Are there areas of high density housing or districts made up entirely of apartments or public housing? Because of the sheer concentrations of people and cars in such areas, they can create concentrations of crime that need to be addressed with different patrol methods.

Knowing the People in Your Community

You need to know the people on your streets as well. What are your city's demographics as far as race, culture, age, education and income? The patrol needs of a wealthy suburban community are quite different from those of a poverty-stricken urban area. What are their expectations of service from you? What is their attitude toward the police? What level and quality of service do they expect? What types of services do they need? And what response times do they demand?

The Heart of Community Oriented Policing

Intimate knowledge of your community is at the heart of community oriented policing. It is what makes a superior patrol officer. These are the types of officers that drive down the street and spot the dumped stolen cars because they know all the cars that belong on that block. They make proactive arrests of robbery suspects, because they see a car parked out of place. They take guns and knives and dope off of suspects on a daily basis, because they see them engaged in activity that doesn't fit the normal pattern of their beat.

The key is to become a great observer and completely familiar with your beat. Get to know the people and places. It takes a lot of work but is well worth the effort.

The first step is to slow down. If you drive through your beat a little slower, you will gain increased acuity for all your senses — better able to see, hear, and smell what's going on around you. Slower speed will also give you an increased ability to react and higher visibility in the streets because you'll have more time to take-in your surroundings.

Commentary driving is another technique that can improve your powers of observation. That's a simple matter of verbalizing, just talking out loud, about the things you see. A typical commentary might sound like this, "I'm approaching Park Street which is a four-way stop. There is a male Hispanic in a white Hyundai already at the intersection to my right. He's come to a full stop and made eye contact with me, and now he's proceeding through. He has a tattoo on his right shoulder, it looks like a "Happy Valley" gang tattoo. I don't know this guy, but the car looks clean, all the locks and windows look intact, I don't see any damage and he doesn't seem nervous at all."

COMMON COMMUNITY POLICING ELEMENTS

Virtually all community policing programs contain the following common elements:

1) There is a shared responsibility for crime between the policing agency and the community.

2) There is the creation of a partnership between the policing agency and the community.

3) The expectations and standards of police performance are changed.

4) Community policing builds understanding and trust between the police and the community.

5) The community is empowered to direct police activities, and strengthen their ability to deal with crime.

6) Both communities and police agencies develop flexibility in their approach to solving problems.

7) Community policing requires a commitment to seeking long term solutions.

8) New resources are developed, both within the community and within the policing agency.

9) Police leaders commit to the community policing concept in order to make it work.

10) Community policing represents a decentralization of power and control over police operations.

11) The focus of the police agency is shifted to proactive, long-term solutions.

12) New skills are developed and nurtured in the police agency and the community.

Community Policing Reassesses Responsibility for Crime

Community policing shifts responsibility, in part, back to the public, recognizing that society and the people in our communities are responsible for the conditions that allow or foster crime. Simply enforcing the laws will do little or nothing to change the underlying reasons that produce crime and social disorder. In fact, specific people in the community such as: parents, teachers, school principals, clergy, politicians, business people, and the directors and members of community-based organizations have to share this responsibility. They are the ones who can make the kinds of changes that might really have an effect on crime. These role models and leaders within each community may be much more important than the uniformed patrol officer in establishing the community's acceptable standards of conduct.

As a patrol officer, you can also play a key role. You are in a unique position to address the real causes of crime. Unlike other leaders, you are available and directly interact with the community everyday. "Policing" is accessible around the clock. You'll have unique first-hand knowledge and insight into many of the problems and issues in the community. Part of your role as a patrol officer includes identifying the persons who might best help resolve the problems you recognize on your beat. As a patrol officer you'll identify important resources which you may bring into the problem solving process.

As a patrol officer, you have to be a teacher. You need to cultivate and encourage the concepts of community policing in your beat. You must heighten awareness of the public's importance in helping you deal with controlling crime. You can't force these concepts on the community. The community must accept their responsibility for maintaining law and social order. Once that responsibility is accepted, they must cooperate with you to identify problems and develop proactive community-wide solutions to these problems.

A New Partnership

Community policing requires that you and your community share the ownership, decision-making, and accountability for crime problems. This requires a long-term commitment from both sides and some major shifts in traditional police management and citizen's concepts of police work. As a patrol officer, you'll have to recognize the fact that police cannot do the job alone. There are valuable resources in your community (and each community is different) that can share in the power to solve community problems. It should be a creative process, with feedback and representation from the entire spectrum of the community.

This partnership requires a transfer of decision-making power to neighborhoods, families, individuals, schools, elected officials, government agencies, organizations, churches and businesses. If they accept responsibility for problem solving, they will need the information that only a patrol officer can provide. They need the power to influence (not dictate) the policy and the goals of the police department.

This doesn't mean a return to frontier or vigilante justice with individual residents attempting to enforce the law. Rather community members should work with you to identify and prioritize problems, develop and implement programs, determine the appropriate allocation of your time and other resources, and evaluate and modify police responses to achieve the community's goals.

Shifting Focus

Traditional police work is *reactive*, focusing on the response to individual incidents and based on priorities that have been determined by the police administration. Reacting to citizen requests for service takes up the majority of an officer's time. The public's expectations of police service has become based on response time and the level and efficiency of that response. This simply perpetuates more demands for service, and officers end up dealing with only the symptoms of criminal activity — the crimes.

Implementing a community policing program requires changing that focus to address the broad problems identified by the community in conjunction with the police. Police can then focus on the overall problem rather than on the individual incidents. Once you begin to focus on the problem, you and the community can work toward solutions that will attack the true causes and thus eliminate and/or reduce crime.

By regular follow up, consultation, and feedback from the community, your actions on patrol can become much more closely aligned with the wants and needs of the community you serve. Instead of dealing with the highly visible crimes that represent threats to life, you deal with the quality of life itself. You affect how people feel about their homes and neighborhoods. A burglar can affect a limited number of victims, but gangs loitering on corners, drug dealing in the parks, noisy stereos and abandoned autos make people feel unsafe and affect the total quality of life within the community.

Community policing deals with those problems which the community has established as most important. It puts your agency in tune with the community, ensures that the public will view your activities as important and effective, and ultimately builds your respect and authority.

That's not to say that community policing should *not* be responsive to crime. Community policing is highly responsive, but not reactive. It is tough on crime and ruthless in the pursuit of criminals, but not blinded by a single mission that excludes the overall needs of the community. By working with citizens for a comprehensive problem solving approach, officers receive more information, have deeper knowledge of the community and its individuals, and thus are far more effective in solving crimes and making arrests.

COMMUNITY POLICING AT A PERSONAL LEVEL

Community policing requires your active participation in the community. You have to practice in your private life what you preach in your professional life. While I no longer live in the community I patrol, I did so for many years, and it was no secret to my neighbors that I was a police officer. I went to church, did my shopping, served as a scoutmaster, attended city council and school board meetings, served on the 4th of July parade committee, joined a service club, voted in every election, and married a local girl. All of which provided me with a large base of community trust. Citizens knew me as an individual and recognized my commitment to the community.

No police agency in the country requires that depth of involvement, and some officers you work with may actually discourage it. I know many officers who take a mercenary approach, keeping their private lives totally separated from their professional lives. Based on my experience, I can tell you that community involvement will enrich your life and enhance your career in every way. You will develop a network of connections and friends in the community that will make you more efficient and effective. The quality of information you receive will be the envy of other officers, and you will find citizens that are there to support you when you're in need of help.

Look for opportunities and be generous with your time: join organizations, be a member, an advisor, an educator or a sponsor, work with Little League or AYSO, be a Scout leader or teach Sunday school. Do things that interest you, but whatever responsibilities you choose, give something of yourself.

As you interact with others in the community, don't be afraid to talk about what you do. I have always been very proud to be a police officer, and I feel there is absolutely nothing I have to hide about what I do or how I do it. Of course you aren't going to tell people about investigations in progress or who you arrested the previous night. However, there is no reason not to tell people about your life at work, sharing your views of the problems the community faces and seeking their input and ideas. The most effective community oriented police officers are those that are, first, members of the community, and, second, "happen" to be police officers.

COMMUNITY POLICING SUMMARY

In 1992, the California Attorney General's Advisory Committee on Community-Oriented Policing & Problem Solving (COPPS) came up with this definition of community policing:

Community policing is a philosophy, management style, and organizational strategy that promotes pro-active problem-solving and police-community partnerships to address the causes of crime and fear as well as other community issues.

Community partnership is a flexible term referring to any combination of neighborhood residents, schools, churches, businesses, community-based organizations, elected officials, and government agencies who are working cooperatively with the police to resolve identified problems that impact or interest them.

Problem solving refers to a process of identifying problems/priorities through coordinated community/police needs assessments; collecting and analyzing information concerning the problem in a thorough, though not necessarily complicated manner; developing or facilitating responses that are innovative and tailor-made with the best potential for eliminating or reducing the problem; and, finally, evaluating the response to determine its effectiveness and modifying it as necessary.

Community policing is what works in your community. It can be overdone, and it is not without its critics. Although the Los Angeles Police Department has been considered one of the leaders in the Community Oriented Policing movement, former Chief Daryl Gates makes some surprising comments in his autobiography *Chief, My Life in the LAPD*. After discussing the leadership role that the LAPD played in developing community-based policing, he said in part, "…we knew the people of Los Angeles wanted more than that. They want their calls answered on time; they want something done about crime and violence. They want balanced policing, and that is what LAPD provided them."

Daryl Gates thought that community based policing would lead to closer relations between the police and their neighborhoods, but he also feared that the citizens were being deceived. He wrote, "At some point, as crime continues to stalk this city, people are going to cry, 'We don't want lollipops! We want arrests!'" It is obvious throughout his book that Gates is a strong proponent of community policing. He also clearly recognized that it must meet the needs and desires of the community. If you thrust an unwelcome program on the community, it will be a program destined to fail.

When community policing works it is because the participants have established a partnership between the law enforcement agency and each and every member of the community: a partnership involving the people, schools, businesses, churches, government agencies, the media, service organizations and the political leadership. Successful programs are often perceived as a threat to police administrators and politicians because it must involve a transfer of police authority. Every member of the community has to be allowed input into determining the priorities of the police department, and with that transfer of authority comes a transfer of responsibility to the members of the community. They accept some of the responsibility for fighting crime. They recognize that in a partnership you share in the victory of success and share in the blame for failures as well.

Community policing is not just a program. It is a total philosophy for conducting law enforcement, and a return of police power to those best able to use it — the citizen and the patrol officer. Properly executed, community policing develops into a lifestyle, uniquely evolved and tailored for every community and every agency, fine-tuned to meet the specific challenges of both. It is a common sense approach and a return to the basic concepts and values of police patrol, all of which is predicated on the basic values of the community being served.

OBSERVATION TECHNIQUES

Ask an experienced officer what lead him to make one of those great, *intuitive arrests*, and oftentimes he will say, "It just didn't look right." That quality of *not looking right* often constitutes lawful probable cause, but sometimes the actual law and facts aren't readily apparent to the officer at the time he takes action. It stems from an experienced officer's intimate knowledge of his community. Since he knows what should "look right" in his beat, it's a lot easier for him to sense when things look wrong.

The officer who knows what "looks right" learns so by being an astute observer. Some of the things that might not "look right" could include: broken windows, missing screens, open doors and gates, pry marks around locks, vehicles parked in unusual areas, or unusual vehicles parked in normal areas, abnormal lighting patterns, pedestrians in unusual areas, unusual sounds, and unusual reactions from dogs and other pets.

Think about how this works. After a long period of patrolling the same beat, you know the people and their patterns. You know the local businessmen, so you know which clerk belongs behind the counter and which attendant should be at what gas station. You learn who hangs out on the corners, who jogs, who walks their dogs, and all the normal patterns of life.

The power of observation is a primary resource to the patrol function. Watch and you'll find some of the best officers never stop moving their head. They are constantly observing and taking-in their surroundings.

Learning the Beat on Your Feet

To learn your beat, you've got to get out of the patrol car, explore the territory, and meet the people. If you want to know which clerk belongs in the liquor store at any given time, you better get out of the car and into the liquor store to meet the clerk before anything happens. If you want to know who's lounging around on your street corners, you better stop and talk to them, find out who they are, find out their names and addresses, and write it all down. Review the names later, recalling them each time you see them, until you've committed them to memory. Get out of the car and walk around buildings (graveyard shift is a great time for this), learn where the walkways connect, where stairways lead, where the doors and windows are located, where you can find ladders leading up to a roof. And always, you have to know where you are at all times — the beat, the street, and the address.

Different beats require different modes of transportation.

PATROL PATTERNS

Traditional "preventative" police patrol has generally been random and reactive in nature. When not reacting to crime by answering specific calls, the officers in the patrol car randomly patrols the assigned area without any pattern. Although not really proactive, conventional wisdom has it that this type of patrol is the best way of fighting crime since the appearance of the patrol car is unpredictable and will end up sometimes surprising criminals in the act.

The Advantages and Drawbacks of Random Patrol

There is probably some benefit to this type of patrol from an officer safety standpoint. Being unpredictable makes it difficult for someone to set up an ambush. But other than that one dubious benefit, the proponents of alternative patrol plans, such as the POP and NOP plans, like to point to the drawbacks. Research from the 1970s and early 1980s seems to indicate that random vehicle patrol has *little* impact on crime, and that rapid response times have almost no effect on the probability of arresting criminals. Yet another study found that, on the average, the typical patrol officer actually surprised a felony in progress about once every five years.

In regards to the second study on response times, their conclusion that a fast response does not increase the probability of arrest appears to be valid. However, from a community policing standpoint, your goal is not to simply arrest the offender. We have to look at the overall service we provide to our community. That includes a swift response to render aid, relieve the victim's fears, give the neighborhood an appearance of security, and the preservation of evidence. It seems obvious to me that swift response times are beneficial to both the community and the policing effort.

Patrolling After Dark

Your patrol patterns and techniques during hours of darkness might be substantially different than those during the day. During the early hours of the morning, I have observed police officers driving down the street in the stealth mode, completely blacked out (no lights showing) and lit up like a Christmas tree with high-beams, spotlights, alley lights, and take-down lights all blazing.

At first look, it was really obvious that the unit with all the lights on was a police car, and criminals would flee long before the officer would ever see them. Similarly, I found that to a person on foot, the blacked out patrol car was almost as identifiable. Even the quietest of cars makes a lot of noise, and a worn out patrol car makes more than most. Patrol cars have a distinctive sound with their de-smogged engines, wide-bore exhausts, squealing brake pads, murmuring radios, and the whistling of wind through the lightbar and antennas. As a patrol officer, I can readily hear when another officer has arrived on a scene — the criminals are just as attuned to those sounds.

What seems to best hide the patrol car at night is to simply act like all the other cars. Drive and brake at normal speeds, and approach incidents with your high-beams on. You'll find that you can see the incident better in the patrol car headlights, and that the high-beams mask the outline of the patrol car better than any other combination of lighting. With this approach you must be extremely sensitive to the possibility of blinding other drivers.

"Democratic Patrol"

Lacking any specific and identifiable crime patterns to pursue, arguably the best patrol pattern for night or day is the "democratic method." Each person in your beat deserves his fair share of your patrol time. That means that you should cover every street and business in your beat. Depending on the size of your beat, that may not be possible, but I always considered it as a source of pride that my patrol car drove past every single house and building in my beat at least once during my shift if it was at all possible. It's a random method of coverage, but one that ensures each person gets a fair share of your patrol time.

SELECTIVE ENFORCEMENT

Most of the time we don't have a clue as to where to find criminals in the act of committing crime so we depend on random patrol. When we do respond to some sort of clue or pattern, we call it *selective enforcement*.

Selective enforcement can be based on any information we have that will help us to better direct our patrol efforts. You may concentrate your efforts on a specific suspect or gang, on a specific high-crime location, or on the profile of specific victims. Your patrol pattern may be altered based on specific times, days, or dates.

For instance, if you have had a series of robberies committed against theater patrons at closing time, you would direct your patrol efforts to the theater district during those specific hours. A series of crimes against elderly in the park might bring about a different patrol pattern, as would a series of car-jackings along a certain stretch of highway.

Selective patrol can be in response to any concern of the community, whether it is a desire for increased police presence during lunch at the local high school or a complaint of commuter traffic running a stop sign in a residential area.

Depending on your perspective, the arrival of a canine unit may make you smile or want to give yourself up.

Fair Use of Resources

What is a fair and equitable use of police resources, and what is a fair and equitable way for you to spend your time on patrol? Should each comparable community receive the same amount of police funding? Should those citizens in neighborhoods with the highest crime rates have exactly the same number of officers per capita and exactly the same amount of patrol time as those neighborhoods with little or no crime? Or should resources be directed to equalize crime, so that by putting a hundred times the officers into the high crime neighborhood you might bring down the rate of murders, rape and robbery to exactly the same per capita amount as in the low-crime neighborhood? While that may seem fair, it is not necessarily the most efficient use of resources. Also, it may not bring the city's overall crime rate to the lowest possible rate.

Proactive vs. Reactive Policing

One way of trying to make more efficient use of these resources is the concept of "proactive policing" versus "reactive policing." Most police patrol in the past has been entirely reactive. That is, you wait for a crime or accident to occur and then react by responding to the location, investigating the incident, and tracking down those responsible.

Proactive policing is preventative in nature. It concentrates on focused patrol, which is directed toward surveillance and the following of known criminals. It includes high patrol activity at locations you can statistically predict crime will occur. Proactive policing seems as though it would be more efficient in protecting and serving the public. However, while it is easy to measure arrests and crimes which result from reactive policing, it is difficult to measure crimes *prevented* and arrests that *don't* occur as a result of proactive measures.

SPECIALIZED PATROL

For most of us, patrol assignment means we will spend most of our career steering a patrol car around the streets and highways. For variety, we might look forward to a foot beat or possibly the occasional use of an unmarked car.

To meet the specialized needs of different parts of the community, there are all sorts of specialized patrol units that sound like even more fun to me. Each is designed to address either a specific geographical area or a unique problem.

Although S.W.A.T. teams are the most well known specialized team, they aren't really classified under patrol.

Patrol Motorcycles and Bicycles

Motorcycle patrol has become firmly established as one of the primary tools of choice for enforcing traffic laws. Motorcycles are exhilarating for the patrol officers — fast, powerful, and just a little dangerous. The officers wear a distinctive uniform, usually with full protection helmets and tall riding boots. They crank out tickets at an impressive rate (one manufacturer told me that if the bike didn't pay for itself in the first week, the officer wasn't doing his job).

Motorcycles also have some major drawbacks. They require a lot of maintenance and training time, function best in fair weather, and are downright dangerous in snow or on ice. They suffer about the same accident rate as a patrol car, but offer virtually no protection to the officer. So motorcycle officers tend to suffer a higher rate of on duty injury than their four wheel equipped peers. The officers tend to be cold and impersonal in their citizen contacts and may leave behind a poor impression with the public. They cannot transport prisoners or carry much in the way of equipment. In other words, they're basically suited for traffic enforcement.

Given the drawbacks of motorcycles, it's surprising that bicycles have become so popular in police work, but virtually every major city (and a lot a minor ones) now offer some sort of patrol on modified mountain bikes. These officers wear a comfortably modified uniform, usually with a T-shirt or polo-shirt, shorts, lightweight nylon gunbelt, and running shoes. They seem to be great for public relations, generally assigned to patrol parks and downtown business districts. Highly mobile, they carry virtually no equipment, so they have to be backed up by regular patrol units. As an added benefit, the officers stay in great physical shape.

Horses, Boats, and Aircraft

Mounted officers on horseback offer another type of patrol. Again, they're great for public relations; everyone loves to see and pet the horse. They're highly effective in a park environment and give the officer the added advantage of great height. Because of the intimidating height and mass of the horse and rider, equestrian units have proven themselves highly effective in policing demonstrations and in conducting crowd control. Horseback patrol is not my personal choice (the term "saddlesore" comes to mind), but I can see how the dedicated cowboy would have a lot of fun.

A motorized version of the equestrian patrol that is popular in many beach communities is an officer mounted on a three wheeled all-terrain-vehicle to patrol the sand and the surf, and on Catalina Island, off the coast of California, the Sheriff's Department patrols the city of Avalon in two golf carts. Again, these officers wear a modified uniform suited for their assignment. I don't know of any studies to show their effectiveness in fighting crime, but it's obvious that they're great for public relations and a lot of fun for the officers involved.

For officers working harbor patrol units, there's even more exciting transportation. Various sizes of powerful patrol boats fill the function of the patrol car, while in warmer climates officers on jet-skis fulfill the marine equivalent of motorcycle officers (colder climates get to use snowmobiles).

Some agencies also have an aero-bureau, patrolling highways or cities by use of helicopters or fixed wing aircraft (nobody uses blimps that I know of, but several agencies have experimented with ultra-lights). Aircraft are great for surveillance missions, indispensable for search and rescue, and the modern patrol helicopter is a miracle of versatility and technology. They can airlift a critically injured victim to a hospital in minutes, light up the night sky like daylight, search for heat-producing targets with Forward Looking Infra Red ("FLIR") units, and capture the entire operation on videotape. They're fun to work with, fun to watch, and an absolute thrill to fly in.

Regardless of your means of transportation, the function of every one of these units is simply to patrol. Each must be responsive to the needs of their respective communities and must work in partnership with those communities to best address the problems they share. Specialized units have the advantage of dealing with specialized problems which are often very narrow in scope. Traditional patrol officers have to deal with the entire spectrum of police and social problems, handling a huge variety of generalized functions in a professional and competent manner. Perhaps the most demanding and specialized patrol of all is the uniformed officer working in a marked patrol car.

DISCUSSION QUESTIONS

1) Why do you think responsibility for public safety has shifted from the individual to the government?

2) If community policing grows and becomes accepted in your community, should police personnel and expenditures increase or decrease?

3) Police officers have always enjoyed privacy in their off-duty lives. How might community policing affect that privacy?

4) Do you think a commitment to community policing would affect recruitment standards? How and why?

5) Why would police managers feel threatened by community policing? What could the community do to lessen those fears?

6) What areas of a police station should remain totally off-limits to the public? Why?

7) The author has suggested the "democratic allocation" of patrol time. What do you think of a "user fee" concept, where patrol time would be based on the actual taxes paid by an individual?

8) When selective enforcement concentrates on a specific individual criminal suspect, do you feel this practice violates his rights?

Salt Lake City police received a call through 9-1-1 from a woman who complained that her husband refused to have sex with her. When police arrived, the nearly nude woman was beating her husband. Hubby's reason for not wanting to participate in the marital act: he wanted to watch an exciting Utah Jazz basketball game on TV.

* * *

Police in Houma, LA, responded quickly to a rare 9-1-1 call but wound up citing the lady they were there to help. Velma Ann Wantlin, 28, punched the emergency line and summoned police because her husband was preventing her from watching the season finale of "Knots Landing." The cops weren't amused. After all, it wasn't "The Young and the Restless."

POLICE COMMUNICATIONS

LEARNING GOALS: After studying this chapter the student will be able to:

- State facts that lead outside observers to believe in the existence of a "police subculture."

- Describe typical police dispatch operations.

- Describe the purpose of having a radio call sign.

- State the purpose of police radio codes.

- Describe how the 9-1-1 system operates.

- List the major computer networks available to police.

- Define a Mobile Data Terminal (MDT) and explain how it is used .

- Identify the new technology available in law enforcement communications.

POLICE JARGON AND SLANG

Sociologists and reporters have often discussed "police subculture," which some believe is an elaborate conspiratorial network of police officers. They feel that police officers must be consumed with stress, suspicion, cynicism, racism, and insecurity. Therefore, these "outsiders" speculate that all law enforcement officers belong to a secret fraternity bound by a "*Code of Silence*," and these individuals rarely venture beyond the comfortable surroundings of other cops for life's needs.

It is easy to understand why outside observers could come to this conclusion. Like most people, police officers tend to form friendships with their co-workers, and, like other jobs, mutual experiences, whether satisfying or tragic, tend to bring those that share these experiences closer. Unfortunately, tragedy and conflict are an integral part of law enforcement. Think of any tragic or "life-threatening" situation you've ever faced. Chances are if you shared that experience you came away "emotionally bound" to one or more of the people involved with you during that experience. Now multiply that effect by the average number of times an officer deals with life-threatening, tragic, emotional and dramatic experiences encountered on a routine basis with his fellow officers. You may now begin to understand why camaraderie between officers usually is so very high.

Doctors and lawyers can unwind in a bar together without attracting attention, but when the public sees cops doing the same thing it's a "choir practice." Doctors and lawyers are bound to keep information on their patients and clients confidential, and rarely discuss their work with outsiders. Police officers have the same professional constraints, but the media tends to treat it as conspiratorial and threatening.

The fact of the matter is, like any other profession, it is very difficult to generalize about any group of police officers. Most officers share the middle class values and beliefs with the majority of persons in the United States. Certain police agencies develop an institutional culture that shapes their officers in unique ways. For every police officer that "talks shop" with his friends, there is an officer that leaves the job behind him in his locker with his duty gun and uniform. For every cop that goes out drinking after work, there are many more that go straight home to family, coach Little League, or attend church, etc.

Unquestionably, those in law enforcement tend to talk in a unique form of slang and jargon that reinforces the public's image of a subculture. All professions have unique technical terms and slang they use on a daily basis. This slang serves a number of valid purposes. It efficiently communicates concepts unique to their jobs, and it lets them communicate more efficiently and effectively with their peers. It also, as with some professions, softens the harsh edge of daily reality.

Thus, a nurse in an emergency room might tell a doctor to get there "stat" (as quickly as you can, it's an emergency) because there's a "Code Blue" (person in full cardiac arrest) enroute by "R.A." (paramedic rescue ambulance). When CPR fails, the relatives will be told something like, "He was unresponsive to CPR," "He expired," or "We did everything possible." Rarely will a doctor come right out and say, "He's dead." Likewise, a prosecuting attorney could tell his secretary he was "on calendar" (scheduled for court) for a "1538" (in California, a motion to suppress evidence based on lack of probable cause) with a "pro per" (a defendant appearing in court and acting as his own attorney).

Similarly, police officers speak a unique language — one that is sometimes impossible for those outside the profession to understand. There are great variations between different agencies and jurisdictions, so a criminal might be a "perp" (perpetrator) on the East Coast and a "suspect" in the West. Cars become "units," "squads," "cruisers," or "prowl-cars." Their conversations with other officers are sprinkled with the penal code sections and radio codes they use constantly. When talking with others within the law enforcement profession, this type of jargon lends itself to effective communication. Unfortunately, when dealing with members of the community-at-large, it can create a barrier to communication.

Like any communicator, you have to know and address your audience. When you talk to members of the public, speak in plain English and make yourself easily understood without simplifying to the point you patronize your audience. For the most part, they won't understand the technical aspects of your job or the intricacies of law. So explain things in terms they can understand. Last of all, when speaking on the radio, use the appropriate codes and procedures your department endorses.

DISPATCH OPERATIONS

Police dispatching has developed rapidly in the past 100 years and continues to accelerate at an incredible rate. In the early days of law enforcement, a citizen had to go find the police officer, either by locating him on foot patrol in his beat or by going to the station house. With the advent of telephones, call-boxes, and alarm systems, dispatching became a more centralized operation.

Even a small agency's dispatch operation can be a complicated matter.

In the early days of law enforcement, many alarms were wired directly to the police station. When the alarm was activated at some location in the city, a bell and an illuminated, numbered light at the police station would alert the dispatcher of the alarm location. A more "sophisticated" system was the Wells Fargo telegraph, which punched out a coded ticker tape. A typical alarm would laboriously punch out holes in a paper tape. A pattern of two holes, followed by five, and then by three, would be read as #253 which would give the dispatcher the location of the alarm. (Sounds like an archaic system, but we had one operational in our department until the mid-1980s.)

Officers were contacted by the dispatcher in the field by signaling devices installed on their beat. Various systems included: having the dispatcher flash the streetlights, activating a special call light at a major intersection, or activating a light atop the beat's call-box. The call-box was the focal point of the foot-cop's beat and a place where citizens knew they could generally find their beat officer. Without radio, officers communicated with each other from beat to beat with a variety of sound-making devices. These included whistles, bells, rattles, striking their nightsticks against curbings in a preset patterned code, and even warning shots.

RADIO COMMUNICATIONS

Radio was first introduced to police work in the late 1920s, a strictly one-way broadcast received on standard AM radios in patrol cars. The dispatcher would broadcast the crime call and hope that cars in the field would hear the call and respond to it. (Remember the radio broadcasts in old gangster movies, where the dispatcher would say, "Calling all cars, calling all cars!"?) Officers who wanted to communicate with the station did so by telephone or by police call-box.

It is hard to imagine a law enforcement agency without radios, but even today it is possible to find places where radio communication is so difficult that police dispatchers still have a physical signal to get the officer to phone for his calls. (Shoshone, California, on the far side of Death Valley, is one such place. The resident deputy, if he can't be reached by phone, is flagged down by a signal at the local gas station.) Radio is a relatively new innovation to law enforcement, and some agencies still work without individual portable radios or "handi-talkies."

As a patrol officer, you will most likely be dispatched by radio. You will also be expected to respond to the radio, answering appropriately, making inquiries and requests, and giving the disposition of your calls.

Depending on the size of your agency, you may be on a non-exclusive single frequency shared with other agencies in the area, on an exclusive single frequency for your own department, or operating on many different frequencies. Most law enforcement agencies have at least three frequencies: a primary channel carrying the bulk of the dispatch traffic, a secondary channel for administrative uses, and a car-to-car channel. Very large agencies such as the Chicago Police Department have over 100 frequencies with separate channels for each of the different divisions, bureaus, details, and specialized units.

Who's Listening Out There?

Police officers tend to have a well-developed sense of humor, and oftentimes this surfaces on the radio. For many officers, there is almost nothing better than getting in a good, humorous line as part of their communication with the dispatcher or other officers. Car-to-car frequencies are even more lively with comedy, commentary and critique of other officers and their handling of calls. It also seems that the later the shift, the more active the comedy. There's nothing like a little joke to liven up a graveyard shift.

A sobering thought to help you keep your radio traffic more professional is to consider exactly who is listening to you each time you speak and how your radio communications are going to affect their opinion of you. In addition to my fellow officers and my supervisors, I always assume the following people in my city *could* be listening:

- The Chief, who lives in town and has radios in his car and home;
- The City Manager, also with radios in his car and home;
- The dispatchers in surrounding cities, monitoring our radios;
- The patrol officers in surrounding cities, monitoring on scanners in their patrol cars;
- Our fire department and ambulance services, all with scanners in their vehicles;
- The local press, in the form of television, radio and newspapers, all eagerly listening to their scanners;
- A local political activist, often attacking our department and an avid scanner listener;
- On rare occasions, the federal government, in the form of the Federal Communications Commission;
- and, based on scanner sales at our local Radio Shack, as many as 60 new listeners in our community every month.

Quite an audience when you think about it. A real inspiration for keeping your radio traffic professional.

Radios

Most patrol officers today will have both a portable radio carried on their "Sam Brown," and a permanent radio in their vehicle. These radios can range from simple single channel transceivers to incredibly complex, digitally synthesized, 100+ channel, scanning, scrambled, and trunked, multi-functional electronic wonders.

Portable radios also can come with an incredible variety of options including: LCD displays, digital keyboards, panic buttons, remote microphones, earphones, privacy channels, and even motion detectors (designed to alert the dispatcher if you fall down and stop moving for more than a few seconds).

What is important to understand is that all radios operate on the same fundamental principles. The basic controls are similar and almost every radio has a microphone, an on/off volume control, a channel selector, and a squelch control.

Radio Procedures

There are certain courtesies and conventions that should be observed when using the radio, whether you are giving or receiving a call. Let's say that you are assigned to a unit with the familiar call sign of "1-Adam-12" (there's more on call signs below). This call sign will be the way the dispatcher addresses you and the way you will identify yourself to the dispatcher.

Radio time is precious time in any agency, so you've got to think out your message in advance. Your radio transmissions should all be calm, clear, accurate and concise. Always try to keep it short, or if you have to give a long message, be sure to pause every 15-30 seconds. Another unit may have a dire emergency and need to jump in with their message. If you go rambling on for two or three minutes, the delay might result in a life or death difference for somebody else.

Practice Makes Professional

Listening and talking on the radio is an acquired skill that takes a considerable amount of practice to master. Other officers and your supervisors will evaluate you on how you communicate via the radio. They will note your wording, your self-confidence, your use of codes and procedures and the pitch of your voice to form an opinion about you before you ever meet. When your high-pitched voice comes across the radio saying, "Uh, 1-Adam-12, uh, we need an 11-41 at our location. No, cancel that, we need a, uh, tow truck," it will produce snickers and head shakes across the city while veteran officers mutter "Rookies!" in their most contemptuous voices.

Under stressful conditions, such as a pursuit or a felony in progress, many officers end up screaming into their radio. Since the microphones are quite sensitive, this produces a condition called "over-modulation," which quite simply means that nobody can hear anything except an unintelligible high-pitched screaming. As you can imagine, over-modulation is counter-productive when you need immediate assistance.

I once heard a young officer who was pinned down behind his car by gunfire. He began screaming at the dispatcher that somebody was shooting at him and he really would prefer that other units join him as soon as possible. Unfortunately, nobody could understand his unit number or his location, so nobody could come to his assistance.

An obviously experienced sergeant came on the channel and took control. In a calm, deliberate, almost drawling voice that I can remember to this day he said, "Now calm down, son, and just tell us where you are." The panicked officer slowed down, dropped his voice a couple of octaves and answered. The sergeant continued, asking, "Now where are the bad guys, and how many of them are there?" That sergeant instantly took control of the situation and coordinated the arrest of the shooters. His controlled voice calmed the officer, the dispatcher, and all the other officers rolling to assist. Your control will have the same affect, keeping everyone else on the frequency calm and, thus, greatly improving your professional efficiency.

As in firearms training, when you talk on the radio you will always instinctively revert to your training when under stress. Practice the codes constantly *out loud!* Think about what you are going to say and how you are going to say it. Practice out loud in your own car. When you drive to work, think about what you would say if the car in front of you suddenly crossed the centerline and hit another vehicle head on. Think about what you would say if you were to conduct a traffic stop on that car — what information and location you might give.

Think about what information you would give if you tried to conduct that traffic stop and the driver took off and you followed in pursuit. What would you say on the radio if the passenger suddenly turned around and shot at you?

I practiced radio traffic like this for the first year or so of my career, and I know that it greatly improved the way I communicated on the radio because other officers complimented me on the way I sounded. However, the real proof came about 18 months into my career. A car stop turned into a pursuit, and I called off the information in a calm and comprehensive manner. Then about three minutes into the pursuit, both the driver and passenger began shooting repeatedly at me. Sure I was excited, and certainly my voice reflected that excitement, but the dispatcher and other officers heard every word of every broadcast of my pursuit which continued for the next 20 minutes. Take your time, keep calm, and keep professional. The best radio system in the world is only as good as the people on either end.

My number one rule is — *never, ever, make your dispatcher angry*. When you're working alone, a dispatcher may be your only partner. You depend on the dispatcher to keep you safe, and if you anger your dispatcher, you will find he can make your life a living hell.

Be courteous and avoid sarcasm. The dispatcher can't see what you're dealing with in the field, and you have no idea of the demands placed on the dispatcher back in the communications center. Speak slowly and carefully, particularly when you are giving information that may have to be written down or entered into a computer terminal simultaneously.

Last, but not least, remember that most agencies keep recordings of *all* of their radio traffic. *All* of your mistakes and attempts at humor may be immortalized for the later listening pleasure of your superiors, higher authorities and investigating commissions. As a rule of thumb, never say anything on the radio you wouldn't want your mother, your chief, a judge, or the grand jury to hear!

Radio Call Signs

Most agencies use some form of identification other than the officer's name on the radio. Generally, the smaller the agency, the simpler the system. If only a few units are in the field, it is relatively easy to keep track of each officer's location and what that officer is doing. In a large agency with thousands of officers in the field, the task becomes incredibly complex. Thus, a number of systems have evolved.

The simplest of these systems might use the vehicle number (anyone driving patrol car #4 would be "Paul 4"), or the officer's serial number (a patrol officer with serial number #52 would be "Paul 52") if assigned to detectives he might be "David 52," and if dealing with the rank of sergeant, "Sam 52"). These systems provide for easy identification of each individual and work very effectively on a small scale.

The Los Angeles Police Department developed a system of identifying their thousands of units based on assignment by either geographic location or function, and that system has been modified and is in use by thousands of other agencies. Perhaps the most familiar police call sign in the world is "1-Adam-12," after the popular television show. In this call sign, the "1" designated LAPD's Central division (one of 18), the "Adam" designated a two-officer patrol unit, and the "12" the actual unit number.

Using this system, any dispatcher, supervisor, or officer can tell a lot about a unit and a call simply by the call sign. A call sign of "6-FB-17" is a foot patrol unit officer working in Hollywood Division. "24-Mary-Queen-4" is a Central Traffic Division motorcycle officer assigned to the Motor Task Force. "4-King-25" is a Robbery/Homicide investigator working for Investigative Services, "2-David-90" a supervisor assigned to the Aero bureau, and "11-Y-32" a Public Affairs officer. The system is extremely flexible and has been widely adopted. In a smaller city, "3-Adam-52" might designate a two-officer unit assigned to the third watch, patrolling in district 5, beat 2.

Radio Codes

Most police agencies use codes to communicate on the radio. Originally, the justification was to save air time and make communications more effective. It was easier and shorter to say "Code 7" than to say "I am temporarily out of service while I'm having lunch, but available for calls if you need me." "Code 4" is a simple and understandable way of saying, "I don't need any further assistance." If your agency does use codes, memorize them, and use them properly. If you need help and can't remember the code, just say it in English.

Everybody will understand you, you will get the assistance you need, and you will survive long enough to go back and memorize the codes.

The Phonetic Alphabet

The phonetic alphabet was designed to avoid confusion between letters that sound alike. The letters "b," "d," "g" and "p" all sound pretty much alike on the radio, and it is difficult to distinguish between other letters such as "m" and "n," or "f" and "s." Getting information like that correct can be important when you get dispatched to a stopped breathing call at 918 "F" Street, Apartment "S."

To avoid the confusion, the dispatcher will use the phonetic alphabet, telling you to respond to "F" as in "Frank" street, apartment "S" as in "Sam." Words that sound alike are often spelled out this way. For example, in my city "Oak" and "Hope" streets are hard to distinguish on the radio and are usually spelled out by dispatch.

The phonetic alphabet is also used to communicate names with unusual spellings. If you give the dispatcher a name like Fred Smith, you can assume she will spell it according to the common spelling, just like it sounds. On the other hand, if you want dispatch to check on someone named Chynnah Micheaux, you're going to have to spell it out. You would tell the dispatcher that the first name of the subject was Chynnah (sounds like China), and then spell it phonetically: "Charles-Henry-Young-Nora-Nora-Adam-Henry." The last name phonetically spelled would be "Mary-Ida-Charles-Henry-Edward-Adam-Union-Xray."

The Phonetic Alphabet

A....Adam or Alpha	H....Henry
B....Boy or Beta	I....Ida or India
C....Charlie	J....John
D....David or Delta	K....King or Kilo
E....Edward or Echo	L....Lincoln or Lima
F....Frank or Foxtrot	M....Mary
G....George or Golf	N....Nora

O....Ocean	U....Union
P....Paul	V....Victor
Q....Queen	W....William
R....Robert	X....X-ray
S....Sam	Y....Young or Yellow
T....Tom or Tango	Z....Zebra

Priority and Status Codes

Almost all agencies use some variation of the following codes, which have been widely used by the Los Angeles Police Department and thus received national exposure from Hollywood. For the most part, these codes are "status" codes. Radio calls are given various priorities, with Code 0, the lowest priority, and Code 3, the most urgent. This type of sorting and prioritization (in hospitals, it's called "triage") makes a lot of sense in a major city where a unit can start a shift with a backlog of a dozen calls. (The LAPD handles so many calls of equally high priority they have developed another level, "Code 2 High." These tend to be real serious calls like shootings and robberies, but the lights and siren are not authorized.)

The 9-Code

The 9-Code and its many variations seem to be most popular with county sheriff's agencies and in rural areas, although portions of the 9-Code are used in many large urban police departments. Although there have been some attempts at standardizing codes, you will find that agencies often make up their own codes, particularly for the more mundane tasks of going to the car wash, picking up prisoner meals, etc. Examples of these codes are as follows:

901 — Paramedic call; also 901A — Attempt suicide; 901K — Paramedics dispatched; 901N — Paramedics requested; 901S — Paramedic call, shooting victim; 901T — Injury traffic accident

902 — Accident; also 902A — Attempt suicide; 902T — Non-injury traffic accident

903 — Aircraft crash; also 903L — Low flying aircraft

904 — Fire call; also 904A— Fire alarm; 904B— Brush fire, 904C— Car fire; 904S— Structure fire

The 10-Code

The 10-Code probably has the widest usage of any of the radio codes. It tends to be particularly popular with large urban law enforcement agencies. It is the **official** code adopted by the Associated Public-Safety Communications Officers (APCO), and is thus the most widely used of the codes. Examples of these codes are as follows:

10-0 — Caution

10-1 — Receiving your radio poorly

10-2 — Receiving your radio well

10-3 — Stop transmitting, or change to another channel

10-4 — Okay, message received

10-5 — Relay message

10-6 — Busy

10-7 — Out of service; also End of Watch (E.O.W.)

10-8 — In service, available for calls

10-9 — Repeat the last message

10-10— Out of service, but available for radio calls

The 11-Code

The 11-Code has a slightly different orientation than the 10-Code. It was designed to cover a wide variety of traffic related situations. This code is best suited for (and typically used by) Highway Patrols and other traffic agencies. Examples are:

11-6 — Illegal shooting

11-7 — Prowler

11-8 — Subject down

11-10 — Take a report

11-12 — Dead animal or loose livestock

11-13 — Injured animal

11-14 — Animal bite

11-15 — Children playing in street

Crime Broadcasts

One of the first responsibilities of officers at the scene of a crime is to broadcast information about the crime to dispatch and other patrol units. This is done so that while you are kept deployed on-scene for the investigation, other patrol units can be out looking for the bad guys, vehicle, etc. you described. As soon as you get basic information on the crime, you should broadcast it on the radio, generally in the following order: type of crime, time delay, location, weapon, loss, suspects, vehicle, and direction of travel. A typical broadcast in which there was very little suspect information might be, "An armed robbery occurred five minutes ago at Doughnut Queen, 1653 Oak Street. Weapon used was a blue-steel revolver, loss was fifty dollars in cash. Suspects were two male Hispanics, last seen southbound on Oak Street."

Both persons and vehicles are broadcast on the radio according to standardized conventions. This makes remembering, recording, and comprehensively describing them easier. Persons are usually described in the following order: name, date-of-birth (or approximate age), sex, race, height, weight, hair color, eye color, clothing, and then unusual features such as glasses, mustache, tattoos, scars, etc.

A typical broadcast might be, "Subject wanted for robbery is Fred Smith, D.O.B. 10-29-55, male, white, 5-09, 300, blond, blue, wearing a white T-shirt and blue jeans. Subject has glasses, shoulder-length hair, and a tattoo of a coiled cobra on his right forearm."

Vehicles are generally described as follows: license plate, year of manufacture, make, model, style (4-door, convertible, pick-up), color, unusual features, occupants, and direction of travel. For instance, a typical vehicle broadcast might be, "Vehicle wanted for robbery is Texas license 2 Sam Adam Mary 123, a 1983 Chevrolet Camaro 2-door, brown, with chrome wheels, occupied by a male white. Last seen southbound on Oak street approximately ten minutes ago."

TELEPHONE COMMUNICATIONS

The most common way in which citizens contact the police department is by the telephone. It is important that every caller be treated seriously, professionally, and with courtesy because that phone call is important to the person making the call. Some agencies have a stated goal of having every phone call answered within a specified number of rings. Others have specific policies stating that you will answer any phone you hear ringing. Such policies and goals recognize how vital the telephone is in responding to the community.

Many departments use a variety of phone lines with separate information lines, business lines, direct dialing to various bureaus, voice mail, emergency lines, 9-1-1 lines, and special lines dedicated to receiving alarm company responses. As a patrol officer, you may well be answering phones as part of your duties. In small agencies, patrol officers are often the relief for the dispatchers — covering for lunches, and sometimes for vacations. In larger agencies, officers can be assigned to handle a front desk, a complaint board, or at the dispatch or communication center.

Regardless of your system and assignment, you need to learn how your agency receives and handles phone calls. By understanding how a dispatcher receives, processes, and broadcasts the information for calls, you'll be a more effective and efficient communicator while on patrol.

9-1-1

The emergency number 9-1-1 is a lifesaver for many, a tremendous tool for emergency service dispatchers, and sometimes a real headache! Introduced about 20 years ago, 9-1-1 combines varying degrees of advanced computer technology with the telephone network.

The basic 9-1-1 system simply routes any 9-1-1 call to the appropriate public safety answering point or "PSAP." Cellular phones route 9-1-1 calls to the appropriate agency and even pay phones will call 9-1-1 without requiring the deposit of any coins. In most communities, this is the law enforcement dispatch center, but it can also be a fire department or a dispatching center independent of law enforcement. In those agencies, the call is screened and then routed through speed-dialing equipment to the appropriate agency (i.e., police, sheriff, fire, ambulance, etc.).

Enhanced versions of the 9-1-1 system identify the number calling, and even more sophisticated versions use a database to produce a complete display on a computer monitor, including the name of the business or residence, the phone number of the caller, the address where the phone is located, and the appropriate emergency services to respond to at that location. An attached printer can print a log of all calls, when they were received and produce a copy of the entire screen. One touch buttons allow immediate transfer or 3-way conversations with surrounding agencies, hospitals, utilities, poison control centers, and a nationwide translator service.

For the patrol officer, this means that the dispatcher can provide better quality information. Also, every 9-1-1 call can be verified, if deemed necessary, with a callback, thus reducing the number of prank calls and needless responses. By providing more and better information, response times have the potential of being reduced.

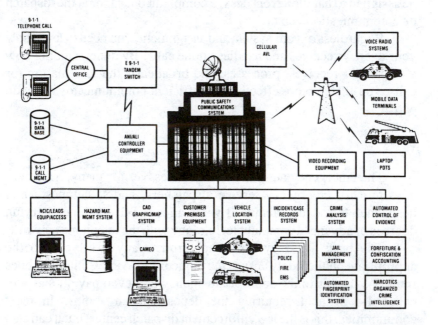

Single point contact public safety system. (Courtesy of Ameritech Information Systems)

In many agencies, 9-1-1 has become an extension of the old call-box system. The system allows any officer in the field to contact his dispatcher directly, without charge, using a secure line that cannot be monitored by others. Every pay phone becomes a police callbox over which confidential information can be sent and received by the officer.

Unfortunately, 9-1-1 is a system that is also greatly abused and can be easily overwhelmed. In major cities, emergency dispatch systems have become jammed with non-emergency calls. In 1989 the Los Angeles Police Department estimated that only 30 percent of the 2.3 million calls they received over 9-1-1 were actual emergencies. People have called 9-1-1 for general information, recipes, the time, weather conditions, and for such important things as noisy trash trucks and stray dogs. Juveniles are notorious for making prank 9-1-1 calls from pay phones. One man called the police more than 500 times in a four week period just to complain about his neighbors. As a result of these inappropriate calls to the 9-1-1 service, response times have slowed. Given the small number of 9-1-1 lines (1 line per 10,000 population seems to be about the average), the lines become easily overwhelmed and the result might be a busy signal for someone calling in a real emergency.

My city of 25,000 has only two 9-1-1 lines. In a major fire or other emergency, it is not uncommon for 20 or 30 calls to come in. Many of the callers receive a busy signal as a result. In most major cities, the problem is even worse. During peak demand times, it is not unusual for 9-1-1 callers to receive a recording stating, "Please hold, all lines are currently busy."

Voice Mail Reports

Nationwide, an estimated 90 percent of all police reports are still handwritten, often in #2 lead pencil which is a time-consuming and inefficient process. Some agencies have long used voice recording devices to transcribe narratives for subsequent report generation by clerical staff. The newest trend is an extension of the voice mail technology for telephones.

The most popular report writing system is presently Digital Express. Officers can use any touch tone telephone to phone in and record their reports. When the officer calls, voice prompts request access codes and specific report information. The officers can then

narrate their reports. They may edit and review reports for accuracy
as needed.

Once the report has been recorded, it is instantly accessible for
transcription by clerical personnel. The departments presently using
this system report increased accuracy and huge efficiency gains in
generating reports. Typically, officers have reported completing voice
mail reports in about one-fifth the time required in the past for
producing handwritten or officer-typed reports.

Cellular Telephones

Cellular phone technology is rapidly moving into patrol vehicles
and has demonstrated itself to be an important tool for the patrol
officer. In addition to offering yet another way to access the station and/
or supervisors, it lightens the demand on radio dispatchers while at the
same time offering the patrol officer greater communication flexibility.

With a cellular phone in the patrol vehicle, officers can actually
call parents or other associates of suspects stopped in the field to verify
identities and question alibis. When dealing with the public, you no
longer have to give those you are trying to help the phone numbers for
resources, you can simply phone those resources and help them
immediately get the assistance they require. You can call credit card
companies, probation officers, parole agents, and parents from your
patrol vehicle, opening up a new dimension of information to assist you
and the community you serve.

One warning about cellular phones. First, always remember that
a cellular phone is not a secure communication. Scanners can be easily
programmed to listen in on cellular phones, and you should assume that
the public, the press, and the more sophisticated of the local drug
dealers might be hanging on your every word. Also remember that
unlike your radio traffic, cellular phone time is not free. Every minute
of every call depletes a little more money out of your department's
budget.

COMPUTER NETWORKS

In the United States today, an incredible network of computer
information is available to law enforcement. The connections can take

an officer in the field and put him almost instantly into both national and international databases. Computers within patrol vehicles provide information on vehicles, boats, aircraft, wanted persons, missing persons, gun registrations, criminal histories, probation information, parolees, property, and hazardous materials. These records are a primary source of information for officers, supervisors and administrators to make discretionary decisions concerning criminal suspects.

The Confidentiality of Computer Records

Unfortunately, this easy access to computer communications is not without problems. Unauthorized information or misuse of information by those with legitimate access is a crime. Computers have long and sophisticated memories. The Department of Justice can conduct a "journal search" (reviewing the activity) on any terminal covering any time period and operates a full time Audit and Record Security Section. Persons who access and misuse criminal justice information risk their careers and face both criminal prosecution and civil liability. Filing of felony charges is a common practice among prosecutors dealing with breaches of computer record confidentiality.

Some of the cases of computer misuse are extreme, and justice has been harsh. In one case, an eight-year veteran detective was caught using a police computer to help her steroid-dealing boyfriend identify undercover agents posing as buyers. The detective would run license numbers to determine if the owner was a police officer or a public agency. An audit of the detective's computer revealed more than 50 uses of the computer for no apparent legitimate police purpose. The now-former detective was arrested and charged with 13 felonies.

In another case, criminal charges were filed against a deputy sheriff for unlawful use of a law enforcement computer in an alleged sexual misconduct case. On eight different dates the deputy used official computers to run records checks on different women. The deputy faces up to a year in county jail.

Your agency can also be penalized for unauthorized access to confidential records. Recently a small rural agency bought computers and placed them throughout the agency. Without permission, but with the best of intentions, a volunteer engineered and connected their computers into the national network. The unauthorized connection was discovered, and the entire agency was penalized by being cut off from the network for six months.

Rank is no protection, either. Recently a chief of police pled guilty to two counts of furnishing state criminal history information to an undercover informant. The chief had been furnishing the information to a business associate who was a private investigator. This 17 year veteran of law enforcement resigned from his department, was placed on two years probation, and was ordered to perform 50 hours of community service.

There's an obvious message here. You are bound by the *Code of Ethics*, which is backed by the full force of the law, to keep all confidential information forever secret. Never use your access to computers or other police records for unauthorized reasons. It's not worth the risk.

The Computer Network

NCIC. While many states operate sophisticated computer networks of their own, the primary national network is the National Crime Information Center (NCIC), operated by the U.S. Department of Justice since 1967. NCIC is operational in every federal law enforcement agency, all 50 states and territories and throughout Canada (through an interface with the Canadian Police Information Centre). It serves law enforcement and related agencies of all kinds including: police departments, correctional facilities, prosecutors, probation offices and the Department of Motor Vehicles. Through the system, any operator can send a message to any other operator. Connections are even available to other countries through INTERPOL.

NCIC serves as an umbrella for a number of other networks, each offering a specific type of information and identified by an acronym or "mnemonic."

NLETS.

NLETS is the *National Law Enforcement Telecommunications System*, commonly referred to as the "teletype." In the early days of computers, this consisted of huge teleprinters that hummed and clanked (literally) out their teletype messages on yellowed rolls of newsprint. Now fully computerized, NLETS has evolved into a means of transmitting administrative or informational messages to a specified terminal or groups of terminals. For instance, given a freeway shooting along an interstate highway, a highway patrol agency could send a teletype to all terminal users along that highway corridor. A description of a kidnap victim's vehicle could be sent to every police agency in the state, or information on a serial murder could be sent to every agency in the nation.

AMIS/USDMV

AMIS is the *Automated Management Information System* ("USDMV" in some areas). It gives access to driver's license and vehicle registration information. With this system, a patrol officer can determine the validity and status of any driver or license plate from any state over the radio. It is a powerful tool for identifying problem drivers with out-of-state license suspensions or revocations.

CJIS

CJIS is the *Criminal Justice Information System,* serving as a master network of other criminal information systems. These other systems include an incredible variety of information on wanted persons, stolen vehicles, property, firearms, restraining orders and criminal history, some of which are described below.

ABS

ABS is the *Automated Boat System.* Of particular use to harbor patrols and marine-oriented communities, it allows inquiries into boat ownership, registration, and stolen vessels.

AFS

AFS is the *Automated Firearms System.* Patrol officers can use this system in a variety of ways. You can run any gun you encounter in the field to determine whether it is stolen and to find the registered owner. You can run specific people (such as those you may be getting ready to arrest on a warrant) to see if any guns are registered to them. With some systems, you can even search by address to determine whether any guns are registered there. It's a tremendous tool for officer safety.

APS

APS is the *Automated Property System,* accessing NCIC's Article File. With this system, officers can run serial numbers and descriptions on a huge variety of objects. The most common use by field officers is to check on stolen stereos and other electronics using the make, model and serial number. The system can also handle pawned items, unique works of art, collectibles, gaming equipment, livestock, credit cards and well-drilling equipment.

CHS

CHS is the *Criminal History System.* This network provides detailed information on a suspect's arrest history; a full "rap sheet" including arrest dates, arresting agencies, charges and sentences or other dispositions. It is also one of the most sensitive sources of information, and is fiercely protected. Officers in the field can only request this information when all three of the following criteria are met:

a) There is **reasonable cause** to believe the safety of the officer and/or the public is at **significant risk**.

b) There is an **immediate need** for summary criminal information.

c) Information from other data bases, such as Wanted Persons or Stolen Vehicles, would **not be adequate**.

Getting information like this would be justified in a hostage situation or when dealing with an armed suspect. Requesting a criminal history would **not** be justified during the course of a routine traffic stop or a routine field investigation. Remember, every such request is audited, recorded, and may have to be justified.

IAFIS

IAFIS is the *Integrated Automated Fingerprint Identification System.* This system is designed to replace the existing system of taking criminal's fingerprints on the 10-print cards presently in use. Instead, prints will be read by live-scan fingerprinting and transmitted electronically to a state identification bureau. If there is no match, the prints will be forwarded electronically to the FBI and returned to the booking station. IAFIS is fully operational in a number of states.

III

III is the *Interstate Identification Index*. This system is used to identify individuals and can access the F.B.I.'s millions of computerized fingerprint records based on the modified Henry System of fingerprint codes.

MUPS

MUPS is the *Missing/Unidentified Persons System.* With this system, not only missing children and adults can be located but unidentified persons, body parts, and the *modus operandi* of serial murderers can all be entered and accessed by detectives.

NCIC-2000

NCIC-2000 allows police officers to identify fugitives and missing persons by placing a subject's finger on an optical fingerprint reader (also known as a "scanner port"). The reader will transmit the image to the NCIC computer at the FBI and will forward a reply to the officer. A printer in the patrol vehicle will make a copy of the suspect's photograph, fingerprints, signature and tatoos. The system is designed to be a centralized repository and clearinghouse for all fingerprint records.

NIBRS

NIBRS is the *National Incident-Based Reporting System,* a function of the *Uniform Crime Reports* (UCR). Every law enforcement agency in the United States reports certain criminal offenses and arrest information to the Department of Justice. These reports are known as the *Uniform Crime Reports* and are used to produce an overall picture of the nation's crime. This system is designed to use that information in different ways, providing data and criminal information to decision-makers including current criminal justice issues such as hate crimes.

ROS

In California, ROS is the *Restraining Order System*. It tracks persons subject to specific restraining orders, such as Domestic Violence and Family Law court orders which involve violence. The system is also used by firearms dealers to prevent selling weapons to any person subject to such orders.

SVS

SVS is the national *Stolen Vehicle System*. License plates, vehicle identification numbers (VINs), engine numbers and components of stolen, embezzled, or missing vehicles are all recorded in this system. SVS is one of the most useful and important tools used by patrol officers due to the number of stolen vehicles encountered on a routine basis.

WPS

WPS is the *Wanted Persons System*. It contains felony warrants from throughout the country. In addition to providing identifying information such as descriptions, tattoos, and scars, the system gives information on bail and extradition.

Given the right information, a dispatcher skilled in operating the NCIC computer terminal can provide you with an incredible array of assistance in your investigations and patrol operations. For example, armed with the Federal Aircraft Administration (FAA) "tail number" of an aircraft, a dispatcher can give you the registered owner and other identification, perhaps vital information towards a narcotics smuggling investigation. Through an inquiry mode, the dispatcher can give you the name, address, and 24-hour telephone number of any law enforcement or criminal justice agency in the United States. Given the identification number from the "Hazardous Materials" placard on a truck or rail car, the dispatcher can identify the material, suggest precautions, and even explain first aid procedures for those exposed to the substance.

While the dispatchers have access to this incredible variety of information, it is absolutely useless if **you**, as a patrol officer, aren't aware of what information is available to you or know the correct procedures for accessing the information. Each inquiry requires specific information. For example, out-of-state license plate inquiries require the number, state, type of license (passenger car, commercial, truck, etc.) and the year of registration. Criminal history inquiries and warrant checks require the name, date of birth, sex, and race. If you don't provide the dispatcher with the appropriate information for which to query the network, you'll probably get a negative response. It's **your** responsibility to learn the inquiry formats so you always provide appropriate information.

The Mobile Data Terminal (MDT)

Police vehicles equipped with Mobile Data Terminals (MDTs) are the wave of the future. In major cities, a computer terminal mounted between the front seats has become the norm. The advent of passenger side airbags has required remounting from the dashboard. These terminals can make inquiries directly into all of the commonly used databases, thus greatly reducing air time and increasing the number of units any given dispatcher can handle. The MDTs also have special function calls to indicate a unit's arrival at the scene and their completion and disposition of a call. The officer only has to press a single button to advise the dispatcher of the majority of routine status transmissions.

Mobile Data Terminal in "Command Console." (Courtesy of Troy Public Safety Products)

MDTs also can be used for computer assisted dispatch, sending the unit all of the information received at the public safety answering point. Sensitive information that could not normally be broadcast by radio can be sent to an MDT terminal with much greater security. MDTs also can be used for communications between units and between officers and their dispatchers. (You should note that all these transmissions are recorded as well and can be reviewed at any time.) The latest trend for MDTs includes DOS compatible computers which can be used for report writing as well.

At present, the capabilities of report-writing MDTs are limited to a few short field reports, but as the technology improves, manufacturers anticipate adding to both the report forms available and the length of the reports than can be completed in the field.

While offering the patrol officer incredible information resources, the MDTs are not without their drawbacks. Reading the screens and sending messages while on the move presents definite problems and has resulted in more than one traffic accident. With the introduction of passenger side airbags, the equipment has generally been located even deeper under the center console or between the seats, making access and input even more difficult.

Some new variations include the Intelligent Mobile Data Network (IMDN), the Portable Data Terminal and the heads-up display. The IMDN integrates the Global Positioning Satellite (GPS) technology into an MDT. Integrated with computer assisted dispatching systems, the GPS can automatically locate and track the positions of a patrol vehicle. Dispatchers then know exactly which patrol unit is nearest any given call and can actually see when units arrive on scene and what positions they take.

The PDT is a hand held unit with all of the capabilities of a MDT but with a smaller LCD type screen and a grid-type keyboard rather than the traditional typewriter keyboard layout. While offering more mobility, entry time is slower and report writing is more difficult.

The heads-up display is a new innovation, derived from the displays in military aircraft. The screen of the MDT is projected on the windshield directly within the driver's line of vision. Readouts from radar displays can also be linked into the display. While such displays may take a little getting used to, they offer officers a greater degree of safety than ever before.

NEW TECHNOLOGY

Law enforcement is experiencing an explosion of technology, offering incredible capabilities that were yesterday's science fiction. The professional law enforcement journals carry regular discussions of fantastic technology that is operational (although under development and not widely available) today. In addition to previously mentioned equipment, new technology includes the use of faxes, satellites, computer scanning and television.

Fax Technology

Cheap fax machines are available almost everywhere, and the proliferation of this technology has greatly benefited law enforcement. Virtually every law enforcement agency has fax machines available for sending photographs, fingerprints, and bulletins at unprecedented speeds. Unlike the NCIC teletype system, fax machines send images. As a patrol officer, you can send wanted posters, photos of missing persons, artwork, unique vehicles and jewelry, counterfeit money, forged documents, and completed crime reports to other agencies almost as easily as making a phone call. As mobile cellular phones are combined with mobile fax machines, the possibilities are limited only by a patrol officer's imagination and agency's budget.

Satellite Technology

Satellite technology has also enhanced law enforcement. Global Positioning Systems, originally developed for the military, has been used to track the position of patrol vehicles using computer aided dispatch and to track drug dealers, their vehicles, boats and aircraft throughout the world. One stolen vehicle recovery system, *TeleTrak*, uses satellites to locate and recover stolen vehicles equipped with their transponders.

In addition, law enforcement agencies are using communications satellites as part of their radio systems, and at least three satellites are presently available with training material allowing police officers to get video training in stations equipped with satellite dishes.

The most broad-based system is the *Law Enforcement Training Network* (LETN), an educational satellite broadcast service. The program provides interviews, training, and up-to-date law enforcement news to subscriber agencies with a variable price based on the number of personnel. The channel provides a cheap and convenient method for conducting roll-call training, and gives access to professional resources beyond the reach of most small agencies.

The Law Enforcement Satellite Training Network is a totally free, but less ambitious project, conducted by the Kansas City, Missouri Police Department and the FBI. They conduct bi-monthly teleconferences on a wide variety of law enforcement topics, available to any law enforcement agency with a C-band dish and tuner.

Scanning Technology

Computer technology, satellites and modems have advanced and combined to produce an incredible potential for law enforcement. Generally, when the word "scanner" is mentioned in law enforcement, we think of radio scanners used to monitor other emergency services in the area. Scanning technology for computers goes far beyond that.

Since fingerprint records have become digitized and available via computer, most checks have been done by inputting traditional inked fingerprint cards through fax machines. An example of recent technology is the "optical port scanner." The optical port is a clear plastic hole in the machine. The person to be fingerprinted simply puts his fingers into the ports where the computer performs an optical scan, producing a digitized image and an immediate computer check for wanted persons. There is also a single port model available for patrol vehicles, in which a suspect places his thumb in the port for immediate recording on the back of citations and an immediate check with national databases.

There is presently technology available that allows a video camera to capture the license plates of passing vehicles at freeway speeds, convert the image through Optical Character Recognition (OCR) software, and check the plate against stolen and wanted vehicle databases. The result is a fixed unit that can identify passing stolen vehicles and notify law enforcement agencies in a matter of seconds.

The test units are presently capturing about 60 percent of the passing plates, however a major limitation is the computer's capacity to handle the high flows of information that are generated. Engineers state that similar vehicle mounted systems are possible in the next few years. Imagine a unit mounted on the front of your patrol vehicle, constantly reading the license plates of every vehicle within sight, and instantly notifying you of stolen cars and wanted vehicles! A complimentary piece of equipment currently being tested would actually disable a vehicle you wanted to stop.

Video Technology

Video recorders have long been used in law enforcement for monitoring correction facilities, security, crime scene investigation, and recording field coordination tests of suspected drunk drivers.

Now this technology has improved and miniaturized to the point where video cameras have become commonplace equipment inside the patrol vehicle itself. The units generally film through the front window of the patrol vehicle, feeding to an armored video recorder mounted in the trunk and feed audio through a remote transmitter worn by the officer. The camera is activated either manually by the officer or when the emergency lights are turned on in the patrol vehicle.

In patrol vehicles equipped with such systems, every Code-3 run, traffic stop, and vehicle pursuit is recorded for evidence and administrative review. Such evidence has prevented many lawsuits and defended officers charged with misconduct. On a few sad occasions (well publicized on television), the cameras have actually recorded the assault and murder of the police officers operating those patrol vehicles, but they have provided evidence for the trial of the killers. Someday, every patrol vehicle will be equipped with such technology.

DISCUSSION QUESTIONS

1) Should police administrators attempt to eliminate the use of jargon by their officers?

2) Do you think that 9-1-1 systems interfere with a person's right to privacy?

3) Should there be any restrictions on who can monitor police radio transmissions?

4) What do you think is the major benefit of this new communications technology to law enforcement?

5) What do you think the impact of new technology will be on law enforcement in terms of personnel and budgets?

6) Do you think that video cameras in patrol vehicles are a good idea? Why, or why not?

Mary Middleton was injured in Batesville, AK, in May, when cars driven by Mary and by Oscar Waymon Middleton (Mary's father-in-law) crashed. After the crash, the two got out of their cars and exchanged gunfire. When family members went to bail out Oscar and Mary, more fighting broke out, and several police officers were injured.

* * *

Gary Blantz, 29, was arrested for kidnapping a bar owner near Lancaster, PA, in February. Police reported later that Blantz shot himself in the foot with is .45-caliber revolver to show the victim what would happen to him if he were disobedient.

* * *

Yes, it still happens — keep your Penal Code handy for those situations calling for knowledge of unusual offenses. After receiving a call regarding a man behaving strangely around some cattle, patrol officers in Atascadero wound up arresting a 17-year-old for sexually abusing a steer. That's one not on your "cheat sheet."

HANDLING CALLS FOR SERVICE

LEARNING GOALS: After studying this chapter the student will be able to:

- Identify a *routine* call.

- List the common procedures used in responding to routine calls.

- Define a *hotshot* call.

- List the common procedures used in any hotshot call.

- Explain the importance of coordinating other patrol units.

- Explain when and why victims and witnesses should be separated.

- Describe how patrol officers minimize detection when responding to calls.

- Discuss the common functions patrol officers perform at every criminal call.

- Define domestic violence and explain how to effectively handle such calls.

- Identify which calls are *high risk* calls, and explain how they should be handled.

- Discuss the best approach when dealing with mentally ill persons.

- List the types of service calls patrol officers routinely handle.

ROUTINE CALLS

Police patrol officers are society's ultimate generalists. As a patrol officer you will be asked to assist others for every imaginable reason. As an officer committed to community policing, you should do your best to see that every person gets the assistance required. A surprisingly small number of service calls are actually related to crime. Much of your time will be devoted to providing service to the public (i.e., handling lost children, disabled vehicles, domestic neighborhood disputes, and injured pets).

Obviously, you need to practice officer safety on each and every call. **There are no "routine calls."** That doesn't mean you need to commando crawl across the lawn on every barking dog call. It does mean that you have to be aware that a barking dog might well indicate an armed prowler. I've responded to neighbor disputes where one of the neighbors thought it prudent to stuff a handgun into his waistband before going out to argue with his neighbor. You don't have to operate in fear, but always maintain your heightened sense of awareness. Approach every call with respect for the unknown. If you're too lax, it could be your last call!

Every call you respond to will require many of the same tactics and techniques. Officer safety always comes first. Operate on the theory that while the public may suffer if you don't catch the bad guy on any given call, they will suffer much more if you are injured in the line-of-duty and can't work tomorrow.

With *every* call you should:

1) Figure out where you're going. After working a beat for a while, you'll have a mental picture of the area to which you are responding. Work out the best route to the call, one that will avoid delays, expedite your arrival, and allows you the best approach.

2) When responding to crimes in progress, think about how the criminal might escape. If you can drive toward the call along the most likely escape route (like the road to the nearest freeway on-ramp) you'll have a better chance of catching the suspect.

3) Slow down. You'll see more as you approach the call and be less likely to be detected by the suspect(s). Sometime on a quiet graveyard shift, get out of the car and listen to the other officers responding to a call. You'll hear the whoops of sirens from blocks away, the distinctive sounds of their engines, the whistling of wind through lightbars and antennas, the squealing of brakes and tires, and the crackling of police radios. Police cars make distinctive sounds, especially when driven fast. Sometimes, if you slow down, you might actually surprise a criminal.

4) Practice situational awareness and control the events that take place on a call.

Look around you as you roll in on each call. It's very easy to develop tunnel vision, your eyeballs tend to lock in on the call location or search for addresses. You should be scanning the *entire* area for cars, people, and things that look out of place.

Listen, once you get to the call. Take a moment to really tune in on what's going on around you. On domestic disputes, you can often listen in on the argument for a few minutes and have a better understanding of the situation you are about to enter. If you listen when you arrive on disturbing the peace calls, you'll be able to tell the disturbing party what it sounds like to the neighbors, and, on crime calls, you'll have a much better chance of finding the suspect if you listen for running engines, cooling metal, barking dogs, and fleeing suspects.

Ask people nearby what's going on. I can't count the number of times when neighbors or casual bystanders have told me exactly what happened and where the suspects went while other officers were fumbling around in the bushes looking for the bad guys. A couple of quick questions like, "What's going on?," "Did you see anyone?," or "Did you hear anything?" can shave hours off your handling of a call. Remember that this information must be scrutinized very carefully because perceptions tend to distort facts, and not everyone can be trusted. Ask the questions, get the answers, and then use your best instincts and judgement.

5) As a fundamental of officer safety, don't park directly in front of the call or drive into the middle of any situation until you know the situation. Although snipers are a possibility, you are more concerned with approaching unnoticed to avoid affecting the dynamics of the call. Parking in front of the location on a criminal call may produce the greatest likelihood that the suspects will see you and escape. On domestic disputes or fights, if your arrival is noticed it will often cause an immediate shift of attention to you. You are far better off parking a few doors away and walking quietly up to the call, unnoticed as much as possible, keeping your vehicle and its associated equipment close enough in case you need it quickly, yet far enough away from the scene so as not to disturb the events as they unfold.

6) **Wait for backup on serious calls.** I know, John Wayne and Clint Eastwood never waited for their backup, but you aren't John Wayne, this isn't Hollywood, and it's your life at stake. There are many officers who arrive at the scene, charge straight ahead, kick in the door, hook up the bad guys and save the pretty girls. If they're lucky, we call them heroes and they get pretty ribbons to wear on their uniforms. If they're unlucky, we call them heroes and their spouses get neatly folded American flags at their funerals.

Sometimes that kind courage is called for and is necessary to save a life (*"Serve and Protect"*). Fortunately, most times charging in without backup will have little or no effect on the outcome of the call and simply makes the world a more dangerous place for you and the public. You are responding to a call, not a race. If a backup unit is rolling, stand by a block away and let them know you'll be waiting for them, then both units can arrive together in a coordinated effort.

7) Don't make unnecessary noise. Cops tend to be noisy people. Their cars have radios, sirens and airhorns, and patrol officers just love to use them. Their bodies are covered with a variety of noise making equipment. Get a group of officers trying to sneak up on a location with squawking radios, squeaky leather, hard soles, jangling keys, clanging whistles, rattling

batons, and it would be difficult to distinguish them from a buffalo stampede. (Okay, the ground trembles less with the buffalo.) Making this much noise is like walking down the hall with a "Kick Me!" sign stuck on your back. It's dumb and potentially self-destructive. There's a lot you can do to control noise.

First, when you arrive, turn your engine off, your unit radio down or off, and turn your portable up just high enough that *only* you can hear it. Don't slam the car doors, either leave them slightly ajar or push them shut slowly (they'll still make a loud *click*). Keep conversations with your partner to a minimum (good partners do a lot of pointing to show where they're going).

Within your department policy, wear soft soles with a good lug sole for traction. Stuff your keys in your pocket (I wear my key fob directly above my rear pocket and the keys are tucked inside and quiet) along with your whistle. (Metal whistles clang like a cow bell; get one that is rubber coated or made of plastic.) Last of all, control your equipment. Proper placement of the right equipment on your belt is essential (there's no excuse for having your baton bouncing off your radio).

8) Don't show unnecessary light at night. Patrol officers seem to exhibit some compulsive behavior to announce to others that they are in the neighborhood. They leave their amber lights flashing on the patrol car (as a warning to criminals, I guess) and their parking lights on (to show other people that they're parked). They shine their spotlights around to find curb numbers and use their flashlights to find the front door of the house. All of this light is very impressive, and probably attractive to male fireflies, but counter-productive as far as catching bad guys.

As long as you are legally parked at a call, there is no reason at all to leave any lights on. They only serve as a distraction, attract attention, and help any criminals to locate you and track your movements against the backlighting of the patrol car. The bright lights reduce your night vision and make the shadows a more hazardous place.

Use your flashlight sparingly, letting your eyes adjust. When you do use your light, use it as a weapon to place the criminals at a disadvantage. Shine it in the dark places where you need to see, but avoid lighting up you and your partners. You don't want to be a target.

In responding to criminal calls, at first it might appear that there are a bewildering variety of crimes, each requiring a unique response to handle the individual elements. In fact, you perform the same basic functions with the same basic priorities on every criminal investigation, with some minor variations. Those basic, common, sometimes overlapping functions include:

1) Coordinating the initial response. This includes getting updated information from dispatch and developing a plan with other responding units.

2) Detaining, restraining, neutralizing, and containing any suspects present. Each suspect and potential suspect should be stopped, handcuffed, searched, and contained either by being placed in a patrol car or guarded by an officer.

3) Getting medical attention for any injured persons.

4) Putting out an initial crime broadcast.

5) Requesting other assistance you require. If you need other officers, supervisors, detectives, fire engines, tow trucks, crime-scene techs, photographers or clergymen, request them and get them on-scene in a timely manner.

6) Securing the scene. You need to preserve the scene and keep the public safe. In some cases, you can just lock the door and go to work. At other crime scenes, one or two officers can establish a protective perimeter. Sometimes barrier tape might be sufficient. At other crimes, you may need many officers and might want to keep an incident log listing every person who enters the crime scene.

7) Gathering information. Get the basic information about what happened, so you can organize your investigation, determine who the "players" are, and determine what evidence and witnesses are important and relevant.

8) Identifying, separating, and interviewing witnesses, reporting persons, and victims. First you need to obtain basic information (name, D.O.B., address, phone numbers) on each witness, so you can find them again and so they can be contacted by detectives, prosecutors, etc.. (A good way to make sure witnesses don't leave the scene before you talk to them is to ask them for a license or other I.D. They usually won't leave if you're holding some of their property). Then, to find out what they saw. It is always best to collect statements individually, out of the hearing range of other witnesses.

9) Identifying, preserving, and collecting evidence. First you need to determine what things at the crime scene are relevant evidence of the crime including those things that might prove the innocence of a suspect. This includes fingerprints and photographs, in addition to physical evidence.

10) Make notifications. Depending on the crime and your department policies, you may have to notify superior officers, politicians, relatives, outside agencies, and/or the press.

11) Document the incident with the appropriate paperwork. This means writing the report, filling out the forms, completing booking paperwork and booking evidence into your property room.

Although the elements of the crimes differ and the evidence and participants of each crime will be unique, this same basic investigative blueprint will serve you well on most every call.

The elements of the same crime will vary from state to state. The definitions of crimes I use below are based on the *Model Penal Code*, statutes proposed for adoption by state legislatures by the National Conference of Commissioners of Uniform State Laws. Just be aware that some states do vary from these definitions.

RESPONDING TO HIGH RISK CALLS

Certain patrol calls represent a higher risk than more routine calls involving property. These we will call *hotshot calls*, in which you

might anticipate a violent confrontation with a suspect, such as any
sexual assault, robbery, burglary, or shots fired call, irregardless of
whether the call is *in progress* or has just occurred. In addition to
normal response procedures, you'll want to add some general methods
when handling any type of high-risk call. Recognize that your goal
should always be to maintain the safety of the officer and the public and,
of course, to apprehend the suspects.

When you first receive the call, you need to visualize the location
and the crime. Consider the area you will have to contain and the
possible escape routes of the suspects. Think about those areas where
it is safe to confront the suspect(s) (i.e., a good shooting background
with few people) and those to avoid (i.e., a crowded mall or a school
zone).

Listen carefully to the descriptions of suspects and vehicles that
might be broadcast, but don't get locked in to the point that you
automatically reject anyone that doesn't *exactly* match the description.
I once responded to a bank robbery in which the suspect was described
as wearing a red plaid Pendleton shirt. I stopped a suspect half a block
from the bank, but he was absolutely eliminated by the bank teller in
a field identification. I felt strongly enough about his evasive answers
to investigate further, and we found his roommate was the suspect who
robbed the bank. Immediately after the robbery the suspect had run into
an alley and changed shirts, the roommate deliberately walked in front
of me to stall my response. Be prepared for suspects who change
clothing, shed hats and wigs, or change cars. If the description is close
and the activity suspicious, stop the suspect, stabilize the situation, and
investigate thoroughly.

As you respond to a hotshot call you need to coordinate with the
other units responding to the call. If it is *your* call, you need to listen
to the other units' locations and response times and assign units to assist
you at specific locations. You might ask the first unit that will arrive
to "take a position south of the bank," or "take a position eastbound
on Main Street at 4th." As the first unit on the scene, you need to advise
other units of information that will help keep everyone safe. Let them
know conditions (Is the bank crowded? Does it look like normal
activity?), your position, and your intentions ("As soon as we establish
a perimeter we will have dispatch contact the bank by phone.")

You must communicate effectively with the other officers. Be
tactful in providing information to other units, be willing to take and

consider suggestions, and don't be afraid to change a plan that doesn't look like it is going to work. The key to a successful response is having the primary unit take responsibility and make assignments. The only wrong assignment is the failure to assign. If the primary unit makes an unworkable or unreasonable assignment (usually due to a lack of familiarity with the location), it is the assisting unit's responsibility to suggest alternatives and make appropriate changes to the plan. Typically, a supervisor will respond to any hotshot call. Therefore, the primary unit usually turns over the tactical response to a sergeant or higher commander quickly.

BURGLARY

When you are dispatched on a burglary call, it will generally be the result of either an eye-witness report or an alarm. Eye-witness reports are great; they can provide you with a description of the suspects, where they entered, and usually what they're driving. Those are the calls where you contain the building with a perimeter of officers and either wait for the offenders to exit, call them out of the location, or go in after them (with a canine or a S.W.A.T. team if needed).

Burglar alarms may be either silent (where a silent signal is sent to the police department or an alarm center), audible (with a ringing bell or a siren at the location), or a panic alarm (one which requires a person to activate the alarm from inside the location). Since well over 95 percent of all alarm calls are false (accidental or due to mechanical malfunction), it is very easy to be lulled into complacency on burglary alarm calls. So many alarms are false that many agencies now charge a fee for each response on an alarm where there is no evidence of a break-in.

On every burglary alarm response, assume that the suspects are there, armed, and ready to shoot. Even an audible alarm is no guarantee that the burglars are going to flee. I once rolled my patrol car into the rear of a restaurant with an audible alarm and found two suspects standing on a milk-crate, attacking the bell with a pickax which they promptly hurled at my patrol car.

As you arrive, note the cars in the area and be alert for anyone acting as a lookout. Establish a perimeter with two or more officers, so the criminals can't escape from one side while you investigate the other. Next, attempt to locate the point of entry ("POE") by walking around the perimeter of the building inspecting every door and window and looking for other means of access such as roof hatches, ladders, and basements. Avoid silhouetting yourself by standing to the side of doors when trying the locks and ducking under the windows. Keep an eye on the areas behind you, many a burglar has escaped from the building and hidden from officers in some outbuilding or tree only a few feet from where the officers were searching.

If the building is found secure, you should check with neighbors to see if they saw anything, and, if possible, wait for a responsible party (usually contacted by the alarm company) to open the building to allow you to search.

When the responsible person arrives, or if you find the structure unsecured, you need to enter the building and search for possible suspects. The preferred method is usually to use a canine to sweep the building. If a canine is not available, always search with at least one other officer. With guns drawn and flashlights as needed, one officer moves at a time, while the other officer covers his movements. You leapfrog through the entire structure this way, protecting each other at every step.

Don't be afraid to use the available lighting. When you use a flashlight, you are an easy target for a criminal waiting in the dark. If you turn on the lights in a room, it puts you and the criminal on equal terms.

Your search has to be thorough, checking every room in a systematic manner, shutting doors behind you to prevent the suspect from backtracking and hiding behind you. Every space has to be checked. I've found suspects hiding under beds, in closets, attics, dog houses, and basement crawl spaces. When officers went to arrest Charles Manson for murder, they found him hiding in a small cabinet under a kitchen sink. I think about Charles Manson and that arrest every time I search; it helps me to be far more cautious and thorough in searching.

If you do locate a suspect, handle him at gunpoint, controlling, covering, disarming and arresting him where he is found. Have other officers come to you and remove the suspect. Then continue your search, assuming there are more suspects waiting for you. Thoroughly check the entire building.

If you do find evidence of a burglary (a point of entry, ransacking inside, missing items, etc.) and the suspects are gone, you need to make

Locate point of entry — here a pried window.

a thorough investigation. Start at the point of entry, and try to determine how the suspects got in. A kicked in door may have a footprint on it, broken glass and painted window sills may have fingerprints, and any tools used may have left distinct marks that could identify it in the future and may match tools in the burglar's possession. Record, sketch, photograph and fingerprint anything that might tend to prove the identity of the suspects. Fingerprint those items which appear the suspects moved, and be alert for items left behind (I've found wallets and keys dropped by burglars in victim's houses). With the owner's assistance make a thorough inventory of the loss, including complete descriptions, identifying features, estimated values, and serial numbers when available.

Last of all, do a thorough check of the neighborhood for witnesses. That means contacting every person who might have had a reasonable chance at seeing the suspects. Sometimes it's frustrating to find a witness who saw the crime but failed to report it. I recall an elderly lady who told me she just knew something was wrong when she saw a young man walking out with her neighbor's television set, but she didn't call the police. I would rather be frustrated than ignorant, however, because that dear old lady wrote down the license plate of the car the young man was driving. Take the time to do your job thoroughly. Did I mention thoroughly? I trust you got the point — thoroughly!

Burglary Tools

Burglary tools are any implements that can be used to commit burglary and are possessed for that *intent*. Because there is a legitimate purpose for most tools (i.e., screwdrivers, flashlights, lockpicks, slide-hammers, slim-jims, etc.), proving the intent (or a lack of legitimate purpose) behind the possession of the tool becomes very important. If you stop a locksmith's truck on the way to a call and find lockpicks and slim-jims, it would be nearly impossible to justify an arrest for possession of burglary tools. Similarly, if you encountered a worker at a body shop with a can of body filler in one hand and a slide-hammer (used to pull out dents) in the other, it is obvious he possesses that tool for a legitimate purpose.

Slide-hammers are also a favorite tool of auto thieves, used to "punch" door and ignition locks. If you find that same body shop worker in an apartment house carport at three o'clock in the morning, he's going to have a difficult time explaining the slide-hammer and flashlight in his hands.

Car thieves know the law as well as you do and often have a seemingly legitimate explanation for carrying those tools. I can't count the number of car burglars I've arrested with a punched lock cylinder still threaded on the slide-hammer and a big can of Bondo™ in the back seat. To make your case, you will have to show the totality of the circumstances to the court, proving the illegitimate purpose of their possession of the tool. Merely possessing a slide hammer won't prove it's a burglary tool, but showing the suspects were trespassing in someone's carport late at night with flashlights, wire-cutters, and broken glass on their upholstery might be enough to *prove,* beyond a reasonable doubt, that their purpose in carrying the tool was to commit a burglary.

Prowler Calls

Prowling is the act of loitering, or wandering on someone else's private property without visible or lawful business with the owner or occupant. In some states the law only applies at night. A *"peeping Tom"* is a prowler who looks into the door or window of any inhabited building while he is on someone else's property. Another term is *voyeur*, a person that gets his sexual gratification by watching others undress or perform sexual acts. Prowler calls are often generated when a resident hears footsteps outside or sees a shadow at his window. As a result, descriptions are often sketchy or nonexistent.

Every prowler is a potential burglar, rapist, or murderer, and should be treated with appropriate caution. Prowlers are often quick and very savvy about police procedures. Sometimes they are local people, often dressed in dark clothing or jogging attire as an excuse for their presence on the street. One prowler even walked a dog to his victim's houses, leaving it tied up nearby while he peeped in windows. Other times they are from far away, and may park a vehicle a block or more away from where they are prowling. Some are armed, some psychotic. Richard Ramirez, the notorious Los Angeles "Night Stalker" was just a prowler until the day he began his sexual assaults, satanic torture and murders.

Catching prowlers requires great stealth on your part. You may have to park well out of sight of the location, and approach silently. I have spoken to prowlers that hid in bushes within a few feet of searching officers and talked to others that have hidden up on roofs or in trees for hours until the officers left. Once you arrive you have to quickly contain the area, and then search it thoroughly.

As you're searching, also be aware of the local wildlife. Animals make the same rustling sounds in the bushes that a prowler might make, and more than one officer has had the unpleasant experience of coming face to face with a bear or a skunk at short range.

AUTO THEFT

When you respond to a car theft call, the car is simply gone and there isn't a whole lot of evidence left behind. Unless the suspect was seen, there will be no description. You should check the area of the car for broken glass (which might indicate a particular window being broken), auto parts, tools, or anything else left behind by the criminals. Some of the information you might ask the owner that could help solve the crime and locate the vehicle includes:

Are the payments current? (If not, was it repossessed?)

Were the doors locked?

Were any keys left in the vehicle?

Are there any keys unaccounted for?

Was the car recently left with a mechanic, in a parking garage, or with a parking valet?

Does the car have the original paint, engine, transmission, and radio?

Does the vehicle have any customization, visible damage, decals, marks, or bumper stickers?

Does the vehicle have a locking gas cap?

Is the vehicle insured, and with whom?

When your investigation is complete, you will generally have the owner sign the report (that's protection against malicious reports by jealous lovers and the like). Then notify dispatch, so the vehicle can be entered in the Stolen Vehicle System as soon as possible (this will also activate the hidden Lo-Jack unit if the vehicle is so equipped). Just as in any other crime, you need to check the area for witnesses, and also check for other stolen cars. Car thieves often will leave one stolen car behind when they "pick up" a new one.

DISTURBING THE PEACE

One of the most common calls you will handle is a call of *disturbing the peace*. Most disturbing the peace calls are *domestic disputes*, or complaints from neighbors about loud radios, televisions, talking, or other noise.

Domestic disputes are often based on seemingly trivial matters. They are not trivial to the parties involved and often simply represent the inability of two or more people to communicate peacefully and effectively to solve a problem. Disputes might involve arguments between spouses, neighbors, or perfect strangers. They may be based on a single moment where a homeowner takes offense at a passerby, or may be the culmination of years of hatred and resentment between neighbors or spouses. As a result, there is great potential for such disputes to erupt into violence and harbor a great potential danger to responding officers.

Your first step, on any dispute call, is to separate the parties. Hopefully, move them to a position where you can watch both parties. Talk to each, individually, without being overheard or interfered with by the other party. If you have a partner, you can position yourselves where you are facing each other, and the parties have their backs to each other.

These are generally people that haven't been communicating with each other very well. Therefore, it's important that they feel they can communicate with you. Be an attentive listener, and attain their view of the problem. Try to summarize, and repeat it back to them so they can see that you understand their side of the story. You can sympathize with their problem, but be careful to remain neutral, and avoid taking sides. You need to listen to each party, in turn, and then take your best shot at resolving the situation.

On calls of loud or excessive noise, the law usually requires the disturbance to be *willful and malicious* in nature. Such calls are generally handled by first finding out who is responsible for creating the noise (often the owner of the property) and advising them that the noise they are creating is disturbing the peace of others. Once they have been told that their noise is disturbing, you can make the assumption that if they continue to make that noise, they are doing so willfully and maliciously. Warn the party that if there are any further calls regarding continuing noise (and a complainant who is willing to go to court as a victim), that you may have to arrest them upon your return.

Disorderly Conduct

Disorderly conduct is often a catch-all statute for any kind of objectionable activity. Violations often include activities that outrage the public's sense of morality (i.e., engaging in sexual acts in public places), or acts that would tend to shock the average citizen (i.e., burning Mother Theresa in effigy outside a Catholic church). It may include disturbing the peace, scandalizing the community, causing public inconvenience, annoyance, or alarm, or offensive language or engaging in offensive behavior. Such calls are handled by arresting the violator. Since disorderly conduct is usually a misdemeanor, you often have the option of simply releasing the violator in the field on a promise to appear in court (citation), or taking him to jail for booking if you feel the offense will continue.

Affray

An *affray* is a fight between two or more persons in some public place. It is a form of *mutual combat* in which the participants have agreed or volunteered to meet and fight. This is very different than an assault, in that there are no victims in the fight (affray) itself. The victims are those bystanders forced to witness the violence of the fight.

In a mutual combat situation, the temptation is to jump in and break up the fight. Avoid doing so unless you have backup. Otherwise, you may find yourself fighting both parties. There's nothing that requires you to jump in and get hurt. Successful strategies include getting their attention. (i.e., I once drove up with my bumper within a few feet of two combatants rolling on the ground and blew the patrol car's airhorns. The fight stopped instantly and both parties were stunned.) Other options include using a chemical weapon such as teargas to incapacitate, or simply waiting until the two parties tire before attempting physical intervention.

Once you break up the physical combat (and get medical attention if needed), you need to separate and talk to both parties and find out why they're fighting. I've broken up fights between lovers, brothers, mothers, and robbery suspects and their victims. If you determine that it is simply a mutual combat situation, you may arrest or cite both parties. Often you will find that neither party wants the other arrested or prosecuted, and the prudent course of action is to take names, have them shake hands, and send them both on their way (in separate directions).

Riots

Although we think of riots in terms of the massive looting and burning experienced in Los Angeles following the Rodney King verdicts, a *riot* is simply a group of people engaged in disorderly conduct. Generally, a riot requires three or more people to assemble and engage in violent acts that are clearly dangerous to persons or property. Meeting with others to *plan* to disturb the peace or to riot generally constitutes "unlawful assembly."

At the preliminary stages of a riot formation, you may be able to disperse the group with a lawful order. Since the right to assemble for lawful purposes is constitutionally protected, your order to disperse requires specific legal wording. In California, the wording would be along the lines of, "I am Officer (*your name*) of the (*your agency*). In the name of the people of the State of California, I am declaring this an unlawful assembly and order you to leave this area immediately. If you do not leave, you will be arrested for *failure to disperse.*" There are specific methods for making sure that every participant in the unlawful assembly would hear you, which will be covered in Chapter 14, *Civil Disturbances.*

At that point all the law abiding participants would immediately leave the area and you would go back to routine patrol. If they don't, then you have a riot and have to use appropriate manpower, planning, and tactics to deal with the occurrence. That will also be covered in future chapters.

DOMESTIC VIOLENCE

Domestic violence is any abuse committed against an adult or emancipated minor who is a parent, child, spouse, former spouse, former cohabitant, or a person with whom the suspect has a blood relationship, has had a child with, or has a dating or engagement relationship. *Abuse* is the intentional or reckless injury of another, resulting in a traumatic condition, or placing another person in imminent fear of that injury. In other words, it's a vicious, self-perpetuating pattern that will continue without strong intervention. It's up to you to provide that intervention.

Spousal Abuse

The most common form of domestic violence is *spousal abuse*, in which one spouse (or roommate) injures the other during some kind of fight. This is a rapidly expanding area of law, with great political consequences and a myriad of laws. As a result, there is wide variation in how different states structure their laws, but all are designed to put an immediate stop to the violence and to protect the victim.

This type of call is considered a high risk call for officers. Always wait for your backup to arrive if at all possible. When both parties in the dispute are present, the risk elevates. This is due, in large part, to the complex psychological nature of these calls. Often the parties turn their aggression onto the officers at the scene.

Your approach to these calls is similar to a mutual combat situation. First, you need to separate the parties, provide medical treatment if needed, determine whether their relationship constitutes one protected by domestic violence laws, interview each party individually, gather any evidence (including photographs of the injuries), and fully document the crime in your report.

In most states you are *required* to arrest a spousal abuser. This requirement is designed to immediately stop the violence. Then you are required to take steps to stop any future violence. These generally include: issuing an Emergency Protective Order (a restraining order keeping the batterer away from the victim), explaining the laws to both parties, informing the victim of his/her legal rights, confiscating firearms or other deadly weapons at the location, and providing assistance to the victim including legal assistance and resources to find a shelter or another secure place away from the suspect.

This is an area where you need to know exactly what your local laws and department policies require and exactly what resources are available in your area (i.e., counseling and shelter programs). Some shelter programs will pick up the victim at the location; otherwise, you may need to provide transportation for the victim.

APPLICATION FOR EMERGENCY PROTECTIVE ORDER

(Name): _____ has provided the information in items 1–6.

LAW ENFORCEMENT CASE NUMBER

1. PERSON TO BE PROTECTED *(name)*: _____
   (Insert in item 1 names of all persons to be protected by this order.) _____

2. PERSON TO BE RESTRAINED *(name)*: _____
   Sex: M F   Ht. _____ Wt. _____ Hair color _____ Eye color _____ Age _____

3. The person to be restrained and the person to be protected are spouses or former spouses, cohabitants or former cohabitants, related by blood or marriage, or they have had a dating or engagement relationship, or the male is the presumed father of a child they have in common.

4. The events that cause the protected person to fear immediate and present danger of domestic violence or child abuse are:
   (Give facts and dates. Specify weapons): _____
   _____
   _____
   _____
   _____

5. ☐ The person to be protected lives with the person to be restrained and requests an order that the restrained person move out immediately from the following address: _____

6. ☐ The person to be protected has minor children in common with the person to be restrained, *no custody order exists,* and a temporary custody order is requested because of the facts alleged in item 4.

7. ☐ The person to be restrained will be arrested and taken into custody.

8. ☐ A child welfare worker or probation officer has advised the undersigned that a juvenile court petition ☐ will be filed ☐ will NOT be filed.

9. Phone call to *(name of judicial officer)*: _____ on *(date)*: _____ at *(time)*: _____
   ☐ The judicial officer granted the **Emergency Protective Order** that follows.

By · ▶ _____
  (PRINT NAME OF LAW ENFORCEMENT OFFICER)   (SIGNATURE OF LAW ENFORCEMENT OFFICER)

Agency: _____ Telephone No.: _____ Badge No.: _____

EMERGENCY PROTECTIVE ORDER

10. THIS **EMERGENCY PROTECTIVE ORDER** WILL EXPIRE AT 5 P.M. ON: _____
    INSERT DATE OF SECOND FULL COURT DAY
    DO NOT COUNT DAY THE ORDER IS GRANTED

11. More permanent protective orders must be requested at *(court name and address)*: _____

12. Reasonable grounds appear that an immediate danger of domestic violence or child abuse exists and this order should be issued against *(name)*: _____

    a. ☐ who must not contact, molest, attack, strike, threaten, sexually assault, batter, telephone, or otherwise harass or disturb the peace of each person named in item 1.

    b. ☐ who must ☐ stay away at least _____ yards from ☐ move out immediately from *(address)*: _____

    c. ☐ who must stay away at least _____ yards from each person named in item 1.

13. ☐ *(Name)*: _____ is given temporary custody of the following minor children *(names and ages)*: _____

VIOLATION OF THIS ORDER IS A MISDEMEANOR PUNISHABLE BY A $1000 FINE, ONE YEAR IN JAIL, OR BOTH. THIS ORDER SHALL BE ENFORCED BY ALL LAW ENFORCEMENT OFFICERS IN THE STATE OF CALIFORNIA WHO ARE AWARE OF OR SHOWN A COPY OF THE ORDER. *(See reverse for important notices)*

Form Adopted by Rule 1295.90 **1295.90** EMERGENCY PROTECTIVE ORDER Code of Civil Procedure. § 546(b)
Judicial Council of California (Domestic Violence and Child Abuse Prevention)
1295.90 (Rev. January 1, 1992) WHITE copy to court, CANARY to restrained person, PINK to protected person 76A838—RD099

Child Abuse

Since children are so much more vulnerable to abuse than adults, special laws are designed to protect them. *Child abuse* is any form of cruelty to a child's physical, moral, or mental well-being. To be defined as child abuse, the act must involve the abuse of a minor child (e.g.., any person under the age of 18 years). It involves sexual abuse, physical abuse, general neglect, mental or emotional abuse, or severe neglect (such as malnutrition). Oftentimes your investigation will begin with a teacher or a school nurse. These investigations require tremendous skill, tact, and expertise. Most child abuse (or suspected abuse) must be reported by police, social service agencies, medical professionals and teachers. It is also cross-reported, so that more than one agency will be involved in any given situation.

In physical abuse cases, you need to inspect the injury, get medical evaluation and treatment if necessary, and carefully interview the victim to determine how the injury occurred. Since children are so vulnerable to suggestion and so imaginative, it is critically important that you avoid leading questions. If you ask, "Did your daddy hit you?," it's very likely that a small child will agree in order to please you, whether or not it is true. Ask open-ended questions like, "How did you get hurt?," and build on those answers to determine the who, what, when, and where. Then you need to make a judgment call as to whether or not you believe child abuse has occurred. Remember, children may try to protect their parents and may mislead you with their answers.

Acts which do not constitute child abuse and are generally not required to be reported include:

1) *Unfounded reports*, that is, reports that have been properly investigated and found not to have occurred, to be a false report, to be factually improbable, or found to be an accident.

2) Acts of *consensual sexual behavior* between minors under the age of 14 years who are of similar age.

3) Acts of *negligence by a pregnant woman* or other person which adversely affect the well-being of a fetus.

4) Adults who report themselves as the victims of *prior* child abuse.

5) *Child stealing,* (still handled as a separate crime, but not necessarily child abuse) unless it involves some other form of abuse.

Corporal punishment is any kind of punishment inflicted on the body. The Supreme Court has upheld the use of *reasonable* corporal punishment by parents and in schools (such as spanking) when it does not result in any traumatic injury.

When you determine that child abuse has occurred, you will generally take the child into protective custody and contact a social agency in your jurisdiction charged with child protection. They may pick up the child, instruct you to return the child to the school or the family, or have you deliver the child to a foster home. Once the child has been cared for, you can continue your investigation with other suspects or witnesses.

Neglect cases require further investigation in the child's home. Most states give you the statutory authority to inspect (technically a search under law) the home to determine whether the child has food, shelter, clothing, sanitary facilities and proper supervision (in the real world, the parents in *Home Alone* would have gone to court). You need to see where the child sleeps, eats, bathes and lives.

You must remember that it is important in such cases to be nonjudgemental and compassionate. There are wide varieties in lifestyles that may be distasteful to you, but adequate to care for the child. Where the child does not have the basic necessities for health and safety, it is often the result of poverty or simply incompetent parenting. Be compassionate and look for solutions. Caring parents need help, and you can be a conduit to resources within your community. On the other hand, children who are neglected and/or abused desperately need your protection.

Sexual abuse of children requires a far more delicate approach and the greatest amount of self control. Again, you need to care for the child first, removing the child from the situation and getting medical treatment, diagnosis, and documentation. This investigation requires a specialist. You will need the help of a skilled investigator (and often a skilled physician to collect the evidence) to investigate and document these cases. Usually the suspect is someone the child trusts: a relative, family friend, neighbor, teacher or babysitter. These relationships create tremendous emotional conflicts for the child and requires the professional assistance of a child psychologist or social worker. Make sure you promptly get the help you need.

Elder Abuse

Senior citizens are vulnerable to specific unique forms of abuse as well, some of which may require reporting. Abuse can result in no physical injury or can result in death. Elder abuse may be perpetrated by others or self-inflicted.

The most obvious form of elder abuse is physical abuse which can include: assault, battery, constraint, deprivation, sexual abuse, medication, isolation, and physical or chemical restraints. Often the named suspects are the care-givers, family members, private nurses, or staff members at hospitals or convalescent homes.

Other forms of abuse to elders include: neglect, abandonment, and mental suffering. Self-inflicted forms of elder abuse include: physical neglect, substance abuse, physical abuse, attempted suicide, and fiduciary abuse.

Because of their special vulnerability, elder abuse cases require the same diligence, compassion, and professionalism in investigating child abuse cases.

CRIMES AGAINST PROPERTY

Grand Theft and Petty Theft

Theft or Larceny is generally divided into varying degrees of seriousness. Minor or *petty thefts* are the simple taking of property without the owner's consent. Part of the theft requires an intent on the part of the thief to deprive the owner of the property and to gain from their loss. These are typically classed as misdemeanors.

Grand thefts or *1st Degree thefts* are more serious and may be based on the way the property was stolen, or the value and type of property. Generally property taken from a person (such as a pickpocket's theft of a wallet) is a grand theft if no force or fear is used. Beating up a person to take their wallet would be robbery. Theft of property valued above a certain amount (ranging from $100 to $1000 depending on the state) is considered a grand theft. These are typically classed as felonies. The dollar cut-off amount is very specific. If your state's limit is $500, a theft of $499.99 is still a petty theft and, therefore, a misdemeanor rather than a felony.

When you respond to a theft in progress call, treat it as seriously as you would a robbery. That same potential for violence exists. Once the situation has been controlled, you will need to determine the nature and value of the stolen property to determine whether it is a felony or a misdemeanor. You'll also need to determine the ownership of the property in order to establish a victim and prove that the suspect did not have permission to take the property. If the owner is a company or corporation (often the case in shoplifting), then list the entity as the victim (such as "Montgomery Ward Store #630"), with the manager listed as a witness to the theft in order to testify on behalf of the store.

Fraud

Fraud is just another form of theft by specifically obtaining property (including money) from another person by deception, trickery, creating a false impression, or hiding information. Some forms of fraud include *bunco* and *kiting* (writing checks against closed or "non-sufficient fund" [NSF] accounts.)

In any kind of fraud investigation, you need to collect all of the paperwork related to the fraud as evidence. This includes: the bounced checks, identification of the suspect, and records from the bank showing the status of the bank account, etc.

Forgery

Generally, forgeries are low-risk calls; you are contacted long after the crime has been committed and the suspect has left the area. As with any crime, it can be a high-risk call when you have to confront the suspect. An officer in a nearby city went to a bank on a forgery call expecting a routine response and contact with the victim. As he entered the bank, the suspect drew a 9mm pistol and shot the officer twice, paralyzing him for life. Just another check forger, but one committed to escaping at any cost. Yes, he was caught and convicted.

When investigating these crimes, your best evidence is the actual identification and documents used by the forgers. It is important to determine whether the suspect merely presented (or uttered) the forged document, or actually wrote or signed the document in the presence of a witness. If a suspect is in custody, you need to have the suspect complete a handwriting exemplar so his writing can be compared to that on the document.

CRIMES AGAINST PERSONS

Assault and Battery

Assault and battery are often lumped together, and the difference is not well understood by the public. *Assault* is the attempt or threat of injuring another, which must be coupled with the present ability to do so. If you raise your fist and tell someone, "I'm going to punch your lights out," you have assaulted them. You have made a threat, you are capable of doing it, and the person has a reasonable fear that you will carry out that threat.

On the other hand, if you said, "I am going to cut your head off with a chain saw!" and you don't have a chain saw at hand, there's no way to carry out that threat and, therefore, no assault. Assault is often divided into *aggravated assault*, where the assault is part of committing some other crime, and *simple assault*, where the general intent is simply to cause pain and injury to the victim (generally a misdemeanor).

A *battery* requires some physical contact that is either offensive or results in injury. In simplest terms, a battery is a completed assault. *Sexual battery* is any unwanted touching of a sexual nature.

Assault becomes a felony based on the intent and the method. Assault with a deadly weapon ("ADW") occurs whenever a deadly weapon is part of the threat, for instance, when brandishing a knife or aiming a gun at the victim. Simply waving a gun or knife around in a threatening manner without making a specific threat is generally called *brandishing*. Assaulting someone for a specific reason is often a separate crime, such as "assault with intent to commit murder," or "assault with intent to commit rape." "Shooting into an inhabited dwelling" would be another form of assault treated as a serious felony.

The crime of *mayhem* is battery in the extreme, the deliberate maiming of another person by removing, disabling, or permanently disfiguring a body part. Mayhem is committed when someone deliberately chops off a person's fingers or hands or bites off a nose or ear. In one celebrated case in Ohio (*Bobbitt* case), a woman who felt her husband was unfaithful cut off his penis while he slept, then fled in her car and threw it out the window. Diligent police officers found the missing organ, and it was reattached after nine hours of surgery. This is a clear case of mayhem.

In any case of an assault, your procedures are pretty much the same as outlined for a mutual combat situation: separation, medical treatment, interviewing, preserving evidence and documentation.

Sex Crimes

Rape used to be a very specific, sexist crime — a male having unlawful sexual intercourse with a female other than his wife, without her consent. Some of the elements of rape included: the female's submission based on the use of force or threat, impairment by the male having drugged or otherwise impaired her ability to resist, an unconscious victim, or a victim below the age of consent. Any penetration of the penis was sufficient to prove rape.

Today's definition of rape has been vastly expanded to include male and female victims of every age, and to include every form of sexual activity. Rape now covers virtually any unwanted or illegal sexual contact between any two persons, whether the same or opposite sex, regardless of their marriage status, and whether the contact involves the genitals, anus, mouth, or foreign objects.

Those who sexually abuse children are called *child molesters.* These are sick, sick individuals. Many are well organized, with rings of similar people providing a network of information and pornography to their members. They even have an organization, *NAMBLA*, the "North American Man-Boy Love Association." They view child molestation as a natural manifestation of love between an adult and child. You view it as a serious crime. There is no acceptable explanation or excuse of any kind for molesting a child. You must be diligent and thorough in your investigation of the offense and the offender.

Child molesters are serial offenders. They will molest again and again until caught and locked away. According to an F.B.I. agent who investigated hundreds of such offenses, molesters have a total obsession with their predatory activity. They will document and photograph their activities, so they can relive the experience again in the future. When locked up, they will think about molesting everyday, and, when released, they will commit more molestations at their first opportunity. Once convicted, they often turn to murdering their victims to avoid being identified again. There is no effective treatment, no cure, no known rehabilitation.

Your thorough and competent investigation is the only way to protect children from future molesters. Give it your absolute best effort. Talk to everyone in the area. In one case, a deputy sheriff looking for a missing girl approached a pickup truck. Inside the cab he saw a man sleeping along with two dogs. There was dog feces all over the cab, and the smell was overpowering. The deputy turned away in disgust and never talked to the man. When apprehended on another child murder, the suspect told investigators that when the deputy approached he was ready to confess to him, and the body of the little girl was in the back of the truck.

You cannot ignore any possible evidence of sexual activity within your search area. Searching for a kidnapped girl, an officer found a pornographic magazine and women's semen-stained panties in a parking area adjacent to the girl's school. A sergeant sent to the scene threw them away after determining that the panties were far to large for the missing little girl. In fact, the killer used the items to masturbate with while watching the school yard, and presumably his fingerprints, blood type, and DNA were thrown away by the sergeant. Although the suspect was convicted (and is currently on Death Row), this could have been important and compelling evidence. If you can determine where the sexual acts took place, you need to collect clothing, bedding, discarded tissues, semen stains, blood stains, pubic hairs, and any other evidence that might identify the suspect.

Part of the evidence in any sexual crime is the victim. Before allowing a victim to shower or bathe, take him/her to the hospital. There a doctor will conduct and document a complete medical examination and collect samples of semen, blood and hair as well.

Robbery

Robbery calls are generated when a passersby observes a robbery in progress or when the victim notifies the police by telephone or silent alarm. Just as in burglary alarms, many robbery alarms are accidental, and it's easy to become complacent in your response. Be particularly aware of lookouts and *lay-off* cars, a car outside of the location and assigned to kill the responding police officers if necessary to effect the suspect's escape.

Your arrival and deployment are just like any other hotshot call: you attempt to arrive silently and unobserved, remain aware of the entire situation, establish a perimeter and contain the scene. Be in a position with a good shooting background where you can challenge and control anyone coming out of the location at gunpoint.

At some point, you need to look into the location. This can be done by binoculars from a hidden position or by a plain clothes unit passing by the front. Be on the lookout for people you don't know, customers or employees being held hostage, and innocent looking customers who might be armed accomplices. If all activity at the location appears normal, or if the caller advises dispatch that the suspects have already left, have the caller describe himself to the dispatcher and then have him slowly step out of the location to talk to you. Generally speaking, you should never enter a robbery location until contact has been made and you have **firsthand knowledge** about what is going on inside.

Once inside, standard procedures apply. Get medical treatment if needed. Separate and interview all the witnesses. Ascertain the loss, particularly the denominations of bills taken and the serial numbers of any "bait" money. Determine the weapon that was used, and get out a crime broadcast. Collect any evidence (i.e., items dropped by the suspect, videotapes from security cameras). Fingerprint counters, cash drawers, doors and door handles, and any other surfaces touched by the suspect.

Kidnapping

Many missing children reports turn out to be kidnapping or child stealing. As part of your investigation, you should always include both the legal and family relationship of the victim and the suspect.

Determine who would want to kidnap that person and why. Collect any evidence, and talk to every person in the neighborhood. Witnesses are the major key in unlocking most kidnapping cases.

Last of all, assume that any kidnapping can turn into a murder. Treat the crime scene exactly as you would in any murder investigation, and be equally diligent in collecting and preserving the evidence.

Murder

When you receive a homicide call, you handle the call using basic tactics: a coordinated response, containment, situational awareness, locating and neutralizing suspects, getting medical treatment, and preserving the crime scene. Unless the person is obviously deceased, paramedics are usually called and will either conduct lifesaving efforts or declare death. If they transport the victim, make sure you continue to preserve the scene after the victim is removed. Leave every rubber glove and bandage wrapper right where it falls, and don't allow anyone to tidy up until you have finished with the investigation.

At a homicide scene, you need expert investigation. These highly-trained specialists will interview witnesses, photograph and sketch the scene, examine the body, and collect, preserve and process the evidence. While waiting for those experts to arrive, your duties as a patrol officer are to control the scene, establish a perimeter, contain and keep separated all possible witnesses, and keep an *Incident Log* listing every person entering the crime scene, their purpose in entering and the time they entered and left. This will prove invaluable to the investigator who is trying to eliminate fingerprints and other evidence left behind.

Controlling the scene is sometimes tough to do. Other officers, public officials, and the media all want to get as close to the body as possible. Be firm, be polite, don't budge. At one homicide scene, I turned away our Chief of Police and the City Manager as neither had any duties at the scene. They were "pissed off," and I wondered if I would still have a job come morning, but, ultimately, I think they respected me for doing my best to preserve the integrity of that crime scene. Use *your* best judgement.

Vice Calls

Vice is a generic term that simply indicates any immoral conduct, practice, or habit. Vice laws include prostitution, bookmaking, and other forms of gambling. All are extremely difficult to work effectively in patrol and are usually investigated and enforced by special vice units. Patrol officers are usually limited to maintaining high visibility on the streets and dissuading potential customers.

What you can do as a community-oriented police officer is to be aware of the activity. Find out who the prostitutes are, where they work, and how they work. Oftentimes prostitutes recognize they have little to fear in terms of arrest from the patrol officers, and establish a "working relationship" in which they are willing to provide good information on other criminals in the area. Likewise, you will learn who the bookmakers and other gamblers are and where they conduct business. They stay in business by avoiding the likes of patrol officers, so don't expect to catch too many suspects in vice investigations. Do be aware and capable of providing competent, fact-based leads to vice units that may work your area.

You will receive calls on narcotics activities and sales and may observe some of this activity on your own. Learn the players in your area, and be prepared to take aggressive action. Given a good description and probable cause, you can be effective in driving drug dealers off your streets. When they move their activities indoors, you can work on their clientele as they come and go. Despite the thousands of officers working specialized narcotics units across the country, the vast majority of dope taken off the streets is still seized by patrol officers as a result of their routine activities. Learn all you can about narcotics activities in your beat, and take aggressive and consistent action.

Under the Influence

A good number of calls you receive will be regarding persons under the influence of alcohol or drugs (symptoms of abuse, appearance, and methods of use are covered at length in Chapter 9 - Substance Abuse). Generally, it is against the law and an arrestable offense to be under the influence of *any controlled substance* (i.e., an illegal drug). To be arrested for being under the influence of alcohol, you have to be in a public place (this includes any area open to public viewing, including the passenger seat of a vehicle), and incapable of caring for your own safety or the safety of others.

What determines whether a person can care for himself? Generally, a person has to be able to function: walking, standing, and talking without endangering themselves. They have to be aware of who they are, who you are, where they are going, what day and what time it is, and have a means of getting where they are going. Simply drinking alcohol and demonstrating a bad attitude to the police does not qualify one for arrest.

Once a person under the influence has been arrested or detained, you have to decide what to do with them. Recognizing that alcoholism is a disease, but also recognizing that chronic public drunkenness is a major social problem, most jurisdictions have a variety of methods for dealing with drunks. These include arrest, sobering up, transportation to court, and criminal prosecution; arrest, sobering up, and release with no further action; and detention and transport to a detoxification facility, again with no criminal record or prosecution.

MENTAL ILLNESS

As a legal term, *mental illness* and *insanity* are pretty much the same. Saying someone is mentally ill is just a nice way of saying they are crazy. A mentally ill person is someone with a condition that makes him unfit to enjoy liberty of action because of the unreliability of his behavior, and the potential danger to others.

Most states have some provision for police officers to take mentally ill persons into custody and to have them committed to a mental health facility against their wishes for a psychological evaluation (usually for 72 hours). This authority to deprive someone of his liberty needs to be taken very seriously. To be committed, a person generally must fit one of three criteria, similar to those used in determining public drunkenness. They must be either:

1) Unable to care for himself or his property (extreme forms of self-neglect such as malnutrition, untreated diseases, or persons living in homes that are unfit for human habitation);

2) A danger to himself (suicidal, attempting suicide, or persons engaging in life-threatening behavior like playing chicken with semi-trucks on the freeway); or

3) A danger to others (engaging in homicidal, aggressive, dangerous, or otherwise harmful activity).

Dealing with the Mentally Ill

Sitting in the patrol car working radar one day I saw a female walking backwards toward the patrol car. She had a white envelope in her hand. As she approached the patrol car, she dropped the envelope in the passenger window and then ran away. It was my introduction to Beverly (not her real name), a mentally disturbed person that I dealt with for years. The envelope contained three pages of handwritten text addressed to the Chief of Police. Here's part of what she wrote:

> Food & Drug Administration: Samples of milk and Orange Juice from their milk + my orange juice. Aug 11 - lasers of left and right clavicle. The reason for submitting samples of the milk and orange juice - the bitter taste in both is similar - transfer of disease - possibility of diseased sperm - AT STEPFATHERS. My stepfather is a heavy smoker. I have never had a positive TB test - Doctor at my request gave me several penicillin shots to counteract the effects of cancerous sperm my stepfather dumped into the potato salad.
> MY PHYSICAL + MENTAL HEALTH REMAINS EXCELLENT. They have kept me from life and living:

1) Narcotics sent through heating system.

2) Laser device-used to scar & cause blood clots.

3) Electrical wire-intense shock under bed.

4) Gas piped into bedroom

5) Wires are hanging from somewhere and hitting metal.

6) 1-foot fissure in bedroom ceiling.

7) Special effects-pink spider on overhead light.

8) Laser bubbled pain (sic) on kitchen window.

> FBI was given a roll of Film Sept. 23 showing
> structural damage. Dead flowers from narcotics poured
> through hose - Lasar damage - kitchen - bubbled paint.
> Gas was turned off - heating vents covered with foil
> baking pans and kitchen foil to prevent effects of
> narcotics. Lasar at arms length could have killed me.

Sound crazy? Of course, but this was real *to her*. She lived in this
world and regularly wrapped her entire body in aluminum foil to fend
off laser attacks, covered all her electrical outlets to prevent gas
attacks, and spread dozens of boxes of Kellogg's Corn Flakes on her
floors to absorb X-rays.

Beverly was not stupid. If you made fun of her, lied to her, or
patronized her, she would be quick to call you on it. She was an
intelligent, articulate woman, who happened to be mentally ill. She was
paranoid and delusional, but she could take care of her needs, dressed
well, did the shopping, took out the trash, kept a neat and tidy house
(she vacuumed and put out new Corn Flakes regularly) and didn't
represent a threat to herself or others. She received regular (although
apparently ineffective) treatment, but she could not be committed. She
just didn't meet the commitment requirements.

Beverly brought me dozens of letters over the years and provided
hundreds of photographs of cars and people she thought were stalking
her — from the F.B.I., the C.I.A., and the K.G.B. Over the course of
nearly one hundred contacts, she ended up being a great teacher and
taught me a lot about dealing with mentally ill persons.

There are some key elements to remember in handling mentally
ill persons. First of all, you have to know what resources are available
in your community to help them. In past years, the Department of
Health Services operated a Patient Evaluation Team (P.E.T.). At the
request of a police agency, they would come to your station, conduct
a brief psychiatric screening of the suspect, and, if appropriate, they
would arrange for the transportation and placement of the suspect in
an appropriate facility.

Budget constraints have ended that program. Now we have to rely
on private insurance and volunteer organizations. Our department
maintains a list of mental health professionals, along with their areas

of specialization. A nearby hospital has its own mental health workers capable of providing services to those with insurance coverage. The county hospital still operates a mental ward, but the officer has to transport the patient to that location, and they are often short on bed space (in Los Angeles County, some estimated 38,000 patients were competing for approximately 3,500 beds).

Knowing your resources will give you more confidence in dealing with the situation. You have to know your community! Within or near our community there are a number of facilities for Alzheimer's patients: nursing homes, halfway houses for drug offenders, and board and care facilities for the more functional of the mentally ill. Most are not "lock-down" facilities, and patients escape or simply wander away. Their unusual and sometimes bizarre behavior can quickly attract attention. With knowledge of these facilities, it is often easy to get them back where they originated with little effort.

When dealing with the mentally ill, there are tactical, moral, and legal considerations. First, you must observe officer safety at all times. Keep a safe position and protect your weapon, remain constantly alert.

That doesn't mean you have to treat mentally ill persons like criminals. You need to treat them with respect and courtesy as you would normally. Avoid exciting them, use restraining force as sparingly as possible, and ignore their verbal abuse. As with Beverly, these people are not stupid; they may be clever and manipulative. They can be highly skilled at provoking a reaction, and may delight in shocking language or anti-social behavior. They can be deliberately insulting and incredibly insightful and accurate in nailing you right in your most sensitive area. Remain professional and deal with their problem.

Last of all, do not deceive the person. Tell them exactly why you are there and exactly what you are doing. I've rarely had a problem in pointing out that their behavior seems bizarre to others and we have a medical professional on the way to evaluate them. You will rapidly get into trouble, and often provoke a violent reaction, if you lie to them about being committed and then suddenly show up with an ambulance and gorilla-sized orderlies in white suits. Treat the mentally ill with trust and respect, and you will typically find them far easier to deal with and resolve the situation.

Particularly in cases where there is a threat of violence or suicide, you may want to remove any deadly weapons from the house of a mentally ill person. In many states, it is against the law for a mental patient to possess any firearms or any other deadly weapon. Police officers are given the legal authority to confiscate those weapons and to hold them until they receive a court order requiring their return. Again, make no attempt to deceive the person. Simply tell him that the law allows you to confiscate his weapons in the name of public safety, and that is what you intended to do. You can let him tell you where his guns and weapons are kept, but, of course, you don't want them to retrieve the weapons. Give him a receipt and book the weapons into property as per your department policies. Don't even make 'any promises about returning the weapons. That is beyond your authority.

Drug Paranoia

An increasing problem is one of drug induced psychosis. This is normally found with users of amphetamines, cocaine and crack cocaine. In addition to being committed criminals and drug dependent, these people develop acute mental illnesses, most often manifesting as paranoia — an irrational fear of being watched and persecuted by others. Because they are often armed, and especially worried about the police, they represent a special danger to you as a patrol officer.

Their behavior may be totally bizarre or calculated and manipulative. I encountered one "crack" cocaine user in our city that had disassembled every wall outlet and ventilation duct in his house looking for possible police listening devices. He later climbed up on his second story roof and did a swan dive onto the sidewalk when the fire department arrived to attempt to rescue him.

In another case nearby, a paranoid crack user tried to flag down a passing officer and lure him to the open trunk of his car. Inside the trunk was a loaded 9mm semi-automatic handgun. When the officer refused to approach, the suspect jumped in his car. A high-speed pursuit ensued that ultimately resulted in the suspect's death.

Such persons, while dangerous, offer you an even wider range of options for handling. You can treat them as purely criminal, purely mentally ill, or somewhere in between. Just treat them all with respect and caution.

Suicide

Suicide tends to be violent and messy. In addition to the traditional and more sedate methods of killing one's self (slit wrists, poisoning, suffocation, hanging, etc.), people have committed suicide by immolation (burning themselves), gunshots, explosives, and deliberate car and plane crashes. Some have planned deliberate, violent confrontations with the police, hoping to commit suicide — death by cop. Unfortunately innocent bystanders are sometimes killed or injured by those attempting to commit suicide. Their deaths may be treated by your jurisdiction as murder, manslaughter, or simply an unfortunate accident that constitutes no crime at all.

Since Dr. Jack Kevorkian began assisting people in killing themselves, states have increasingly passed laws designed to deter assisting such efforts. Depending on your jurisdiction, persuading or aiding another person to commit suicide can be charged as murder, manslaughter, a separate and specific crime, or no crime at all.

When you respond to a possible suicide in progress, you can generally plan on talking to a person who qualifies as mentally ill. Use the guidelines above, talking them toward a solution in a calm, rational manner; never lying to them, always remaining respectful, never compromising your safety.

When you respond to the scene of an attempted suicide, you will generally be responding with medical assistance. If the victim is still alive, make sure you and the paramedics are safe, but basically allow the ambulance crew to handle the call as a medical emergency. Assist them in any way you can.

If the person is already dead, treat the scene as a homicide until you can positively rule out murder. Some of these scenes are relatively straightforward; a history of depression, a suicide note left pinned to the chest, a gunshot wound to the temple, and a handgun left clenched in one hand. You photograph, document, gather the evidence, and call the coroner.

Other cases are like a jigsaw puzzle: hugely complicated, mysterious, and convoluted. In one case, the body of a young East European doctor was found in his locked apartment, floating in a bathtub overflowing with hot water. His face was under water, and his body severely scalded. There was a half empty bottle of wine on a nearby table and an empty package of some medication from Europe in the trash which we could not identify. He left behind a note written entirely in German, which none of us could read. Fortunately, his German girlfriend arrived and helped us translate the suicide note. Unfortunately, we couldn't entirely believe her since she had previously been convicted of attempting to murder the doctor. In contacting a family friend, the friend immediately claimed the doctor had been murdered by the KGB, since the doctor's father was an important diplomat.

I had a very competent coroners' deputy assisting me that day, and we were able to establish suicide beyond any doubt. The doctor had a history of depression and attempted suicide, the bottle and note had only his fingerprints, the handwriting proved to be his, and the note detailed his intention to take a fatal dose of the drug, wash it down with alcohol, and go to sleep in a hot bath to ensure his death. Up until that note was translated, however (with a little assistance from the State Department), we treated the scene as if it were a homicide.

HOMELESSNESS

It used to be that patrol officers had to deal with hoboes (mobile, seeking work), tramps and transients (mobile, not seeking work), and bums and vagrants (non-mobile, not seeking work). Now we deal with the *homeless*, a broad term covering a wide variety of people, circumstances, and differing levels of personal hygiene.

As a result, most laws affecting the homeless have been repealed, leaving the patrol officer with few resources to deal with such persons except when they violate specific laws. In my city it was once unlawful to loaf or loiter in public, and state law made "vagrancy" a crime. Every person was required to present I.D. on demand by a police officer. That is no longer the case, and homeless people have taken up permanent residency in various places throughout our city.

The law now treats homelessness as a status (sometimes as a protected status) rather than a crime. You need to know what resources are available in your community, so that you can direct them to places where they can sleep, eat, bathe, or receive health services. Most communities have established rescue missions, soup kitchens and similar institutions to meet this need. They are often operated by churches or organizations such as the Salvation Army. Know these resources and learn what they can do for you in various situations.

You also need to know what laws you can use that may apply specifically to homeless people. Some of those most frequently used include: trespassing, prowling, theft (of food, or water), hitch-hiking (or walking in a roadway), and shopping cart theft.

Many of the homeless are alcoholic or mentally ill and can be referred or transported to some agency for assistance. For those that are willing to work, sometimes your best tool can be knowledge about who in town might hire them for temporary or long term employment. Sometimes the homeless may pretend to be mentally ill. Feigning insanity can be a convenient way of being left alone. I learned that one night as a rookie when I met with a crusty old veteran police sergeant. We had just started talking when a transient in the next booth started babbling away in a loud, obnoxious voice. The sergeant just turned around and in his best command voice ordered, "Shut the hell up! I don't have to listen to a crazy man in *my* doughnut shop. Now you either shut your mouth or leave."

The man sat there in stunned silence for the next half hour. My sergeant had accurately assessed his behavior and made an appropriate tactical decision. It is not a tactic that would work with every individual, but, since that time, I have found that ordering someone to act in a rational manner often works well.

NON-TRADITIONAL AND SOCIAL SERVICES

As previously mentioned, a great deal of your time will be spent on non-criminal calls. These calls often deal with threats or potential threats to the public safety or welfare, or simply with providing unique expertise to assist citizens in need. Without spending a great deal of time or space on them, let's examine some of those calls.

Animal Calls

Since animals can represent a threat to public safety and health, the police are the ones first called to respond. Many agencies operate the local animal shelter and perform all animal control functions. Other agencies may depend on private organizations.

Animal calls are infinite in variety. Some that I have handled include: dead, stray, rabid and injured dogs and cats, deer hit by cars, horses stuck in mud, an escaped pet rattlesnake, bees swarming in walls, trapped skunks and a possum with his head stuck in a can.

Animals are dangerous. They can bite, claw, sting, infest you with fleas and give you infectious diseases. As a general rule, unless you are required to do otherwise, just keep back and protect yourself and others from harm. If the animal is on the loose and truly vicious, you may have to kill it to prevent injury to others. Unless that is the case, just wait for the real experts to arrive and handle the wildlife.

Business Disputes

Oftentimes disturbance calls at commercial establishments turn out to be business disputes. People have paid for goods and services that have not met their expectations or customers have used the goods and services and not paid for them. In each case, unless you can prove some kind of *fraud* (a deliberate, willful intent to cheat one party or another), these calls are generally non-criminal.

You should not be the one interpreting contracts and warranties, torts and liabilities. Separate the parties, listen to each side, and then send each packing off to their attorneys for advice or to Small Claims Court for a judge to settle the matter.

Dead Bodies

Like income tax, death is inevitable for everyone. Everyone dies, by old age, natural causes, disease, accident, or criminal homicide. When people die, the police investigate the circumstances, and the coroners' office investigates the body and determines the cause of death.

Usually, you will have a quick feel for how the person died. You may have ruled out homicide or suicide, and there's the body, collapsed on a floor, slumped in a chair, or peacefully in bed. The person is either obviously dead, with rigor mortis (stiffening), lividity (settling of blood into the lower parts of the body), or putrefaction (rotting), or a doctor or paramedics have responded and declared death.

Some agencies will defer to the coroner, others will require you to investigate. In my city if we get a doctor to certify the cause of death (based on recent treatment of a life-threatening disease) a simple officer's report with only the most basic information will suffice. If no doctor is willing to certify the cause of death, the officer writes a more comprehensive report, and the body is picked up by the coroners' office for autopsy.

Fire Department Assists

Frequently, police officers are dispatched on fire department calls. Since the police are already out in the field, they can usually respond in much shorter time, assess the situation, and often take immediate action.

It's important to understand the limits of our training and equipment in this area. We wear flammable uniforms, carry no breathing apparatus, and wear various volatile fluids and explosive devices around our waists. That's not the ideal situation for encountering extreme heat and fire.

Stay back and let the experts (F.D.) do their job.

As a first responder, you need to remain safe and keep the public safe. Where possible, you will probably evacuate burning buildings, keeping as low as possible, feeling for heat on doors before opening them, and getting out in time to save yourself. Smoke inhalation and burning are not good ways to die. Unless the fire is very small, using a garden hose or a fire extinguisher on a building is generally a waste of time.

Car fires represent a special hazard. Full of plastic, rubber, resins and fluids; a burning car puts out a potpourri of potentially deadly vapors. Exploding tires, batteries, and fuel tanks can send burning debris flying for hundreds of feet. Stay back from a burning car and keep others back until the fire department arrives.

The same tactics apply for downed power wires, leaking gas, and hazardous materials. Get back and keep others back until the experts arrive to handle it. Notify responding agencies if hazardous material placards are evident and take appropriate action.

First Aid

Police officers are also often the first responders to accidents and medical emergencies. Depending on your department and the response times of ambulances, you may be a full paramedic or simply a basic first aid provider. Generally, your care is limited to life-saving emergencies such as: stopped breathing, no pulse, or heavy bleeding. You should have a few basic supplies to help you: a CPR face-mask, a blanket and some large bandages.

In our agency, a paramedic ambulance is usually only minutes behind the officer and nothing other than immediate life saving measures are required by our officers. If that is not your situation, you need to acquire the necessary skills and equipment to handle the calls you might normally receive.

Missing Persons

By law, most police agencies are required to accept missing persons reports by any person. These reports include:

1) runaway juveniles (minors who have left home without their parent's permission or knowledge),

2) voluntary missing adults (those who have left of their own free will),

3) parental abductions (a juvenile who has been taken by a parent or family member),

4) non-family abductions (where a known abductor from outside of the family took the juvenile),

5) stranger abductions,

6) dependent adults (missing persons with physical or mental limitations),

7) lost (whereabouts and circumstances are unknown),

8) catastrophic (missing after a plane crash, earthquake, flood or other disaster), and

9) unknown circumstances.

In each case, you must document the incident and make the appropriate entries into the computer network. You need to make an immediate and comprehensive investigation and search anytime there is an indication the person is "at risk." At risk persons would include or indicate the person was or has been:

a) the victim of a crime or foul play,

b) in need of medical attention,

c) has no pattern of running away or disappearing,

d) the victim of a parental abduction, or

e) mentally impaired.

Missing children are particularly critical. You need to get whatever manpower you need, (I've called out the Fire Department, Water Department, Explorer Scouts, and the High School Football Team to help) and then conduct an organized search.

Start with the child's house, the vast majority of time you will find small children hidden in a closet or under a bed. Then work your way in overlapping teams through each and every adjacent property in every direction, recording each address searched and person contacted. Search every bush, tree, trash can and hole in the ground. (We found one missing three-year-old that had crawled in through a neighbor's doggie door). Again, remember that every missing person is a potential kidnap or murder victim.

Resident Services

Depending on your department's resources and orientation, you may be asked to help people locked out of their cars or homes, conduct safety inspections, abate nuisances (such as abandoned refrigerators), help handicapped people back into their beds, or notify them of the death of a loved one. No matter what the call, always do your best. Remember the first lines of the *Law Enforcement Code of Ethics*: "As a police officer my fundamental duty is to *serve mankind*." Do your best, every day, on every call.

DISCUSSION QUESTIONS

1) To what degree does your local law enforcement agency specialize? What specific experts (homicide investigator, photographer, crime scene tech, etc.) are available to patrol officers?

2) Do you feel that *NAMBLA* (the North American Man-Boy Love Association) should have a constitutionally protected right to exist?

3) Should prostitution be illegal? Why, or why not?

4) Should alcoholics *ever* be treated as a criminal problem? Given a limited budget, would you choose to deal with public drunkeness solely as a criminal problem, or solely as a social problem?

5) Do you think that law enforcement agencies are the appropriate organizations to deal with the mentally ill? Why, or why not?

6) Should homelessness be a criminal problem? How else could we deal with the problem?

7) Why do you think the police should be the organization handling runaway juveniles?

8) What do you think of the mixture of law enforcement and social services police agencies provide? Should these functions be separated?

Mayor Luther Meadows of Nixa, MO, was charged in December with assault on a police officer after being stopped for suspicion of drunken driving. After some arguing, Meadows allegedly leaned into a patrol car and punched the officer in the chest. However, Meadows claimed he was only touching the deputy's shirt to see whether or not it was foreign made.

VEHICLE OPERATIONS

LEARNING GOALS: After studying this chapter the student will be able to:

- Analyze the relationship between a patrol officer's driving and the public's image of the police.

- List the basic principles of defensive driving.

- Identify the liabilities an officer is faced with when driving a patrol car.

- Describe how patrol officers conduct traffic stops.

- Define a "high risk" stop, and explain how it is conducted.

- Define "Code-3," and list the important factors in driving under emergency conditions.

- Discuss why vehicle pursuits are of such concern to the public.

- Identify factors an officer should consider before engaging in a pursuit.

- List methods that can be used to terminate a pursuit.

- Name the primary safety rules for transporting prisoners in a patrol car.

SAFE DRIVING

You've seen it a thousand times on television stunt shows — the Amazing Barzini Brothers make a car tilt up and drive on only two wheels while jumping 14 buses and passing through a burning hoop. Just before they complete their incredible feat, the host makes some disclaimer such as, "Kids, don't try this at home! These men are highly trained professionals using specialized equipment. Were you to attempt this stunt on your own, it could result in death or injury." Even a simple television commercial showing a new car driving along a twisty mountain road carries a subtitle reading "Professional driver on closed road!" The driver is shown in a full-face helmet, driving gloves, and flame-proof driving suit.

If you think about it, both of these situations are utterly absurd. Do the television producers really expect that some idiot is going to get together a couple of busses and a flaming hoop to try to duplicate the Barzini Brothers? Do car manufacturers really expect us to wear helmets and other safety equipment every time we drive on a twisty road?

The answer is no, and yes. While they don't expect the average consumer to attempt to duplicate their stunts, they do expect accidents to happen, and they expect to get sued by any idiot that crashes his car and says, "Well, I saw it done on TV!" So manufacturers and broadcasters try to limit their liability by suitable warnings. Consider this a warning for every patrol officer: every time you drive a vehicle owned by your department, you must think of the liability.

This chapter will teach you a lot about driving tactics: strategic ways of thinking, planning and carrying out your driving chores as a patrol officer. It is not intended to teach you driving techniques such as: how to steer, brake and shift. So remember, "Kids, don't try this at home…"

Also remember that every time you drive a police car, you are driving 3,000 pounds of highly-visible advertisement for your department. People are going to judge your entire agency based on their observations of your driving. During normal patrol, you should be polite and courteous and obey every traffic law. Instead of using your steely law enforcement stare on every driver, try a smile and an occasional wave. A deputy sheriff in Los Angeles once supposedly failed to return the sheriff's greeting which generated a terse department-wide memo stating, "Any deputy too busy to wave is too busy to be a deputy sheriff." Point well taken!

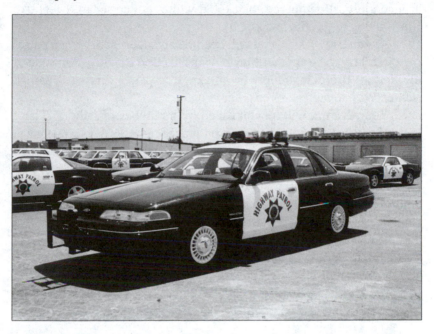

The above could become the below very quickly.

The average urban patrol car averages about 10 miles an hour in between calls. That's still about 400 miles per week, 1600 miles per month, 19,200 miles per year. After more than a decade of pushing around a big, ill-tempered, black and white, police sedan, I feel like I'm *starting* to get the hang of it.

As a patrol officer, you will become an expert at driving a patrol car. Don't try to be another Mario Andretti, Bob Bondurant, or one of the Barzini Brothers; simply be an expert at patrol driving. That's a tremendous advantage over other drivers.

Your driving will be controlled by a number of factors. These include your common sense and experience, city attorneys, state laws, department policy, and your community's expectations and norms. I've watched films of officers in highly congested eastern cities where they considered the sidewalk simply another lane for their use in emergency calls. In my community, passing another vehicle on the right even with the amber "excuse me" lights on will often generate a complaint call to the watch commander. You have to know the standards in your community, and stay within their expectations.

Last, but not least, most officers' injuries on duty are the result of traffic accidents. Traffic accidents are the leading cause of on-duty officer injuries. Get the point! Prepare for this inevitability.

Defensive Driving

Your greatest safety lies in developing defensive driving habits early in your career. It's easy for patrol officers to develop aggressive, almost belligerent styles of driving. Patrol cars, with their lightbars and markings, tend to intimidate other drivers. People will often yield their lawful right-of-way to an aggressively driven patrol car, scrambling out of your way. They will refuse to pass you in traffic and hang back a long way from your rear bumper. It becomes easy for you to take unfair advantage over their "black-and-white fever," and develop driving habits that are simply rude and obnoxious. Knowing that you are pretty unlikely to be pulled over and cited, patrol officers are often chronic speeders, rolling through stop signs and pushing through red lights at the very last minute. It's a kamikaze "hot dog" mentality that hurts the image of the department and compromises your officer safety.

If you want to be a successful, well-accepted patrol officer in your community, learn to be a polite driver. If a driving act is rude — it's usually wrong. Make eye contact with other drivers, smile, and wave them through the intersection when they have the right-of-way and they hesitate. Drive looking well ahead of your patrol car's hood, drive at the speed limit, and observe all laws. Assume that the other driver will not yield the right of way, that other drivers won't see you in time and that their reactions will be illogical and wrong. That way you won't be taken by surprise and end up embedded in a couple of tons of crushed steel. Always be looking for an escape path for your patrol car, by leaving plenty of reaction time between yourself and other vehicles. At every intersection, assume at any moment that you might get the most important Code-3 call of your life. That way you can position yourself to react, instead of leaving yourself boxed in by other traffic.

Vehicle Inspection

In previous chapters, we talked about inspecting the patrol car. But before you take off on patrol, you need to do a few more checks. Your basic patrol inspection made sure the car was properly equipped, that there was oil in the engine and the tires were properly inflated. You checked that everything worked and that nothing was obviously damaged. If any damage was found, you reported it to your supervisor.

Before starting the engine, check the safety belt and put it on. As you start the engine, a modern patrol car will check both the air bag restraints and the anti-lock brake systems and give you an indication on the dashboard. Once those lights go out, you need to conduct a basic road check. As you pull out of the parking lot, see how the vehicle operates and feels. Does the engine run smoothly without unusual noises? Check the tires and brakes for squeals, rumbles, and vibrations. See if the vehicle tracks straight or pulls to either side; then check it again while braking. Check the steering, to see if it feels tight and responsive without excess play or vibration. Only after you have completely checked the condition of the vehicle are you capable of making informed decisions about how to respond to calls.

Broken Patrol Cars

The reality in many agencies is that patrol cars are often high mileage vehicles in terrible condition. Unless the car is genuinely unsafe to drive, you may be forced to patrol in the vehicle they assign you. Over the years I've had to take out cars with no heaters or air conditioners, cars with holes rusted through the floor, cars with seats rotted to the springs, cars so slow a bicycle could outrun them, and cars without operating lights or sirens. If no other cars are available, you generally write up the problems and hope that someday the car will be repaired or replaced. Meanwhile you go out on patrol in your assigned unit, recognizing the limitations and driving accordingly. That means using common sense and not taking risks, advising the dispatcher you are incapable of emergency responses, and ignoring traffic violations that you otherwise might stop.

VEHICLE STOPS

Assuming everything works on your patrol car, you are now equipped to make a vehicle "*stop*," (pulling over another vehicle). We live in a mobile society where we depend on our patrol car to respond to crimes. Because of that mobility within society, many of our contacts with citizens and criminals are related to vehicles.

Burglars, bank robbers, rapists and murderers all may drive to and from their crimes. As a result, every vehicle stop you make is an unknown. You may know that you are only stopping the car for a broken tail-lamp, but the driver of the car may be heavily armed and fleeing from the scene of a crime. That is what happened one morning near my city when a motorcycle officer from the Highway Patrol stopped a car for speeding. The officer thought it was just another speeding ticket; the driver thought he was being stopped for the armed robbery he had just committed in another city and immediately shot the officer in the face. The officer survived the wound, but was retired on disability. I can vividly remember escorting the officer to the hospital. I visualize those terrible images and use them as a reminder that every car stop can turn deadly.

Routine Stops

We call them "routine stops," but, in truth, they are often anything but routine. A routine stop is a basic, low-profile stop for a traffic violation you have observed or an investigation of a suspicious person. For whatever reason, you have probable cause to stop and talk to the driver or passengers of the vehicle.

The first thing you have to do is position your patrol car directly behind the suspect vehicle. In most cases, this is just a matter of maneuvering through traffic. If the vehicle is going in the opposite direction, a traffic signal separates you, or traffic conditions are heavy, it can be a lot more difficult to accomplish. If the other vehicle gets a signal ahead of you, you have to make a decision. Are you justified in using your lights and siren to get to the other vehicle? Would it be legal and within department policy? Is it worth the risks you expose yourself and your agency to every time you drive Code-3?

Once you are behind the vehicle, you need to position your patrol car so the other vehicle can see your lights. This will vary based on your speed and the traffic conditions, too close and the other driver's field of vision through his mirrors might cut off his view of any emergency lights on your roof. You also need to leave yourself enough room to safely stop in case the other driver suddenly stops. If you place your patrol car too far back, the driver may not realize that you are trying to pull him over or may use the distance to try to escape. You'll learn proper distance while at the academy and during on-the-job training.

Once your patrol car is properly positioned, you can usually pick a location to conduct the stop that is most advantageous to you. Try to stop the other vehicle in a place that is legal and safe with a minimum exposure to traffic hazards and other risks. For example, you may think a stretch of red curb is a perfect place for a car stop, but many drivers won't stop at a red curb. They may think that stopping here would be committing another violation. Instead of stopping where you planned, they may end up stopping directly in the traffic lane or pulling into a parking lot or alley where you can rapidly lose control of the situation. Just because you know the scenario for how a traffic stop should go, don't assume the other driver is following the same script and be aware of the possibility that you may be being set up for an ambush.

Having planned where to stop the vehicle, go ahead and call off your radio traffic. Advise dispatch, in whatever radio terminology is appropriate, that you are making a traffic stop and give the license plate and the location. It's important to get the radio traffic out of the way before you stop the car. If the stop goes sour and you end up in a fight, crash, or shooting, it's going to be difficult to put out that information while you're trying to stay alive. If the location changes or the driver fails to yield, you can always modify the broadcast. It's always a good idea to write down the license number on a pad inside your vehicle.

Now, you need to get the driver to stop. Most officers use progressive levels of equipment to get another driver's attention. If the driver is looking in his rear view mirror, you might simply gesture to the side of the road with your hand and effect a successful stop. With a less attentive driver, you will turn on your emergency lights, your headlights or high-beams, your spotlights, and then sound your horn or siren. Your use of equipment often affects the other driver's attitude; he may equate the equipment you use with the seriousness of his offense. In general, use as little as needed to get his attention.

As the driver comes to a stop, you need to position your patrol car in the safest possible position, 10—15 feet behind the other vehicle, and offset to the left by 3-4 feet. Assuming you're at the curb, this will create a safety zone (a small area beside his driver's door in which your car protects you from passing traffic) in which to contact the other driver. Consider the danger from passing traffic when you position your patrol car on a freeway or other high speed road. Any offset into traffic might increase the danger to you, so use your judgment.

Watch all occupants of the vehicle carefully. Are they behaving "normally?" Sometimes occupants make "furtive" movements as they try to hide guns, alcohol, or other contraband. Sometimes occupants

A correct position for a car stop.

make very similar movements in trying to sneak on their safety belts to avoid a citation. Some drivers become very nervous, and police officers and experienced felons often make a show of keeping their hands in plain sight. Watch all occupants and try to interpret their actions. It's difficult to do, especially as you get out of the patrol car. Vans, tinted windows, and campers pose a special problem, and your agency will assist you on the proper technique for these stops.

Give approaching drivers maximum warning, leave on the rear amber lights on the lightbar and leave either your left turn signal or the 4-way hazard lights on as well. You need to put the car in "park," turn the wheel to the left, and remove the key from the ignition. Placing the wheels in this position gives you the maximum protection from potential gunfire from the suspect vehicle and also steers the patrol car away from you and the car you've stopped if it gets hit from behind.

After you have removed your safety belt, check for traffic in your mirror, turn on your portable radio, and grab your flashlight, baton and citation book, if you need them. Then open the car door, transfer everything to your non-gun hand, and step out of the patrol car. Close the door behind you, approach the driver of the other vehicle. Usually he will remain behind the wheel, but sometimes he will get out and try to meet you in the street. If he does, you have to evaluate his attitude and motivations, and either direct him back into his vehicle or up to the sidewalk. You can't stand in the street between the vehicles; that's an invitation to become the filling for a chrome sandwich if your patrol car gets hit from behind. Also be aware of others on the sidewalk or surrounding area that may pose a threat.

Assuming the driver remains behind the wheel, you should walk past the front of your patrol car and step to the right into the "safety zone" you created. Continuously scan the car and its occupants, check for anything usual: license plates, tags, damage, locks, window glass, lighting, tires, and other equipment. Most officers pause at the back of the suspect vehicle and touch the trunk lid. This makes sure it is shut and locked (armed suspects have ambushed officers from the trunk), and lets you feel the vehicle to determine whether the engine is running, and whether there is movement in the vehicle that doesn't match the movement of the occupants you see. As you walk up slowly to the driver's door, scan the interior, look for each occupant's hands, search for weapons, alcohol, drug paraphernalia, stolen items and other contraband. If you have a partner, he should parallel you on the opposite side of the car, and look for the same things.

As you approach the driver, stay clear of the driver's door so that you would not be hit if he suddenly opened the door. Usually the driver will have the window open, but sometimes you have to knock on the window and get the driver's attention to conduct business. As you do, keep your gun hand free while observing the driver's hands, and check the steering column and ignition for any signs of damage or tampering.

Your first contact with the driver is usually a professional greeting ("Good morning," etc.), and a request for a driver's license and vehicle registration. You may ask the driver to turn off his engine if it is running (although in very hot or cold climates it's appropriate to let him leave on his engine to keep the air conditioner or heater working). Again, watch the hands very closely. The action of pulling out a wallet is almost identical to drawing a gun, and guns and drugs are often hidden in the glove compartment along with the registration. Be alert. Once you've obtained identification, take a look at it and see if it appears to match your driver. Check the registration as well. Does it match the car you've stopped? Does the driver know who the car belongs to? Once you're assured you know who and what you're dealing with, you should explain the purpose of the stop to the driver ("I'm stopping you for excessive speed", or "We received a call about …").

If you're investigating suspicious activity or suspect the driver might be under the influence of alcohol or drugs, you should separate the driver and each passenger before asking any questions. To do so, ask the driver to step out of the car and up on the sidewalk. When you do, control his actions. Open the door yourself, direct him to the spot you want, and follow him so that you never turn your back on the suspect. If you are concerned about weapons, you can frisk him briefly on the sidewalk before continuing. Then get information from him that you can compare to the passenger's stories. People that are telling the truth will generally be pretty consistent, but liars will almost always screw up the details when you start asking the right questions.

For most routine traffic violations, the driver will remain behind the wheel of his car. Obtain the information you need to write the citation, and then give him specific instructions (i.e., "Stay right here, I'll be back in a few minutes.") before backing away from his driver's door. I learned this lesson through experience. I stopped a driver, and then I told him I was going to issue a citation. As I returned to the patrol car, he drove away. I chased him down a few blocks later, stopped him, and demanded to know why he took off. "I told you I was going to write you a citation," I said. "Yes," he replied, "but you didn't tell me I had to stay." Although it seemed obvious to me that he wasn't free to leave, it wasn't obvious to him. Never assume anything and learn to be very specific in your instructions.

Weather permitting, stand behind the open passenger's side door of the patrol car while writing a citation, a field interview ("F.I.") card, or while running a person for wants and warrants. This offers a number of advantages. It's a good vantage point to continue to observe the occupants, You are protected from traffic, and the door provides some additional cover. Also, I have easy access to the patrol car's radio and shotgun, and can hear the unit radio in case your portable fails (it seems like the battery life on some portables is calculated to die when you need it the most). When it's cold, you can leave the heater on and stay fairly warm in the open doorway. At night, the patrol car's take-down lights provide enough illumination to write without trying to hold a flashlight at the same time. Once you start writing, try to look up at the suspect vehicle at the end of every line.

If I have a partner, I like him to stand somewhere further to my right so that he has a continuous view of the occupants. Partners should be close enough to communicate with each other but far enough apart that they don't make themselves easy targets.

In bad weather, you may have to write your citation from the inside of the patrol car. This makes you an easy target for assault. You place yourself in a confined place, generally well illuminated, and with a limited ability to hear and see around you. To give yourself more reaction time, leave a lot more room between the stopped vehicles, as much as four or five car lengths.

After completing your work, you need to return the driver's identification and complete your contact. You should return to the driver with the same caution and techniques you used on your initial contact. If you issue a citation, obtain the driver's signed promise to appear and issue him his copy. Then release him from your custody with something like, "Thank you for your cooperation. You are free to go now." Keeping an eye on the driver and any approaching traffic, you can return to your patrol car and leave.

Night Stops

At night, your routine in stopping a vehicle will vary slightly. You should consider lighting as a factor for picking the location for a car stop. For high-risk stops, you may want to choose a dark location, giving you a greater advantage of concealment behind the patrol car's lights. For low-risk stops, you may want the maximum illumination from streetlights so that you can conduct an investigation or field sobriety test with minimum use of your flashlight. Your stop location depends on your situation — use your best judgement.

Use every source of illumination possible on the patrol car when making night traffic stops. Place both spotlights on the suspect vehicle, the left aimed at the outside left mirror, the right on the center rear-view mirror. Turn on the take-down lights in the lightbar, the 4-way hazard lights, and leave the solid red light on (rotating lights if the unit is within a traffic lane). The result is a blinding display of light that conceals your movements as you approach a suspect vehicle, thus effectively destroying the suspect's night vision and allowing you to control the action. Approach the driver carrying a bright halogen flashlight in your non-gun hand, usually held at shoulder level. This bright light further reduces the suspect's night vision. This gives you a better opportunity to visually sweep the interior of the car and improves safety.

High Risk Stops

High risk, or *felony*, *stops* are those traffic stops where you know there is increased danger to you and the public because the suspect is either armed or may have committed a serious offense. Stolen cars, felony suspects, offenses involving weapons, and suspects involved in pursuit are all handled as high risks and use very different techniques.

First, generally try to avoid stopping the suspects until one or more back-up units have caught up to you. Just follow the suspect at a comfortable distance and wait for as much backup as possible. What's the hurry? If you have the luxury of a lot of back-up headed in your direction, give everyone a chance to get in position before initiating the stop. You control the timing to your advantage.

Second, you should carefully choose the location for your stop. Wait to pull over the suspect vehicle until you have the maximum advantage. Wait for an area with the best possible control of the suspects, traffic, and innocent bystanders.

Once you decide to stop the high-risk vehicle, turn on your lights, and wait for it to yield. The first unit generally positions itself about 10 feet from the curb and 3 to 4 car lengths behind the suspect with high beams on. This allows the second unit to park parallel and to the right of the first unit, side by side with room between the units for the officers to work. Additional units can be positioned anyplace that is out of the other officer's potential line of fire, yet still offers a clear view and a safe shooting background on the suspects. Once the suspect vehicle is covered, units can be assigned to traffic control at both ends of the roadway, preventing innocent motorists from driving into the middle of your stop.

Felony stop with two car response.

The primary objective of a felony stop is for the officers to remain in a protected position while carefully controlling the suspects. Rather than approaching the suspect vehicle, each suspect is slowly brought back to the officers and dealt with individually where the officers have the maximum advantage. If the suspects flee on foot, it's important to have a plan. Another suspect may be hiding in the vehicle, waiting to ambush any officers that run by in foot pursuit. Don't let the suspects "sucker" you into doing something that isn't safe. If the suspects bail out, the primary unit has to maintain control of the suspect vehicle and carefully clear the vehicle before chasing the suspects, but other units positioned ahead can chase the suspects or establish a perimeter in the meantime.

Each officer should have specific responsibilities. One officer will control the stop, issuing commands to the suspects over the patrol car's P.A. system. One or more officers will do nothing but keep the suspects covered with their weapons. One or more officers will do nothing but arrest and handle the suspects. Additional officers can be assigned as observers or to traffic or crowd control. All officers try to make the maximum use of cover, generally crouched down behind the doors of the patrol cars with their weapons aimed at the suspects.

The arrests are made by bringing the suspects back to the officers, generally to a position in front of the patrol cars. This keeps potentially armed suspects in front of the officers' guns at all times. The suspects are then ordered to either lie down in the roadway or kneel so they can be arrested. I prefer to arrest each suspect, handcuff, search, bring him back to the patrol cars, and then question him before dealing with the next suspect. In some jurisdictions, officers prefer to bring all the suspects out of the car, and place them in front of the patrol cars, and then have the arrest team handcuff and search all the suspects at the same time. Depending on your manpower, either system will work effectively.

If you are giving the commands, make them specific, brief, and uncomplicated. Start with a warning: "You in the red Honda. You are in a stolen car. Do exactly what I say when I tell you to, and you will not be harmed. If you do not do what I say, you may be shot." Then neutralize the suspects. Order each of them to place their hands on their heads, flat against the windshield, or held out the windows. This allows all officers to see that their hands are empty and they don't represent a threat. Next, neutralize the vehicle. A typical series of instructions might be as follows:

> "Driver, using your left hand only, remove the keys from the ignition." (You may have to skip this step if the car is stolen and no keys exist. After your first command, the suspect will usually tell you he has no keys.)
>
> "Driver, hold the keys out the window where I can see them."
>
> "Driver, throw the keys out the window to your left."

The next step is to carefully remove and arrest each suspect, generally starting with the driver. You control each and every action, providing maximum safety for the officers in bringing the suspect back to the arrest team. You have to assume that each suspect is armed and willing to kill you and your partners at any opportunity. Be careful and be specific.

"Driver, with your left hand, reach out your window. Use the outside door handle and open your door."

"Driver, use your right hand to unfasten your safety belt."

"Driver, step out of the car with your hands over your head."

"Driver, take three steps to your right."

"Driver, slowly turn to your right so I can see you are unarmed. Keep turning until I say stop."

"Stop!"

"Driver, walk backwards toward the sound of my voice until I tell you to stop."

"Stop!"

"Driver, slowly drop to your knees. Now lie face down on the pavement. Put your hands out to your sides, palms up. Cross your legs at the ankles. Don't move!"

At that point, the arrest team can move forward to control, handcuff, and search the suspect. Additional passengers can be brought back to the arrest area and positioned where you need them. As each suspect is handcuffed, they can be placed in separate patrol cars or held by officers. When all the known suspects are removed from the car, you need to "clear" the car of any potentially hidden suspects. Each of the suspects already in custody should be asked if anyone else is in the car and reminded that a hidden suspect could be shot if they suddenly appeared. If all suspects deny that anyone else is in the car, you can try a bluff. Use the P.A. to order them out. "You in the car. We know you are in there. Come out with your hands up!" Sometimes the occupants don't speak English or pretend they don't. Have a back up plan.

Ultimately, a team of officers has to approach and visually clear the suspect vehicle. They should advance carefully, keeping their weapons pointed at the car, and use all available cover. Once they have checked both the interior and the trunk, they can give the "all clear," and you can get on with the business of suspect interviews, evidence collection, vehicle impounds and bookings.

Obviously, felony stops on motorcycles, vans, buses, campers, motorhomes or trucks require variations on these procedures. Officers should coordinate with each other and have a general plan in mind, but you have to be flexible because anything can happen. Units should be positioned to give you the maximum coverage of any doors or windows on the vehicle, and you have to recognize that larger vehicles may have numerous hiding places (often best searched by a K-9) or be equipped with roof hatches or trap doors. The suspects may not be following the same plan you are, they may not cooperate, and they may attempt to escape or assault you at any time.

Anything can happen in a felony stop. I've had an armed robbery suspect stop, lower his hands, and start screaming, "Just shoot me!" (We had a team of four officers wrestle him to the ground.) I've had a passenger in a stolen van claim that the door was broken, so he couldn't open it. (He had a loaded gun on the center console, we made him crawl out the window.) I've had a car with six juveniles simply ignore us and refuse to obey any of our commands. (We sprayed a lot of tear gas into their car until they "got with the program.") And I've cleared a felony vehicle of suspects only to discover a huge pipe bomb in the back seat (successfully disarmed by the bomb squad many hours later).

In the academy, cadets see a lot of films about felony stops and practice the procedures time and time again. We know how the stop is *supposed* to go. It's easy to forget that the suspect hasn't seen those same films. We give all these commands and expect them to be followed. The reality is that the suspect may be deaf, intoxicated, or may speak a foreign language. Just take your time, adapt the procedures as you go, and maintain tight control for your safety.

ROUTING TO CALLS

The vast majority of calls to which you respond will be non-urgent in nature. They are routine reports in which the suspect is long gone, calls in which citizens need advice or minor assistance, neighborhood disputes or business problems. While the citizens expect you to respond in a timely manner, you should drive normally. There is no excuse for speeding, tailgating, or passing traffic illegally. You should obey each and every traffic law including finding a legal parking place once you arrive at the call. In my city, a police car on official business may park at a red curb and so can U.S. mail carriers and utility companies. Nonetheless, this perfectly legal parking by police officers generates complaints from citizens who don't understand that the police unit is exempt. Do your best to meet your community's expectations.

The more urgent the call, the more tempted you will be to drive faster and break traffic laws to get there and catch the bad guys. Unless you have actually been dispatched on a Code-3 call, authorizing you to use your lights and siren, you will be violating the law just like the people you cite every day. I've been passed on the way to prowler calls by officers traveling at 70 mph on city streets with their amber "excuse me" lights flashing to the rear (sometimes called "Code- 2 1/2 by the officers). That's inexcusable! The city and the officers are strictly liable for any accident that occurs and enjoy only limited protection when responding Code-3 on an authorized call. Like most jurisdictions, we have specific guidelines for which calls are dispatched Code-3, and then only dispatch a single unit.

Most agencies only dispatch a unit Code-3 when there is a great threat to human life. These include: structure fires, injury auto accidents, armed crimes in progress, assaults in progress, and officer needs help calls. Then only one unit is dispatched. That unit gives its location, allowing a closer unit to "buy" the call, and allowing the dispatcher to advise other responding units (such as fire engines and ambulances) of their route, so they can avoid collisions.

EMERGENCY DRIVING

In every jurisdiction, certain laws exist to permit the safe and efficient operation of emergency vehicles of all kinds including the patrol car you will be driving. These laws are designed not only to protect the physical safety of those traveling to emergencies but to protect the public from danger in the operation of emergency vehicles.

Only when you conform precisely to your jurisdiction's laws and your agency's policies will you enjoy the law's full protections and exemptions. In every emergency response you undertake, it's vital that you remember your mission to help and assist the public. You won't do anyone any good if you don't make it to the scene. Safety should always be given priority over the speed of your response.

Yielding to Emergency Vehicles

The laws in virtually every state require that when any driver observes an emergency vehicle approaching which is displaying emergency lights (solid red in California, flashing red and/or blue in many other states) and sounding a siren as is reasonably necessary, that driver shall yield the right-of-way. *Yielding* means pulling as far to the right as possible and coming to a full stop. Since they are required to yield by pulling to the right, it is critically important that you make every effort to pass other traffic to their left. Otherwise, an accident might occur as a driver did his duty, pulling to the right as you tried to pass.

Your use of the siren falls back on the "reasonable" test. In a high speed pursuit on the freeway, you are often overtaking other vehicles at such a high speed that they have no opportunity to hear or react to the siren until you are well past. In such cases, the use of the siren may be a liability. Similarly, in rural areas of the United States, a patrol officer may be responding to the scene of an emergency for several minutes without ever seeing another car.

The frustrating reality of urban traffic is that many people don't yield to emergency vehicles. Sometimes there is no room for them to pull out of the way, other times they simply ignore the lights and siren, and the patrol officer is forced to either tag along behind the idiot or take the risk of passing by crossing onto the wrong side of the road.

Although patrol cars are exempt from stopping at red lights and stop signs, they need to approach every intersection with extreme caution. Often that means slowing; sometimes it requires coming to a complete stop. Modern cars are increasingly well sound-proofed and modern stereos can easily overpower the sound of sirens. Likewise, on a major emergency, the sound of a siren might well block out the sound of other approaching sirens.

Exemption from Traffic Laws

When driving an authorized emergency vehicle in compliance with state laws, you are exempt from most of the provisions of the *Vehicle Code*. These specifically include laws pertaining to speeding, right-of-way, traffic signals, signs, and other rules of the road, but this exemption only applies when in "actual pursuit" of a violator (or suspected violator) or when responding to a call of a fire, rescue, or other emergency.

The definition of *emergency* is pretty broad and includes: injury traffic accidents, medical assistance calls, and felonies in progress. Remember, the exemption from traffic laws only applies when you are properly using your lights and siren, and when you are responding on an authorized call. As a supervisor, I once arrived at the scene of an injury traffic accident before the assigned unit and looked up the street to see four of our units driving Code-3 in a caravan toward the scene. While appreciating the officers' willingness to all share in handling the incident, only the first unit was authorized to use Code-3. Once he arrived, he would be free to ask for the assistance of other officers, even requesting them Code-3 if there was a continuing threat to life at the scene. The other units were not exempt from liability, since they were not authorized Code-3 under our department policy. They should have proceeded to the scene at normal speeds, obeying all laws.

Exemption from Civil Liability

In most jurisdictions, patrol officers enjoy certain immunities and exemptions from civil liability when they are operating their police vehicles under emergency conditions. Typically, the law exempts the driver of an authorized emergency vehicle when responding to an actual emergency call, and when showing emergency lights to the front and sounding a siren when necessary. The exemption from civil liability is not a blanket exemption for any kind of driving. Your duty is still to exercise reasonable care to avoid collisions, driving with due regard for the safety of all persons using the highway, and not imposing an unreasonable risk of harm upon others.

The courts hold the operators of emergency vehicles strictly accountable for operating those vehicles in a safe manner. In one infamous case, the driver of a 40-thousand-pound fire engine was asked in court whether he had seen the red signal light at the scene of a fatal traffic collision. His contemptuous reply was, "We carry our own red light." His city paid nearly 3 million dollars for that callous, unreasonable statement.

Remember, in order to enjoy the exemption, you have to be responding to an actual emergency call or actively in pursuit of a violator, not simply engaged in some arbitrary use of your lights and siren because you're in a hurry to get to a non-coded call.

Officer Needs Help Calls

Generally, there is no call that will get your blood pumping and your common sense thrown out the window like an *"officer needs help"* call. The instinct of every officer that hears that call is to get there as fast as possible to help their fellow officer. All too often, officers crash into each other or into other cars and never make it to the call. A number of officers have died in utterly senseless collisions where they both approached the same intersection Code-3 at high speed. It's a stupid way to die.

If you're dispatched to an *officer needs help* call, get there as quickly as you can in a safe manner. If you aren't dispatched but are nearby, get headed in that direction, — but do it safely and don't use lights and siren unless you are specifically authorized to do so. If you want to really be sure you can help your fellow officer, take it slow enough to make it safely to the scene. Go to the officer's assistance as quickly as you can, but don't go running into a totally unknown situation alone. If your fellow officer is dead, his condition is unlikely to deteriorate if you pause a few seconds to assess the situation.

Stay off the radio and listen; the officer in peril may be trying to get out information or the first arriving unit may be broadcasting. If you are not needed, your presence at the location will only complicate matters, draw more attention to the incident, and create another disciplinary problem (you) for your sergeant.

Escorts

In most jurisdictions, emergency vehicles are forbidden to use their lights and siren or to violate any traffic laws when serving as an escort. An exception exists when escorting supplies and personnel for the armed forces during a national emergency or for the preservation of life.

Generally speaking, police escorts are a poor idea. Imagine trying to lead a group of disaster relief vehicles, none of which are equipped with emergency equipment. Using your lights and siren, traffic might yield for your patrol car, but their tendency would be to pull right back into traffic after your passing and right into the middle of your convoy.

The most common use of patrol vehicles as escorts is for ambulances and fire equipment. It is not uncommon for patrol cars to precede ambulances with critically injured patients (particularly with injured officers) blocking traffic at key, busy intersections. As the only means of protecting firefighters and getting them safely to the scenes of hundreds of arson fires and medical incidents, during the 1992 Los Angeles riots, patrol officers ran non-stop escorts for fire units.

The Patrol Car as an Ambulance

A police car is not an ambulance. It's not equipped as an ambulance and generally should not be used as one, but sometimes you have no other choice. I will never forget rolling in on the scene of a wild shoot-out between a narcotics team and drug dealers. Two officers were down with gunshot wounds to the head, a third officer suffered multiple wounds. Two suspects were dead at a second nearby location, a third suspect was critically wounded but survived to stand trial for murder. Officers and paramedics were desperately attempting CPR. The surviving officer was wisely placed in a patrol car for a quick trip to the hospital, saving precious minutes.

No jurisdiction has infinite resources to deal with medical emergencies. When the medical emergencies start stacking up, paramedics and ambulances may not be immediately available. There you are on the scene, doing CPR on an infant, two minutes away from a hospital and the dispatcher advises you that the E.T.A. of the nearest ambulance is 15 minutes. All of the sudden your patrol car is an ambulance.

Over the years, I've taken injured officers and dying children to the hospital. I've driven firefighters in my backseat as they assist a pregnant woman in delivery. The only time such transportation can be justified is during a dire medical emergency, where the delay in transportation will mean greater injury or death to the victim. Then it is time for the utmost caution. With your supervisor's approval, you'll be rolling Code-3, but you must be conscious every moment that a collision will totally defeat the purpose of your transportation, possibly with fatal consequences for those being transported.

PURSUIT TACTICS AND PROCEDURES

Police pursuits are undergoing scrutiny like never before because of one simple fact — police pursuits kill people. They kill officers, suspects, and innocent citizens alike. In California, the Highway Patrol requires all law enforcement agencies to submit a report on every pursuit. This program has resulted in some interesting data. Statistics based on 7,323 pursuits reported in 1992 showed that roughly one-fifth (22 percent) of all California pursuits resulted in a collision. The really bad news is that 17 percent resulted in injury, 0.4 percent (or roughly one in every 250) resulted in death. The good news is that over three-quarters (77 percent) resulted in the arrest of the suspect. That's a pretty effective arrest technique with a relatively low probability for death.

California has very high standards of training for their officers and some very restrictive laws requiring specific pursuit policies from their police agencies. Combined with the tremendous advances in traffic safety (mandatory safety belt laws, ABS braking, and the proliferation of airbags), these statistics represent a vast improvement over similar studies conducted just 10 years ago.

Who dies in a pursuit? On the average, 288 people in the United States lose their lives in pursuits each year. Fourteen percent of the time, it is you, the patrol officer, that become the fatality. Fifteen percent of the time it's an innocent citizen that dies, and 70 percent of the time the suspect dies.

Although you probably enjoy statutory immunity for damages resulting from a pursuit, case law has required that each law enforcement agency adopt a pursuit policy and take steps to ensure its compliance, specifying minimum standards and giving officers adequate guidelines. Only through such guidelines can the officers make informed decisions and exercise appropriate discretion as to when to initiate and when to discontinue a pursuit.

Entering into a pursuit is a decision-making process that includes the partnership of the officer, the dispatcher, and the supervisor. All must continually determine whether or not the risks involved in conducting the pursuit outweigh the public benefit of apprehending that particular suspect. In addition to specific laws for your area and the policies of your agency, some important factors must be considered by officers and their supervisors:

1) The seriousness of the violation for which the traffic stop was originally being attempted.

2) The safety of the public in the immediate area of the pursuit.

3) The safety of the officers involved in the pursuit.

4) The volume and patterns of traffic in the area.

5) The volume and patterns of pedestrians in the area.

6) The location of the pursuit (i.e., jurisdictional boundaries, residential, commercial, freeway, etc.)

7) The time of day.

8) The weather conditions and visibility.

9) The road type and conditions.

10) The capabilities and limitations of the police vehicle and the officer driving.

11) The familiarity of the pursuing officers (and supervisors and dispatchers) with the area of the pursuit.

12) The quality of radio communications between the pursuing unit, dispatch and the supervisor.

Consider the following example:

You observed a Pontiac Trans Am speeding at roughly 70 miles per hour through the central business district at 11:00 p.m. The streets were dry, the weather warm and perfect. You pulled in directly behind the Trans Am as it turned onto a six-lane street, separated from opposing traffic by a wide center median. From that position, you radioed the vehicle's description and the license plate. Other traffic was extremely light, and you had your sergeant and two other units behind you when you attempted to stop the vehicle.

Unknown to you, the driver was a drunken ex-convict who had kidnapped, raped, and repeatedly stabbed two young girls. In his car was various police equipment that allowed him to impersonate an officer including a police scanner tuned to your frequency. He had no intention of stopping when you "lit" him up.

You were able to stay with his car for about three blocks before you began to lose sight of him. The patrol car was topped out at about 110 miles per hour, the Trans Am at about 130. Partly due to his speed, but mostly due to his .12% blood alcohol level, the suspect hit the only other vehicle you passed in the entire pursuit. The Trans Am disintegrated, but the suspect was virtually unharmed and arrested without problem. The victim he hit took a rocket sled ride as his vehicle was propelled through an intersection, into a vacant lot, over a cliff and into a tree. It took almost 15 minutes to find the victim's vehicle, and it took the fire department over an hour to extract the seriously injured victim. Ultimately as a result of the pursuit, the suspect driver was convicted on multiple counts of kidnap, rape, and attempted murder and received a long prison sentence.

This illustrates one of the great dilemmas of deciding whether to pursue any given suspect. You don't always *know* why the suspect is running. All you had, initially, was a traffic violation. If you worked in a jurisdiction with a "no pursuit of traffic violators" policy (a number of agencies are considering such policies now), this major felon might never have been brought to justice. If the traffic violation was indeed the only offense the suspect had committed, it would be difficult to justify the serious injuries suffered by the innocent victim for what would only have been a traffic ticket.

There is always a great deal of risk in every pursuit. Your life and the lives and health of others will be at risk. There is great potential for property damage and great potential for economic damage to your city. Many attorneys make their livings from police mishaps, and jurors often show a natural empathy for innocent third parties harmed as a result of police activities.

PURSUIT DRIVING TECHNIQUES

The best tactic for surviving pursuits is to avoid them entirely. There are some situations in which you can almost predict that a pursuit will occur. If you know you're stopping a felony vehicle, a stolen vehicle, a wanted person, or a vehicle that has already passed you at high speed; you can reasonably predict that a pursuit might occur. There are some sound tactics that you can use to make a pursuit less likely.

1) *Pick the location for your stop.* Wait to try to pull over the suspect vehicle until you have the maximum advantage.

2) *Wait for as much backup as possible.* One of the biggest mistakes that officers commit in attempting to make high-risk stops is to attempt to stop them prematurely.

3) *Get close to the suspect vehicle.* If you ever want to *create* a pursuit, just let the suspect think he has every opportunity to escape. Chances are he will take advantage of your offer. I've seen officers "spook" a suspect by lighting up Code-3, lights and siren, while still more than two blocks behind the suspect. That's an invitation for a pursuit. On the other hand, you have a good chance of avoiding a pursuit if you give the suspect every reason to think that you can fully identify him and his vehicle and that you have covered every possible escape route.

4) *Don't be afraid to quit.* Patrol officers are supposed to exemplify courage. Sometimes the bravest thing you can do is to know when to back out of a pursuit.

Once you're in the pursuit, the suspect vehicle is going to dictate when, where, and how fast you're driving. Make sure your safety belt is still fastened and any loose gear is secured (I've seen officers throwing flashlights and cite books into the back seat: you don't need gear rolling under the brake pedal in a pursuit).

Use the most comfortable and familiar driving technique. Most experts now recommend keeping both hands relatively low on the steering wheel and "shuffling" the wheel back and forth, never crossing the hands. Don't let the suspect sucker you into driving beyond your experience and ability. If you are driving a one officer unit and are the only unit in the pursuit, you will have to handle the radio. Wait for straight sections of road and call off your position every time the suspect turns, or in a rural setting every mile or so. Ideally a helicopter or one of the secondary units can handle all the radio traffic for you.

You need to keep the suspect in sight, but don't stay too close to him. You want to keep enough room between his car and yours that you won't become a permanent part of his trunk when he broadsides a semi-truck at an intersection. Give yourself the maximum space possible to escape any possible hazard by sticking to the center of the road. When approaching a turn or a corner, use maximum braking just before the turn and then accelerate as you come out of the turn. (ABS brakes will allow you to actually brake safely through the turn.) Don't cut corners, stay off of shoulders, curbings and sidewalks, and avoid sudden, jerky movements. The best speeds in pursuit driving are usually attained by officers with the smoothest driving style.

These techniques will eat up a lot of distance between you and the violator. Remember, this is not a race in which you want to win first place. You win in second place, by simply keeping the suspect within your sight. Let him make the mistakes; you just want to be in a position to observe and take him into custody when he screws up and crashes or bails out of the car.

TERMINATING PURSUITS

Once you're in the pursuit to stay, you better start thinking in terms of how you are going to end the pursuit. Are you going to wait until the driver crashes or decides to stop, or are you going to force him to stop? Terminating a pursuit by forcing the other vehicle to stop has been held to be a seizure under case law. Since the Constitution guarantees citizens the right to be protected from unreasonable search and seizure, even the termination of a pursuit becomes a complex legal matter with the potential of being sued by the violator if a court were to find your termination of the pursuit to be a violation of the rights of the suspect.

The decision to attempt to forcibly stop a pursuit has to be based on very careful consideration of all the facts apparent to the pursuing officer and usually requires a supervisor's permission. Often the deliberate termination of a pursuit has resulted in damage to patrol cars and injury or death to the pursuing officers. It is often best to simply follow the suspect vehicle until he stops. Eventually he will crash, surrender, or simply run out of gas.

Generally, terminating a pursuit should only be considered when the officer feels that any continued movement of the suspect vehicle will place others in immediate danger or when the apparent risk of harm to the public is so great as to outweigh the risk of harm in making the forced stop. Some of the techniques available for terminating a pursuit include: boxing, channelizing, ramming, roadblocks, and gunfire. These often require supervisor approval.

Boxing

Boxing is done by literally surrounding the suspect vehicle with police cars and then slowing as a group to a stop. This technique is generally only successful at very slow speeds and is sometimes used with grossly intoxicated drivers. Some cities in New Jersey have reported great success with boxing in juvenile car theft suspects using unmarked (and already beat-up) patrol cars. This technique offers the suspect the opportunity to damage all four patrol cars creating the "box," so it is generally not a favorite of budget-conscious police administrators.

Channelizing

Channelizing consists of deliberately directing a vehicle into a given path or location such as an unpaved roadway, dead-end or parking lot, and by using stationary objects (such as barricades, patrol cars and semi-trucks) in the path of the pursued vehicle. It is important to make the suspect clearly see the "escape route" leading to the take-down area. It is this aspect that is very different from a roadblock which offers him no escape.

Ramming

Ramming is simply running into the other vehicle in a manner designed to force him to stop. There is a real art to the technique of ramming that results in disabling the suspect vehicle without destroying the police vehicle. The risks are tremendous, and, as a result, ramming usually requires the approval of a supervisor and careful orchestration with other units so that they can continue the pursuit should your unit be disabled.

Ramming is best done at low speeds because at high speeds the patrol car is too unstable. Not every vehicle is a candidate for ramming. Unless the weight of the patrol car is greater or close to that of the suspect, chances are you're just going to chew up your patrol car by ramming. Thus the patrol cars chosen for ramming are usually large sedans rather than smaller pursuit cars such as the Ford Mustang, and large suspect vehicles such as motorhomes and trucks are stopped by other means.

Successful ramming usually takes place at relatively low speeds under braking or turning maneuvers. Braking and turning causes weight transfer and makes it much easier to affect the course of the suspect vehicle. A typical ramming may take place as a suspect attempts to exit a freeway. At the base of the offramp, the suspect slows and turns, causing a weight shift to the front and side of the vehicle away from the pursuing officer. At that point, just a little nudge on the corner nearest the patrol car will generally break the traction of the suspect vehicle and cause it to lose control. This is called a **spin-out technique**.

Obviously, this has to be carefully planned and choreographed. You don't want to send the suspect spinning into a group of pedestrians or other cars, and you want to leave room for yourself to brake and avoid entanglement in the collision.

Roadblocks

Roadblocks are used primarily in rural areas with very limited routes in or out of an area. The logistics simply make it an impossible technique in large cities, and the manpower and equipment requirements make it difficult to use along major highways. Imagine how many officers and cars it would take to effectively block a modern interstate highway.

Roadblocks have been effectively used in such areas as the Grand Canyon and Yosemite National Park where there are only a few narrow roads in and out of an isolated area. You might effectively block a rural two lane road with a few vehicles and officers, but unless heavily manned and well-armed the roadblock leaves the suspect with all the advantages. He knows what he is facing - you have to screen each car and individual. Against a determined aggressor, you may apprehend him but sometimes at a terrible cost.

Physically blocking the roadway also creates great potential for death and injury. Think of the mayhem that would be caused by a fleeing suspect hitting the parked patrol vehicles at a hundred-plus miles per hour. In one case, a deputy sheriff I knew in a desert community was killed at a roadblock. A fleeing motorcycle was approaching the roadblock at high speed. The deputy took shelter behind some rocks more than a hundred feet away, but was still killed (as was the cyclist) by flying debris from the motorcycle at impact. Obviously, it is a technique with limited use and great risk.

Spikes

A far lower risk alternative to the roadblock is the spike strip which is currently deployed by a number of highway patrol agencies. The strip consists of either a lattice or roll of material that can be rapidly deployed across an entire roadway. The material has hundreds of small hollow spikes, designed to perforate the tires of the pursued vehicle.

Spiked strips have proven tremendously effective. They can be carried in the trunk of a patrol car and deployed ahead of a pursuit in less than a minute by a single officer. As the suspect vehicle passes over the strip, the spikes penetrate the tires and rapidly release the air, often flattening all four tires of the suspect's vehicle and bringing it to a halt within a few hundred feet. An officer in position at the strip is supposed to yank it off the roadway as soon as the suspect passes over the device.

Unfortunately, in their zeal to pursue the suspect, excited officers often follow across the strip, flattening all the tires on their patrol cars. Still the technique is far more cost effective than even a single patrol car collision.

A spike strip in use. (Courtesy of Stinger Spike Systems, Inc.)

Gunfire

Some state laws and department policies allow for shooting at a suspect's vehicle under the gravest of circumstances. Not only do you have to comply with every facet of law and department policy, but you will have to demonstrate that using deadly force was the only reasonable method of stopping the suspect, and that allowing the suspect to escape represented a far greater danger to society than your gunfire and the possible results.

Think of the danger to the public represented by a several thousand pound vehicle, suddenly completely out of control because you shot the driver. From a technical standpoint, shooting at a moving vehicle while driving a patrol car is nearly impossible. As a passenger officer it is extremely difficult; many officers who have attempted such an act have only managed to perforate their own windshields or hoods. Your best chance for shooting and incapacitating another vehicle is from a stationary position.

In an isolated area, with an excellent shooting background and no possibility of the vehicle harming others, it would be far easier to justify shooting at a vehicle. Similarly, if a vehicle was headed straight toward you with the obvious intent of striking you and no means of escape, you might effectively fire at a moving vehicle and be capable of justifying your actions. Generally speaking, however, this should be the technique of last resort for stopping any vehicle.

TRANSPORTATION OF PRISONERS

In some cities, patrol officers have the luxury of a prisoner transportation unit or wagon that picks up all prisoners in the field. Chances are, however, that you will have to drive your own prisoners to the jail and other locations.

Transporting prisoners is an inherently dangerous activity. Most of your prisoners have no desire to go to jail. Some will be actively looking for any opportunity to escape, others will be violently resisting at every step of the process. Some may have accomplices, friends or family members looking for opportunities to rescue them from your custody. Countless officers have screwed up and been killed while on a "simple" prisoner transportation detail. As a result, there are a number of important rules to follow whenever you transport any prisoner.

RULE #1: Always search the back seat of your patrol car (the front seat if you transport prisoners there) thoroughly, both before and after every prisoner transportation. I have found guns, ammunition, knives, keys to stolen cars, hypodermic needles, stolen jewelry, heroin balloons, handcuff keys, razor blades and bindles of cocaine lying on the floorboards underneath prisoner's seats. Only by checking before and after each prisoner can you say in court that the contraband could only have been left by that one prisoner.

RULE #2: Never, ever transport any prisoner you have not personally searched for weapons. I don't care if you are picking up a prisoner from a jail, accepting a prisoner from your FTO, or taking a traffic warrant suspect to jail. You must search each and every prisoner before you place him in your car. It's *your* life at stake.

Male officers are often reluctant to search female suspects, and females are reluctant to search male suspects. Taking advantage of this, female gang members frequently conceal weapons in their bras, and males often place small guns and drugs in their groins. Each can be searched adequately by officers of any sex when properly done. Always do your search in public, with another officer as a witness, using the back or edge of your hand to run over the suspect areas. This avoids any charges of groping or sexual assault.

RULE #3: Never transport any prisoner who is not handcuffed (and double-locked) with his hands behind his back. Check the cuffs yourself to make sure they are tight enough, properly applied, and double locked. Even so, you will find prisoners who will escape from handcuffs. Some suspects are expert at picking the locks and ratchets of handcuffs and will conceal a lockpick or handcuff key on their person, usually near their waist at the rear. Some people have exceptionally small or limber hands and can easily pull through a standard handcuff at its smallest ratchet setting (plastic flexible handcuffs can be applied to those who appear to have this ability). Similarly, many people are limber enough to pull their feet up and slip the handcuffs under their feet and to their front. In this position they can escape, and even drive a vehicle. Seat belting will reduce their ability to "slip" the handcuffs.

If you have a cage or other barrier between the front and rear seat, the prisoner should be in the back seat on the passenger side, securely seat-belted. If you have two prisoners, they both should be in the back seat, again, handcuffed behind their backs and secured with safety belts.

If you are operating as a single officer unit without a cage, you should transport a single prisoner beside you on the front seat. The prisoner must be handcuffed behind his back, and securely seatbelted. This position is extremely dangerous, as even a secured prisoner can interfere with your control of the patrol car. I've seen prisoners who kicked out windshields and destroyed radios and dashboards.

If you have two officers and two suspects without a cage, generally the partner officer sits directly behind the driver officer. This prevents the driver from being kicked or otherwise interfered with by the rear seat passenger and also allows a clear shooting angle at the front seat passenger should it become necessary.

RULE #4: Always take the keys. Not too long ago, a deputy sheriff in a nearby city watched in frustration as a suspect he had placed in the rear seat of his patrol car drove it away.

Leaving the key in the patrol car while it is occupied by a prisoner is unacceptable under any conditions. Once you take a prisoner into custody, you are responsible for his safety. He shouldn't be in a place where you need to leave the lightbar running. When the prisoner goes into your car, do yourself a favor: if you're not leaving the scene immediately with the prisoner, park the car in a safe location, and take the key out.

An alternative used by our agency, and widely available, is a simple switch in the ignition circuit. Marketed under "Secure-A-Car" and several other names, a flip of the switch leaves the engine running (along with the air conditioner and other accessories), but allows you to remove the ignition key, leaving the steering column and gear shift locked. If the brakes are applied, the horn sounds and the engine dies. It's a simple system, easily installed, highly effective, and much cheaper than a new patrol car.

RULE #5: Always roll up the windows and lock the doors. Most modern patrol cars are ordered from the factory with the rear door and window handles removed or inoperative and the rear interior locks removed or concealed. Electric windows and locks can still be controlled by the driver's switches, but in cars with cages this effectively locks the prisoner into the rear, both preventing his escape and his rescue from outside.

Take the time to lock your car every time on every call. It will keep valuable property such as your flashlight and ticket book from being stolen, keep your patrol car from being vandalized, and keep your prisoner where you put him.

RULE #6: Never engage a combative or unrestrained prisoner alone. Despite your best efforts, someday you will face a prisoner on the loose in your patrol car. It's not a time to be macho or proud. Engaging the suspect one-on-one would be foolish, giving him all the advantages and possibly resulting in your death. Instead, pull over, stop the car, and radio for assistance. Once you get additional officers, you can worry about regaining control over your prisoner.

RULE #7: Never leave a hobbled prisoner alone. Occasionally you will have to hobble a combative prisoner, tying his legs together and connecting them to his handcuffs. This is a very dangerous position, particularly for a heavy suspect, and it has resulted in a number of deaths due to suffocation and heart failure.

If you must place a hobbled suspect in your patrol car, you need to place him on his side (never face-down) and monitor his breathing and pulse continuously until he is released from that position. Similar precautions should be taken with any suspect complaining of or suspected of having a medical condition or injury.

DISCUSSION QUESTIONS

1) What do you think motivates citizens to complain about a patrol officer's driving?

2) Why does the law exempt police officers from liability in some emergency driving situations? Do you think this should change?

3) Based on your observations, which are the safest drivers— ambulance drivers, fire fighters, or police officers? Why?

4) You conduct a traffic stop on a vehicle with an expired registration. The driver is an elderly female, who refuses to roll down the window, unlock the door, or even acknowledge your presence. What would you do?

5) Should police agencies restrict, or even eliminate, pursuits? Why or why not?

6) You conduct a felony stop on a stolen car with disabled license plates. When you order the driver out of the car, he shouts out that he cannot comply because he has no legs. What would you do?

7) Once you arrest the legless suspect above, he demands that you bring along his electric wheelchair which is also in the car. What would you do?

8) In your opinion, what is the most dangerous means of terminating a pursuit?

A woman assaulted a Glenville, NY, police officer with a cheesecake after receiving several traffic tickets from the officer.

* * *

Police in Kewanee, IL, charged Michael Runyon with drunken driving this summer after he accidentally drove a lawn mower into the path of a freight train. Runyon, who escaped injury when the train flipped the 5 horsepower mower 10 feet into the air, had used the vehicle for transportation after his license to drive a car was suspended.

* * *

A drunken driver allegedly was at the wheel of a stolen pickup that slammed into a police trailer at a sobriety checkpoint in Garden Grove. The driver was held in connection with the 2 a.m. Sunday incident and for investigation of a Saturday armed robbery during which the truck was stolen, a police spokesman said. Two officers who had just closed the checkpoint were uninjured.

TRAFFIC

LEARNING GOALS: After studying this chapter the student will be able to:

- Explain the purpose of traffic enforcement.

- Describe how speed laws are enforced.

- Explain how traffic laws are enforced.

- Define a citation, and explain how one is given.

- Discuss why patrol officers impound vehicles.

- List the elements of a drunk driving arrest.

- Name and describe the symptoms of alcohol impairment.

- Explain how field coordination tests are performed.

- Evaluate the purpose of traffic accident investigation.

TRAFFIC LAWS

Imagine what the United States would be like today without any traffic signs, controls, or laws. Millions of vehicles scrambling at every intersection, using any available road surface in any available direction to get where they wanted to go. The result would be total chaos, destruction of property, death, and injury; our entire economy would grind to a halt.

Obviously, there is a valid purpose for traffic laws. Obedience to those laws serves a vital national interest. The vast majority of persons who drive to work depend on traffic laws to expedite their safe journey. Those who use public transportation and those who walk to work equally depend on the protection of traffic laws to move from one place to another. Virtually everything we consume and use daily is shipped to its final destination in a vehicle.

Traffic laws exist to allow movement on our vast transportation network in the most efficient, cost-effective, and as safe a manner as possible. Given the size and complexity of our transportation system and the incredible array of technologies used in our vehicles, it is inevitable that thousands of laws have been created to protect our lives and our economic interests. It's often been said (and bragged about by motor officers) that a well-trained police officer can stop any car, any time, any place, and find at least three violations of law. It's probably true considering the incredible number of traffic laws.

For example, the *California Vehicle Code* is composed of 42,277 sections covering 1,032 pages. It's followed by 383 pages listing various other state laws dealing with motor vehicles including: the Business and Professions Code, the Civil Code, the Code of Civil Procedure, the Commercial Code, the Constitution of the State of California, the Education Code, the Fish and Game Code, the Food and Agriculture Code, the Government Code, the Harbors and Navigation Code, the Health and Safety Code, the Insurance Code, the Labor Code, the Military and Veterans Code, the Penal Code, the Public Resources Code, the Public Utilities Code, the Revenue and Taxation Code, the Streets and Highways Code, and the Welfare and Institutions Code. And if that weren't enough, our city code lists over a hundred additional local vehicle laws.

Every imaginable act is covered in infinite detail by law. Some, such as speed laws, drunk driving, manslaughter and stop signs are pretty obvious. Others are not so obvious such as the operation of motorized skateboards on equestrian trails (forbidden), the speed of vehicles using metal tires (6 MPH), or cheating on your driver's test by the use of crib sheets (up to one year in jail). Every part of every vehicle is defined, described, and regulated. The vehicle code specifies the color of radial tire inner tube valve stems (red), the exemptions from littering (clear water and chicken feathers), the design of radiator ornaments, and the establishment of golf-cart crossing zones.

TRAFFIC ENFORCEMENT

The vast majority of laws in the vehicle code are administrative or procedural in nature. Only a small percentage are enforcement sections which can be violated and incur a penalty. In most states' vehicle codes, there are only about a thousand or so enforcement sections ranging from felonies, such as manslaughter, punishable by long terms in prison, to simple infractions punishable only by fine. Violations are generally grouped in some logical fashion into three broad categories: document violations, equipment violations, and moving violations.

Document violations are those where the driver you stopped doesn't have all his paperwork in order. Typical violations are for unregistered vehicles, expired registration, expired driver's licenses and no proof of financial liability (insurance). In some cases, such as when the registration is expired more than one year, you may be able to impound the vehicle. Most of the time you will issue a citation to the person which can be cleared by paying a fee or fines and producing the appropriate paperwork in court.

Equipment violations are things that are wrong with the vehicle itself. Bald tires, burnt out lights, broken windshields and leaky mufflers are all good examples, but the laws are very exacting. For example, tow trucks may be required to carry a broom and a bucket of sand, and trucks hauling hazardous materials must be clearly marked with placards in a specific manner. Each of these are equipment violations. If the vehicle is so unsafe as to represent a hazard to others, you may impound the vehicle on the spot or order the driver to take it directly to a repair facility. Fortunately, for the vast majority of equipment violations, you will simply issue a citation and require the person to correct the problem and prove they have fixed the car before they go to court.

Moving violations include the violations of the rules of the road committed by the driver. Besides driving under the influence of alcohol or drugs, there are eight major driving offenses that are the principal accident-causing moving violations. These violations include:

1) excessive speed,

2) failure to yield right of way,

3) following another vehicle too closely,

4) improper turning movements,

5) driving on center lines,

6) failure to heed stop signs,

7) improper passing, and

8) disregarding signals.

Citations

The principal tool for traffic enforcement is the *citation*, also called a *ticket* or a *notice to appear*. Most police officers are generous in giving warnings to people for low grade violations of law, but are increasingly inclined to issue a citation as the danger to the public increases. Rolling a stop sign in the wee hours of the morning will usually get the offending driver a warning, the danger to other persons is minimal. Running a red light at high speed during rush hour is close to suicidal and will surely generate a citation from any patrol officer.

Citations vary substantially from state to state but are generally uniform within each state. Most citation forms are multipart forms made with carbons or NCR paper. The top copy goes to the courts, the second to the violator, the third to the department and sometimes a fourth copy to the officer. Care should be taken to write on a hard surface such as the plate in a citation book and to write on just the one citation to avoid defacing the citations underneath.

The top line of the citation usually has the time and date and is followed by blocks to fill in descriptive and identifying information about the driver and the vehicle. The center portion of the citation usually has lines to list the violation sections and a description of the violation followed by checkblocks to note the traffic, roadway, lighting and weather conditions, along with posted speed limits and the suspect vehicle's speed. The bottom portion of the citation has a place for the officer's signature, information about when and where the violator is to appear, and a place for his signature.

Technically, the violator is under arrest at the time that you stop him. You release him from custody on his "promise to appear,"— his signature agreeing to show up in court. Right above the signature line our citations read, *Without admitting guilt I promise to appear at the time and place checked below.*

Contacting the driver is one of the most dangerous points of a vehicle stop.

If a person has no proper identification, if you have some other reason to believe they might not go to court, or if the person refuses to sign the citation, you can place him under arrest and take him immediately before the next available magistrate. If court's in session and nearby, it may not be terribly inconvenient, but if it's a late Friday night in a rural area the driver might well spend the night in jail if he cannot post cash bail.

Many people think that officers have some type of *quota* — a specified number of tickets that they have to write. Let me tell you that they are absolutely correct. Administrators will deny the existence of any quotas, and, indeed, you will find no department policies or rules that specify a set number of tickets that have to be written by their officers. But realistically, supervisors and administrators use numbers to evaluate their officers.

If you are a patrol officer, you will find your sergeant telling you that he expects you to work for a living. That includes writing tickets, and unless you are overwhelmed with reports or partnered with a seeing-eye dog, you should be able to write one to two tickets each day. Sound reasonable? Certainly, but by specifying his expectations of your performance, he has set a quota of 20 to 30 citations each month.

If you are a traffic officer, all you do is stop motorists for violations and write accident reports. What is a reasonable number of citations for a traffic officer to write in an eight-hour shift? Personally, I'd feel cheated if a traffic officer couldn't manage one ticket per hour, and his performance evaluations would reflect such. So here's another quota, this one is eight citations per day or 160 per month.

Quotas are also set by peer performance. If all the other officers on your shift are writing 20 citations each month, you can bet that there's some bean-counter in administration figuring out the average per officer and ranking you against that average. If you write less than that, your sergeant will probably start scrutinizing your logs and other activity to find out where you spend all your time. If you write more than that, the other officers may resent you for "raising the average." Quotas are unhealthy, counterproductive and illegal — but very real. Be aware of your department's expectations and your peers' performance levels.

Speed Violations

Rural agencies and highway patrols spend much of their enforcement time devoted to speed violations. Speed violations are of three basic types: *maximum speeds*, *prima facie speed limits*, and *basic speed limits*.

Maximum speeds are the highest speed a driver can go at any time in the state. Most states have established a maximum speed limit of 55 miles per hour (with some interstates at 65 mph). It is important to use such laws properly. If you have someone driving at 70 mph in a 25 mile per hour zone, you should write them for violating the 25 mile per hour limit (with their fine based on exceeding the limit by 45 miles per hour) rather than citing them for exceeding the maximum speed limit (and basing their fine on exceeding the speed limit by 5 miles per hour).

Prima facie speed limits are speeds specified by posted speeds or laws that are always applicable unless posted otherwise such as a 15 mile per hour limit for alleys or a 25 mile per hour limit for residential roadways.

The *basic speed laws* are really the logical heart of speed enforcement. The typical wording of a basic speed law reads:

> No person shall drive a vehicle upon a highway at a speed greater than is reasonable or prudent having due regard for weather, visibility, the traffic on, and the surface and width of the highway, and in no event at a speed which endangers the safety of persons and property.

In other words, you can't drive at an unsafe speed. On a wide open, totally empty, six-lane boulevard in the middle of the night, 55 miles per hour may be perfectly safe and legal under the basic speed law, despite a posted 35 mile per hour speed limit. Conversely, on the very same roadway under heavy fog conditions, a speed of 5 miles per hour may be unsafe. Your purpose in enforcing traffic laws is to make the world a safer place. Always keep that foremost in your mind when you are doing speed enforcement, and you will find yourself treating people fairly.

Radar

Before the development of radar, all speed enforcement was conducted by pacing — matching the speed of the patrol car to a violator and checking the speedometer. For many officers this will still be the primary method of speed enforcement, but generally traffic officers use radar or other devices as a scientific means of validating their observations of speed. *Radar units* are electronic devices used to measure the speed of moving vehicles. There are a variety of styles and types, moving radar and stationary radar, hand-held and vehicle mounted. All work on the same basic principle.

Radar in operation. Note the gun is shooting backwards and the officer is reading the display with the car mirror.

Radar transmits a signal on one of several frequencies. That signal strikes a moving target vehicle and returns to the antenna. The signal returns at a different frequency because of the relative motion between the radar unit and the target vehicle.

With moving radar units, a second signal reads the speed of the patrol vehicle and subtracts it from the closing speed between your patrol car and the violator. This returning signal is compared to the original signal and the difference between them (known as a "Doppler shift") provides the basis for determining the speed of the violator. A computer translates the Doppler shift into miles per hour and displays that speed on a screen. An audio signal is also produced representing the Doppler shift, to give the operator a second indication of how fast the violator is traveling. The clarity and strength of that audio tone is an indication to the officer of the strength of the radar signal and the identity of the target. The higher the pitch of the signal, the higher the speed of the target.

The new laser devices work on a similar operational principle but use light instead of radio waves. Vascar is a timing device used to compute speed and distance. With Vascar, distances are measured between landmarks with the patrol car and then compared with the speed of other vehicles traveling that same distance to derive their speed.

VEHICLE IMPOUNDS AND SEARCHES

As a patrol officer, you will often find yourself taking cars and other vehicles away from people. When you make arrests, and under certain other conditions, you will take custody of every kind of transportation you can imagine. It's your responsibility to keep your beat free of stolen and abandoned cars and to expedite the smooth and efficient flow of traffic. As a result, patrol officers have very broad authority for removing vehicles. Under typical laws, patrol officers and/or other employees of law enforcement agencies can impound, store, move, or remove a vehicle under many circumstances. Examples are:

- When the vehicle has been abandoned on any public or private property.

- When the vehicle is found obstructing traffic on a bridge, viaduct or tunnel.

- When the vehicle is found obstructing traffic on any highway.

- When the vehicle has been reported as stolen or embezzled.

- When the vehicle is illegally parked and/or blocking a driveway.

- When the vehicle is illegally parked and/or blocking a fire hydrant.

- When the vehicle is parked within 7-1/2 feet of a railroad track.

Now that you're familiar with possible instances regarding when to tow a car, the question is how? In most areas, you contact dispatch for either the next available tow truck (if your agency rotates through a list of local tow companies) or for the official police tow service. I always like to call the tow company before starting the paperwork because I would much rather have the tow driver waiting for me to finish the paperwork than have me wait for the tow driver.

Vehicles that are reported as stolen, stored, or impounded are generally reported to your state's Department of Justice and the F.B.I. via your dispatcher's entry of the vehicle into the computer. You will fill out an appropriate form, which gives you authority to take the car and a complete description and inventory of the car. For most agencies, this is just a matter of checking "yes" or "no" on a series of check-blocks and drawing in any dents and scratches on a diagram of the car's exterior. It's important to note such body damage since the car is in your custody, and you don't want to be held responsible for damaging the vehicle. You also need to conduct a complete inventory of the vehicle's interior, glovebox, and trunk, all in accordance with your department's policies.

All searches must be thorough.

The court has held that it is perfectly legal for a patrol officer to search a vehicle in order to inventory the contents prior to towing as long as that is the policy of the agency. As a result, any contraband you find can be used in court against the driver/owner of the vehicle.

DRIVING WHILE INTOXICATED

Drunk driving is a term that will be used throughout this text for any driver whose blood alcohol level (BAC) exceeds the allowable percentage for his state (usually from .05% to .10%). You should recognize that a person whose BAC is above the legal limit isn't necessarily "drunk" in the falling down, slurred speech, public drunkenness sense of the word, and may in fact be quite functional in most respects. In order to differentiate driving with a BAC above the legal limit from being drunk, most states use politically correct terms like DUI (Driving Under the Influence) or DWI (Driving While Intoxicated). For purposes of this text, I will use the term "drunk driving." Feel free to replace it with "DWI driver" if you're offended by the term.

Every drunk driving arrest is composed of four key elements. These elements are:

1) driving behavior (or an accident),

2) objective symptoms of intoxication,

3) field coordination tests (FCT's, also called *field sobriety tests* or FST's in some areas), and

4) chemical tests.

Never base a drunk driving test on any one of these elements alone. Rather make your decision to arrest on the totality of your observations of all four elements.

Alcohol's Effect

Alcohol is a central nervous system depressant. Differing amounts affect different people in different ways depending on their particular physical makeup. After one or two drinks, reason, caution, intelligence and memory begin to be affected. Inhibitions are released, people become sociable and talkative, may appear more self-confident, but suffer loss of attention and judgment. With three or four drinks, there is a noticeable loss in self-control and judgment. Reaction times are greatly slowed, memory is impaired and muscular coordination suffers.

With five or six drinks, the senses begin to be impaired, the vision and hearing so critical to driving tasks become less acute, along with losses in taste, smell, and touch. Drivers become mentally confused, dizzy, and less sensitive to pain. With seven or eight drinks, coordination begins to suffer substantially, drivers show poor balance, a staggering gait, and slurred speech; and with nine drinks the sense of balance is completely lost. This is the point at which drunks fall down, but, unfortunately, you don't have to be able to stand to drive a car.

Beyond that, at 10 or more drinks, the vital centers of the body begin to shut down. The person may be stuporous, unable to stand, vomit, or fall asleep. If you exceed this level, coma and death may follow.

Drunk Driving Behaviors

Detecting drunk driving used to be a "seat of the pants" intuitive process of police officers. After years of stopping various vehicles for various violations or other driving behaviors, police officers learned which driving behaviors most likely result from drunk driving.

In many communities, there are definable patterns to the drunk driving arrests and accidents. In my city, there is a very popular British-styled pub just north of our city on a major street. Every night at closing time the patrons of the bar leave for home, and there is a sudden increase in the number of drunks on the road. We don't profile the drivers based on the bar they attend, and we don't stake out the driveway of the pub, but we are certainly aware that right around two in the morning that particular street is a good place to hunt for drunk drivers.

There are some 20 cues which have been developed by the *National Highway Traffic Safety Administration* for police officers to use in detecting nighttime drunk drivers. These cues were developed from a combination of interviews with a variety of experts in drunk driving, from a detailed analysis of more than one thousand drunk driving arrests, and from a field study in which more than six hundred patrol stops were correlated with the driver's BAC. These cues represent the most systematically developed method available for visually predicting whether a vehicle operated at night is being driven by a drunk driver or a sober driver. A few examples follow.

Probability values given after each visual cue are the percentage of probability that a driver exhibiting that cue has a BAC of .10% or greater.

65% — Turning with Wide Radius: This is simply a turn wider than normal traffic, often crossing the center of the roadway on one or more of the intersecting streets.

65% — Straddling Center or Lane Marker: Here the vehicle is moving straight ahead with the center line or the lane marker centered between the wheels.

60% — Weaving: Zig-zagging down the roadway, alternately moving from one side to the other. This can be a mild movement within a lane, or a very violent movement with squealing tires.

55% — Driving on Other than Designated Roadway: Here the vehicle is seen driving on the shoulder, through turn-only lanes, or one other non-traffic areas such as fields or railroad tracks.

55% — Swerving: A swerve is an abrupt turning movement. Drunk drivers most often swerve after a period of drifting, when the driver suddenly realizes an impending collision and makes a sudden correction.

Objective Symptoms of Intoxication

Once you stop a suspected drunk driver, you will generally contact that person behind the wheel. You will approach as usual, but all of your senses are critical in checking for the symptoms of intoxication. What you are looking for are deviations from what you have come to expect as normal. One or two of these signs may mean nothing, but when numerous symptoms of intoxication are present the probability is far greater that the person is drunk.

Initially, as you scan the car, you should be looking for open containers of alcohol. Look for open bottles or cans on the floorboard or the seat beside the driver, and be alert to suspicious wet spots on the floor. Many drunk drivers will scramble to stuff an open bottle under the seat, spilling all the contents in the process.

Your nose should be in overdrive, checking for the odor of any alcoholic beverages within the car. You will note that I say "beverages." That is because any defense attorney will tell you that alcohol is odorless. As a result, many officers feel compelled to write their reports saying, "I detected the odor of an alcoholic beverage on or about his breath or person." That sounds silly to me. As an adult, you know what beer smells like, and you know what "alcohol" smells like on a person's breath. If you smell beer on a suspect's breath, your report should read, "I smelled beer on the suspect's breath."

Be alert for other odors as well. The smell of vomit or urine can be quite distinctive and should be noted in your report. The smell of burned marijuana might lead your investigation in other directions, and the smell of mint, ether, or ammonia might lead you to suspect PCP or methamphetamine intoxication.

When you talk to the driver, you should listen carefully to how he speaks and his speech patterns. An intoxicated person may respond slowly or inappropriately, and his answers may be thick, slow and slurred, or very rapid. Fast or slow, it is important to note that it represents an alteration from the norm.

As you listen to the driver, you may see altered emotions. Drunk drivers may react inappropriately by laughing, crying, or expressing rage or depression. There is a normal range of emotion that you can expect on a traffic stop. These include being concerned, frightened, angry or even lightheartedness about the violation. What you need to be looking for are abnormal extremes.

You should be asking yourself if the driver *appears* drunk. I've found drunks immaculately groomed and attired, but I have also found them with disheveled hair and rumpled clothing. I've stopped drunk drivers covered in vomit or stained with their own urine or feces. I've stopped drunk drivers who were dressed up in costumes and drunk drivers who were totally nude. All represent something different than the norm.

As you talk to the driver, you should be looking at his eyes and complexion. A drunk driver's eyes may be bloodshot, watery, glazed, or exhibit a specific type of twitching called *nystagmus* (we'll talk more about nystagmus below). His complexion may be very pale, ruddy, florid, or sweaty.

As he looks for his driver's license and registration, you will have an opportunity to observe his coordination and motor skills. A drunk driver typically fumbles through his wallet and glovebox, often passing by his license a number of times, dropping other items, and removing his license only with great difficulty.

At this point you should have a fair idea of whether or not a person appears to be under the influence and will decide whether to move on to the field sobriety tests. You will ask the driver to step out of the car and to walk to the sidewalk or other level place to conduct those tests. When he does so, you will have another opportunity to observe his coordination impairment. He may stagger to one side or another, fall against you or the door, be unable to get out of his safety belt, hold onto the car for balance as he walks, or exhibit "moon-walking" (an ataxic gait in which the feet are lifted too high as a result of the person's altered depth perception) or some other altered way of walking.

Nystagmus

Nystagmus is the involuntary jerking of the eyes which occurs as the eyes move toward the sides. It is a natural, normal phenomenon that happens to everyone all the time. Your eyes naturally and involuntarily jerk as a way of keeping the sensory cells from fatigue. These tremors are generally too small to be seen with the naked eye. Alcohol or drugs don't cause nystagmus, but they exaggerate it to the point where it is easily seen, and, thus, it is a reliable, objective symptom of intoxication.

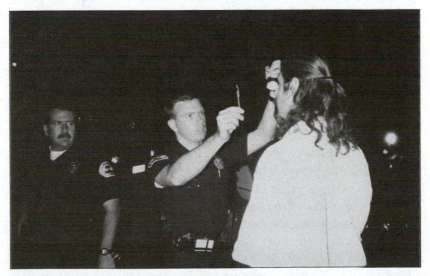

Nystagmus test being administered.

There are a number of different types of nystagmus. As police officers, we are concerned with the three types of "gaze" nystagmus— the jerking that occurs as the eyes move away from center. Those three types are: horizontal nystagmus, vertical gaze nystagmus, and resting nystagmus.

Horizontal nystagmus occurs as the eyes move from side to side and represents the most valid test for determining blood alcohol levels. Horizontal nystagmus is also present under the influence of PCP, certain inhalants, and depressants.

Vertical nystagmus occurs as the eyes move up and down. This type of nystagmus is generally associated with PCP but can also indicate very high levels of alcohol, inhalants or depressants.

Resting nystagmus is a jerking or twitching of the eyes as the person stares straight ahead. This condition is rarely seen and usually indicates high doses of PCP.

Nystagmus can be caused by certain rare medical conditions and diseases such as brain tumors and inner ear diseases. Unless the driver tells you about these conditions during your initial questioning, you probably don't need to worry about the possibility of their existence. At that point it becomes an interesting potential argument between medical experts in court and really won't affect your decision making process in the field.

To examine for nystagmus at the roadside you will have the driver follow a pen, penlight, or even the tip of your finger with his eyes. You will be looking for three signs. First, the suspect cannot follow a slowly moving target object smoothly with his eyes. Second, a distinct and pronounced jerking motion will be evident when the eye is held at maximum deviation to the side. Third, the more intoxicated a person becomes, the less movement to the side is required before this jerking begins. When a person's blood alcohol level is .10% or greater, the jerking will begin before the eye has moved 45 degrees to the side.

Real experts on drug recognition and drunk driving will continue with additional tests, estimating pupil size, testing for convergence (the ability to cross your eyes), taking pulse and noting pupil reaction to light. Leave those tests to the experts. Once you have examined and noted all the objective symptoms of intoxication given above, you should ask the suspect to perform some field coordination tests (FCT's).

FIELD COORDINATION TESTS

Many departments use a variety of tests to determine the level of intoxication of a suspect. Some have been scientifically substantiated, and some have not. Some are accepted in local courts, and some are not. I've seen tests that involved the alphabet forward and backward (difficult if English is not your native language), palm-slapping and finger counting, tongue-twisting phrases and picking up various coins from the hood of the patrol car. Interesting tests of skill and coordination, but perhaps not the most valid indicators of sobriety. If you have a difficult time doing the test sober, chances are you'll be called to demonstrate it in court and end up looking silly.

The most reliable and useful tests are those who employ the concept of divided attention, requiring the suspected drunk driver to concentrate on two things at the same time. Driving is a very complex divided attention task. The average car has upwards to 50 different controls presented to the driver. In order to operate the vehicle safely, the driver must simultaneously control steering, acceleration and braking, react appropriately to ever-changing traffic and environmental conditions, and perform many other tasks. Alcohol, along with many other drugs, reduces a person's ability to divide attention among such tasks, causing the driver to ignore the less critical tasks and concentrate on a single task.

To drive safely, a person needs to constantly balance various tasks and possess critical capabilities such as: information processing, short-term memory, judgment, balance, reactions, clear vision, small muscle control and coordination.

The experts now recommend that you consistently use four *Standardized Field Coordination Tests* (or "FCT's") to evaluate the divided attention impairment of any drunk driving suspect. The tests should always be given exactly the same way, in exactly the same order, instructed the same way, evaluated the same way and recorded the same way. These will give you specific clues to determine to what extent the suspect is impaired. These four tests are the Romberg

Balance, the Walk and Turn, the One Leg Stand, and the Finger to Nose.

Ideally, these tests should be administered on a flat, level, well-lit surface. The reality is that sometimes you don't have any choice as to where the tests will be performed. If your traffic stop is on a lonely, snowy mountain road, you have to pick the best spot possible and take the conditions into consideration.

You need to ask the suspect some preliminary questions about his physical condition to ascertain that he is normally capable of performing these tests. I have administered the tests in a modified form to people with their legs in casts and people with no legs at all. Use common sense and take what they say into consideration.

These tests can be virtually impossible to perform in certain types of shoes such as cowboy boots or high-heels. If you notice unusual footwear, comment on it, and ask if they wish to remove the shoes and perform the tests in their socks or bare feet.

It's not easy to give these tests consistently, with the same instruction, in a specific order and manner. You have to practice. Practice demonstrating the tests yourself, and practice administering the tests to your partners, your friends, and your family. In addition to providing a certain amount of amusement, practice will make you smooth and professional both in the field and in court as you demonstrate and discuss these tests.

Suspect Interview

Before beginning the tests, there are a few simple questions you should ask the suspect. There is no need to give the suspect his *Miranda* advisement, since these questions are directly related to your interpretation of the field coordination tests and are not questions about the "crime" (of drunk driving). The questions you should ask are:

"Are you sick or injured?" (If yes, find out what is wrong.)

"Did you drink alcohol today?"

"What kind of alcohol, and how much?"

"Where were you drinking?"

"What time did you start?"

"What time did you stop?"

"Do you feel the effects of the drinks?" (If yes, "How?")

"Are you a diabetic or epileptic?"

"Do you have any disabilities or conditions that might affect your coordination?"

"Have you taken any medication or drugs?"(If yes,"What?","When?", "How much?", "Time of last dosage?", and "Do you feel the effects of the drugs?").

Many agencies have these or similar questions preprinted on an arrest form. If not, incorporate them into your report. After asking these questions, you are now ready to move on to the FCTs.

Romberg Balance Test

This test (sometimes spelled "Rhomberg") requires the suspect to stand with his feet together, his head tilted slightly back, and his eyes closed while he estimates the passage of 30 seconds. When the suspect believes that the 30 seconds have passed, he should tilt his head forward, open his eyes, and say, "Time's up."

The Romberg test being administered to a DUI suspect.

During the test you should look for eyelid tremors, muscle tension, and any statements or unusual sounds made by the suspect. Anything you observe that is abnormal should be noted on your report. It is critically important that you record test performance in a standardized manner. Most agencies will have you use a form with various blocks for each test performed. For the Romberg Test you need to record the number of inches of sway you observed both from front to back and from side to side. You should also record the actual number of seconds the suspect stood with his eyes closed.

Walk and Turn Test

This test requires the suspect to stand heel to toe with his arms at his sides while a series of instructions are given. Then, the suspect must take nine heal to toe steps along a straight line, turn in a specified manner, and take another nine heel to toe steps along the line. You can use a painted line on the roadway, a crack in the sidewalk, or an imaginary line if necessary. All of this must be done while he is counting the steps aloud and keeping his arms down at his sides. The suspect must not stop walking until the test is completed.

During the test, you should record every instance where the suspect stopped walking or stepped off the line. While he is listening to the instructions, note any instances in which the suspect cannot keep his balance, or starts too soon.

There are six specific clues you need to watch for and record during the test. These clues are:

1) Suspect stops walking.

2) Suspect misses heel to toe.

3) Suspect steps off line.

4) Suspect raises arms while walking.

5) Suspect takes the wrong number of steps.

6) Suspect turns improperly (usually staggering).

If the suspect is unable or unwilling to complete the test for any reason, be sure to note why. If the suspect appears so impaired that he might harm himself or you (by falling over or staggering into traffic) you should stop the test and note why.

One Leg Stand Test

This test requires the suspect to balance on one leg while extending the other leg stiffly in front of him with his foot about six inches above the ground. The suspect is to stare at his elevated foot and count out loud for 30 seconds in this fashion: "One thousand and one, one thousand and two, one thousand and three,...." The suspect will perform this test twice, first standing on his left leg, then standing on his right.

It's important that this test last for the full 30 seconds; most suspects begin losing their balance right around 25. You have to track the time, and stop them when 30 seconds have passed if their counting is slow, or tell them to continue counting if they count too fast.

After the suspect completes the test on his left leg, let him relax for about ten seconds and go through the same instructions for the right leg.

The primary clues to impairment for this test are:

1) swaying while balancing;

2) using the arms to balance;

3) hopping; and

4) putting the foot down.

Your report must indicate how many times you observe each of these clues for each leg. You should also note the type of footwear worn by the suspect (you're unlikely to remember in court, and the defense attorney may very well bring it up). During the test, pay attention to the suspect's general appearance and behavior. Note any body tremors, muscle tension, or unusual sounds or statements, and include them in the report.

Finger to Nose Test

In the finger to nose test, the suspect is required to touch the tip of his nose with the tip of his index finger. The test is performed with the suspect's eyes closed and his head tilted back, identical to the stance used for the Romberg Balance Test. The suspect attempts to touch his nose six times, three with each hand. You will instruct the suspect as to which hand to use, always using the sequence of "left, right, left, right, right, left."

A person who is impaired by alcohol or drugs will often use the wrong hand or miss the tip of his/her nose entirely, touching his/her lips, cheek, eye or forehead. Note on a diagram or in your notes exactly where he/she touches his/her fingertip with each command, and which finger was actually used. In addition, note body sway, tremors, eyelid tremors, muscular tension, and any unusual sounds or comments.

Arrest

At this point, you have to make a decision as to whether to arrest the suspect or release him. Your decision is not based on passing or failing any one test, or on the presence or absence of any one clue. Your decision should be based on the entire picture, the combination of all of your observations: the driving, the objective symptoms, the initial statements, and the field coordination tests.

Your decision cannot rely on any one factor alone but should give emphasis to the field coordination tests. Some experienced drinkers may seem sober but are actually impaired and, therefore, unsafe to be on the road. Since the FCT's examine physiological factors which are often beyond the driver's conscious control, impairment can still be accurately detected.

If you've made the decision that the driver is *not* legally under the influence, thank him for his cooperation and send him on his way. Don't get into a situation where you tell a *borderline* drunk driver, "You really shouldn't drive," and then leave him there with the vehicle. Either he's too drunk to drive and is going to jail or he's sober enough to drive and should be released.

When you arrest, do so safely and by the book. Tell the suspect exactly what you are doing, saying, "You are under arrest for driving under the influence." Ninety-nine percent of the time your arrest is as simple as telling the offender to turn around and put his hands behind his back. One percent of the time the fight is on and you and your partner will have to arrest the suspect using physical force.

However the arrest goes, you must ultimately handcuff the suspect. Double lock the cuffs and frisk the suspect thoroughly, then place him in your patrol car.

At this point you can make a thorough search of the suspect's vehicle without a warrant, since the search is contemporaneous with your arrest. You want to thoroughly search the interior of the car for any evidence related to the driver's identity and his use of alcohol or drugs. You need to search anything large enough to contain a small quantity of cocaine, and seize any item that would tend to support your drunk driving arrest. In most jurisdictions, you will then impound or store the vehicle at the police tow lot, using the appropriate forms and procedures.

Chemical Tests

Following your arrest, you will give the suspect an admonition or warning regarding chemical testing to determine the amount of alcohol in his blood. Most states have an *implied consent law*. That means that everyone who exercises the privilege of driving is understood to agree to a chemical testing of the alcohol or drug content of his blood if arrested for driving under the influence. About 90 percent of all arrested drivers do take a chemical test. When a driver refuses or fails to complete the test, the arresting officer's sworn statement is used by the licensing authorities of the state to revoke or suspend the person's driving privilege, and his refusal can be used in court as evidence of his awareness that he is too drunk to drive.

The purpose of the implied consent law is to obtain the best possible evidence of intoxication at the time a driver is arrested. A chemical test gives an objective evaluation and is a scientifically accurate way to decide if a driver is intoxicated. It also protects drivers who have alcohol on their breath and gives the appearance of intoxication, when they may, in fact, be below the legal limits for drunk driving.

In California, the Chemical Test Admonition is specified in law and should be read *verbatim* (exactly) to the driver. Until you've done it a few hundred times, don't trust your memory, just read it from the card. The law reads as follows:

You are required by state law to submit to a chemical test to determine the alcoholic content of your blood.

You have the choice of taking a blood, breath, or urine test.

If you refuse to submit to, or fail to complete a test, your driving privilege will be suspended for one year or revoked for two or three years. A two year revocation will result if the refusal occurred within seven years of a separate violation of driving under the influence and/or such a charge was reduced to reckless driving, or vehicular manslaughter which resulted in a conviction or an administrative determination that you refused testing or were driving with an excessive concentration of alcohol on a separate occasion. A three year revocation will result if you had more than one of these violations or administrative determinations within the last seven years.

Refusal or failure to complete a test may be used against you in court. Refusal or failure to complete a test will also result in a fine and imprisonment if this arrest results in a conviction of driving under the influence.

You do not have the right to talk to an attorney or have an attorney present before stating whether you will submit to a test, before deciding which test to take, or during the test.

If you cannot, or state you cannot, complete the test you choose, you must submit to and complete a remaining test.

You then ask the driver which test he chooses. If he refuses, you ask him specifically, "Will you take a breath test? Will you take a urine test? Will you take a blood test?" If the answer is no, take it as a refusal. There is no need to give him a second chance, and no need for you to try to convince him to take any test. Just read the forms and submit the paperwork on the refusal.

If they agree to the test, then you have to follow proper procedures in your area for administering the test. These vary widely, so we'll stick to some generalities in describing them. Whatever tests, equipment, and procedures you use, take the time to fully explain them to the suspect. This will help to eliminate fear on his part, get greater cooperation, avoid confusion, and make your job easier.

Blood tests are generally done at the local hospital or other medical facility, but may be done in a large jail with its own medical staff. The blood sample has to be taken by a medically qualified person such as a doctor, nurse, or lab tech. The site on the suspect's arm has to be sanitized with a non-alcohol based antiseptic, usually aqueous zepherine or hydrogen peroxide. The blood is usually taken in a sealed vacuum container containing an anticoagulant and should be gently rocked back and forth to mix after the sample is taken. The tube should be labeled with the suspect's name, booking number, time and date. You must observe it all, initial the sample, and take custody of the sample to preserve the chain of evidence. Being conscious of the possibility of AIDS contamination in any bodily fluid, you should always handle the sample with rubber gloves. The tube is generally sealed in an envelope with your initials and then booked into evidence for later testing. Results from the crime lab generally take a week or more.

Urine tests are handled in a similar manner, but require far less medical expertise. Urine samples are generally obtained in the jail. The driver is first required to drain his bladder and then to provide the urine sample 20 minutes or later. You have to observe the giving of urine (obviously, male officers should observe male suspects, and female officers should observe females) to ensure the sample is valid and not contaminated or diluted, while still providing enough privacy to maintain the suspect's dignity. The amount of urine required is small, generally about three fluid ounces are required for testing drugs, less for alcohol.

The driver should urinate in the specimen bottle, screw the lid on, and then hand it to you. Using gloves, you should then seal and label the bottle, just as with a blood sample. The urine is then booked into evidence, and again the results from the crime lab usually take a week or more.

The last test is the breath test, usually performed by officers at the station or jail facility but occasionally available in the field with a mobile unit. State laws require two separate breath samples which cannot differ from each other by more than .02 percent. You have to continuously observe the suspect for at least 15 minutes prior to the test, to make sure that the results won't be affected by ingesting additional alcohol. You should make sure the suspect doesn't eat or drink anything and doesn't vomit, belch, burp or smoke. Once the time is up, use the proper procedures and have the driver blow into the machine at the appropriate times.

Make sure that every driver gets a sanitary tip to blow into the machine, and wear rubber gloves to avoid contact with his saliva. Again, you don't have to beg or plead with the driver who won't blow hard enough for the machine to register, just tell him that if he can't blow hard enough it's the same as a refusal. Don't ever take it personally, it's just part of the test and doesn't affect your report or your case. After completing the procedure, the machine will print out the test results. Fill in any needed information, initial the sheet and attach it to your report.

Sometimes you have a grossly intoxicated person who will show no blood alcohol on a breath test. That should lead you to believe the person might be under the influence of drugs, and you will need either blood or urine samples for testing. You have the legal right to demand a second test under those circumstances even though the driver has completed the breath test.

Roughly 10 percent of the time, the drunk driver will refuse to take or complete a test. Under current case laws, all of the following represent forms of refusal:

Directly answering, "No."

Shaking his head no, a hand gesture, drawing back from the equipment or walking away from the testing apparatus.

Refusing to blow into the machine.

Responding to requests with silence.

Demanding to take all three tests.

Demanding to talk to an attorney first.

Demanding to be tested by a physician.

A minor requiring parental consent, when the parents are unavailable or unwilling to sign the medical consent.

Fighting with the officers.

Refusing to cooperate.

Once you have the results of a breath test showing a BAC above the legal limit, or once you have obtained the blood or urine sample, then you can proceed with your normal jail booking procedures. In some areas, drunk drivers automatically spend the night in jail, in others, they are processed and released as soon as possible.

DUI CHECKPOINTS

An alternate method of finding drunk drivers is the DUI checkpoint. Strictly controlled by the courts, such checkpoints are basically roadblocks looking for drunk drivers, established at locations with past histories of DUI-involved collisions or arrests.

DUI checkpoints are very common during the holiday season.

Key to the checkpoint concept is heavy publicity to deter drunk driving and the notion that it is voluntary and random, thus avoiding issues of search and seizure. Checkpoints are always constructed with advance warning signs and escape routes such as a side street or a turn-around prior to entry into the checkpoint lane. No driver is forced to drive through a checkpoint.

At the point that vehicles are actually stopped by the officers, cars are stopped on a random basis. Depending on traffic flows, that might be every other car, every fifth car, or every tenth car. Screening officers greet the driver and hand them informational materials. If no DUI signs are observed, the driver is sent on through. Those with objective signs of intoxication are directed to a side area for additional investigation, field coordination tests, and possible arrest.

DUI checkpoints have proven to be an effective tool against drunk driving, but depend on strict policies by the agencies operating them. Know your department's policy before attempting to organize or participate in such an operation.

ACCIDENT INVESTIGATION

When all of our preventative measures fail, accidents happen and patrol officers respond to investigate. If there are injuries at the scene, you may be dispatched Code-3. As you arrive at the scene, you will have to handle the situation in a safe and effective manner. Your priorities will include the following eight steps:

1) A quick assessment of the scene.

2) Requesting the assistance you need.

3) Assisting those that are injured.

4) Protecting persons and property.

5) Protecting the public.

6) Removing any situations that may have caused the accident.

7) Containing all witnesses, drivers, and suspects at the scene.

8) Documenting the accident on the appropriate reports.

To new officers, the tangled wreckage at an accident scene seems like an impossible task to handle. In fact, traffic accidents are similar to many other incidents you handle. With a cool head and common sense, you'll make quick work out of any traffic accident.

As you first arrive on the scene, you need to make a quick assessment. Check to see what streets are blocked, what vehicles are involved, what persons seem to be involved, and how much help you are going to need. During this time, you will probably get a gut feeling about what happened and why. The majority of time, that gut feeling will be absolutely correct.

Good accident investigation becomes an acquired skill.

As a first priority, start by getting the assistance you are going to need rolling. The assistance you need may include: more officers for traffic or crowd control, ambulances for the injured, fire department personnel for trapped persons and tow trucks to clear the road. Many of these may take time to get to your location. Have the dispatcher get them rolling as soon as possible.

Your next priority is to assist those that are injured. Life threatening emergencies such as stopped pulse, stopped breathing, or heavy bleeding have to be dealt with immediately. Put on protective gloves, get out your CPR facemask and start to work. You may have to sacrifice making an arrest or losing a witness in order to save lives at the scene. Non-life-threatening injuries can wait for treatment from the paramedics, but those persons still need your care and reassurances. Do what you can to make them comfortable and to reassure them that help is on the way.

Next you need to protect persons and property at the scene. Accident scenes are volatile, dangerous places. You need to protect the injured persons, witnesses, cars, and emergency responders as they arrive. You do so by placing your patrol car with the lights flashing to protect yourself (think of it as a three thousand pound highway flare) and by placing flares, cones, or other traffic control around the scene. Generally injured persons should not be moved, but if they are lying in a pool of gasoline, it may become necessary. Damaged cars may have to be pushed to the side of the road.

Once you've protected the scene and yourself, think of how you can protect the public. Does this accident represent a danger to observers or passersby? If so, you need to take immediate steps of evacuating or rerouting traffic.

Often accidents are caused by some condition, such as a fuel spill on a roadway. If that is the case, it could easily happen again. You have an obligation to remove any situations that may have caused the accident that still represent a hazard.

In order to handle an accident report, you need to talk to the people that saw it, both witnesses and drivers. Long before you arrive on the scene, your witnesses and passengers may start evaporating from the scene. Containing all witnesses, drivers, and suspects is a challenge. As a general rule, handcuff and detain those identified to you as suspects, and immediately collect I.D. from anyone who says they saw the accident or were part of the accident. Those parties rarely leave the scene once you have a piece of their property, and it leaves you free to do other duties until you can get back to them.

Your very last priority is to document the accident on the appropriate report forms for your department. Some major agencies do not handle or even respond to non-injury accidents, while others take motor vehicle accidents on private property and courtesy reports from other jurisdictions. Know your department policies and the expectations your citizens have.

The basic accident report is pretty much standardized from state to state. In every report, you will need to document all the information to identify every driver, passenger and witness, and every vehicle involved. You will need to establish exactly where the accident occurred and how it occurred. You will document who was injured and what their injuries were. Based on your interviews of the persons involved, combined with the physical evidence of skidmarks, damage and debris, you will need to come to a conclusion about why the accident occurred, who was at fault, and what sections of law they might have violated.

Every year in the United States, we kill about the same number of people in traffic accidents as we lost in the entire Vietnam war. The loss to our society in death, injury, property damage and lost time is in the billions of dollars. Obviously, there is a huge need for us to investigate traffic accidents, and your report may serve as the basis for arrests, convictions, prison sentences, and multi-million dollar lawsuits.

Your investigations will result in arrests for drunk driving, auto theft, and, perhaps, even murder. You will touch people in need and, perhaps, be a person's last comfort before he dies. Give your best, know the procedures, and do the job right.

DISCUSSION QUESTIONS

1) What is the primary purpose of traffic enforcement?

2) Traffic fines generate considerable revenue for cities. Explain why they should be eliminated, directed to other agencies, or left alone?

3) Should the enforcement priorities of a traffic unit be established by members of the community or by the police? Why?

4) Do national maximum speed limits make sense to you?

5) Do you believe that the use of radar is fair to the public? Explain.

6) Do you feel law enforcement, as a whole, is over emphasizing drunk driving enforcement?

7) Do you think that DUI checkpoints violate a person's right to privacy?

In Los Angeles, an 18-year-old gang member, probably leaning out a car window to position himself for a drive-by shooting, said police, was killed when his driver drove too close to a parked car, sending his head through the rear window of the other car.

* * *

Drinkers do some pretty weird things sometimes, and glue-sniffers get even crazier. But in Springfield, OR, a glue-sniffing drinker proved he could outdo both categories.

A man taking his dog for an early morning walk near a boat landing heard a male voice call for help. He tracked the plea down to a pit toilet. When he opened the door of the concrete block pit outhouse, he saw the top of a man's head — and an arm — sticking up out of the toilet tube. The man explained to his rescuer that he'd been sniffing glue and drinking the night before, and hallucinated that someone else was calling for help from the bottom of the toilet.

Naturally, being a good samaritan, he jumped right in. He had been stuck since then, with his head level with the toilet seat. The rescuer kindly offered the rest of his morning coffee, then went to call firefighters. Emergency personnel had to break the toilet fixture to get a strap around the man and pull him out. Then they gave him a ride — after hosing him off.

SUBSTANCE ABUSE
AND GANGS

LEARNING GOALS: After studying this chapter the student will
be able to:

- Define substance abuse.

- Identify procedures used to determine if a community has a
substance abuse problem.

- Define controlled substance.

- List the symptoms of substance abuse.

- Identify roles that substance abuse plays in crime.

- Describe a proper method used to recognize and approach a
drug suspect.

- Identify the roles gangs play in substance abuse.

- List alternatives to arrest that a patrol officer can offer to the
community.

As a patrol officer, you will deal with substance abuse every day in your community. From drunks on the corner to gang members; from experimenting juveniles, to bored Yuppies; from middle aged professionals to pot-smoking grandmothers — you will deal with people who use alcohol and drugs to ease their pains, alter their realities and screw-up their lives. More than half of all of your arrests will be related to the abuse of alcohol or drugs; and countless murders, assaults, robberies and burglaries that you investigate will be the result of the use of drugs, the desire for drugs, and the abuse of drugs. When you deal with a prostitute, a pimp, a burglar or a robber; you are likely dealing with someone working to support a drug habit. In some agencies, virtually 100% of your patrol time will be dealing with drugs.

The people leading your community will largely determine how much time is truly dedicated to the substance abuse problem. The effectiveness of your time will be determined by community support and your agency's leadership, training, and policies. When I started as a rookie patrol officer, I dealt with substance abuse everyday. Drug usage was rampant, but I was told, "We don't work drugs here, our city doesn't have a drug problem." That was official policy and reflected the mindset of the community leaders who thought of our city as something portrayed in a Norman Rockwell painting. Since we didn't have a drug problem, there was no need to enforce drug laws, investigate drug sales, conduct surveillances, or serve search warrants. The local high school dealt with students under the influence of drugs by simply sending them home. They didn't want police on campus, fearing the "chilling effect" that might have on education. Obviously, this taught students an important lesson.

I once met with an association of parents supposedly dedicated to controlling substance abuse among their children. They congratulated themselves (and rightly so) on their efforts to curb teenage drinking. They had set up alternative parties, chaperoned social events, conducted Safe-Ride programs, and initiated education programs about alcohol abuse. Then they asked my opinion. I told them that they had really done some great things, and now they needed to work on the methamphetamine problem, since I was encountering their children under the influence of "meth" on an almost daily basis.

They looked shocked, said "Metha-what?," thanked me for my time and showed me to the door. Later that night they voted to disband their organization, feeling that they had effectively dealt with the problem of drug abuse in the community and "saved" their children.

How much you do, and how much you are allowed to do will largely depend on your community's perceptions of the problem. If the community at large will not support your efforts to curb substance abuse and the sale of drugs, you will find it very difficult to make arrests and conduct investigations. On the other hand, if the community perceives the problem is of great magnitude, you may be able to devote a huge amount of time and resources to your efforts.

A perfect example of this type of support occurred in Los Angeles under Chief Daryl Gates when crack cocaine took over the streets. There was a huge public outcry about *crack houses* — fortified homes with iron bars and armored doors where cocaine was sold. These locations presented tremendous problems for patrol officers, so Chief Gates was given the resources and freedom to attack the problem. He used specialized narcotics teams to conduct drug buys, SWAT teams to conduct search warrants, and an armored personnel carrier (labeled "RESCUE VEHICLE") with a huge battering ram mounted on the front to knock holes through the front of crack houses.

The Los Angeles City Council provided the police department with abatement laws that ultimately allowed the city to condemn and bulldoze crack houses. Both the battering ram and the abatement procedures were effective, although controversial, measures. They were widely publicized and fairly popular with the majority of the community but roundly condemned by members of the press and the ACLU. Ultimately, the legal challenges and negative publicity brought about a shift in public opinion and the practices were discontinued. Police actions controlled by the community, like it or not, are going to be the reality of police work for the foreseeable future.

CONTROLLED SUBSTANCE LAWS

Every community in the United States has a substance abuse problem. Some problems may be bigger or more obvious than others, but the problem is there. Every law enforcement agency in the world deals with substance abuse, whether they recognize it or not. By some estimates, one out of every six persons in the United States makes more than casual use of illegal drugs; as many as one out of four abuse alcohol. That works out to over 75 million people with some degree of a substance abuse problem.

In talking about drugs, we make a distinction between over-the-counter items such as aspirin and cold capsules and drugs that are controlled by law (either totally forbidden or requiring a prescription). We call these drugs *controlled substances*. A controlled substance is any drug, substance, or immediate precursor (a chemical compound that will ultimately produce the drug) contained in various "schedules" initially established by the *Comprehensive Drug Abuse Prevention and Control Act of 1970* (commonly called the *Controlled Substances Act*). This act was the cornerstone of the federal government's efforts in the treatment and control of drug abuse. The federal agencies charged with enforcing it are the Food and Drug Administration (FDA), the Drug Enforcement Administration (DEA), and the Department of Justice. Under the act, which has been uniformly incorporated into the laws of every state, all controlled substances are placed in one of five schedules-the most dangerous in Schedule I, the least in Schedule V.

The schedules are very specific as to the exact drugs on each list, so they have to be updated constantly as new drugs and variations are developed on the street. You need to know the classification of a particular drug on the schedule in order to charge a suspect with the appropriate offense. As a police officer, you will deal primarily with high profile drugs (i.e., cocaine, heroin, methamphetamine, PCP and marijuana). These drugs will occupy the bulk of your time and investigations, and as a result of your focus on these drugs, it will be easier for you to miss the signs and symptoms of other, less-popular drugs.

Prescription drugs are also controlled substances, and their possession without a prescription is generally a felony. For the identification of pharmaceutical drugs, the *Physicians Desk Reference* or *PDR* is absolutely indispensable. This book has photographs and listings for more than 2,500 common prescription drugs, along with listings by manufacturer, product name, product category, and generic and chemical name. It's an indispensable tool for identifying drugs and determining how your laws classify that particular drug.

In addition to the controls on prescription drugs, the use, possession, alteration and misuse of prescriptions, prescription pads, and related documents are strictly controlled. Usually the mere possession of a blank prescription by anyone other than a doctor is a felony.

The possession of any controlled substance, except with a prescription, is a felony. The wording of *California's Health and Safety Code Section 11350* is typical of most state laws:

> "Every person who possesses any controlled substance (listed in specific sections), unless upon the written prescription of a physician, dentist, podiatrist, or veterinarian licensed to practice in this state, shall be punished by imprisonment in the state prison."

It is also illegal to sell, furnish, transport, administer, or give fake controlled substances. In other words, if you find someone who is selling phony cocaine, it's just as illegal as if it were real cocaine. You treat the sale of fake drugs just as seriously and in just the same way that you treat the sale of real drugs. The section on possession of controlled substances is followed by additional prohibitions which include:

- Possessing controlled substances for the purpose of selling.

- Possessing cocaine base.

- Transporting, selling, or giving away controlled substances.

- Selling heroine.

- Involving children with controlled substances.

- Selling on school grounds or public playgrounds.

- Possessing opium pipes.

- Possessing syringes and needles.

Marijuana is also illegal to possess and sell, and it is usually punishable as a felony. "Personal possession" of marijuana has been "decriminalized" in many states. In California, possession of less than 28.5 grams (one ounce) of marijuana is a misdemeanor punishable by a fine of not more than one hundred dollars (unless you have three or more convictions of the same offense in the previous two years).

For a patrol officer, this means that a suspect found with a few "joints" will receive a *notice to appear,* much like a traffic citation, and cannot be arrested if the possession of marijuana is the only offense.

Any other possession of marijuana or its products is certainly arrestable. These include:

- Possessing cannabis or hashish.

- Cultivating, harvesting, or processing marijuana.

- Transporting, selling, importing, or giving away marijuana.

- Selling marijuana to children.

- Selling marijuana on school grounds and playgrounds.

Outside of opium pipes (this includes a "crack pipe") and injection devices, most drug paraphernalia items are not illegal to possess (unless they actually contain drugs). Merchants and "head shop" operators generally can't allow minors to loiter, or even enter establishments specializing in these items, unless accompanied by their parent or legal guardian. Society's message seems to be that dope is okay if your parents approve. Just tie a red ribbon around that bong you buy for Christmas.

While the mere possession of "drug paraphernalia" may not be illegal, it doesn't mean that it can't be a powerful tool for the patrol officer. Where there's drug paraphernalia, there's a good chance that it represents probable cause that will allow you to search for drugs. When you find drugs, you can then seize the paraphernalia as evidence. Be attuned to the presence of such items, and use them to enhance your investigations.

The legal definition of *drug paraphernalia* includes all equipment, products, and materials of any kind which are intended for use or designed for use in planting, propagating, cultivating, growing, harvesting, manufacturing, compounding, converting, producing, processing, preparing, testing, analyzing, packaging, repackaging, storing, containing, concealing, injecting, ingesting, inhaling, or otherwise introducing into the human body a controlled substance.

Under the Influence

When driving a motor vehicle, we know that you are not legally "under the influence" until the point where your blood alcohol concentration exceeds your state's legal limit, usually .08 to .10%.

A person on the street can be under the influence of alcohol, and it is perfectly legal unless they are intoxicated. A typical definition of "drunk in public" reads as follows:

> (Every person is guilty of disorderly conduct, a misdemeanor) who is found in any public place under the influence of intoxicating liquor, any drug, controlled substance, toluene, or any combination of any intoxicating liquor, drug, controlled substance, or toluene, in such a condition that he or she is unable to exercise care for his or her own safety or the safety of others, or by reason of his or her being under the influence of intoxicating liquor, any drug, controlled substance, toluene, or any combination of any intoxicating liquor, drug, or toluene, interferes with or obstructs or prevents the free use of any street, sidewalk, or other public way.

This section is limiting in many ways. You can't arrest someone simply because they have been drinking, or because they are under the influence of alcohol. You have to meet the much higher standard of showing they are incapable of caring for themselves. This same standard does not apply to being under the influence of a controlled substance. No matter how functional or safe you might be, the mere fact that a person has a controlled substance in his or her system is sufficient to justify arrest. For controlled substances, the wording of the law is as follows:

> No person shall use, or be under the influence, of any controlled substance, except when administered by or under the direction of a person licensed by the state to dispense, prescribe, or administer controlled substances.

The vast majority of the time, you will be contacting a person under the influence for some other reason. You may contact them because of some criminal activity, as a result of a traffic stop, or while responding to a loud party of a neighborhood disturbance. The key is to have adequate probable cause to be where you are, doing what you are doing, and keeping an open mind about the situation so you can look beyond the initial radio call, and recognize the symptoms of substance abuse when you see them.

SYMPTOMS AND CHARACTERISTICS

Our courts require some proof that a person was under the influence of a controlled substance beyond the mere opinion of the officer that a person was intoxicated in some manner. You establish that proof by carefully noting all of the symptoms in an attempt to identify the drug being used (the officers that are really good at this are those who have completed a D.R.E. or "Drug Recognition Expert" program). Once you have narrowed down the potential list of substances, it's a lot easier to obtain chemical proof by sending the urine or blood to a laboratory for analysis.

Your best guide to determining drug use is experience. You will rapidly learn what drugs are commonly abused in your community. Watch other officers, particularly as they conduct under the influence investigations, and watch everyone you contact for symptoms. When I first started police work, PCP was just starting to hit the streets. It scared a lot of police officers because suspects often exhibited bizarre behavior and superhuman strength and a lot of officers were injured when making arrests.

Eventually, we learned what PCP was, what symptoms to look for, and what tactics were likely to work. Special classes were held, and I found myself successfully arresting PCP suspects on a regular basis. I talked to suspects about drugs and learned what I could about how it was packaged, sold, and used. I learned it's street names, packaging, prices, and availability. Just by virtue of normal in-service training and a lot of arrest and reports, I found myself qualified in our local courts as an expert witness on PCP. You will also become an expert on the drugs you encounter on your beat.

Some drugs will be much easier to identify than others. A classic "hype" or heroin addict may exhibit any or all of the following symptoms:

1) pinpoint, non-reactive pupils.

2) slow and deliberate speech.

3) impaired balance.

4) slow, lethargic movement.

5) droopy eyelids.

6) nervousness.

7) profuse perspiration.

8) runny nose.

9) itching.

10) yellowish complexion.

11) puncture wounds, ulcers, and scars on veins.

Obviously, if you encountered a person exhibiting all of these symptoms in any area known to be frequented by hypes, it would be easy to deduce that he was under the influence of heroin. You could ask a few quick questions about his physical condition (just to rule him out of being a kidney dialysis patient or the like), and you would likely have enough information to form the opinion that he was under the influence of heroin. Other drugs will be far more subtle and require careful investigations on your part.

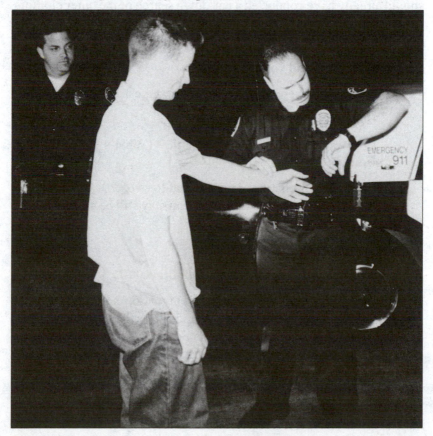

Elevated pulse rate is a common symptom of drug use.

Experts typically divide drugs into eight broad categories: alcohol, depressants, hallucinogenics, inhalants, marijuana, narcotics, phencyclidine, and stimulants. Typically, you will have to get by, like other police officers, with a few reference books, some in-service training, and a little experience in order to become truly effective at recognizing symptoms. Bear in mind that symptoms may vary substantially from person to person depending on mental condition, physical condition, dosage, purity, and the combined use of one or more substances.

Handling Persons Under the Influence

Once you've formed the opinion that a person is under the influence of a controlled substance, you can then arrest him. You should already have conducted a pat-down search of the outer clothing for weapons, now you can proceed with a more detailed search and questioning. You can ask very specific questions like:

"How much did you use today?"

"When and where did you last inject, ingest, or inhale?"

"How long have you been using?"

"How are you supporting your habit?" (What's your source of income?)

"Are you on probation or parole, and for what?" (Although you might not have a good drug case, you may still be able to violate him on his probation.)

"Where did you obtain your drugs?"

"Are you going to suffer from withdrawals?"

You can also ask hypes about different marks and scars, for some reason they seem to freely discuss how and where they shoot up. If you do get this type of information, you should use a standardized chart to show all marks, tattoos, scars, cuts, burns, and puncture wounds and photograph the most recent marks.

You can also proceed with a detailed search of the person you have arrested. You can ask the person to roll up his sleeves for you to inspect his arms, you can take everything out of his pockets and fully search a purse. You can also search the interior and trunk of the suspect's vehicle for evidence (the drugs) or instrumentalities (needles, cooking spoon, cotton balls, hype kit, etc.) of the crime.

Once taken to the station, you can demand that the suspect take a urine test. In California, there is a specific admonition called a "Sudduth" advisement, that explains both the purpose and legality of a urine test. The Sudduth admonition reads as follows:

> "You have been arrested for violating Section 11550 of the Health and Safety Code, "Under the influence of a controlled substance." You are now required to take a urine test to determine the presence of drugs or controlled substances in your body. Under the law, you do **not** have the right to refuse to take such a test. When you take the test, the results will be available to you, and if the test shows no controlled substance in your body, you may use such evidence to demonstrate your innocence; but if the test indicates a controlled substance in your body, it will be used against you in court.
>
> "If you refuse to take a urine test, it is a wrongful refusal to cooperate with a law enforcement investigation and your refusal will be used against you in court as an indication of your consciousness of guilt in attempting to suppress evidence.
>
> "You do not have the right to talk to an attorney or to have an attorney present before stating whether you will take a test or during the test.
>
> "I have been told by (your name) of my obligation to take a urine test. Having this obligation in mind, I choose to (submit, or refuse to submit) to a urine test."

Most states have some similar laws and admonitions and may have specific forms you need to fill out or sign. Once you have completed your interview, search, collection and disposition of evidence, and booking, your investigation is complete. Now you have to decide what to do with the suspect.

The vast majority of drug suspects are simply going to be placed into a cell until they sober up and either go to court or are released on a promise to appear. Procedurally, these suspects need constant supervision. Both overdoses and withdrawals from drugs can result in death. Anytime you have a suspect under the influence of any substance, he needs constant monitoring (most agencies use 15 minute jail checks) and medical attention if there are any problems.

If there are any indications that a suspect is in need of medical help, follow your agency's procedures as far as having paramedics respond to the jail, or transport the suspect to a hospital or jail infirmary. The days of having an addict go "cold turkey" in a cell are long gone, and the days of police officers being named in multi-million dollar lawsuits are here. A person in your custody is totally dependent on you for their care, regardless of what they may have done to themselves. Make sure you know exactly what your department requires in caring for intoxicated persons and those in need of medical care.

ALTERNATIVES TO ARREST

So far, we've talked about substance abuse from a pretty punitive standpoint: use a drug, go to jail. The fact of the matter remains that most of the law enforcement actions we take have little effect on the use and abuse of drugs and alcohol in our society. The trend is increasingly toward treating substance abuse as a medical problem, and some futurists project the total repeal of all drug laws within our lifetime.

Detoxification programs are becoming commonplace as alternatives to arrest, primarily for drunks. The authority to take a person into custody and leave him in a detoxification center have to be codified as law; otherwise, it would be difficult to differentiate a transportation to a detoxification facility from kidnapping. A typical statute might read:

> "When a person is found in any public place under the influence of intoxicating liquor, any peace officer, if he or she is reasonably able to do so, shall place the person in civil protective custody. Such person shall be taken to a facility for the 72-hour

treatment and evaluation of inebriates. A peace officer may place a person in civil protective custody with that kind and degree of force which would be lawful were he effecting an arrest for a misdemeanor without a warrant. No person who has been placed in civil protective custody shall thereafter be subject to any criminal prosecution or juvenile court proceeding based on the facts giving rise to such placement. This section shall not apply to:

(1) Any person who is under the influence of any drug, or under the influence of intoxicating liquor and any drug.

(2) Any person who a peace officer has probable cause to believe has committed any felony, or who has committed any misdemeanor in addition to being intoxicated in public.

(3) Any person who a peace officer, in good faith, believes will attempt escape or will be unreasonably difficult for medical personnel to control."

Your ability to take someone to a treatment facility rather than to jail will depend largely on what facilities are available. A person with great financial resources (or appropriate medical insurance) may voluntarily go to an expensive private facility (such as the world-famous Betty Ford Clinic). A transient will likely be at the mercy of the limited availability of public services.

At treatment facilities patients generally receive a medical evaluation and go through comprehensive screening and detoxification processes. Most are then encouraged to enter some form of long term treatment program. Unfortunately, the best of these claim success rates of less than 25 percent.

TREATMENT PROGRAMS

Probably the world's most popular treatment program is Alcoholics Anonymous, but it is just one of many programs which deal with a variety of substance abuse problems. A quick look through the Los Angeles phone book reveals hundreds of hospitals, clinics, treatment centers, and telephone hotlines, most eagerly proclaiming "All Major Medical Insurance Plans Accepted!" There are hotline numbers for Al-Anon Family Groups, Alcohol Recovery Centers, Alcoholics Anonymous, Cocaine Abuse, Drug and Alcohol Treatment, the National Council on Alcoholism & Drug Dependency, the National Drug Abuse Treatment & Information Service, and the Heroin Hotline. There are advertisements for therapeutic communities, Methadone maintenance and detoxification programs, drug-free outpatient services, half-way houses, residential treatment programs, and centers for every problem known to man.

Almost every treatment regimen is dependent on the same key concept — the person must admit he has a problem. Then, and only then, can he deal with the problem.

As a patrol officer, you have to know what services and assistance are available in your community. You can't force someone to admit he has a problem, but you can provide those who recognize they have a substance abuse problem with the means to get assistance. You should carry a list of hotlines and services to refer people to, know what they do and do not offer, and establish relationships with those service agencies. Then you can offer the victims of substance abuse and their families some type of alternative that offers the best chance for controlling the problem.

GANGS AND DRUGS, DRUGS AND GANGS

You're probably wondering what the heck a section on gangs is doing in the middle of a chapter on substance abuse. The answer is all too simple — drugs and gangs are interdependent. You almost can't have one without the other. Gang culture is dependent on drugs, and drug culture is dependent on the gangs.

Gangs have always been around, in one form or another, in the United States. They have evolved over the years just as law enforcement has evolved. Early gang members were called "outlaws" or "hoodlums," but they represented the same kind of organized criminal enterprise we have today. Instead of carjacking and drive-by shootings, gangs practiced horse thievery and bush-whacking. One hundred years ago the media and the public romanticized Jesse James, Billy the Kid, and the Dalton Gang; today it's the Crips, the Bloods, the Mexican Mafia, and video stars like Ice-T and Marky Mark.

In California today, there may be as many as 95,000 Hispanic gang members, 65,000 black gang members, 15,000 Asian gang members, and 5,000 white gang members. They range in age from 10 to 40, and the gangs vary in size from about 15 to over 1,000. That's 180,000 gang members in a state with about 20,000 police officers, and many gang experts admit their numbers may be off by as much as 100% (so there could be as many as 360,000 gang members in California alone). Not great ratios.

Both the modern and historical gangs represented very real threats to society: killing innocent citizens, challenging law enforcement, and causing fear and economic grief to everyone. And like the gangs of a hundred years ago, the media has romanticized and fictionalized gang life, tried to make heroes out of criminals, and hyped their viciousness beyond any reason.

Black Gangs and the Narcotics Trade

Gang crime is still expanding far beyond its traditional boundaries. Gangs have operated *rock houses* to shelter their drug sales and use. Non-gang members are being murdered over drug transactions and rip-offs. Innocent civilians are being caught in the cross fire of drug dealer shoot-outs. Extortion has become prevalent.

In the traditional black street gang, there is no one person in charge, no rank structure or leader. There are members with more influence than others, usually based on their age, stature, arrest record, and/or their reputation for violence. Now, the drug trade has made money the greatest factor in establishing gang leadership. Power can be earned, bought, and sold.

As gang members become successful in their drug operations, they tend to drift away from the actual gang and its related activity. The dealer's loyalty to the gang can still be demonstrated by providing drugs, guns, and money to a gang and its members, but close personal contact represents an added risk to the dealer. The organization he forms will most likely be made up of trusted gang members who will be used for street dealing, intimidation, protection, and killing. The more money the dealer has, the more influential he will be within the gang and within your neighborhoods. Successful drug dealers have become role models, prominent leaders within their neighborhoods, driving expensive cars, and often performing local charity efforts. Once again, these drug dealers are following the classic profile of the Mafia bosses, assuming the role of a Godfather who not only controls crime but becomes the social leader and patron of the neighborhood.

In Los Angeles County alone, approximately 280 black gangs are involved in dealing narcotics, each using three to five rock houses or stash houses to conduct their operations. Each location will involve 15 to 30 gang members selling narcotics or guarding the location. These gang members are paid by the dealer. Three or four high level members transport and supply narcotics and pick up the money from the locations. The gang members are usually indifferent about who the dealer is or where the drugs come from, as long as money is produced for the gang and its members.

The drugs are transported by a "Roller" (fancy cars, money and jewelry), usually in the early hours of the morning, often escorted by a second vehicle with armed gang members for protection. The cars can be heavily modified, with full bullet resistant glass and panels, secret compartments, even electrically operated trap doors. They generally communicate with each other and between locations with cellular phones and are sophisticated in the use of sending coded signals by beeper. A typical delivery would be an ounce of rock cocaine, for which the Roller gets paid about $100 (prices fluctuate depending on supply and law enforcement activity).

Drug Couriers

Beyond the "rollers" of the local distribution network, gangs transport large amounts of drugs from their delivery points to distribution centers throughout the United States. Their methods are complex and varied and may range from a single individual in a car to a huge organization with semi-trucks. At present, the majority of large seizures by patrol officers, like you, are as a result of stopping the middle-level courier in automobiles, vans, and even in rental trucks. While there is no specific profile or identifying characteristics of drug couriers, there are a number of signs that should alert you to the possibility that you have stopped a drug courier. Using these signs can then lead you to investigate further. Here are some of the things you can look for:

1) Poor Identification: Drug couriers want to avoid being identified in the field (since many have arrest backgrounds for drugs) and, if arrested, hope to make bail before they are fully identified, thus avoiding arrest on warrants or bail enhancements because of prior arrests. They will often present no identification, forged identification, "green cards" (immigration), out-of-state or foreign I.D. (particularly those without photos), or identification cards issued by commercial enterprises such as check cashing centers or video rental companies.

2) Not the Vehicle Owner: Couriers like "cold" cars that can't be traced back to them. That way they can ditch the car or simply abandon it if drugs are discovered in their absence. The cars they drive may be new (and unregistered), rented, borrowed from a friend or relative, stolen, or simply unknown to the driver. Oftentimes, the courier has the car provided to him by the distributor and has no idea at all who owns the car. This makes it easier for you to search, since the driver can't object if the owner gives permission.

3) Nervous Driver: The courier knows he's carrying drugs and doesn't want to be arrested. That makes him nervous and dangerous. Your alertness level should always go up a couple of notches when the driver is nervous. It could be someone who just doesn't want another traffic ticket, or it could be someone who is hiding guns or drugs or both.

4) Nervous Passengers: When the passengers are nervous, it's *really* time for you to be alert. If they're worried, it isn't because they fear a ticket, it's because they're afraid they're going to jail. Separate the driver from the passengers. Check to see if they give conflicting stories, or stories that match a little *too* well. Be concerned if

the passengers want to get out of the car or want to stay within hearing of the driver.

5) Communications Devices: Drug couriers use communications to enhance their security and the security of their drug delivery network. Sometimes they are simply given a beeper and a number to call when they reach their destination. The local distributor calls back the beeper with a pay phone number and makes contact with the courier. Simple, secure, and difficult for law enforcement to penetrate. Couriers also travel together, sometimes in several cars, sometimes with a "gun-ship" full of armed gang members to protect the shipment from rip-offs and the police, sometimes with a decoy car to suck you into a pursuit or a traffic stop if you start showing too much interest in the courier. Pay attention to surrounding traffic on every stop. Watch for beepers, C.B. radios, cellular phones, police scanners and mobile radios. Oftentimes these are temporarily mounted using magnetic antennas.

6) No Luggage: Drug couriers travel light and generally drive straight through to their destination. When you stop somebody from California giving New York as his destination, you should wonder if you don't see any luggage in the car.

7) Fast Food Trash: Since a load of dope may be worth millions of dollars, generally drug couriers are forbidden to park the car out of their sight. They'll be dining in the car on food from fast-food drive-up windows and gasoline station mini-markets with the trash thrown casually to the floor.

8) Sleeping Items: Since the courier can't leave the car, you may find the courier or his passenger sleeping in the vehicle. You'll find them sleeping in parks or alongside the highway. Look for pillows, blankets, and sleeping bags. Be curious and extra alert when handling accidents where the driver fell asleep behind the wheel.

9) Odor Masking Agents: Drugs stink. That's not a philosophical statement, simply a physical fact. From the damp moldy smell of marijuana, to the mint or ether of PCP, to the "cat piss" ammonia smell of methamphetamine; drugs produce distinct odors. Even when heavily packaged, couriers know that trained canines can

sniff out tiny amounts of drugs. To fool you and the canines, they may try to mask odors with soap-powder, coffee grounds, vials of perfume or cans of disinfectant. It is not unusual to find a drug courier with dozens of cardboard air-fresheners hung throughout the car.

10) Single Ignition Key: Oftentimes, a drug load is carried primarily in the trunk of a car. The courier may not have access to the load. By giving him just the ignition key, the distributor knows the driver has no access to the load, and it becomes more difficult for the police to search. Keeping the car keys separate from house or business keys also makes it more difficult to tie the courier to a property location that could be searched and potentially seized. This single key may also show the car was borrowed. Couriers sometimes will carry the trunk key in their pocket.

11) Road Maps: Frequently couriers make deliveries to new locations where they have never been before. Look for maps and be particularly alert for highlighted routes, circled cities, and notations of addresses, phone numbers, and beeper instructions. Check the driver's story and see if what he tells you about his destination and intentions matches what is shown on the map.

12) Mileage: Drug couriers drive a lot of miles in very short order. As a result, they may often have very high mileage on very new cars. Meaningless information by itself but significant when combined with other information.

13) Trunk Items: If you see a jack, spare tire, and jumper cables in the back seat of the car, you should be wondering what is taking up all the room in the trunk.

14) Cash: Drug couriers don't want to leave a paper trail for law enforcement of gasoline and food charge slips. They use cash for nearly all their purchases. Likewise, when they deliver drugs, they often pick up cash — lots of cash. This may sometimes be hundreds of thousands of dollars neatly packaged in plastic bags or briefcases. Incredibly, when asked about the cash, couriers will often deny knowing anything about it. Oftentimes this cash can be legally seized by the agency. You may find cash in a hidden compartment or in plain sight. Can the driver explain it logically?

15) Appearance Conflict: Last of all, does the driver seem to "go with" the vehicle? If you have an 18-year-old, unemployed, uneducated gang member driving a $50,000 BMW, you should wonder why. Similarly, if you have a well-dressed person, loaded with thousands of dollars in jewelry and driving a poorly maintained junker, you should be curious and looking for a logical explanation.

None of the items above are probable cause in themselves to search for drugs. They are simply warning signs for you to look for and be aware of. They may allow you to take advantage of a warrant arrest or an arrest for unlicensed driver and turn it into the drug seizure of the century.

Weaponry

The level of violence in black gangs is extremely high, so high that the national figures are skewed to make murder the number one cause of death for black males ages 15-25. The Crips and the Bloods are traditional enemies as entrenched in their positions as the Hatfields and the McCoys. They will fight and kill each other over seemingly trivial matters.

As the black gangs have grown financially, they have purchased advanced weaponry from both legal and illegal sources to protect their operations from competitors and the police. Ten years ago, the primary weapons faced by the police were Saturday Night Specials (cheap, small caliber weapons). Today, many gang members wear the same type of ballistic vest you do, and they are armed with sophisticated assault rifles, high-capacity shotguns, and various semi-automatic handguns. The specific weapons carried have become status symbols within the gangs.

The preferred rifles are semi-automatic assault rifles, often modified for full-automatic firing. The Soviet AK-47, 7.62 mm rifle and its variants are the most popular, although M-16 or AR-15 type .223 weapons are also very common. Uzi and Mac-10 "machine pistols" are also popular, and 9mm and .40 caliber pistols are much sought after, with the Glock being the most popular weapon today (in the Los Angeles area the gangs avoid using Berettas, because they are used by the police).

It is not uncommon to find AR-15 weapons with 100 round magazines, an AK-47 with 30 and 40 round magazines, and smaller 9 mm weapons with 15-30 round extended magazines. Drive-by shootings are often done by spraying an area with gunfire, sometimes leaving as many as 80-100 expended casings at the crime scene. The hazard that this type of weaponry represents to you, as a patrol officer, is obvious.

Other Gangs

While the Crips and Bloods clearly dominate the media, particularly in the Southern California area, there are countless other gangs, almost all of which are involved in drug usage and sales. No matter what aspect of law enforcement you enter, you will deal with gangs and gang members. As a patrol officer, it is vital to know the gangs in your area and as much as possible about the way they operate. These gangs cross all racial and geographical boundaries but seem to have divided up much of the drug trade market.

As indicated above, the black gangs seem to dominate the present cocaine trade in the United States but also deal extensively in PCP and marijuana. Hispanic gangs also deal in PCP and marijuana and control most of the sales of black "tar" heroin (out of Mexico), hashish, and peyote. Here the language and connections are a real advantage in doing business south of the border. White "Stoner" and motorcycle gangs seem to specialize in LSD, amphetamine, and methamphetamine sales. If that isn't enough, Asian gangs seem to be dominating the sale of Asian heroin and opium.

Hispanic Gangs

Hispanic gangs are a major criminal enterprise, particularly in the western states. Most gang members are second and third generation Americans far removed from the country of their heritage. They have a tight structure with well established leadership and social stratification and a very definite code of ethics that stresses loyalty to the death.

While black gang members often deny their gang affiliation, most Hispanic gang members express supreme pride in their gang and their neighborhood. They are highly protective of their turf and their families. To many of them the gang **is** their family, and they think of every other member of the gang as a brother.

Hispanic gang members frequently use drugs in the gang setting, particularly marijuana and PCP. They use the drugs recreationally and to prepare themselves for conflicts with other gangs. However, because of their particular code of ethics, they often try to shelter their families and children from drugs. As a result, sales by Hispanic gang members are far more subtle than with black gangs, sometimes restricted by specific gang rules regarding sales to outsiders and other gang members.

Hispanic gangs frequently fight with other gangs, usually over turf, women, or perceived insults such as spray painting over another gang's graffiti. They are often armed, sometimes with homemade guns and improvised blades. The baggy clothing they frequently wear provides excellent opportunity for concealing weapons and calls for extra caution on the part of patrol officers.

As a patrol officer, you need to be particularly sensitive to gang members' sense of values and ethics. Recognize that they have values (although very *different* ones than your own) and treat them with respect. Treat them fairly, no matter what law enforcement actions you are taking, and many Hispanic gangs will treat you with respect in return by providing you with information and assistance with crimes that affect the welfare of their neighborhoods. I am not saying that you should in any way tolerate their criminal activities. Simply treat them with dignity, and chances are your job on patrol will be easier and safer.

Asian Gangs

All across the nation there are highly active Asian gangs, generally centered around a shared ethnic heritage. There are Cambodian, Cantonese, Filipino, Japanese, Korean, Laotian, Samoan, and Vietnamese gangs, and many have members of various mixed nationalities. They are opportunistic gangs, generally preying on people of their same nationality. They terrorize their communities committing residential home invasion robberies, rapes, and business extortions. They control drugs, prostitution, and gambling within their communities and they recognize, and readily exploit, the fact that these victims may have a cultural distrust of the police and insurmountable cultural and language barriers making their crimes unlikely to be reported.

A typical Asian gang is the Tiny Rascal Gang (TRG), a Cambodian gang with as many as 500 members in organized sets.

Formed in Long Beach, California around 1988, sets have now been located throughout the state, as well as in Seattle, Washington; Portland, Oregon; and Lowell, Massachusetts. Less involved in the drug trade than some other Asian gangs, TRG members often prey on other Asians with home invasion robberies, extortions, auto thefts and drive-by shootings. They have threatened their victims with torture and have been responsible for a number of murders.

Nearly every Asian culture has its gangs. Within the Japanese communities, Federal authorities estimate there are 2,500 "Yakuza" groups with membership approaching 1,000,000. Gangs with names like Inagawa Kai, Matsuba Kai, Sumiyoshi-Rengo Kai, and Yamaguchi Gumi control prostitution, gambling and narcotics often fronted through legitimate businesses. Their ornate tattoos of eagles, dragons, hawks and the like are used to flash and intimidate their victims.

Vietnamese gangs trace their origins to the streets of Saigon. These gangs tend to be loosely knit, highly mobile, nomadic groups likely to travel considerable distances to commit crimes. Typically a group comes together for just the duration of the crime (often a residential burglary) then the "Hasty" gang separates and disperses to different cities or even states. Coming from a war-torn society, Vietnamese gangs are known for their extreme violence. Skilled with weapons, booby-traps and torture, they are often used as contract killers by other gangs. Some of the dominant Vietnamese gangs include: Catalina Boyz, Frogmen, Lunes, Paratroopers, Pink Knights, Saigon Cowboys and Tai Chem.

Other mixed Asian gangs include the "Wah-Chings," "Joe Boys" (formerly the "Joe Fong Gang"), and many smaller sets such as Notoma Boys, Asian Boyz, Oriental Bad Boys, Oriental Killers, King Cobra Boyz, Cheap Boys, Silver Middle Girls, Innocent Bitch Killer, China Town Rulers, Hung Pho, All Brothers Together, Ninja Clan Assassins, Exotic Foreign Cambodian Coterie, Black Dragons, and the Teaser Mohawk Boys. Make no mistake, despite their seemingly whimsical names, these gangs are lethal, well-organized criminal organizations. The Wah-Ching is a nationwide, organized criminal group that has formed powerful alliances with foreign-based Chinese criminal groups.

Many of the Asian gang members, and particularly those with Vietnamese affiliations, affect punk or new-wave hair styles and dress, but that style can be quickly and easily changed to make them indistinguishable from a run of the mill college student. They often carry sophisticated weapons, sometimes carried by female gang members, sometimes hidden within vehicles. These guns may be hidden in specially built compartments, inside the engine compartment, and occasionally even attached by magnets to the underside of the body or fenders.

Colors and Dress

Most gang members are proud of their gang and openly show their membership by the way they dress. Hispanic gang members have long worn baggy khaki trousers, white T-shirts, Pendleton shirts and knit caps to show their gang affiliation. Black gang members favor athletic attire with team logos and, increasingly, gang members even have custom silk-screened or embroidered shirts and jackets with their gang names or logos on them. Asian gang members are less inclined to dress in a distinctive manner, but many have adopted the baggy style of Hispanic and black gangs. Most gang members seem to treat black as a neutral gang color with the Raiders being the most popular logo.

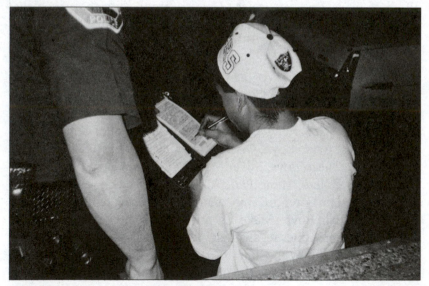

Always look for insignias on clothing.

Green is also a "neutral" color, and green caps are often worn with other gang attire to indicate the wearer handles the money for the gang.

Gang members frequently write their gang name and home street under the bill or on the side of the cap, something that can be an important source of information for you as a patrol officer. Drug dealers will often embroider marijuana leaves or dollar signs on their caps as well.

Tremendous rivalries exist between the Bloods and the Crips, a passionate hatred that has killed hundreds of gang members. Each gang deliberately does things in a different manner. For years, Crips have worn blue as a distinctive color, "dressed down" in blue from head to toe. A Crip member may be carrying or wearing a blue bandanna, blue jacket, blue socks and blue shoelaces. Their preferred shoes are British Knight running shoes, emblazoned with the B.K. logo. The Crips assert this stands for "Blood Killer," and frequent Burger King restaurants as well since that chain began using "B.K." in their advertising. One source in Chicago alleged that locally the Crips favored Nike shoes, bragging that Nike was an acronym for "Nigga I Kill Everybody." Crips may also wear blue New York Yankees or Los Angeles Dodgers caps and jackets.

Blood sets wear red clothing, caps, and bandannas, and often wear Columbian Knight sports shoes (with "C.K." for "Crip Killer"). A favorite cap is the Cincinnati Reds cap, worn by Bloods because they have a "C" on them which shows great disrespect for Crips.

Graffiti

Graffiti is the most highly visible and widespread by-product of the street gang culture. If you can read and understand it, it will provide you with a wealth of information about what gangs are active in your community, what their membership is like, and what the relationship between various gangs may be. The bulk of gang graffiti is written by black and Hispanic gang members, and their style of graffiti is quite different and distinctive.

Hispanic gangs often show the traditional gang philosophy. They prefer stylized script letters, most often in spray paint. Many are elaborate and even artistic. Their graffiti is a source of pride and a means of marking their territory and memorializing their membership. A typical "placa" might feature the gang's name (like "Dogtown," or sometimes just the initials "VNE" for "Varrio Nuestra Estrada."), a stylized logo, their subset (like "Tiny Locos"), and then a list of gang members' names. Sometimes the names will be just the members present when the placa was written, but other times it may be an elaborate listing of every member in rank order of importance.

The names shown will be their gang nicknames or "monikers." Most Hispanic gang nicknames are based on physical attributes or characteristics and may be a mix of English and Spanish. Some typical names might be Casper (pale complexion), Chino (someone with pronounced Oriental features), Cyco (crazy), Flaco (skinny), Silent (shy), Spooky, Weasel, or Wolfy.

Much black graffiti is loaded with profanity and expressions of racial prejudice and black power. There are often challenges to other gangs, such as "Death to Bloods," and "187" (the California Penal Code section for murder). Common motifs include crude drawings of knives or guns sometimes with a stream of bullets directed toward another gang's name.

Relations between gangs can be deduced by such challenges along with cross outs. If one gang's graffiti has been crossed out, oversprayed with another gang's graffiti, or defaced with obscenities, it means the gang ownership of that location is being contested. Depending on the relations between gangs, it can be a direct challenge or a deadly insult that will result in murders on your beat.

Graffiti is a sure sign of gang activity.

Tattoos

Many gang members wear tattoos with pride, and hard-core members may tattoo their neck, back, and belly as well as their arms. They are most common among Hispanic gang members but becoming increasingly common among blacks. The tattoos proclaim gang affiliation (members of the "Five-Duce Broadway Gangster Crips" might have the tattoo "5BGC2") and their nickname. Along with tattoos, scarring has become more common, using cigarettes and lighters to create scars in specific spots on the hands and arms. A common method of scarring among Asian gangs now is to heat up a half-dollar and then press it into the flesh of the inner forearm, creating a burned scar image of the eagle.

Tattoos can range in quality from crude home-made tattoos, to highly professional prison tattoos with beautiful girls or images of barred doors and guard-towers as popular subjects. They can range in size from a tiny dot in the web of the hand to a massive placa covering the entire back. They can be as subtle as a cross on a female's hand or a teardrop under an eye. Never insult a person about his tattoos, always treat him with respect, and often you will gain a wealth of information.

Interview Tactics

Extreme care and meticulous officer safety have to be observed when dealing with gang members. Every confrontation with a street gang has the potential to turn to violence so you have to act decisively, call for backup when needed, and respond with appropriate force when necessary.

As a patrol officer, you will be evaluated in terms of your fairness and professionalism by the gang members in your area. You have to establish your authority and gain the gang member's respect, doing what you have to do, issuing citations when appropriate, and making arrests as needed. You must always behave in a fair manner consistent with the *Code of Ethics*.

Gangs operate under a certain set of rules and ethics, as warped as we may view them. For the most part, there seems to be an understanding that police officers are out there doing their job. A gang member may resist arrest with all his power and weaponry, but once the situation is under control and the suspect under arrest it isn't "personal." If the gang sees you act in an ethical manner and your actions seem fair and warranted by the circumstances, they will respect you and your authority, and eventually you may establish rapport with some members of the gang.

With a few exceptions among their top leadership, most gang members are followers, proud members of their gangs, proud of their gang names and their accomplishments. If you cater to their vanity, they will often brag to you about the people they have killed and the deals they've done. It is essential to isolate gang members from each other when you interview them and to do so safely, frisk each member for weapons before doing any interviews.

Always ask a gang member for his set, his neighborhood, his "tag" or nickname, and look at his tattoos and clothing for verification. Generally, his possessions will be marked with the same gang initials and his tag. Look for these markings inside of clothing and hats, on address books and other papers in the gang members possession. Know your local gang sets, their colors, hand signs, and symbols before you attempt to talk to them at their level. If you don't know the gangs in your community, you'll just sound stupid when you interview a gang member.

Once you find out their gang name, use it and ask them how they acquired it. "Why do they call you Sniper?" you might ask. They'll lie about it, but often provide you with valid information in the process. If a gang member is flashing a lot of gold jewelry, cater to his image of himself as a businessman. Ask him about his car and his prosperity. You'll be surprised at how much he may tell you.

As you work your area, you will learn the gang members, patterns, graffiti, families, cars and hangouts. It's invaluable information for effectively patrolling your community and priceless in controlling the flow of drugs through your beat.

DISCUSSION QUESTIONS

1) Does your community have a substance abuse problem? What drug is most commonly abused?

2) What resources are available in your community to fight substance abuse?

3) What resources are available on your campus to assist students with their substance abuse problems? What do you feel is the most commonly abused substance on your campus?

4) Does your community have a gang problem? Is your local law enforcement agency devoting appropriate resources to the problem?

5) Many school districts across the country now forbid wearing "gang attire." Do you agree with these policies?

6) What do you think about the idea of the police using armored vehicles, such as the LAPD's battering ram, to attack crack houses?

7) Marijuana has been decriminalized in many states so that possession of small amounts for personal use is punishable only by a fine. Do you think marijuana should be totally legal? Should other drugs be decriminalized?

8) Should a patrol officer be concerned with the rehabilitation of drug offenders, or should his role be limited to enforcing the laws?

L.A. police nabbed a robbery suspect in North Hollywood on Thursday night and hauled him downtown for questioning. They kept at him for several hours before deciding he wasn't the culprit.

That's when they found out that they had caused him to miss his wedding.

Did this realization leave them guilt-ridden? We don't know. But we do know that they summoned the bride, who responded with some reluctance, and called in a police chaplain, then pulled duty as witnesses while the couple were married right there in the dingy, crowded police station lobby early Friday.

Explained police Sgt. Ray Davies: "We're just full-service type of place-police work, wedding chapel. We do tune-ups too."

FIELD INTERVIEWS

LEARNING GOALS: After studying this chapter the student will be able to:

- Describe a field interview.

- Differentiate between an interview and an interrogation.

- Define a consensual encounter.

- Define a reasonable suspicion.

- Identify a detention and how much force is appropriate for a detention.

- Define probable cause.

- Define an arrest.

- Analyze what role race and your experience play in establishing reasonable suspicion and probable cause.

- Use appropriate techniques for stopping a suspect and conducting a field interview.

- Explain how and when you conduct a patdown search.

- Describe an F.I. card.

- Demonstrate how to conduct a showup.

- Identify when can you move a suspect you have detained.

- Recognize the maximum amount of time you can spend on a detention.

As a patrol officer, you will spend your day dealing with people. Your contacts will vary — talking to informants, contacting suspicious persons, making arrests, assisting citizens, and gathering information. If you do your job properly as an active member of the community, you'll spend a lot of time talking with the people in your assigned area, getting in contact with *their* needs, views, and concerns. You should go out of your way to meet as many people as possible: residents, business people, teachers, community leaders, and the people of the street.

Much of the time, you will be seeking information. When you seek information from a suspicious person or a suspect in a crime, your questions will go beyond conversation and, thus, constitute a "field interview," or a "field interrogation." Generally, the word *interview* implies a two-way conversation, while *interrogation* means a more formal, adversarial type of questioning.

From a legal standpoint, the law will classify every one of these contacts in one of three ways: a *consensual encounter*, a *detention*, or an *arrest*. Each has very specific legal implications, and it's important for you to understand how your actions will be interpreted by the courts.

Consensual Encounter

Most of your contacts during a shift are with persons who are not suspected of any specific crime(s). You don't need any justification or specific reason for initiating these types of contacts because you don't intend to restrain the person or exert any *authority* over him. This is the key to a *consensual encounter* — the other person remains totally free to leave, to ignore you, or to otherwise not cooperate with you. Of course, once you initiate such an encounter, it may very well lead you to detaining or arresting the person, but the initial contact is still legal and valid if that person remains free to leave. You have no specific powers to frisk or search during a consensual encounter, but any contraband or evidence you see in plain sight can be seized and may serve as your *probable cause* to make an arrest and search incidental to that arrest.

When you initially suspect the person is involved in a crime, it will be a lot more difficult to convince a judge and jury that the encounter was consensual. Nonetheless, you can approach an individual in a public place, identify yourself as a police officer, ask for identification, and ask the person a few questions while still maintaining that consensual status. Even shining a spotlight on a person at night, or asking a person to take his hands out of his pockets is permissible in a consensual encounter since those requests (not demands) are reasonable to maintain your safety. The key is always that the other person remains free to leave or ignore your requests.

In a consensual encounter, it's important that you not communicate to the person that you are requiring compliance with your requests. Ask, don't demand. To make things perfectly clear, you can actually tell the person, "You are not being detained and you are free to leave, but I would like to ask you a few questions." Most of the time, you will find that people cooperate.

This notion of consensual encounter extends to your patrol vehicle and how you use it. With a person, an encounter is consensual as long as you don't restrain the person or exert any authority over him. There's a parallel concept in your patrol car. If you're in your patrol car, you can pull up behind or alongside another vehicle and have a consensual encounter as long as they aren't blocked in and they are still free to drive away. If you follow a vehicle and they pull over of their own accord, you can stop and talk to them on a consensual basis.

You can even flash your high beams or shine a spotlight into a car and still keep it a consensual encounter. The courts have viewed it this way since the person in the other car has no legal authority that he's required to submit to when illuminated by white lights. However, once you turn on your red or blue emergency lights, the other driver is required by law to pull over and stop. That's using your lawful authority to restrain a person, and at that point he is no longer free to leave. Once you use that authority to limit a person's freedom, you've gone beyond a consensual encounter and upgraded to a "detention."

Detention

A *detention* is the temporary stopping of a person by exerting your authority. It is less than an arrest and more than a consensual encounter. You need no justification to initiate a consensual encounter, and you need probable cause to make an arrest. For a detention, you need "reasonable suspicion." Both the quality and the quantity of information you need for reasonable suspicion is considerably less than the probable cause you would need to arrest, but the authority you exert is far more than anything you might employ in a consensual encounter.

You have made a detention whenever a reasonable person that you contact might believe that he is no longer free to leave. Their belief might be based on you physically restraining them in some way, giving them some specific order or command that they feel obligated to obey, or your questioning or actions that clearly indicate you are investigating them as the suspect in a specific criminal act.

Arrest

An *arrest* occurs when you actually take a person into custody in "a case and in the manner authorized by law." This requires that you either physically restrain the person by touching, a control hold, handcuffing or other use of force, or that he submit to your authority. You may always use the reasonable force necessary to effect an arrest, overcoming resistance and preventing escape.

Without a warrant, you can only arrest if you have probable cause to believe the suspect committed an offense. *Probable cause* to arrest means you need enough factual information to make the average reasonable person with your same training and experience believe that the individual is guilty of a crime.

This doesn't mean you have to prove beyond any reasonable doubt, that's a different standard that applies only at trial. The information you use for probable cause is not limited to admissible evidence. You may consider the "totality of the circumstances." That means you can take into consideration not only the facts, but your knowledge, training, expertise, experience, and observations. You can also use information given to you by other officers, citizens and informants. As long as all the information you possess meets the standard of probable cause at the moment of custody, your arrest is reasonable. If it doesn't meet that standard, your arrest is unreasonable, and all evidence becomes inadmissible. That is why it is *critically* important to understand the difference between a detention and an arrest. Make sure you act appropriately and consistently with your intent to detain or arrest.

Use of Force in Detentions

In order to stop a suspect for a detention, you should avoid using force if possible. Physical restraints, handcuffs, or displaying your gun may indicate to a suspect that he is being arrested, not detained. This can cause a lawful detention to turn into an invalid arrest and cause the loss of an otherwise excellent case in court.

Despite this cautionary note, you can and should use appropriate precautionary safety measures to protect you and the public. In the middle of a street fight in a tough part of town, you may be perfectly justified in handcuffing a suspect, placing him in a patrol car, or even holding him at gunpoint.

Once you stop the suspect, you can then take whatever investigative actions are reasonable under the circumstances. You can question the suspect about his identity and conduct. You can contact other persons to confirm the story, to verify the identification, and to determine if the person has any outstanding wants or warrants. You can check nearby buildings and properties to determine whether a crime occurred, contact neighbors and other individuals, and examine any objects in the vicinity that might be relevant to the crime or circumstances you are investigating. You can also bring a victim or other witness to a suspect for an in-field "showup."

PROBABLE CAUSE LAW

"I just had a hunch." Playing hunches always worked well for movie detectives but rarely plays well to judges in court. Most judges give "two thumbs down" to using hunches as the basis for an arrest. But what, exactly, is a hunch? The dictionary definition reads, "a guess or feeling not based on known facts."

Other officers have attributed great arrests to "a sixth sense," "luck," or have stated, "it just didn't look right." Yet all of these officers possessed unique skills, knowledge, education and experience. They all had good, legal, probable cause but simply did a poor job of articulating their reasons why probable cause existed.

That hunch, lucky guess, sixth sense, weren't arbitrary, they were specific sets of facts applied to specific situations that led these unique professionals to make the reasonable assumption that a particular event occurred. You must be able to articulate those specific facts in your report and under questioning in court. The court will look at "the big picture," or as they phrase it in case law, "the totality of the circumstances." Instead of looking at any single fact, the court will look at all the facts, including how they relate to one another.

Bullet holes are always great P.C.

Reasonable Suspicion

For any detention to be valid, you have to have a "reasonable suspicion." The two-point test used by the courts is that you, as a police officer, must believe that:

1) Criminal activity may be taking place, and

2) The person you detain is somehow connected with that possible criminal activity.

You cannot make a detention based on simple curiosity, instinct, intuition, rumor, or a hunch. You've got to have facts, and articulate those facts. Here's some examples of fact patterns and how they have been interpreted by the courts:

Reasonable Suspicion:

The detention of a known drug addict who was carrying a pry bar in early morning hours.

The detention of suspects who were loading a television into a car late at night, then looking shocked when they saw the police and ran.

The detention of a suspect inside a hotel room, when the officer who was there for other purposes, saw drugs and a syringe.

The detention of a suspect sitting at a red light who looked drunk, with his eyes closed, his hair disheveled, and his head resting, even though his driving was normal.

The detention of a suspect who was showing others something in a paper bag, then yelled, "Police" and ran inside.

Unreasonable Suspicion:

The detention of the occupants of a car in a convenience store parking lot who ducked down when the officer passed by in his patrol car.

The detention of two youths walking through a high burglary area during school hours.

The detention of suspects in an alley in a known drug-use area when the suspects refused to identify themselves to the police officer.

The detention of suspects in a back yard when the officers were investigating an anonymous tip about drug sales, and they recognized a suspect they knew did not live there.

The detention of a group of men officers saw gathered during the evening in front of a liquor store who fled when the police officers arrived.

The Role of Experience in Probable Cause

Your experience as a patrol office can be a highly important factor in the court's determination of how reasonable it is for you to detain any individual. As a police officer, you possess highly specialized knowledge about your community and its particular criminal patterns. The courts won't turn a blind eye to that type of experience. If you see someone you know is a drug-using gang member paying cash out to someone you know to be a drug seller on a corner on which you have previously arrested a dozen people for hand-to-hand drug sales, you may well have the probable cause to stop those suspects and investigate further. A brand new officer who doesn't know the suspects or the location doesn't have the same facts you possess. Based on his experience, all he saw was one citizen handing cash to another which is hardly enough to suspect criminal activity.

Your experience outside of law enforcement can also come into play. One of my officers ran his own auto body shop for years before joining our department. He has a vast pool of expertise in automobiles, particularly in dealing with stolen automobiles. He can spot a VIN-switch or a substituted part at a glance, and develop probable cause to arrest that which would elude other officers. Other officers have worked in restaurants, as bank managers, credit card investigators, computer programmers, electricians, laboratory technicians, tax accountants, chauffeurs, bartenders, and construction workers. Some are combat veterans in the military with ordinance and explosives expertise. Each have unique life experiences that they can apply to particular cases. You have unique experiences as well, and you will find ways to apply that knowledge to your particular duties.

How well you know and become involved with your community will determine how effective you are in discharging your duties. Every fact you know about your assigned patrol area adds to your base of experience and information that can result in reasonable suspicion or probable cause. Knowledge like this is an invaluable resource when patrolling the streets. It can make the difference between being an average officer known for simply working hard and an exemplary officer known for making great arrests and having a *"sixth sense"* about crime.

The Use of Second-Hand Information

In addition to your own information and experiences, you can base a detention on information you have received from others, even though you don't have direct knowledge yourself. This can be information from a witness, another police officer, a dispatcher, a crime bulletin, or a broadcast from another agency you receive on a scanner. Even an anonymous tip *may* justify a detention, depending on the quality and quantity of information and how reasonable it is for a person in your position to believe that information.

No matter how large an area you live in, it is amazing how small the world really is and how well contacts can pay off. Several years ago, I rode along with a police officer I knew in a small community in Northern California, more than three hundred miles away from my city. While he wrote a report, I thumbed through local wanted posters and came across a murder suspect I had stopped and conducted a field interview on just the previous week. When I returned to my city, I asked a neighbor to keep an eye out for that same car and suspect. Within a week I found him, detained him while we verified with the Northern California agency, and then arrested him for murder. My probable cause for arrest was a crime bulletin that I stumbled across by accident and information given by a detective 300 miles away and relayed to me by my dispatcher. That would be strictly hearsay evidence in a trial, and completely inadmissible, but great reasonable suspicion for a detention, and perfect probable cause for arrest out on the streets.

Here it paid off to be an active, integral part of my community. The neighbors that spotted the suspect were people I knew through local Boy Scout events and members of a local service club. They were people I already knew by name, people that I had helped in the past, people that I trusted and people that trusted me. Every contact you make with a person on your beat (patrol area) is a potential resource. The vast majority of the people you serve are decent, caring people who hate crime as much as you do. You'll be amazed at what they can tell you and at the probable cause they can generate to help you do your job more effectively.

Flight and Suspicion

One of the quirks of law enforcement is that people run away from the police. You can just drive around a corner and suddenly people are running inside, jumping over walls, or climbing into vehicles and leaving. Running, jumping and leaving are not crimes. They spark your curiosity, but they don't provide you with the reasonable suspicion you need to detain unless you have other facts as well.

In general, flight alone is not enough to justify a detention, but flight combined with any other suspicious factors or activity can help to provide you with the probable cause to detain the individuals that flee. If you know the person running is a burglar and you see him throw jewelry into the street as he runs, the court will likely find it reasonable for you to detain him. If the group is committing some other crime in your presence, such as trespassing at a location you know they do not belong or drinking in public, you are well justified in detaining them to investigate those crimes. If the vehicle leaving a location commits a traffic violation, you can stop and detain for the length of time it takes to issue a citation or deal with that offense.

Fleeing from the police is an act that makes it clear the person is not being detained. Even if you make such authoritarian gestures as aiming a gun at the suspect or yelling, "Police, Freeze!" (a tactic I have found often fails to impress suspects much less stop them), no detention has taken place until the suspect *submits* to that authority. If you feel like exercise, you can chase after every single person that runs from you to satisfy your curiosity. Just chasing after someone does not constitute a detention. However, once you catch the suspect all of the requirements for a detention have been met. You will have exercised legal authority over him, or he will have submitted to your authority, and you better be sure you had the reasonable suspicion you needed to detain or you risk losing your court case and probably being reprimanded.

The same concept applies to a vehicle. If a vehicle flees when you try to stop it, no detention has taken place. There must exist either a physical restraint or a submission to your authority.

Every suspect you chase has the obligation under law to stop and has no legal right to resist a lawful detention. When he flees, you may use whatever physical force is reasonable and necessary to make him stop. If your detention begins in a public place, a suspect cannot escape by running inside a private place. You have the right to pursue him into a residence, business, club, or any other place he runs to.

How the Area Affects Probable Cause

Where you contact a suspect can add to your reasonable suspicions and probable cause. The fact that it is nighttime or that there is a documented history of narcotics traffic, auto burglaries, or street robberies all can add to your probable cause but alone are not enough to support probable cause.

Let's say that you are working a particular street in the early morning hours specifically looking for auto thieves. You've lost at least one car every night from this same street. At three o'clock in the morning, you spot a man walking down the sidewalk. That alone would not be enough to detain, but it is certainly enough for you to initiate a consensual encounter to satisfy your curiosity. Instead, you wait a little longer. If the man stops and looks into a car, you have a reasonable suspicion to contact him. If he has a police scanner and a crowbar on his belt, you have reasonable suspicion to detain, and with just a little more information you can investigate and may well develop probable cause to arrest.

The fact that it was nighttime and a high crime area would not be sufficient alone. But those facts combined with the scanner and tool make it entirely reasonable to detain that suspect and find out what he is doing.

The Role of Race in Probable Cause

The race of the suspect is irrelevant as an independent issue of probable cause unless race was part of the description of a specific suspect. If you received a call regarding a robbery and the suspect was described as a male white, you could stop any white male that you could place in proximity to the crime. On the other hand, if that same person was simply walking through a neighborhood you knew was populated solely by Hispanics, there would be no justification for stopping him simply because of his race.

In one California case, a deputy stopped two male black juveniles based on their race, since he knew the neighborhood was all white. The juveniles were burglars, but the courts barred all the subsequent evidence as the fruits of an illegal detention. It wasn't that the deputy did a bad job. He was looking for burglars and he found some and arrested them. What he did wrong was to detain them prematurely, before he had developed reasonable suspicion based on facts other than race. Had he stopped them because of the burglary tools they possessed, or some other suspicious activity, he might have had an easy conviction. As it was, the burglars walked free.

FIELD STOP TECHNIQUES

Now you have some idea of the legalities of various kinds of field contacts. Just curious about some person or activity? You can always pull up for a consensual contact and just talk with the people involved. Reasonable suspicion? Now you can detain and investigate further. Probable cause? Make the arrest as authorized by law. The remaining question is, "How?"

Approaching the Suspect

Your initial contact with any suspect can set the tone for the entire encounter. You should be polite, but firm. Be professional, take care of business, and move on. Your safety should always be a primary consideration. A popular bumper sticker of the 1960's proclaimed, "Today is the first day of the rest of your life." You should remember that the next field contact may be the last contact in your life. In 1991, the first LAPD female officer to die in the line of duty was shot to death when she and her partner contacted two pedestrians for drinking in public. One immediately pulled out a handgun and shot the officer in the head before being killed by her partner. You don't have to do a SWAT crawl up to every suspect you contact, but you do have to take reasonable measures to protect yourself.

Once you've identified a person you want to contact, ask yourself what kind of contact you intend. Is this a consensual encounter, detention, or arrest? Based on the answer, you can determine how much force you might use, and how you are going to legally respond to a lack of cooperation, resistance or flight. Have a plan in mind before you ever initiate your contact.

Pick your spot. Ideally, you want a location where the suspect has limited places to run, making it easier for you to contain or catch him. Look at the lighting, potential hiding places, and the other persons and vehicles nearby. Check to see what cover and concealment are available for you. Sometimes you might want to take a suspect by surprise, letting him walk right past a driveway or alley and contact him from behind. Other times, you might want to let him get a long look at you as you approach head on in the patrol car, giving you a chance to observe his reactions. Neither is right or wrong, they are just different techniques for different situations.

Always, always, always notify your dispatcher (or type in on your Mobile Data Terminal) where you are, what you are doing, and a description of the suspect being stopped. If there is any question of a confrontation, ask for back-up. Then wait until your radio traffic is acknowledged before making your approach.

I have seen countless officers make their approach in the car, by pulling up beside a suspect and calling him over to the car — and I have seen officers buried who died in their patrol cars. While you can use the car for cover (a place to hide behind if the suspect opens fire), you should always be out of the car, on foot, when you approach a suspect. Again, the situation will dictate your tactics. Pull to the curb behind a suspect and challenge him ("Police! Stop right there!") from behind the car. Pull into a driveway to block the path of a suspect on a sidewalk, again placing yourself on the opposite side of the car. Pull around corners and stop, wait on foot for the suspect to arrive. All of these are good tactics depending on the situation.

Contacting the Suspect

Once you make contact with a suspect, your first words and his reaction will determine the course of the interview. You can be very friendly in a consensual encounter, starting off with a simple, "Hi, I'd like to talk to you for a minute." Understand that if all you have is your curiosity, you may have to let the suspect walk away from you if he doesn't want to talk to you.

If you are going to make a detention, you can immediately exercise authority with "Police. Stop. I need to ask you some questions." A good technique for detention is to have the suspect sit on the curb, legs in front of him crossed at the ankle. That makes it very difficult for him to run or assault you without telegraphing his intentions. Or, given probable cause to arrest for a violent felony, you can immediately use force, draw your weapon, point it at the suspect, and order him into compliance with, "Police. Don't move! Do exactly what I say, or you may be shot!"

The point of any contact is generally to gain information. With that in mind, the less authority you have to use, the better. Be as pleasant and friendly as possible, but don't be afraid to escalate to higher levels of force and authority as the situation dictates.

Always maintain your safety zone when contacting suspects.

I have found that suspects are usually far more cooperative when I explain exactly what I am doing. "We just got a phone call from a citizen that said you were walking in their driveway. I want to talk to you to find out what you were doing there." Generally, you'll get an immediate explanation, or a baldfaced lie. Either one is a good springboard for further questioning, and, in my experience, a suspect that is actively talking to me is less likely to assault me or to flee.

Patdown Searches

During a detention, you have no legal authority to conduct a full exploratory search of the suspect. However, if you have any reasonable suspicion that the person might be armed, or if you are making an arrest, you can always conduct a patdown search to check for weapons. Reasonable suspicion can be supported by the type of suspect (any suspected dangerous felon is fair game for a patdown) by the type of activity the person is involved in (assault, fight, a robbery suspect, etc.), by the people he is associated with (gang members known for violence), by seeing an object that could be a weapon, or by the suspect's behavior toward you. An angry, aggressive suspect can and should be immediately searched to lessen the threat to you.

Unless your department policy forbids it, you can search members of the opposite sex for weapons as well. Just be professional, avoid anything that might be interpreted as sexual, but be thorough. Your life depends on it!

Your patdown should be systematic. Start behind the person, and by controlling the hands, either behind his head with fingers interlaced, or behind his back. You may want to pull him back into you, causing the back to arch and throwing him off balance. This, of course, is a greater level of force, and its use will depend on the type of detention. The technique you use will also vary based on your size, suspect's size, and the situation.

Holding the suspect's hands with your left hand, begin searching with your right. Start at the top, with a hat or the collar, and work your way down all the way to the ankle. You need to run your hand across every likely hiding place, checking pockets, across the chest, into the armpits and around the waistband. You should go far enough around the front and back to ensure that you will overlap your search from the left side. Once you have completed the right side, switch hands, controlling the suspect with your right hand, and search top to bottom down the left side.

If you are searching a suspect of the opposite sex, hold your hand flat and search with the edge of the hand. While your sense of feel will not be as acute, you will easily identify anything that might be used as a weapon.

Remember the huge variety of weapons available. Widely marketed catalogs have holsters for small handguns disguised as beepers and belt buckles, and knives and swords concealed in hair brushes, combs, pens, umbrellas and canes. As you search a suspect, any hard object that can conceivably contain a weapon should be removed and secured either by handing it to your partner or by tossing it out of easy access by the suspect. Once you've determined the suspect has no weapons to use against you, you can release him and ask for identification.

Suspect Identification

During the course of any detention, you have the authority to determine who you are dealing with during that detention. If the suspect provides you with a driver's license or some equivalent government-issued identification, you can confirm that through dispatch. If you have further suspicions, you may take further steps to ensure the accuracy of the suspect's identification.

You can't search a suspect for identification unless you can show some legal justification for doing so. Some good reasons might include:

1) A suspect who admits he has identification but refuses to produce it.

2) A suspect that provides you with false information or forged documents, thus providing you with probable cause to arrest him and search for other identification.

3) A suspect that insists he has no identification, but you can clearly see has a wallet in his pocket.

4) A suspect who says he has no identification, but you can feel a wallet in his pocket during a frisk for weapons.

Asking for identification serves several purposes besides identifying the suspect. First, it gives the suspect something to do with his hands. He has to get out his wallet and fish out his identification, all of which makes him less likely to assault you with those hands. Second, once he hands you his identification, it makes him less likely to flee or assault you. You possess a valuable little piece of him at that point, and generally he won't leave without it.

When you do get some sort of official identification, you want to verify its authenticity. Most documents have some official secrets to help you spot forgeries and alterations. Driver's licenses have seals, signatures that overlap onto photos, special laminations, and coded numeric sequences that correspond to names and dates of birth. Forgeries are common. In my area a forged social security card is a bargain at five dollars, while drivers licenses and alien registration cards run from fifty to two hundred dollars depending on quality.

You will be very familiar with your own state's licenses and identifications cards, but verifying out of state I.D.'s can be difficult. The guide I carry has actual photographs and detailed security checks for all of the I.D. and license plates from each of the fifty states and Canada along with military I.D.'s, federal documents, social security documents, and bank cards. It's a tremendous tool, generally available at your local law enforcement supplier.

If the suspect can't come up with some type of official identification, ask him if he has anything with his name on it. I'll take a video rental card, library card, credit card or a letter from his mom. Anything that will provide me with a name, address, date of birth or other information. If he has no wallet or identification, I have the suspect write down his name, address, phone number and date of birth. If he can't write, I ask him the information verbally and write it down. Anything you can get provides a starting point. It mentally gets the suspect in the mode of providing information and answering questions and begins the process of providing facts for you to verify, investigate, challenge or prove false.

Once you get the basic information, you can compare it with things you know to be true. If there are multiple suspects, ask each suspect the other's name (out of each other's hearing) and compare the answers, or use his phone numbers to contact a relative and try to verify the information. If you suspect a made up address or date of birth, ask the suspect again a few moments later and see if he gives the same answer. If your dispatcher can locate a driver's license, compare the physical description with your suspect. If you suspect he is giving you someone else's information, ask him about his citation or accident history. Those are things usually only the driver will know about his license record.

Once you establish the suspect's identity, you can have dispatch check the person for any wants or warrants, and you can then begin investigating his activity.

INTERROGATION TECHNIQUES

Your position when talking to a suspect is important. You have to be close enough to talk, yet far enough away to give you a little reaction time (six to eight feet), keeping yourself as safe as possible. When alone, you should be facing the suspect and offset about 45 degrees to the suspect's side. Since most suspects are right-handed, I prefer to stand to the suspect's "weak hand" left side. Your own "strong hand," the side you wear your sidearm on, should be away from the suspect with the foot on the side slightly back. That makes it more difficult for the suspect to take away your gun, and gives you a little more time to draw and control the weapon should the need arise.

If there is a second officer on the scene, he should stand behind the suspect and to the same side as you, thus avoiding a cross fire situation. Your partner should stay mobile, moving around enough so the suspect is never exactly sure of that officer's position. This accomplishes the dual purpose of reducing the chance for aggression by the suspect and helps produce enough of a distraction to make consistent false statements by the suspect very difficult. Your hands should be in front of your body, no lower than your waist and no higher than your chin. As you write down information, keep your hands in that position, in front of your body. That allows you to react to attacks or to readily control the suspect. No doubt you've seen sloppy officers writing field interview cards on the trunks of their patrol cars with their backs to the suspects, or talking to suspects with their hands in their pockets, but sometimes appearances can fool you. I've talked to suspects on a cold evening with my hands jammed in my jacket pockets with a hidden handgun in my hand aimed directly at the suspects. Use the techniques that seem suitable for the situation.

Field Interview Cards

Your questioning of a suspect begins at a very basic level. Initially, you will ask things like: "What are you doing here?" "Where were you coming from?" "Why are you hanging around here?" and even more specific questions like, "What were you doing over there by that Rolls Royce?" Ask the questions that satisfy your suspicions and follow up on what you are told. If the suspect says he was visiting his cousin down the street, it should be an easy matter to determine if his cousin does live there and if the suspect was visiting.

If you have suspicious activity, you will want to complete an *F.I. Card* (also referred to as a "Field Interview Card," a "Field Interrogation Card," and a "Field Interview Report" or "F.I.R."). These are simple, fill in the blank type cards that document specific information. Typical information might include the following:

1) The date, time, and location of the field interview.

2) The suspect's full name, including first, last, middle, and additional information such as III, Jr., etc.

3) The suspect's nicknames, gang names, monikers, and gang affiliations.

4) The suspect's date of birth and age.

5) The suspect's driver's license or identification card number.

6) The suspect's physical description, including sex, race, hair, eyes, height, and weight.

7) The suspect's residence address.

8) The suspect's occupation, and business address or school.

9) The suspect's social security number.

10) The clothing worn, including the color and style of shirt, pants, shoes, etc.

11) Any physical oddities such as glasses, facial hair, deformities, scars, marks, and tattoos.

12) Why the suspect was contacted (loiterer, prowler, solicitor, hitchhiker, etc.)

13) Whether the suspect has a criminal record, and whether he is on parole or probation.

14) Any other associated records such as reports, arrests, bookings, or citations.

15) Any persons with the suspect.

16) Complete vehicle information including license, make, model, year, style, color, interior, damage, customization, wheels, windows, and stickers.

Your completed card is then typically routed to a clerk for computer entry or may be sent to your detective unit. In either case, remember that this represents you, the quality of your work, and the quality of your investigation. Make it neat and complete, and copy it over if needed.

Like everything else, whether you can extend a detention in order to fill out an "F.I. card" depends on the circumstances. In general, if there is a specific crime you're investigating or if there are specific facts you can describe tying this suspect to something criminal in nature, you are justified in taking the time to complete an F.I. card.

You have to continually keep in mind the purpose of your original detention and not detain the suspect any longer than it takes to complete your investigation into that particular matter. Of course, if your investigation leads to uncovering additional criminal information, you can extend the detention while you further explore those areas.

The *Miranda Warning*

On television, it seems like police officers are always reading suspects their rights. In the old *Dragnet* series, Jack Webb turned the *Miranda* warning into a high ritual and a dramatic moment. Television is **not** the real world. Generally speaking there is **no** requirement to give *Miranda* warnings in the following situations:

1) When you have detained a person on reasonable suspicion,

2) When you have detained a person for an offense for which you intend to issue a citation and release at the scene, or

3) When you are making inquiries about a person's identity or other similar information at the scene of a crime.

Pre-*Miranda* questions such as "Who are you?" "Where are you going?" and "Where are you coming from?" are generally admissible in court. Similarly, when investigating a possible drunk driver, no *Miranda* warning is required for questions such as "What did you have to drink?" and "Where are you coming from?"

Miranda warnings **are** appropriate once you've developed enough probable cause to arrest, when the length of the detention becomes unreasonable, when you use force to detain the subject you are investigating, and when the suspect is clearly in custody and the focus of the investigation is aimed at him. *Miranda* warnings may also be required by your departmental policy or by your state laws when you make an arrest. Different rules may also apply to juveniles (i.e., a juvenile's request for a parent is treated the same as an adult's request for his attorney). If you are detaining a suspect you clearly believe is responsible for a specific crime regarding his participation in that crime, you should read him his *Miranda Warning* admonition of rights as follows:

"You have the right to remain silent."

"If you give up the right to remain silent, anything you say can and will be used against you in a court of law."

"You have the right to speak with an attorney and to have the attorney present during questioning."

"If you so desire and cannot afford one, an attorney will be appointed for you without charge before questioning."

Some states add the additional statement that, "You can decide at any time to exercise these rights and not answer any questions or make any statements."

After the admonition has been given, you need to ask the following questions:

"Do you understand each of these rights I have explained to you?"

"Do you wish to give up the right to remain silent?"

"Do you wish to give up the right to speak to an attorney and have him present during questioning?"

If a suspect then says, "No, I don't want to talk to you." the interview is over. If he waives all his rights, carefully document his responses (tape recorded if possible) and then continue with your interview.

Remember, *Miranda* only applies when a suspect is in custody. If you call a suspect on the phone and talk to him, there is no need to give the *Miranda* warning. He is obviously free to leave or stop talking, so no warning is needed. You can achieve the same thing in the field or in the station lobby as long as you carefully explain the situation to the suspect. I've told suspects in all truth, "Look, you are not in custody. You are not under arrest. You are free to leave at any time, and you don't have to talk to me, but I would really like to hear your side of the story." *Miranda* does not apply, and, most of the time, the suspect has given me his side of the story.

LINE-UPS, SHOW-UPS, AND FIELD I.D.'S

A *lineup* can be either a physical grouping of people or a group of photographs presented to a witness for the purpose of trying to identify a suspect.

A *showup* is a one-on-one viewing of a suspect by a witness often conducted in the field. This is sometimes called a *curbside identification* or a *field lineup*. Showups are frequently conducted as part of a field interrogation.

In general, the courts prefer a lineup (picking out one suspect from a group of similar looking persons) to a showup in which there is only one suspect. However, the courts recognize that a showup held shortly after the crime benefits everyone involved. This is when the witnesses have the suspect's image fresh in their minds, innocent suspects can be released immediately with little infringement on their rights, and the police can continue with their investigation in other directions with a minimum of delay.

The sooner the showup takes place, the better. In an ideal situation, you stop a suspect a short distance away from the crime and, within minutes, the victim is able to identify the culprit or clear an innocent party. Any showup within an hour or so of the crime is probably reasonable, but as time passes, the legality of a field showup becomes more and more questionable (although a delay of nine hours was upheld in one case).

You can detain a suspect for the purpose of conducting a showup any time there is a reasonable suspicion to believe the suspect committed a crime. The showup is a practical and effective way of making sure you have detained the correct person. The courts require that you inconvenience the suspect as little as possible when conducting a showup. That means bringing the witness to the suspect rather than taking the suspect to the witness and not conducting a full-scale search of the suspect unless you already have probable cause to arrest and do so. (Of course, you can still pat down the suspect for weapons, and you can conduct a full scale search with the voluntary consent of the suspect.) There are three exceptions in which you can bring a suspect to the witness for identification:

1) When you have probable cause to arrest the suspect, you can take the suspect to the witness for identification.

2) When you obtain the valid, voluntary consent of the suspect to take him to the witness (always get it in writing or tape record the consent!).

3) When it is impossible or simply impractical to bring the witness to the suspect. Good examples are when the witness is injured or incapable, undergoing medical treatment, or when you just don't have enough officers to do the job.

The Supreme Court has held that it is an unfair violation of a suspect's rights to due process if the police suggest in any way to a witness that a suspect observed in a lineup or showup committed the crime. You must avoid doing anything that might influence or affect the witness' decision. If you do, you can jeopardize the whole case because your influence on a witness can "poison" his ability to ever identify the suspect again. The court describes this as "giving rise to a very substantial likelihood of irreparable misidentification."

When conducting a lineup, you, as an officer, cannot do anything that might draw the attention of the witness to any suspect. The best way to avoid mistakes is to simply say nothing and do nothing during the actual identification process.

If you have more than one witness or victim, each of them needs to view the lineup or showup separately. You cannot permit any witness to hear any other witness' comments or to compare notes about the description of the suspects. This includes both before and after the identification and remains so until the court trial is complete.

Do's and Don'ts

Prior to the identification, you can **never** tell a witness any of the following:

1) That you caught the person who committed the crime.

2) That you think you caught the person who committed the crime.

3) That you found the victim's property in the possession of the suspect.

4) That the suspect admitted anything.

5) That the suspect confessed.

6) That the suspect is a suspect. You have to use words like "person," "subject," or "young man" to describe the person to be viewed.

Prior to the identification, you should *always* tell the witness all of the following:

"We have stopped a person that we would like to you to take a look at."

"You should keep an open mind."

"The person who committed the crime may or may not be among those present."

"It is just as important that innocent persons are cleared and set free, as it is that guilty persons are identified."

"You should make no assumptions about this person's guilt just because he is in our custody or because he is wearing handcuffs."

"You should not talk to any other witness about your identification."

These items are particularly important in a showup, since there is just one person to look at and he is almost always in the custody of the police. That makes showups *automatically suggestive* and less powerful as evidence than a lineup.

The mechanics of a showup are pretty simple. You have the suspect standing at the curb, looking straight ahead. At night, you can illuminate him with patrol car spotlights or a flashlight. The witnesses are driven individually to a point where they can see the suspect, and tell the officer whether it appears to be the same person they saw commit the crime.

Even after the showup, you still need to be careful. You can't tell the witness that he picked the right or the wrong person without jeopardizing the admissibility of later identifications performed in court. On the other hand, if your witness fails to identify the suspect or seems uncertain, you can question him if you think he actually recognized the suspect.

Even when a witness clears a suspect, it is important to fully identify the suspect. Failing to do so could seriously confuse issues in a trial should you later arrest another suspect. Sometimes witnesses fail to identify the correct suspect out of fear, reluctance to be involved, or simply by mistake.

Moving the Suspect

You should always avoid transporting the suspect during the course of a detention. That will almost always turn a detention into an arrest. There are a few recognized exceptions other than those previously mentioned:

1) You can move a suspect for either your protection or his protection (due to a gathering lynch mob, unsafe traffic conditions, or some other physical danger such as a fire or flood).

2) You can move a suspect to avoid embarrassment to him (i.e., he might object to being detained out on a public sidewalk in front of a church or school).

Allowable Time for Detention

A detention is a temporary event and can last no longer than it takes you to carry out your purpose in stopping the individual. If you detain a suspect too long, it may be interpreted as an arrest by the court. As always, the standard is what is *reasonable* under the specific circumstances.

Many times what you see and hear after the initial detention makes you more suspicious than ever. In talking to the suspects, you note nervousness, agitation, lying, or even physical evidence of a crime. As an example, we stopped a pedestrian one cold evening following a report of a prowler nearby. The suspect said he was just out for a walk. In talking to him, we noticed he was sweating so much that steam was rising off his head and shoulders, he had blood spattered all over his pants and shoes, and he had several knife cuts on his palm. Given those facts, we were well justified in an extended detention while we investigated (and later arrested him for a bungled contract murder).

On the other hand, if a suspect answers all of your questions in a satisfactory manner, you have to let him go once your suspicions have been laid to rest. At that point, you need to complete your interview and get back on patrol.

Completing the Interview

There are really only two possible outcomes at the conclusion of the interview. Either you have probable cause to arrest the suspect and will do so, or you have determined that you lack probable cause and are going to release the suspect. Whatever the outcome, take care of business in a professional manner. If the suspect is to be arrested, take him into custody and take him to jail. If he is to be released, thank him for his cooperation, explain once again why you contacted him, and let him know what you are going to do with the information you gained.

The field interview process is an important function, both for the department and for you as a patrol officer. For the department, it creates a database and a means of communication that allows you to tell the detectives and patrol supervisors what is happening in your beat. If you were to interview a dozen gang members a day, every day for a month, it would be difficult for anyone to ignore the fact that you have a gang problem in your beat. F.I. cards can serve to document any problem you and the people you serve want the department to address (i.e., homelessness, loitering, truants, prostitution, illegal vendors, etc.) If you take the time to document the problem, it's much easier to get the resources you need to solve that problem.

Last of all, field interviews make you a better officer. You can't imagine how much more effective you can be when you already know the people on your beat, where they live, what they do, where they work, and with whom they hang out. Field interviews put you in tune with your service area, let you get a grip on problems before they get out of hand, give you invaluable practice in one-on-one tactics, and make you a better police officer in every way. Constantly gathering information is essential. The more you know, the better you can serve and protect.

DISCUSSION QUESTIONS

1) You contact a motorcyclist who has his hands in the pockets of a bulky jacket. Can you order him to remove his hands without turning a consensual encounter into a detention?

2) What does the word *interrogation* mean to you? Does it have positive or negative connotations? Why?

3) What experiences do you have, other than those related directly to law enforcement, that you think you might be able to use in establishing probable cause?

4) Juveniles often have no official identification. What ways could you use to establish a juvenile's identity in the field?

5) While conducting a patdown search for weapons on a person loitering outside of a market, you encounter what feels like

packages of fresh meat hidden on his person. Can you seize the meat as evidence?

6) Do you think that field interviews build better community relations? Why, or why not?

7) Have you ever been detained for a field interview? How did the process make you feel?

8) Do you think that officers should be limited to frisking only suspects of the same sex? Why or why not?

After attacking two Indio police officers and getting shot in return, a wayward pit bull apparently had had enough — so he surrendered by jumping into the front seat of a patrol car.

As officers recounted the tale of the dog, the canine was licking his wounds at the Riverside County animal shelter in Indio. The encounter with the pit bull began when officers responded to a report of armed youths gathered in front of a home.

As police neared the address, they received reports of shots fired and then spotted a car leaving the area. Officers pulled the car over, but two youths fled into a storm channel. As officers gave chase, one of the teenagers suddenly stopped and screamed that a dog had attacked him.

A moment later, the pit bull — a four foot chain dangling from his collar— jumped one of the pursuing officers, knocking him down. The officer threw the dog off and fired at the pit bull, which attacked a second officer, who also drew his handgun and fired, police said.

Grazed in the chest by one bullet, the pit bull ran to a patrol car and jumped through an open window into the front seat. The pit bull was treated by a local veterinarian for the gunshot wound and then taken to the animal shelter. The dog was quarantined there until further notice as a precaution against rabies, police said, adding that it appeared someone owned the dog because of the collar and chain.

ARRESTS

LEARNING GOALS: After studying this chapter the student
should be able to:

- State the legal requirements for making a valid arrest.

- Identify who can make an arrest.

- Describe what force can legally be used to make an arrest.

- Explain when and where you can make an arrest.

- Identify the principals in a crime.

- Describe diplomatic immunity. Explain how it affects an
  officer's ability to arrest.

- Define an arrest warrant and explain how is it obtained.

- List the basic concepts used in every arrest situation.

- Illustrate control holds and how they are used.

- List the fundamentals of gun retention for police officers.

- Name the common restraint devices used by police officers
  and explain how they are used.

- List the basic rules for transporting arrested persons to jail.

- Demonstrate the typical procedures used for booking a prisoner into a jail facility.

PROBABLE CAUSE REVISITED

To make an arrest you need *probable cause* (termed "reasonable cause" in some cases, but, for all intents and purposes, it means the same thing), a substantially greater level of justification than "reasonable suspicion."

Probable cause has been variously defined by the courts as: "such a state of facts as would lead any man of ordinary care and prudence to believe and consciously entertain an honest and strong suspicion that a person is guilty of a crime"; "Facts, or apparent facts viewed through the eyes of the experienced officer which would generate a reasonable belief that a crime has been or is about to be committed"; and "The reasonable ground or suspicion which justifies an arrest without a warrant is a state of facts which would lead a person of ordinary care and prudence to believe or entertain an honest and strong suspicion that the person is guilty of an offense." Take your pick, they all amount to about the same thing: you need facts that clearly indicate to any reasonable person that the person you arrested is involved in a specific crime.

LAWS OF ARREST

Now you have developed probable cause. You've focused on a specific individual and believe you have sufficient facts at hand that any reasonable person would believe he is guilty of an offense. Now you need to go through the mechanics and formalities of making an arrest.

In order to make a lawful arrest, you must take the person into custody "in a case and manner authorized by law" — anything else may constitute a *false arrest*. A *false arrest* may be a crime, a violation of civil rights, the source of a civil lawsuit, and may result in the loss of valuable evidence when it is excluded from the trial.

We've all heard the term "citizen's arrest" (although legal types prefer the term "private person's arrest" since you do not need to demonstrate citizenship to make an arrest). Private persons can generally arrest another person in only three specific circumstances:

1) For a public offense committed or attempted in the private person's presence.

2) When the person arrested has, in fact, committed a felony although not in the presence of the private person.

3) When a felony has been committed, and the private person has reasonable cause to believe the person arrested committed it.

Coupled with these powers for a private person to arrest comes a duty. A private person who has arrested someone must immediately take the person arrested before a judge, or deliver him to a police officer.

When a private person presents you with a person he has arrested (a very common situation when security guards arrest shoplifters), you have specific duties as a patrol officer as well. As long as you believe the arrest was lawful, you are required to take custody of the person and take him before a judge. By accepting the private person's arrest, you remain free of civil liability for false arrest.

As a police officer, you have much broader authority to arrest than private persons. Police officers in most jurisdictions can arrest a person when:

1) the officer has a warrant for the person's arrest,

2) the officer has probable cause to believe that person has committed a felony,

3) a crime was committed in the officer's presence, and

4) specific misdemeanors have been committed outside of your presence (in California, these include juvenile offenses, some DUI situations, battery on school grounds, and carrying a loaded firearm in a public place).

Your "presence" includes anything apparent to any of your senses. That includes your hearing, smell, touch, taste, and sight. Your presence can be enlarged by the use of electronic devices such as "big ear" microphones, telephones, and binoculars. If you're watching a market for shoplifters through binoculars from across the street, any crime you see occurs in your presence.

How to Make an Arrest

To demonstrate to the suspect and the court that you have established custody, you have to actually touch or restrain the suspect (unless he makes some clear indication that he is voluntarily submitting to your authority). Usually, you are going to handcuff the person and put him into your patrol car. Clearly, that demonstrates restraining the person.

You can use whatever force is reasonable and necessary to make the arrest, to overcome the suspect's resistance, and to prevent that suspect from escaping. That force must always be reasonable. If you use excessive force in any arrest, the suspect can legally resist with enough force to resist your excessive force, and then his attorneys can sue you, your sergeant, your chief, and the entire city for millions of dollars.

Felony kneeling arrest position — always control the suspect's hands first.

If the suspect resists, you are entitled to go to increasingly higher levels of force (if reasonable) until you make that arrest. Just because a person resists or threatens to resist doesn't mean that you have to back down, retreat, or desist in your efforts. While it might make sense to back away and wait for assistance, the law says you don't lose your right to self-defense by the use of force to effect the arrest, overcome resistance, or prevent the suspect's escape. In almost every case, the suspect's actions will dictate the level of force you use to arrest him. When a suspect arms himself with a deadly weapon, it is generally reasonable for you to respond with deadly force.

When your force is reasonable, the suspect has a duty under law to submit to your arrest, even if he thinks (or knows) the arrest is unlawful. Anything else is a separate crime of resisting arrest.

To establish a lawful arrest, you need to tell the suspect three things:

1) Your authority ("Police Officer!")

2) Your intent ("Don't move! You are under arrest...")

3) Your reason or cause for the arrest ("... for burglary.")

You don't have to comply with these three steps when the circumstances are obvious to a reasonable person. If you are in a distinctive police uniform, you would be excused from stating that you are a police officer. If you catch him crawling out a residential window with a TV under his arm, it's obvious he's being arrested for burglary, and you *may* be excused from stating that obvious fact. If you knock on his door and he flees into the house, it's obvious that he knows you are the police and you don't have to advise him any further. On the other hand, if any suspect you arrest asks you specific questions ("Are you really a cop? Am I under arrest? What am I being arrested for?"), you are legally obligated to answer.

Once you have placed the person under arrest and have him restrained, it is reasonable for you to search the person for dangerous weapons if you have some reason to believe he might possess one. More than one sloppy officer has had his brains splattered all over the windshield of his patrol car by failing to search a felony suspect for weapons. Don't make that same mistake!

When you do find a deadly weapon, remove it, and get it away from the suspect. Then continue searching for more weapons. Once you have thoroughly searched the prisoner, then you can worry about securing those weapons in a safe place, booking them into evidence, etc.

Where You Can Arrest

There are some limitations as to where you can arrest a person. The U.S. Constitution and resulting laws have always protected homes from intrusion by the government, so some special rules are in place to limit your actions. As a general rule, you must have an arrest warrant in order to arrest someone inside his home, and you must normally comply with the "knock and notice" rules. The rules for homes generally mean any place the suspect resides and can include tents, motel rooms, boats, vans, and even a homeless person's park bench. Police are simply not allowed inside a person's home without the judicial authorization of a warrant, an emergency situation (*exigent circumstances*), or the valid permission from the occupant (*consent*). You are also limited by your *jurisdiction*, (the geographical boundaries of your agency). The places and situations where you **are** allowed to arrest a person include:

1) a public place (which includes a person in a vehicle on any public highway).

2) a person inside his home (or someone else's home, business, or hotel room) if you have an arrest warrant and you reasonably believe the suspect is inside.

3) a person inside his home when you have the consent of the owner (or other person legally in charge) to enter.

4) a person inside his home when *exigent circumstances* exist. (***Exigent circumstances*** means that some emergency situation exists that requires immediate action on your part because of the possibility of danger to life, serious damage to property, the imminent escape of a suspect, or the destruction of evidence or property.)

5) a person inside his home when you are already lawfully inside for some other reason.

You can arrest a person outside of your jurisdiction only when:

1) the crime was committed in your agency's jurisdiction,

2) exigent circumstances exist, or

3) you have the consent of the agency within whose jurisdiction the arrest is taking place.

To make an arrest in a person's home, you can break open the door or window of the house in which the suspect is hiding as long as you have reasonable grounds for believing the suspect is inside and as long as you have given *knock and notice*. **Knock and notice** means that an officer must knock, identify his authority and purpose ("Police officer, we have an arrest warrant for John Smith!"), demand admittance ("Open the door!"), and then wait a reasonable amount of time before entering.

The amount of time that is reasonable is a judgment call on your part. At 3 o'clock in the morning, two or three minutes might be prudent to give the suspect long enough to wake up, throw on a robe, and get to the door. On the other hand, if you can see a person inside or believe he might arm himself or destroy the evidence (flushing dope down the toilet has always been popular), a wait of only a second or two might be appropriate. The standard, as always, is what would a reasonable person with my training, knowledge, and experience do in this situation?

When You Can Arrest

The law also places some limitations on when you can arrest a person. In most jurisdictions, you cannot make an arrest for a misdemeanor or infraction during the night (generally between 10 p.m. and 6 a.m.) unless:

1) You are accepting a private person's arrest;

2) The arrest is made in a public place (streets, cars on streets, and any premises such as restaurants or theaters that are open to the public);

3) The crime occurred in your presence;

4) The person is already in custody (or in jail) on some other charge (that's similar to #2 above, since jails are essentially public places in which a suspect has little or no expectation of privacy); or

5) You have a misdemeanor warrant that is specially "endorsed" by a judge for nighttime service.

In misdemeanor cases, you also have to arrest a person at the time the crime is committed in your presence or within a reasonable amount of time from when the crime was committed. Unless you are in fresh pursuit of the suspect (i.e., actively investigating and searching for the suspect), any delay will require you to wait until you can take your evidence before a judge and get a warrant for the person's arrest.

For felonies, there are no time restrictions; you can arrest at any time of the day or night, with or without a warrant.

Who You Can Arrest

You can arrest any of the parties to a crime, specifically any *principal*, *accessory*, or *accomplice*. These terms may vary considerably from state to state with terms like *perpetrator*, *abettor*, *accessory after the fact*, and *co-conspirator*, but most of the fundamental concepts remain the same.

The California Penal Code defines a ***principal*** as someone who:

1) commits any crime,

2) aids and abets in committing any crime,

3) advises and encourages committing any crime, or

4) uses some innocent person to commit a crime.

The actual wording is a bit more specific and confusing, stating:

> All persons concerned in the commission of a crime, whether it is a felony or a misdemeanor, and whether they directly commit the act constituting the offense, or aid and abet in its commission, or not being present, have advised and encouraged its commission, and all persons counseling, advising, or encouraging children under the age of 14 years, lunatics or idiots, to commit any crime, or who, by fraud, contrivance or force, occasion the drunkenness of another for the purpose of causing him to commit any crime, or who, by threats, menaces, command, or coercion compel

another to commit any crime, are principals in any crime so committed.

An accessory is someone who helps out a felon after the crime. You have to prove the accessory had knowledge that a felony had been committed, that the person he was helping was wanted for that felony, and that aiding him might let the suspect avoid arrest, trial, conviction, or punishment.

The actual wording in California law reads:

> Every person who, after a felony has been committed, harbors, conceals or aids a principal in such felony, with the intent that said principal may avoid or escape from arrest, trial, conviction or punishment, having such knowledge that said principal has committed such felony or has been charged with such felony or convicted thereof, is an accessory to such felony.

An accomplice is simply a principal who testifies against another principal. Again, California law is a little confusing but states, "An accomplice is hereby defined as one who is liable to prosecution for the identical offense charged against the defendant on trial in the cause in which the testimony of the accomplice is given." Because the courts don't trust criminals all that much, the testimony of an accomplice is insufficient to convict a principal unless supported by other evidence.

Who You Can't Arrest

As nutty as it sounds, there are certain people you generally can't arrest, and others you generally shouldn't arrest, because they are legally incapable of committing a crime (but you can take them into custody). To be guilty of a crime, there has to be "a unity of act and intent." In other words, you have to want to commit a crime and then take action toward committing that crime. Some people can't form that unity of act and intent. If you think arrest is appropriate, go ahead and arrest because most of these exceptions are legal defenses in court but don't prohibit you from making an arrest. However, if you have clear evidence that the person who committed the act falls into one of these classes, you are generally better off not arresting. Document the incident, and then submit it for filing. Those classes of people include:

1) Children under the age of 14, unless you can show proof that they knew what they did was wrong.

2) Idiots. While it can be tempting to classify many of the people you meet as idiots, the legal definition is someone with an I.Q. below 26 ("average" persons are between 90 to 100) and are thus incapable of knowing right from wrong.

3) Persons who commit the act through ignorance or mistake. This doesn't include ignorance of the law, but rather someone who makes "an honest mistake," taking property he mistakes as his own, trespassing on property he believed was public land, etc.

4) Persons who commit the act unconscious of their actions. A person who was sleepwalking, slipping into a diabetic coma, or drugged by another person is not responsible for his condition or for acts while in that commission.

5) Persons who commit the act through misfortune or by accident. A person driving at a safe speed with reasonable care who kills a child who runs out from between two cars isn't a murderer.

6) Persons who commit the act under threat to their lives (except for acts punishable by death). If someone stands behind you in line at the local convenience store with a knife in your back and tells you, "Take all the clerk's money and get a medium cherry Slurpee or I'll kill you," it's a reasonable and valid defense for you to feel your life is threatened and carry out the act.

Immunity

In the United States there are approximately 120,000 individuals who are entitled to some degree of special privilege under international law. There are ambassadors, consuls, secretaries, attachés, military liaisons, blatant spies and various flunkies, along with their wives, children, nannies, servants and janitors. For each of these categories of persons, different degrees of immunity may apply. Unless you're working in a major international diplomatic community such as New York City or Washington D.C., you have very little chance at remembering all the specific levels of immunity enjoyed by each person in each position.

In general, persons who are covered under full diplomatic immunity (generally only heads of state and the most senior diplomats such as Ambassadors) are not prosecutable for any crime or tort they commit. That doesn't mean they can't be stopped, detained, cited, or arrested just like anyone else; they simply are not liable for prosecution. Once arrested, the matter is referred to the Department of State, and for serious offenses the diplomat may be declared "persona non gratis" and effectively "booted out" of the country.

When you do encounter a diplomat, he will often be driving a car with "Diplomat" or "Consul" license plates and will offer you special I.D. issued by the U.S. Department of State. It's not a "Get Out of Jail Free" card, it's more like a "Quick, Call the Feds" card. You have an absolute right to protect other people and the public safety. Only when your sole purpose is to interfere with diplomatic processes could you be guilty of a federal offense.

In my career, I've encountered a number of diplomats and many more persons who claimed diplomatic immunity. These included the Ambassador from China (a real diplomat), a car full of gentlemen from the former Soviet Union that I swore were from the K.G.B. (with limited diplomatic immunity), and the son of a Kuwaiti oil engineer who tried to claim immunity for his drunken crimes at a fraternity house (no immunity). If you contact a person who claims diplomatic immunity, you should treat the person with respect, but go ahead and ask for his Department of State identification, and then take the action you think appropriate as far as detaining the offender. Then, immediately notify your supervisor. Diplomatic immunity is not intended to serve as a license to mock the law or to allow individuals or their countries to escape responsibility for the crimes they commit.

Last of all, recognize that you may deal with our own politicians. Treat them with the respect due any citizen, and always notify your superiors, but do your job. Although the U.S. Constitution seems to indicate that U.S. representatives and senators cannot be arrested for misdemeanors (U.S.C.A. Const. Art. 1 Sec. 6, cl. 1.), that is not the case. The ranks of former senators and mayors in prison stand as testimony to their lack of immunity in felony matters. U.S. senators and representatives do enjoy some limited privilege from arrest during their actual attendance at a session of Congress. Chances are that unless you're working within the District of Columbia, you won't encounter that particular problem. You do your job in protecting the community, and let your superiors and the politicians argue about the politics of prosecution.

Certain witnesses are also immune from arrest. In general, a person who enters your state in obedience to a court order or a subpoena cannot be arrested for any crime committed prior to his coming back into the state. Similarly, witnesses passing through your state on the way to or from testifying in obedience to a subpoena in another state cannot be arrested for crimes committed prior to entering the state. These laws simply exist to expedite court cases by encouraging people to appear as witnesses. If they enter the state and then commit a crime on the way to the trial, they are fair game for arrest for any crimes they commit.

Warrants

As a patrol officer, you'll deal with arrest warrants in a number of ways. First of all, you'll "run" a lot of persons you contact and detain to determine if any warrants exist for their arrest and "serve" the warrant by arresting the suspect and taking him to jail. When you develop probable cause to arrest a suspect in one of your cases, you may go before a judge to obtain an arrest warrant. When you've filed completed criminal cases with a named suspect who is not yet in custody, judges will issue warrants for the suspect's arrest. And last of all, you will be given arrest warrants on other cases and assigned to go looking for that specific suspect.

You need not have the actual warrant in your possession to arrest a suspect. Sometimes you will have a warrant "abstract" (a summary of the information on the warrant), but even just your good faith knowledge that a warrant exists is sufficient to make the arrest.

Warrants are justification in themselves for immediate arrest, because probable cause to arrest has already been established before a judge. This can be as a result of a complaint being filed that satisfies the court that the offense has been committed and that there are reasonable grounds to believe the named suspect has committed the offense, or it can be obtained before the complaint is filed.

These warrants (often called "Ramey" warrants after a California Supreme Court case) are issued on affidavits (sworn statements) by police officers (the "affiant") establishing their probable cause. The judge evaluates the officer's affidavit and, if he finds sufficient probable cause, can issue the arrest warrant even though no criminal complaint has actually been filed.

Generally, arrest warrants are valid until they are recalled by the judge. Nonetheless, mistakes are made and sometimes warrants don't get "pulled" from computer systems after service. Always verify a warrant with the issuing agency as soon as possible after service (and beforehand if you know you are going after a specific suspect). In addition, courts like to see "good faith" efforts to serve warrants by going after the suspect. It's a good practice to attempt to serve known arrest warrants to demonstrate to the court that you are actively pursuing the suspect in the case.

A typical affidavit might read as follows:

State of California
County of Los Angeles
**AFFIDAVIT IN SUPPORT OF
PROBABLE CAUSE ARREST WARRANT**

Your affiant, Officer Mary Black, is employed as a peace officer for the Metropolitan Police Department and has attached hereto and incorporates by reference official reports and records of a law enforcement agency. These reports were prepared by law enforcement officers and contain factual information and statements obtained from victims, witnesses, and others which establish the commission of the following criminal offense(s): PC 459 -Residential Burglary, by the following person: John DeHaviland Smith.

WHEREFORE, your affiant prays that a warrant of arrest be issued for said person.

(signed) Officer Mary Black.

MECHANICS OF ARREST

As a police officer, you are bound and constrained in your use of force by law (the Penal Code), your department policy, and ethics. Keeping that in mind, you must always understand that force is a part of law enforcement. Some degree of force is used in every arrest. The only question is the amount of force to be used. If you start to lose control of a suspect, you must automatically increase force levels to stop that suspect's aggression and escape. If you begin to lose control and cannot or will not rise to a higher level of force, you must back away and safeguard your own life. Coming home at the end of your shift represents a win for you. You must win every single day or there will never be another. You must want to survive more than the bad guy. Nothing can be more important to you than the will to survive and win.

Part of survival includes career survival. To continue your career and to stay out of federal prison, your use of force must always be reasonable. In order for it to be reasonable, you must master a wide variety of weapons, tactics, techniques and restraints. Like anything else, practice counts. The more you do something, the more automatic it becomes and the better equipped you are to handle arrests.

Your knowledge and use of arrest techniques must be similar. There are hundreds of techniques — control holds, twist locks, wrist locks, take-downs, leg sweeps and pain compliance holds. There are bar-arm holds, carotid holds, and modified carotid holds. There are punches, jabs, feints, kicks, and throws. Some or all of these tools may be allowed by your particular agency; some may be forbidden. These are the tools you use to arrest people, and just like your gun and baton, you need constant practice to keep your skills at a proficient level.

Unless you are a martial arts expert and work out an hour or more a day, you will likely not be able to keep a high level of expertise in every technique. You are better off learning and practicing a few techniques that work consistently for you, and learning some general concepts of self defense that you utilize in every situation. At the same time, you have to be aware that in jails and prisons all across America, there are inmates conducting role-playing training and practicing techniques to counter everything you know. Be flexible and alert, and practice, practice, practice.

Basic Concepts

There are six key concepts to keep in mind for every arrest situation.

1) Prevent problems before they happen. Taking control of the suspect from the first moment of encounter will help avoid assaults. Establish firm control by placing suspects where you want, preferably sitting down with their hands in sight. Think ahead and keep control.

2) Maintain situational alertness. You must keep your focus on the situation at hand, monitoring the suspect's hands at all times, being aware of all other persons in your proximity.

3) Don't over-commit. Never jump into a situation you aren't sure you can handle on your own. If you're going to arrest a large unruly suspect, wait until more officers arrive to help you. That way the outcome will be obvious to both you and the suspect. If you get in over your head, don't be afraid to back away and wait for help.

4) Never meet an attack head-on. Deflect blows to the side, and if attacked, side-step and allow the suspect to pass by into a more vulnerable position.

5) Always use superior force. The suspect's resistance will dictate what force you use. With no resistance, a few simple commands will establish control and allow you to arrest. Meet physical resistance with a baton or chemical weapons. If attacked by a knife, use your gun, and stop that attack. You must survive every attack, you must win every fight. To not win may mean death.

6) Take the suspect to the ground. Whenever you engage a suspect in a fight, take the suspect down to the ground. Use your weight, use your partners, use your weapons and keep him on the ground. It's far safer for you, and far easier to effect most arrests, with a suspect on the ground.

Control Techniques

Most officers are not experts on control techniques. Ninety-nine percent of arrests are made by establishing verbal control and talking the suspect into handcuffs. It's a simple matter of projecting total self-confidence (backed up by a lot of experience and training), informing the suspect that he is under arrest, and ordering him to turn around, and either place his hands behind his back or on top of his head. Then handcuff, search, and stuff him into the patrol car.

There is, however, that one percent of arrests when you may have to use force. Know and practice a few simple techniques which usually combine a foot sweep with a take down or pain compliance hold to bring the suspect to the ground. Then apply your weight to some portion of his body to convince him to submit. Only on rare occasions is some additional convincing needed.

You need to be highly flexible and capable of adapting your tactics to the situation. I was once faced with a very large man in the center of the rear seat of a taxi. A half-dozen cops were standing around trying to figure out what to do with this man. He was refusing to get out, had both arms locked down to his sides with his hands deep in the crack of the seat gripping the metal supports. He was a big guy and breaking his hold would be difficult. I needed something that would get his hands free so I could grab him and yank him out. I told him if he didn't immediately get out of the taxi, I was going to grab him by the nose and yank him out. He told me I wouldn't dare, so I immediately reached in and grabbed his nose as hard as I could. He did the predictable response, he let go of the seat and grabbed for his nose. I grabbed his free hand and yanked him out of the car and to the ground.

The "nose take-down" is not a technique you can learn in an academy class. It was a great and effective tactic for that particular situation, but nobody taught it to me. All I did was apply my basic principles: apply pain compliance to break a hold, grab a hand, and take the suspect to the ground. It worked well for me, because I practice those principles. You have to learn tactics that work well for you given your particular size, physical abilities, and the time commitment afforded to train and practice.

Officers don't really like control holds, because it ties them up physically with the suspect. It is much better to gain control verbally from a safe distance, direct the suspect to a position you like, and then only engage him when handcuffing.

Good control techniques make your job much safer and easier.

The tactics you use will be limited by law, department policy, your training, and by community attitudes. For example, during the 1970's the Los Angeles Police Department still taught and used a variety of chokeholds, applying pressure to a suspect's neck to cut off the blood supply to the brain, rendering the suspect unconscious. Obviously, that's a serious level of force, and with some six thousand officers in the department it was inevitable that some suspects died after being restrained by those holds. The media publicized the deaths, and political pressure brought about restrictions, modification, and then finally a total ban on all forms of chokeholds.

Even if your department teaches and allows these holds, you have to know how your community will feel when they see them used. Restraining a drunken biker at a bar fight with a modified carotid might be perfectly acceptable, but using the same hold on a drunken school teacher on a street corner at noon might outrage the citizens. As always, you have to be in touch with the community you patrol and modify your tactics accordingly.

Gun Retention

In every fight with a suspect, possession of your gun should be the number one thought in your mind. If the suspect gets your gun, you're at his mercy and your parents or spouse may be getting a neatly folded flag as the guest of honor at your funeral. There are several key concepts to keeping your gun out of a suspect's hands.

1) Always keep your gun side away from suspects, dropping your strong leg back to protect your weapon.

2) Use a safe, well-made, well-maintained holster with a sturdy safety strap and other retention devices.

3) Keep your distance. You should never let a suspect get within arm's reach. Generally, six to eight feet is a safe distance to interview suspects.

4) Wait for back-up. The greatest deterrent to someone going for your gun is the presence of someone else to shoot him if he tries.

5) Disable and cuff (behind the back) every arrestee before searching. Double-lock every time you cuff.

If a suspect does manage to grab your gun, you have only two options — either disengage (get away from the suspect) or engage (take the suspect with you and incapacitate him). In either case, you must retain control of the gun. He will be focused on that gun and gaining control of it. If you can keep yourself under control, you can use his focus to your advantage, attacking him where he least expects it.

If your gun is in its holster when grabbed, use your hand to pin his hand (or hands) and your gun tightly to your body. Then use your body weight to twist into him, bending his wrist backward. At the same time, kick him in the crotch or jab the fingers of your weak hand as hard as you can into his eyes or throat. As you attack with your weak hand, shift your grip on the gun hand to grab one of his fingers. Rip backwards as hard as you can, with the intent of breaking that finger and causing as much pain as possible. As he releases, kick away from him and get some distance between you. Remember, you are fighting for your life and fighting over the device that can kill you. A very high level of force is completely reasonable. Be utterly ruthless — survive!

The second option is to engage the suspect, attaching yourself to him and not letting go. You use the same techniques, clamping down on his hand, twisting, and attacking with your weak hand. Now as he reacts to the pain, keep his hand clamped down and use your body mass and weight to drive into him, pushing him backwards, off-balance, and down, while simultaneously bending his wrist backwards until you can peel it off your gun and into a control hold. If you need to, use your weight and take the suspect to the ground. Continue your weak hand attack until he is incapacitated and down, and then bring his hands behind him and cuff.

If you are fighting for an unholstered weapon, the principle is the same. Whether it is a handgun or a long weapon such as a rifle, use both hands to bring the weapon to your chest, and clamp it to your body. Now you can use your entire body weight, turning your body to aim the gun at the suspect and away from you and others. Try this; practice it. Make the weapon a part of your body. No one can wrench away a gun that weighs two hundred pounds (or whatever you weigh). If the suspect continues to fight you, simply pivot your body with the gun clamped to your chest until the muzzle is facing the suspect, and then pull the trigger. You may receive a burn from the muzzle flash. The suspect will receive a point-blank bullet hole. You go home for dinner — he doesn't.

Restraints

When we talk about restraints in police work, most of us think in terms of metallic handcuffs connected by a metal chain. Indeed, handcuffs are the primary restraint tool you will use day after day in patrol, but the list of restraints used by law enforcement also includes: handcuffs joined by hinges and cables, non-metallic handcuffs, leather cuffs, thumbcuffs, disposable restraints, handcuff bags, body wraps, straight jackets, gang chains, waist chains, transport belts, nylon straps, hobbles, and seatbelts.

Like every other tool in your inventory, it's up to you to become an expert with the restraints you carry. Learn the restraints you are allowed to carry. Know how they work, and practice their application. Used properly, they will keep you safe. Used improperly, you are simply providing the suspect with another weapon to use against you.

You should also think in terms of multiple suspects. How many people can you reasonably be expected to arrest? I carry two pairs of handcuffs on my Sam Brown (one standard, one hinged), two extra pairs in my patrol box, along with two hobbles and a dozen plastic strap restraints. I can arrest a whole group of people. It may seem like over-reaction, but I've been on party calls where we've made dozens of arrests and utilized every restraint we had.

The most common restraints used by patrol officers are handcuffs (either hinged or standard), plastic strap restraints ("Flex-cuffs"), hobbles, and leg irons.

Standard handcuffs will fit 95% of all suspects. Some small, limber persons will be able to fit their hands through the smallest opening and escape (plastic straps are a good alternative) and some very large people will have wrists too large to be handcuffed (again, you can interlink two plastic straps with one on each wrist and arrest anyone smaller than Godzilla).

The *standard handcuff* is made of high grade steel and consists of two ratcheting bracelets, each with a hinged portion with about twenty teeth. The bracelets have a swivel at their base and the two swivels are connected by two links of chain. A very strong suspect can sometimes break standard handcuffs, but it's rare.

Hinged handcuffs (sometimes called "Gorilla Cuffs") are joined at the bases with a hinge and are much stronger. The bracelet themselves are about 25 percent larger and accommodate much bigger suspects. Because there is no pivot, you can place one bracelet on a suspect's wrist and then rotate the other to gain pain compliance.

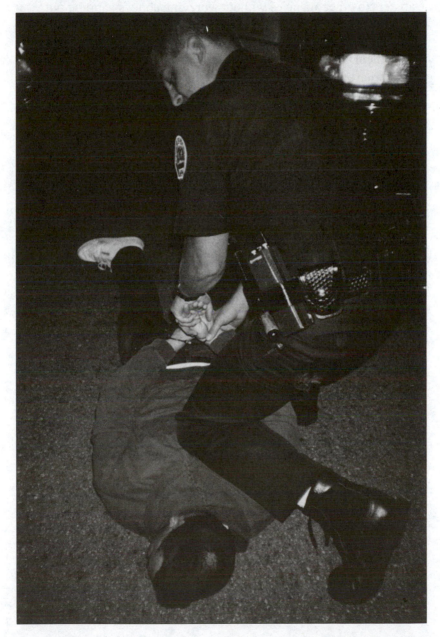

A knee between the shoulders pins the suspect while you secure the restraints.

Plastic strap restraints are concealable, disposable, and incredibly strong. They are cheap, so they can be used for mass arrests or transfers to other agencies without worrying about swapping out your handcuffs to avoid losing your equipment. They are light and easy to carry; many officers tuck some under their keepers on their Sam Brown or coil them in their hat. Use them just as you would handcuffs, placing one loop around each wrist, back of the hands together, behind the back. Care has to be taken to apply them tight enough to avoid escape without cutting off circulation. They are easily removed by cutting with a knife or scissors. I have also used them as leg-irons to secure one of multiple suspects to a fence in a foot pursuit and to lock up a stolen bicycle while I went to look for a suspect.

Hobbles are simply a nylon strap or rope with a clip at one end, and either a clip or a loop at the other. Since PCP first started hitting the street, most officers have carried one on their Sam Brown (a leather, single-carrier for a .45 semi-auto seems just about the right size.) They are used primarily to "hog-tie" a violent already handcuffed prisoner. The usual procedure is to loop one end around a suspect's ankle, bring the strap around the other ankle (generally looping around both ankles like a cowboy roping a calf), then through the middle of the ankles, clipping the loose end to the chain of the handcuffs. This forces both the ankles and the hands down toward the buttocks, and prevents the prisoner from kicking and running.

Several suspects have died of suffocation and/or heart attacks in the back seat of patrol cars while restrained in this manner. It seems more likely to occur when the suspect is intoxicated or under the influence of drugs, and more likely to occur when the suspect is overweight. Anytime you are forced to restrain a violent prisoner in this manner, he should be placed in the patrol car on his side (never face-down) and monitored continuously for breathing.

An alternative is to place the hand-cuffed suspect upright in the patrol car, then loop the hobble around the ankles and to a seat mount, keeping the suspect upright in the car. Hobbles can also be used as a gang-chain, connecting two or more prisoners together by the handcuffs. They also make a good dog leash for those stray Rottweilers you encounter on duty.

Escapes from Restraints

Properly applied handcuffs are a great tool for 95 percent of the population. Then there's that 5 percent that seem to spend a whole lot of time figuring out how to get out of them. Magicians have made a career out of removing handcuffs, something easily done with a lock-pick or even a straight pin if you know how. It is always a relief to get a suspect into handcuffs, but even a handcuffed prisoner must be watched constantly to avoid his escape.

Many suspects carry handcuff keys or lock picks. One juvenile I arrested had his key taped to the inside of his belt at the center of his back. (I later found out his mother, a former police officer, had given him the key.) I've found other suspects with cuff keys, shims, and lock picks in their back pockets or hidden in seams.

Look at the one lonely tooth on a handcuff key, and you can see that the lock mechanism in a pair of handcuffs is very simple. (There are some high security cuffs with fancier keys available). Any thin, stiff object could be used to pick a set of handcuffs. Prisoners have been known to open handcuffs with a standard plastic pocket comb and with the insert from a ball point pen.

Any reasonably agile suspect can "slip" the cuffs, bring his hands around his buttocks and step through the cuffs, and bring his hands up in front of his body. In this position the suspect can attack you, shoot you, or drive away in your patrol car (which would likely bring about some thought-provoking memos from your chief).

Suspects with small hands, or those who are highly flexible or double-jointed, may be able to simply slip their hands out of the handcuff bracelets.

Particularly strong suspects, or those under the influence of alcohol or drugs to the point of feeling no pain, have on rare occasions been able to snap the chain on a pair of standard handcuffs. Oftentimes this ends up breaking their wrists, but, feeling no pain, they don't care and may assault you despite their injuries.

Seatbelts have proven to be a handy tool for escape. Prisoners have used the flat blade portion to pry the double-finger portion of the handcuff apart, releasing the single-finger at the hinge and allowing the bracelet to fall apart. They have also used the square hole in the blade portion of a seatbelt as a wrench to twist apart the stud. You need to watch a handcuffed prisoner every minute.

Handcuff Application

There are many different ways of putting handcuffs on a person you arrest, and the methods you use are going to depend on your size, the suspect's size, the nature of the arrest, the environment, how much back-up you have, and how aggressively the suspect is resisting. If you're wrestling a suspect to the floor in a dark bar, you'll count yourself lucky to get the handcuffs on the suspect instead of your partner. Once you get the cuffs on and the situation better under control, you can always adjust them.

Ideally, a suspect should be handcuffed behind his back, with his palms facing outward. This position makes it more difficult to extract a hidden key, or to use a key or a pick on the handcuffs. The cuffs should be positioned with the keyholes facing up toward the elbows. This makes it a lot easier to remove the cuffs safely and more difficult for the suspect to use a key or a pick on the lock mechanisms.

The cuffs should always be double-locked (by sticking the little pin on the handcuff key into the holes in the base of the locks). The cuffs should be fit snugly around the wrists, without cutting into the skin, and provide just a tiny bit of slack. Many suspects will complain that the cuffs are too tight. Don't take their word for it, it's a common ploy to give them a little more room to escape. Handcuffs weren't designed for comfort, they were designed for your security. If they aren't cutting into the skin, they aren't too tight.

Since you need two hands to handcuff a suspect, you can't hold a gun on a suspect at the same time. You are always safer with a minimum of two officers — one to handcuff, the other to cover. If you are the handcuffing officer, holster your gun and snap the restraining strap in place. This gives both you and your partner time to react in case the suspect goes for your gun.

There are two primary handcuffing techniques. The first is the kinder and gentler of the two and assumes a certain level of cooperation from the suspect. With the suspect standing, you order him to turn around (facing away from you) and place his hands behind his back with the palms facing outward. You secure your gun in its holster, pull out your handcuffs with your strong hand, and hold them by the chain with the keyholes facing upward and the single-fingers facing toward the suspect. Then you simply push the cuffs onto the suspect's wrists, securing each bracelet snugly around the wrist and then double-lock.

The second is a higher profile, more secure method. Order the suspect to place both hands on top of his head with the fingers interlaced. You can use this method with a suspect that is standing, sitting, or kneeling. You approach the suspect from behind and grab his interlaced fingers with your left hand. This gives you a little bit of control over the suspect, but, more importantly, it lets you feel his hands and makes him more likely to telegraph any attack to you. If the suspect's wrists are covered by his cuff or sleeve, push it back toward the elbow with your right hand. Pull your handcuffs out with your right hand, and hold the base of one cuff in your hand with the two-finger side of the bracelet up. Place the single finger side against his right wrist and snap down smartly. (Since roughly 90 percent of the population is right-handed, you want to immobilize his strong hand first). This will cause the cuff to flip around his wrist and lock. Tighten the cuff around his wrist if needed.

Now you bring his right hand down and behind his back, by pulling on the unused cuff. This is the most dangerous moment, since he has the opportunity to break away and use the cuff as a weapon to strike you with. As you pull his right hand into his back, you are essentially in a control hold. Use the your right hand to position the unused cuff above the suspect's right wrist, with the single finger facing toward you. Then bring his left hand down and toward his back, snapping it into the unused cuff. You should end up with both hands cuffed, palms facing outward, key holes facing up. It takes practice to do right.

Transportation of Prisoners

Now that the suspect is handcuffed and has been advised why he has been arrested (the charge), you need to get him to jail. There are a number of things you need to do to get the prisoner safely to jail. Of course, the primary rule is that anyone you transport is handcuffed. I once refused a direct order from a lieutenant to **not** handcuff a prisoner. I just flatly refused to do so (I think I told him I wasn't going to play Russian Roulette if he ordered me to either). He was really upset at me and ended up driving the prisoner to jail himself. I am alive to tell you about the incident and have no regrets about refusing to compromise on a critical point of officer safety. I was lucky, too; I never got reprimanded or punished, but my evaluations suffered for a little while.

Once you handcuff a prisoner, he needs to be searched again. With your partner covering, you want to carefully search his entire body, removing anything that represents a danger to you. Virtually any hard object can represent a weapon, and anything thin and pointed could be used to attack the handcuffs. Usually I ask a suspect, "Do you have anything that might hurt me? Any needles, razor blades, or knives?" Some suspects will tell you, and you can prevent being injured. Others will tell you to go to hell. Regardless of the response, check carefully, starting at the top of his head and working your way down every pocket, seam, and belt loop.

Once he has been searched, you need to search the patrol car where he'll be sitting. You need to check the floor and under the seat, first to make sure that he's not going to find any weapons (I've found guns lost by officers in the back seat of patrol cars) and second, so that if some evidence shows up after the transportation run, you know that only your suspect could have dropped it there.

Ideally you will have a cage in your car, making any transportation a lot safer. With a cage or a second officer, the suspect should be placed in the rear on the passenger's side. Without a cage, your partner will sit in the rear directly behind the driver. This provides better protection for the driver against attack or interference with his driving.

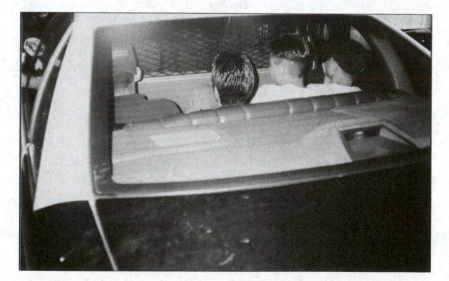

Sometimes you will transport more than one prisoner at a time.

If you're working a one-man unit without a cage, you will have to place the suspect in the front seat. Always secure the suspect with a seatbelt, both to protect him from injury and to restrain his movements. Remember, since he is in custody, you are totally responsible for his safety.

Generally, you will have informed the dispatcher that you have made an arrest. Anytime you are going to transport a juvenile or a suspect of the opposite sex, you should also tell the dispatcher the time of your departure for the jail and the mileage on your patrol car. Give the same information on your arrival at jail, thus you have a complete record of the distance you covered and the time it took. Suspects know it's to their advantage to claim you violated their rights. They may claim you stopped to beat them, question them, or sexually assault them. Having a dispatch record of your time and mileage can help to lay to rest any false charges.

JAIL AND CUSTODY PROCEDURES

Once you arrive at the jail, officer safety should remain your primary concern. At many jail facilities, you will drive into a secure area, either a fenced courtyard or a sally-port (sort of an armored garage). You should secure all weapons and unnecessary keys. (Assume the worst — that as soon as you enter the jail you will be taken hostage by prisoners. Get rid of your guns, knives, batons, tear gas, and car keys.) Usually there is some kind of gun vault, individual safes where you lock your stuff up and take the key. In some facilities, you will have to make do with locking your weapons in the trunk of your car.

When you are ready, go ahead and open the rear door and help the prisoner out. One of you should retain control over the prisoner while the second does a quick search of the rear seat where the prisoner was sitting. If you search carefully, you may find rocks of cocaine, paper bindles, cash, keys, evidence, and weapons: all sorts of things the prisoner doesn't want you to know he possessed.

Most jails have careful security — gates, guard shed, fences, etc.

Prisoner Movements

Your prisoner is your responsibility until the jailer takes over. You have to move him through the facility to the booking area, keeping control over him. In your own facility, you may well have keys to all the doors, and you will have to protect them carefully. In a large jail, control officers will open and shut doors for you, allowing you to move through the jail.

Once in the booking area, you can begin to process the prisoner. In a large jail, you may have to wait for your turn in a long line of officers. In a smaller jail, you may have to do all the booking yourself.

Different prisoners are segregated into different areas of the jail. Males and females are separated, as are juveniles and adults (for example, in California, juveniles generally cannot be held for more than six hours in a local jail, cannot be handcuffed to any stationary object, cannot be in a room with a locked door or outside of direct adult supervision). Rival gang members may be housed in different modules of the jail. Those with medical problems and contagious diseases will be isolated, and efforts will be made to keep gays and straights apart.

Booking Searches

The first step is a thorough search of the prisoner (generally, you will always use an officer of the same sex as the prisoner to conduct booking searches). Protect yourself with rubber gloves. You should remove every piece of property from the prisoner — the contents of his pockets, any jewelry, belts, watches, rings, etc. All these items should be bagged, labeled, and inventoried in accordance with your agency's policies. Often your policy will be to discard certain items such as open foods, cigarettes and matches.

Only after searching should you remove the handcuffs. You need to be wary of assault, since uncuffing a prisoner gives him the freedom to attack, and an open handcuff can be a dangerous weapon. To remove the handcuffs, I generally place the suspect against the wall with his legs spread wide (you can also have him stand with his legs crossed, giving him a much more awkward stance to attack from). Tell him you are going to remove the handcuffs. If you've placed the cuffs with the keyhole up, it should be easy to remove. If you placed the keyhole down, you will have to bend down while pulling the prisoner's hands upward in order to insert the key. It's a dangerous and uncomfortable position for both of you, easily avoided by putting the cuffs on correctly the first time.

Place the weak hand on his head or up high on the wall. Remove that cuff and then remove the second cuff, telling him to do the same with his strong hand. As he is occupied with the movement, step away from him and secure your handcuffs.

For certain arrests, such as narcotic sales, you may need to conduct a strip search as well. While protecting the prisoner's right to privacy, you will have him remove all of his clothing, and then do a thorough visual search, inspecting inside his mouth, under his genitals, and between his buttocks and toes. As distasteful as this sounds, all are common hiding places for narcotics, weapons, and other contraband. Because of the sensitive nature of such searches, they must exactly follow your state laws and department policies. Remember to document everything you do.

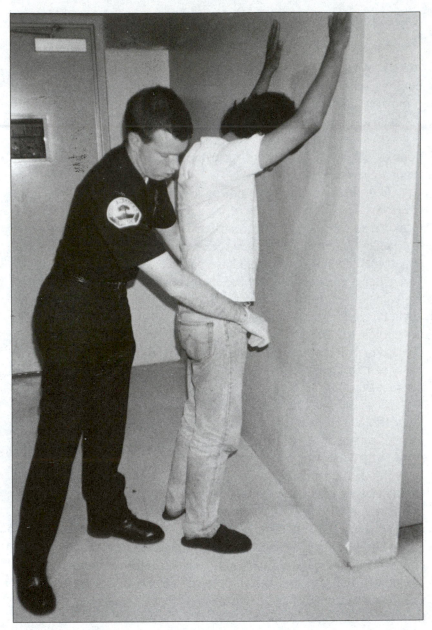

Booking search.

BOOKING PROCEDURES

At this point, the prisoner is usually secured in a holding cell, or sometimes just handcuffed to a bench, while you gather booking information. It's just a matter of filling in the appropriate forms with such items as name, aliases, address, date of birth, place of birth, descriptors (sex, race, height, weight, hair, eyes, scars, tattoos, birthmarks, clothing description), occupation, phone number, social security number, driver's license number, and emergency contacts. You will use any identification in the suspect's wallet to verify, or you may have to fax his fingerprints to some other agency in order to find out who he really is. You will also ask about his medical condition and whether or not he has specific diseases such as: AIDS, tuberculosis, venereal disease or hepatitis (take appropriate precautions if he does have those diseases). Your processing will also include taking the suspect's fingerprints and photograph so that he can be identified in the future.

Once the suspect's identification is verified, he will be carefully checked for wants and warrants, and those additional charges will be added to your original arrest. The booking information will be entered into appropriate ledgers, records, or computers, and then the suspect will either be released or placed into his assigned cell.

Releases from Custody

Obviously, some prisoners will remain in a jail facility through the trial and until they are acquitted or their sentence is finished. These long term custodies will be either in a county jail or a state prison. You may also have some "holds" on a prisoner that require you to keep him in custody. A typical hold might be a parole hold on a person on parole from state prison, an immigration hold on a foreign national, or an extradition hold on a person wanted in another jurisdiction. In a local jail, the majority of prisoners get released from custody under a wide variety of authorities (i.e., bond, bail, O.R.).

DISCUSSION QUESTIONS

1) Do you think the present arrest powers given a private person are adequate?

2) What effect do you think recent national gun control efforts such as the "Brady Bill" will have on private person arrests in your community?

3) Why do you think that police officers are mandated to accept arrests from private persons?

4) The 8th Amendment of the Constitution prohibits excessive bail. Under what situations do you think "no bail" warrants are appropriate?

5) In some countries, every arrestee is stripped naked and searched upon entry to a jail. Under what circumstances do you think strip searches should be conducted in your jurisdiction?

6) What organizations, agencies, and forces in your community tend to shape your local law enforcement agency's use of force policies?

7) Give an example of how you may arrest and book a suspect for disorderly conduct and public intoxication.

Cops in Radnor, PA, just smirk and shrug when asked about it, but the story just won't go away. It seems two officers were questioning a suspect and getting nowhere. Finally, they put a metal colander on his head, ran two wires from it to a nearby photocopy machine, and told the suspect he was rigged to a lie detector. They had placed a simple typed message in the machine, and every time the suspect made a statement, they pressed the "copy" button. Out would come a sheet of paper that read, "He's lying."

The suspect finally confessed.

* * *

Assistant Police Chief B.W. Smith said it was the first such robbery he'd ever heard of, but he had to believe it. The victim knew it sounded weird but claimed "That sucker was going to bite me. They put him right up to my face." It was Balch Springs, Texas' first "robbery at turtle-point."

Domino's Pizza delivery man, Troy Brewer, said he was making a call at a pay phone when two suspects thrust a "big, huge, ugly" snapping turtle in his face threatened severe bites and nips if he didn't surrender his cash bag. "Don't move or you're gonna get bit," they told him.

Brewer gave up $50 to the turtle-wielders, and despite his doubts that anyone would believe him, reported the robbery to the police.

My personal favorite stick-up man was the guy in Georgia who would walk up to attendants at lonely rural gas stations with a big pile of dog excrement in his bare hand. "Gimme the money or I'll make you eat this," he'd tell them. Then there was the guy who stuck up beauty salons with a power stapler threatening to "pin some ears back" if he didn't get the loot. Now that's some class.

INVESTIGATIONS AND REPORTS

LEARNING GOALS: After studying this chapter the student will be able to:

- Explain the purpose of a police report.

- Explain the purpose of field notes and identify when they can be destroyed.

- List the essential elements of every report.

- List three common characteristics of good police reports.

- Identify when it is appropriate to put your conclusions and opinions into a police report.

- List some of the basic steps in investigating any crime scene.

- Name the basic tools needed to assist in crime scene investigation.

- Describe the methods used to collect, identify, preserve and package some common types of evidence.

- Demonstrate how to organize a police report.

- Explain why reports are written in natural language, first person, active voice, and chronological order.

CRIME SCENE INVESTIGATION

In previous chapters, we've discussed specific ways for field officers to investigate specific crimes. Now you have to marry your investigation to a report. As a patrol officer your objectives are well defined — solve the crime and arrest the suspect. If you are incapable of solving the crime, you need to collect all of the evidence and information that will allow other investigators to solve the crime in the future.

You already have learned the basic priorities after arriving at the scene of any call: giving aid, calling for assistance, identifying and apprehending offenders, interviewing witnesses and victims, and protecting evidence. Now we will move onto the crime scene itself — how to identify, examine, document and collect evidence.

Preliminary Assessment

The first thing you need to do is find out what you have. If you have statements from witnesses, victims, or suspects, you may already have a good idea of what you are looking for and where you can find various pieces of evidence. In any case, you need to carefully walk through and inspect the crime scene. If possible, try to retrace the routes of the suspects and victims. Try to visualize what the scene looked like before the crime, and visualize what exactly took place within the crime scene.

As you walk through the crime scene, you should be looking carefully to identify any items of evidence related to the crime. These might include: weapons, broken items, money, property, blood, scuff marks, fingerprints, footprints, hairs, pieces of fabric, or anything out of the ordinary.

Before moving or handling any evidence, make a sketch and/or take notes. I find it useful to simply do a quick and crude outline of the building or room and locate evidence with notes. In an ideal world, you should measure, sketch, and/or photograph all items of evidence before you collect them. Ideally, before you photograph the object (preferably with a 4"x 5" view camera and perfect lighting), you would make complete notes as to where it was found, who was present, the exact measurements from permanent objects, and all identifying marks and numbers.

In the real world of restricted time, budgets, and resources, you need to use common sense and evaluate each piece of evidence. You need to ask yourself some questions: Is this a solvable case? Is this an important case, in terms of the priorities of the community, agency, and the courts? Will this piece of evidence be an important factor in obtaining a conviction? If the answers are all "yes," then you obviously want to photograph and carefully document that item of evidence. If the answers are all "no," you may want to save your time and the department's money by simply noting the location of the evidence and collecting it for later study.

In a busy police department, you may handle a dozen crime reports in a day, collecting evidence at many of them. Most of the evidence will be bagged and tagged, and noted in the report with a statement like, "I checked the point of entry for evidence and found 2 latent prints (cards submitted to I.D. Bureau) and a 1/2" flat-blade Craftsman screwdriver directly under the window (booked into evidence)."

There is a methodology to getting through a crime scene such as this one.

COLLECTION OF EVIDENCE

Few things are more convincing in a trial than physical evidence. Witnesses can make mistakes and change their minds, they can become sick or scared or stupid when you need them for a trial. Evidence is there to see and be evaluated by the judge and jury, intact and unchanged from the time you collected it. How they evaluate that evidence depends on how well you located, collected, handled and preserved it. Given adequate equipment and some basic training, you should be able to handle 99 percent of the evidence you will ever encounter.

Evidence Kits

Below are some of the items I've found useful for evidence collection. I won't tell you that every evidence kit has to contain these items; some you will find useful, others you might never use. I carry mine in a large sports bag. I've seen other officer's evidence kits so full of black powder they looked like the inside of Mount Vesuvius, ruining all the equipment. I keep the bag clean. Here's some items for you to consider:

Camera: I've found one of the compact, automatic 35 mm cameras (about $150 or so) with the automatic date imprint and built in flash works great for evidence. It won't work well at night for large scenes, but it's great for inside work and close-up evidence. Make sure you have extra batteries and film. Higher speed color film is your best bet (ASA 200 - 400).

Cotton Pads: Good for collecting some fluids (blood, semen, PCP) for packaging in other containers.

Evidence Tape or Labels: For sealing containers or bags, labeling items, and labeling items to be photographed.

Fingerprint Kit: Containing at least black powder, white cards, some brushes and tape. Some officers like the fancy magnetic powders, silver and white powders, black cards and other gizmos.

Flashlight: If you don't routinely carry a good rechargeable flashlight, you will need to carry a flashlight (with fresh batteries).

HazMat Suits: Disposable full coverage overalls are now available at relatively low cost. They're a good bargain when handling a major crime scene (like a murder), reducing the chances of you being contaminated with blood, and reducing the chances of you contaminating the crime scene.

Knife: A small pen knife or craft knife is invaluable for trimming fingerprint tape and other materials.

Magnifier: For the close examination of fingerprints and other trace evidence.

Marking Pen: Get the sharp-pointed, permanent, waterproof pens for labeling evidence for later identification in court. I've also tried china markers and grease-pencils, but both tend to melt down in a hot car.

Paper Bags (clean): Grocery-sized paper bags are great for packaging clothing and other bulky evidence items, and will still allow wet items to dry (wet things can mold or mildew in a plastic bag. Manila envelopes can also work well.

Plastic Bags (clean): We have pre-labeled evidence bags that are useful and convenient for storing small evidence items.

Plastic Jars (clean): For protecting fragile evidence or dangerous things like PCP-laced cigarettes.

Rubber Gloves: Like Karl Malden used to say, "Don't leave home without it!" Rubber gloves are essential to avoid contamination from body fluids and the like. I carry two different kinds, some heavy industrial models for picking up dead animals and the like and disposable surgical gloves for fingerprinting, handling dirty objects, and touching suspects.

Ruler: For measuring small objects and for using as a scale in photographs (You can also use a PR-24 in a photo to show a 24-inch scale).

Screwdriver: For prying and taking things apart during searches. Some guys that are really into searching cars like the cordless power screwdrivers.

Scribe: For permanently marking evidence.

Surgical Masks: Anytime you are exposed to biological hazards (blood) or environmental hazards (dust, molds, fingerprinting powder) a surgical mask is very useful. They can also help to make terrible odors (from dead bodies in particular) a little more bearable.

Syringe Tubes: This is a plastic tube with end-caps and safety seals used for safely storing and carrying syringes with needles attached. If you deal with a lot of hypes, this item is important for your health.

Tape Measure: To measure large items and place them accurately on sketches and diagrams.

Tweezers: Surgical tweezers are the best, letting you pick up delicate evidence without damaging it or disgusting evidence without getting "cooties."

Collection of Physical Evidence

The different types of evidence you discover have to be handled in very different ways. As a patrol officer, you may not have to collect obscure types of trace evidence like semen and DNA. That type of collection will often be left to homicide investigators, evidence technicians, or other experts. Nonetheless, every item of evidence you recognize and desire to collect for your case needs to be packaged in an appropriate manner.

You package evidence to isolate it from other evidence, protect its value and integrity in court, and avoid deliberate or accidental contamination. In the list below you will find most of the common evidence encountered and collected by patrol officers. If you don't see a particular item of evidence, look for something similar below or call your sergeant.

Once collected, you need to mark the evidence for later identification in court. Most evidence is marked by attaching a tag or label, or by placing it into some kind of container with a tag or label. Typical labels have the case number, date, time, location collected, type of case, description of the evidence, and your name, initials, and I.D. numbers.

Sealed by _____

FOLD HERE

EVIDENCE

Case Number _____

Pouch Number _____

Type of Offense _____

Description of Evidence _____

_____

_____

Suspect _____

Victim _____

Date and Time of Recovery _____

Location of Recovery _____

Recovered By _____

Reason Seized

☐ Analysis ☐ Trial ☐ Safekeeping

CHAIN OF CUSTODY

Received From _____ By _____

Date _____ Time _____ AM PM

Received From _____ By _____

Date _____ Time _____ AM PM

Received From _____ By _____

Date _____ Time _____ AM PM

Received From _____ By _____

Date _____ Time _____ AM PM

Received From _____ By _____

Date _____ Time _____ AM PM

Physical evidence bag.

ADHESIVE TAPE: May contain fingerprints or trace evidence such as fibers, dust, or powder. Remove carefully without contaminating. Then carefully place between two supports (across the top of a box would work fine) or place on waxed paper.

AMMUNITION: If you remove it from a gun, package each round separately and describe where you found it (in the chamber, in the magazine, in which position in the cylinder, etc.). Pack the rounds in tissue, soft paper, or cloth in a small box or envelope.

ARSON DEBRIS: Label carefully as to where you found the evidence, and note if you smell some accelerant such as gasoline. The preferred container is a clean, empty, metal paint can.

ASHES/BURNED PAPER: Pack loosely on soft cotton, placed in rigid container. Clearly mark as "FRAGILE," and hand carry to the lab.

BLOOD (Sample): Use a sterile tube with heparin or EDTA, rock gently to mix, and refrigerate if you have no preservatives available. Label the vial with the name, case number, date, time, and person who collected the specimen, along with your initials for identification. Some agencies provide a paper envelope to seal the tube in. Handle it carefully. A paper evidence envelope dripping blood is an ugly sight. You can also wrap it in tissue or foam and place it in a box.

BLOOD SPATTERS: Photograph and make notes on the pattern size and location. If dried, and the object cannot be removed, scrape and place in a paper bindle or clean glass vial. If more than one source is suspected, use a clean object to scrape off each sample.

BLOODSTAINED OBJECTS: If the object is small enough, submit the entire object intact. Package to prevent the stained area from rubbing against any other surface.

BLOODSTAINS: Submit entire stained item, allow to air dry, place in paper bag.

BULLETS (Expended): If embedded in wood or plaster, cut around the bullet until it falls free. Handle carefully to avoid disturbing trace evidence. Do not attempt to mark (I know you saw somebody scratch their initials into the base in an old movie, this isn't Hollywood). Air dry if bloody, and do not lose adhering fibers or debris. Place in soft tissue or paper (not cotton, it sticks into the soft lead of the bullet) and secure in a hard container like a small box or jar.

CARTRIDGE CASES: Handle the same as bullets. Take care not to disturb possible prints on the outside of the case, and try not to damage possible scratches or dents on the end. Remember, brass is a soft metal and can be easily deformed and damaged. That makes it good evidence, but evidence that is easily destroyed.

CHECKS: Same as "Documents," below.

CHEMICALS: Place in a glass bottle (plastic bottles can be used unless the chemical is an acid or solvent) and mark clearly on the outside as to what type of chemical you think it is.

CLOTHING: Mark directly with a permanent marker on waistband, collar, cuff, etc. Avoid contaminating with other clothing and do not wrap in plastic bags. If wet, hang to air dry, then fold neatly. If bloody, place clean paper between folds before folding and refrigerate if possible. Wrap each individual item in a paper bag. Label the bag.

DOCUMENTS: Items such as demand notes or extortion letters might contain fingerprints. Don't handle with your bare hands, place carefully in a paper envelope without folding the letter. You may need to protect the envelope between sheets of cardboard.

DRUGS (Liquids, powders, and pills): Place in original container (bindle, baggie, or jar) and place in a heavy plastic evidence envelope. Seal the envelope (with a heat sealer if available) and clearly label. (Nobody wants to be surprised with a faceful of PCP, make sure you warn lab personnel about what is inside!)

EXPLOSIVES: Includes blasting caps, bombs, dynamite, grenades, pipe bombs, and plastic explosives. Don't touch, don't move, just evacuate the area and call the Bomb Squad.

FIBERS: If firmly attached to the object, photograph, diagram, and submit entire object. If not attached, you can collect fibers individually with tweezers, and package in a plastic or glass jar or vial.

FIREARMS: Handle the weapon as little as possible, touching only surfaces that will not take a print such as the edges of the trigger guard or checkered grips. Unload the weapon if possible, noting the position of all live rounds. If the weapon cannot be unloaded, do not submit to the lab until you receive specific instructions. Handle gently. If fingerprint evidence may be present, package in a tight-fitting box.

GLASS: If looking for fragments on shoes or clothing, submit the entire item, wrapped separately and tightly in the smallest container possible. Do not pack with cotton or foam. Larger fragments should be placed on soft material to avoid further breakage. Clearly label the package to avoid injury to lab personnel.

HAIR: If attached to object, submit entire object. Photograph and package to prevent hair loss enroute to the lab. If not attached, remove and place in paper bindle, clean envelope, or small plastic bag. If searching for pubic hairs or other hairs on clothing or blankets, carefully fold the items inward, and wrap individually in clean paper bags.

PAINT CHIPS: Place on tissue or foam, insert in small bag or folded paper bindle, package in rigid container.

PRINTS/IMPRESSIONS: "Plastic" fingerprints, shoe prints, and tire tracks should all be protected against damage and the weather. Fingerprints should be isolated and handled by a trained technician if possible, but if you have to handle it, collect the entire object. If the object cannot be moved, photograph it carefully. Shoe prints and tire impressions are normally photographed with a ruler in the picture to give accurate scaling. After photographing, plaster or resin casts can be made.

ROPE, STRING: Preserve hairs, fibers, or skin that might be adhering to surface, place in an envelope or wrap in paper.

SEMEN: Handle like blood, take biological precautions.

SOIL/DEBRIS: Allow to dry thoroughly, then place in box.

TOOLS: Place in envelope or folded sheet of paper. Take care not to disturb tip to prevent damage and loss of adhering paints, etc. Wrap each tool separately.

TOOL MARKS: If removable, cover marks with soft paper and then place in box. Send in the tool if found.

WIRE: Can be compared to the cutting tool, label the end you believe was cut off, handle like rope and wrap securely.

THE PURPOSE OF POLICE REPORTS

You can be the greatest patrol officer your community has ever known, you can do fantastic investigations, but if you can't write a decent report, you will be totally ineffective.

Your fellow officers, and perhaps your sergeant, may see you operate in the field and judge your performance on that basis, but most of the rest of the world will judge you and your investigations on the quality of your reports. Your arrest takes only an instant, but the report may occupy hours of your time. It follows your case through the entire system — approved by your sergeant or lieutenant, reviewed by detectives, presented to the district attorney for filing, reviewed by judges for warrants, and, finally, presented before attorneys and a jury at trial. More than anything else, the report is your work product and is the finished article by which others will judge the quality of your work. Make sure every report reflects your **best** effort.

Generally speaking, you will have a superior officer reading and approving your reports before they can be filed with the district attorney. This is the stage where he should catch spelling and grammar errors, poor writing, inaccuracies, and incomplete information. He'll generally meet with you and return the report to you for corrections. He'll also be forming opinions about you and your work habits, and use that information in your evaluations for pay increases and promotions. Try to impress him. Make your report as neat as possible. If you are a poor speller, use a dictionary or electronic spelling device.

Write every report as if it were the most important case in your career, with the knowledge that you may have to support and defend every word at trial. If more than one officer is reporting on the same incident, you must assume that each may have a unique perspective and viewpoint. Talk over the case in detail before you ever write a word, and make sure you resolve any apparent discrepancies.

The defense attorney will also be rating you as a potential witness by your report. He'd just love to put some inarticulate clown in front of a jury to represent the "People's" case. On the other hand, a well-written, error-free, concise report is the defense attorney's nightmare. The better you write your reports, the better chance you have of getting a conviction, and the less likely a case is to ever go to trial.

FIELD NOTES

For most officers, the report begins with field notes. These are often taken on a pocket-sized pad of paper (sometimes called a "buddy pad" or a "cruiser pad"). Your memory is not perfect, most people can retain only about 10 percent of what they hear. Unless you are one of those rare persons with a truly photographic memory, you need to write down all the pertinent facts you encounter on any given case. This will ensure that you have accurate information regarding times, statements and events when you go to write your report.

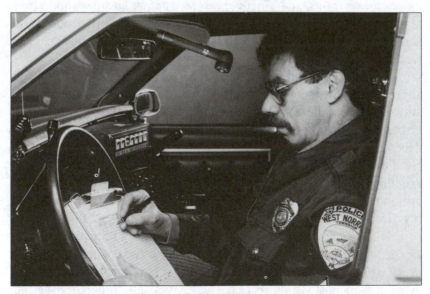

Good reports start with good field notes.

Some of the information generally entered in notes includes: names and descriptions of suspects, victims and witnesses; dates and times of occurrences; addresses; case numbers; serial numbers and notes on evidence. When you first start, you will need to take a lot of notes, and when you go to write your report you will find, inevitably, that you have neglected to write down some vital piece of information while collecting a lot of unusable trivia as well.

With experience, you will have a lot better idea about what kinds of information are needed for specific types of crimes and incidents and be a lot more selective as to what you record. You'll always need to write down statements that you intend to quote, especially any admissions, alibis, confessions, eyewitness accounts, etc. Outside of those types of statements, many experienced officers simply use the appropriate form and record factual information directly onto the spaces in the report at the scene. This avoids writing the information twice, reduces transcription errors, and saves a lot of time and effort.

Field notes certainly have some limited value in court as evidence. There once was a time when it was considered tremendously important to save such notes for ever and ever, and diligent officers had shoe-boxes full of the damn things hidden away in their closets. Today, some departments have a policy requiring you retain your notes or place them in the file with the report, and even without such a policy it certainly wouldn't *hurt* to save your notes. However, no less an authority than the U.S. Supreme Court has declared that you can throw away your notes when you're done with them, provided you meet a few conditions:

1) Any notes you destroy must be destroyed in "good faith" (it would be bad faith if you destroyed them to prevent facts from being entered into your report or to cover up some other false information).

2) The information from your notes must be entered into a formal report (thus preserving the facts you recorded).

3) The formal report you write must accurately reflect the contents of the notes you destroyed.

4) The prosecutor must turn over a copy of your formal report to the attorneys for the defense before the trial (and if you retain notes, you would have to provide those to the defense as well).

ESSENTIAL ELEMENTS OF REPORTS

Police reports represent a real paradox. It's extremely difficult for a supervisor or field training officer to communicate what he wants in a report when every single report is different — deals with different fact patterns and requires you to establish various elements of hundreds of different crimes. On the other hand, there are tremendous similarities between reports, and if you can learn some fundamental principles of report writing, you can produce a competent report to document any imaginable subject.

For example, the thought of writing a fatal traffic accident report is pretty intimidating to a new officer, but writing a non-injury fender-bender is pretty easy. I found long ago that there is little difference between the two. You investigate in the same way but, obviously, in much greater detail for the fatal accident. You still do your best to document the physical evidence and establish who is at fault and conclude why the accident happened.

Characteristics of Good Reports

All good reports share certain common characteristics. They must be legible, clear, concise, accurate, complete, objective, and contain good grammar and spelling.

Legible means that the report must be neat and readable. A word processor coupled with a high quality printer is really the ideal because it allows you great freedom in revising and correcting. Second best is a typewriter (assuming you're a decent typist), but a thick layer of correction fluid flaking off the page can ruin the effect. The next choice would be black pen, but if you make a lot of corrections this can look terrible. The last choice for legibility is the most common method required by law enforcement agencies — a #2 pencil. Pencil can smear and be too light to photocopy, but God knows it's easy to erase and change, and pencils tend to have low maintenance costs. If you must use pencil or pen, print neatly in block letters, erase your errors completely, and make your report as easy to read as possible.

Clear means that you must communicate the facts of the case to any reader (including the housewives and construction workers that might make up a jury) in an understandable, sequential manner.

Always write your reports in chronological order (the order things actually happened), **not** the order they became apparent to you. Most cases begin with a crime occurring and a victim or witness seeing or experiencing some event. The crime doesn't begin when you arrive, in fact the crime is often over before your arrival. Why begin a report with your arrival? Start in order with the first event, and work your way through all the facts and events in the order they took place.

Concise means that you are specific and get to the point without burying the reader in trivial information and useless verbiage. Use short, simple words. Use them in short, simple sentences. I once described a man that burned to death as being "in a pugilistic stance." That's a very specific description of the classic boxer's pose, with the hands clenched into fists and drawn up to the chin, and a very common description of people who die in fires. Any coroner or arson investigator would understand exactly what I meant, but probably no one in a jury would have a clue as to what I meant.

Unless you are quoting someone, avoid the use of slang and jargon. Avoid describing people with letters and numbers, and unless they are abbreviations recognized by everyone (including the average person in the jury), don't use any. Use the simplest word possible. I can't count the number of reports that read something like, "Victim Smith related the following information verbally to me, in substance," and should have said, "Smith said." Don't write, "Upon arrival undersigned officer exited from the patrol vehicle," write "I arrived and got out of the car."

Accurate means getting the facts right — checking every name, address, phone number, and date of birth. It means taking good notes and accurate quotes, thus avoiding later surprises in court. It means telling the truth about what happened, every time, with no shading, no underestimation, no exaggeration.

Complete means including all relevant information. It means covering every element of the crime you're investigating, contacting every potential witness and getting their full information, and completing every investigation in a thorough manner so that nobody has to come redo your work or clean up your mess.

Objective is defined as "without prejudice or bias," and means you deal with all facts and issues fairly and without prejudice. You aren't the judge, you are simply the recorder of the facts. Record all the relevant facts, whether they tend to prove or disprove your case.

Some of those facts may include your *subjective* interpretation of events reported in an objective manner. Only by doing so will the judge and attorneys respect you as a professional and respect your report as a professional product.

At the beginning of an investigation, it's impossible to know what seemingly insignificant facts could ultimately become important. Better to have too many details than too few. By recording even details that tend to prove a suspect's innocence, you gain in several areas:

1) The prosecutor can be better prepared to counter those arguments in court by knowing all the facts from the start.

2) The jury may be favorably impressed by an officer who records all of the facts, instead of those just proving the suspect's guilt.

3) If you are aware of evidence favorable to the defendant and withhold it, the case may end in a mistrial, reversal, or dismissal.

Good grammar and spelling means that your report should look like a business professional's report, not like a third grade book report.

The heart of the report is the narrative, which should contain all of the elements and details of the crime, using the sequence of events as they occurred. It is essential that you lay the legal and logical foundations to show the reasonableness of your actions throughout, showing your legal right to be where you were and your probable cause and reasonable beliefs to proceed with contacts, detentions, arrests, and searches.

You must remember that your report is a blueprint used by investigators and prosecutors to bring those responsible to trial. Issues of probable cause and the elements of the crime will be argued in court based on what you have written. Both the district attorney and the defense will use it as a script for your testimony in justifying your actions. It is essential that you show the facts as you knew them at the time you took such actions as arrests and searches. To show what you believe happened, your report should be based on all the information you had, the evidence you discovered, and your investigation.

Who

Your report should include all of the relevant parties, identified both by their name and their role (suspect, victim, witness, party, reporting party, informant, passenger, etc.). When you first mention a name, give the full name ("I arrived and spoke to Victim #1-Judith Ann MITCHELL"). After that, you could simply call the victim "MITCHELL." If there were more than one Mitchell in the report, you should make it plain to the reader which one did what ("Judith MITCHELL told Frank MITCHELL to put the axe down").

Some agencies use abbreviations ("RP told U/S that V-1 told S-2 to put the axe down.") (Translation: "Reporting party told undersigned that Victim #1 told Suspect #2 to put the axe down.") Sure it saves time and space, but how does this sentence sound to a jury of laymen? Does the similar sentence in the previous paragraph paint a better picture in your mind of what really happened?

Also, avoid the pronouns: "he," "she," "they," "we." Using pronouns instead of names in the same phrase as above, you would write, "She told him to put the axe down." If you have more than one person of each sex within the report, you can only guess at who did what. Use proper names whenever possible to keep the clearest picture of what took place and who did what.

Part of "who" includes being able to identify the person and to find him or her again. As a result, you should obtain phone numbers and addresses for both home and work (or school for students), the date of birth, race, physical description, occupation, and identifying numbers such as drivers licenses or social security.

"Who" should also include who owned property, who was injured, who took them to the hospital, who treated their injuries and who can describe them in court.

What

The "what" question is the heart of the crime, where you prove the elements of the crime and the *modus operandi*. Make sure you cover all of the "whats," starting with "What happened?" You need to detail what specific crime you are investigating, what elements are present proving that crime, what type of property was taken or recovered, what the value of that property is and how it could be identified in the future.

When a particular crime involves several offenses, be sure that you document all of the elements and charge each and every offense. If a traffic violation led to your initial contact with a suspect, write the details of that violation into your report and file for the traffic violation as well. If a person was raped at knife-point, you would have to cover all of the elements of rape, assault with a deadly weapon, and possibly kidnap or sexual assault. If a suspect was booked, you should book under all the applicable charges, ensuring that the public is protected by an appropriate amount of bail for the crimes he actually committed.

What damages or injuries occurred as a result? Did someone die or require medical treatment? In addition to items stolen, was there damage (window smash, kicked in door, bullet holes, etc.)? Your victim may need this as documentation for his insurance company or for court-ordered restitution.

What clothing was the suspect wearing, what exactly did he say and what did he do? Did he have any particular accents, speech patterns, or physical abnormalities?

What statements were made by the suspects, victims, reporting party, and other relevant persons? What type of business or property (residence, apartment, grocery store, bank) was involved? What did the suspect use for transportation (describe whether he was on foot, skateboard, bicycle, or vehicle)?

Where

Your report should describe in detail exactly where every part of the crime took place which is a critical issue in determining the legal jurisdiction of both you and the court. Did it take place in your city, your county, your state? Did it start in another jurisdiction or on a state or federal highway?

For burglary reports, you will need to describe the point of entry, and for accident reports, you will need to locate the point of impact (or area of impact). In a city setting, you may measure exact distances in feet and inches from specific curbings. In a rural area you may measure distances to the nearest milepost on a highway or use a power pole, irrigation ditch, or other permanent landmark. You should also describe the type of area in which the crime took place. Was it on a public street, in a carport, in a park, or in a business district?

Why

"Why did this crime take place?" Sometimes this can be the hardest question to answer. Was there a specific motive expressed by a suspect or victim such as financial gain or revenge, or was the event an accident? When someone tells you they did something (particularly when their actions don't seem to make sense), ask them why. "I told Frank to drop the axe." Why? "Because I was afraid he was going to hit me." With this simple why question you have established her motive and shown her state of mind (fear of being struck by a deadly weapon). Showing this state of mind could provide you with an element of the crime (i.e., the fear or force required for proving robbery), or with a defense in court (i.e., the fear needed for a shooting done in self-defense).

When

Time is an important element in your report. Noting the time can help to prove what happened, how it was possible that it happened, and allow the prosecution to eliminate alibis. Your report should list the exact times (or your nearest approximation) that calls were received and dispatched, when you arrived, the time that victims were contacted, suspects arrested, and evidence was located.

Noting the times as precisely as possible can help in preventing future crimes. When did the victim park his car, last see his property, or lock and leave his house? When did the suspect say he left his house, ate dinner, met a friend, or did some other potentially alibi-providing activity?

How

How is the heart of the "modus operandi," "method of operation," or "M.O." — the way in which the criminal committed that particular crime. Some crimes seem to be generic (i.e., window smash auto burglaries of cars with pull-out stereos seem pretty common place and the suspects leave behind little in the way of evidence). Look carefully beyond the obvious, and you may note specific details in common with other crimes.

Does the thief target one particular make, model or color? Is he targeting a particular style or make of stereo? Does he break the same window in the same manner? Is the window shattered by impact (scattering glass across the car) or by prying (a quieter method that drops most of the glass straight down and may leave a pry mark)? Does he like certain areas, lighting conditions, buildings, or districts? Then your M.O. may be "right windwing window smash of German cars for Blaupunkt stereos, parked to rear of bars during late night business hours." That's a lot more specific and a lot more identifiable.

In robberies, the "how" is even more distinctive. How does the robber approach and leave? Does he display a weapon? How and in what hand? How does he demand the money or property — by note or verbally? How is the demand worded, and how is it presented to the victim? How does he carry away the loot, and how does he disguise himself? The F.B.I. finds bank robbery suspects so distinctive that they often name them after distinctive features or parts of the M.O. We've had the "Old Man" robber, the "Southern Gentleman," and the "Blue Toyota" robbers working our area. Noting how the crime occurred can help tie a suspect to many other crimes.

You also need to report on how you know something. When you write in the report that "Investigation revealed the suspect entered through the unlocked kitchen door," you tell the reader nothing about how you obtained this knowledge and how you can prove it in court. Say what you learned and how. The telling details would be, "Mr. Smith told me he always left his kitchen door unlocked, and I could find no other sign of entry into the house. I saw one set of muddy footprints leading into the house from the backyard and through the kitchen door. Mr. Smith told me the footprints were not his."

If someone else saw, heard, or felt something you mentioned in your report, say who the person was and how they knew what they told you.

Statements

When a witness' or suspect's statement is used, you must describe when and where you heard that statement. If you use a witness' statement, be sure to include how and when the witness observed what he described to you. If the statement is from a suspect and his *Miranda* rights were read to him, indicate in your report when, where, and how those rights were read, who read them, who was present, and what the suspect's exact answers were.

Property Descriptions

Always list all of the property involved along with serial numbers, trade names, model numbers, and identifiable marks or flaws. Remember, an inaccurate description or incomplete list of property may hurt your case. I saw one auto burglary case in which the officers from another jurisdiction did a really poor job of describing a victim's stolen stereo. Not only did they lose the case in court, but when the defendant was acquitted the judge ordered the agency to return the stereo to the defendant. That's humiliating.

You also need to describe the specific location and circumstances under which any items of property were searched for, found, located or seized.

Opinions and Conclusions

In general, police reports should document facts not assumptions, opinions, conclusions or theories of the officer or anyone else. Your opinions are a calculated risk that may be proven wrong in court and tear away at the rest of your case. When you have to assume something, it often means you aren't certain beyond a reasonable doubt, so don't expect a judge or a jury to be any more certain than you when it comes to trial. There are some limited exceptions:

1) You may give your opinion when it is required by department policy.

2) You may give your opinion when your opinion or interpretation of facts or events provided your probable cause for arrest, searching, or seeking a warrant. When you do take action based on probable cause, your reports should show the reader exactly what you were thinking and why. As an example, you might write, "At that time I placed MAHONEY under arrest for burglary. My probable cause was:

a) MAHONEY's physical description was similar to the suspect description given to me by JONES."

b) MAHONEY's clothing was identical to the suspect description given to me by BROWN."

c) MAHONEY is the registered owner of the blue Ford with license 1SAM321 that BROWN saw leaving the scene."

d) computer equipment similar to the loss reported on the radio was in plain sight on the back seat."

e) MAHONEY's statement about where he had been at the time of the burglary was inconsistent."

3) You may give your opinion when writing traffic accident reports, and your opinion is used to determine the cause of the accident.

Use a conclusion only when it really seems necessary and would add to the reader's understanding of your actions. A valid conclusion might be, "Based on my investigation, I believe this reported crime is unfounded."

REPORT WRITING STYLES

Traditional Report Writing

Police reports have long been written in a very formal style, filled with big words and technical phrases guaranteed to mystify anyone outside of law enforcement (and probably mystifying a few in law enforcement too, though they may be embarrassed to admit it). Recognizing the shortcomings of the formal style, most agencies have changed to the informal style of writing.

Informal language does not mean substandard or idiomatic. It is the language that educated people use who know how to communicate with others. Words are short and direct. Contractions and common abbreviations are used where they make sense. Sentences are simple and short. Some grammatical rules may be bent where they communicate greater meaning, and idioms and everyday words understood by anyone are used throughout. Informal writing is direct, sincere, and credible. It will give your reports greater credibility, because your report will sound the way that you speak. On the witness stand your report will sound like you — real, human, and understandable.

Get Organized

If you're going to write a report, the first thing you have to do is get organized. Report narratives should always be written in exactly the order that they happened. Don't mix up the dates and times; usually things started happening long before your department received a phone call and long before you got to the scene.

Start at the beginning, with the first event that took place. If a lot of things happened in the case, you will need to make a chronological outline of the events before starting on the narrative.

As an example, on a typical call, you might handle a stolen car report. You are dispatched to the victim's location, where he tells you when and where he parked his car and when he found it gone. If you check the spot, you might find some physical evidence. The victim will sign your report, and afterwards you may make a crime broadcast and have the Records Division enter the vehicle into the Stolen Vehicle System.

Now you have to write the report. Organize the events into a chronological order:

1) The victim parked his car.

2) The victim discovered his car was gone.

3) The victim called the police.

4) You were dispatched and arrived at the scene.

5) You discovered some evidence.

6) You wrote a report and the victim signed the report.

7) You made a crime broadcast.

8) The car was entered into SVS.

With a simple outline like this, you can then write a cohesive narrative, plugging in the facts you gather and telling the complete story to the reader. Your narrative might sound something like this:

On 083094 at about 0800 hours V-David BLACK
parked and locked his 1993 Saturn Coupe (license
#XYZ987) in the carport at 736 Main Street. On his
return at 1500 hours BLACK found the car gone and
he called the police.

I drove to his location and spoke to BLACK. He
told me that no one else had keys to his car or
permission to take the car, and he signed the GTA
report. I checked the carport for evidence and found
some broken window glass on the driver's side of the
parking space along with a portion of a General
Motors ignition lock with a screw inserted into the
keyway. I took the lock as evidence, and I broadcast
a description of the car. When I returned to the station,
Clerk James entered the car in SVS.

Putting things in chronological order makes report writing simple
and straightforward. You can take hundreds of events and facts, put
them into an outline, and still write a comprehensive narrative report
that makes sense.

The First Person

At some point in the dark ages of law enforcement, someone
decided that words like "I" and "we" were unprofessional, informal,
lacking in credibility, and too subjective. Government writing, in
general, and police reports, in particular, were written in the third
person point-of-view, and pseudo-scientific big words were thought to
sound the most professional of all. Instead of the first person statement,
"I never saw a purple cow," a true law enforcement professional would
say, "The undersigned officer had not previously observed a lupine-
hued bovine."

This nonsense persists in many agencies today. If the GTA report
above were written in the formal third person, it might sound like this:

On 083094 at about 0800 hours Victim-David
BLACK parked and secured his 1993 Saturn Coupe
(license #XYZ987) in the carport at 736 Main Street.
Upon his return at 1500 hours, victim discovered his
vehicle was gone and notified the police.

Undersigned officer responded to the above referenced location in response to a dispatched radio call and contacted BLACK in person. Victim verbally informed this officer that no one else had keys to the vehicle in question, or permission to take said vehicle, and aforementioned victim signed the requisite Grand Theft Auto report. It should be noted that officers checked the carport for evidence, and undersigned officer discovered what appeared to be broken window glass on the driver's portion of the parking space within said carport, along with a portion of a General Motors ignition lock with a screw inserted into the keyway. This officer took the lock as evidence and then broadcast an all points bulletin description of the vehicle. Upon return to the station, Clerk James was detailed to enter the reported vehicle into the Stolen Vehicle System computer.

Compared to the previous narrative, did using the third person, formal style add anything at all to your understanding, or did it simply confuse the reader and make the facts unclear?

The Active Voice

Reports should always be written in what is called the *active voice*. *Voice* indicates if the subject of a sentence is acting or being acted upon. When the subject of the sentence acts, the verb is active. When the subject is acted upon, the verb is passive. Writing in the passive voice will just bulk up your reports, making them far longer than needed, confusing the reader, and burying important information. Avoid starting any sentence with "there" or "it." Following are some examples of the active and passive voice. Notice how the passive voice is almost always longer and more ambiguous and how the active voice always presents more information about who did what:

PASSIVE: A call of a fight was broadcast at that location.

ACTIVE: I heard a radio dispatch of a fight at 358 Monterey Road.

PASSIVE: It was alleged that SMITH verbally assaulted the victim.

ACTIVE: Victim BROWN told me that SMITH yelled at him.

PASSIVE: It should be noted that prints were wiped off the crowbar.

ACTIVE: BROWN told me he saw SMITH wiping his prints off the crowbar.

PASSIVE: It was determined that the victim suffered a head injury.

ACTIVE: I could see that BROWN was bleeding from a cut on his forehead.

PASSIVE: SMITH was taken into custody and placed into a patrol car.

ACTIVE: I arrested and handcuffed SMITH, and Officer Matranga put him in the back seat of my patrol car.

PASSIVE: SMITH was transported to the station for booking.

ACTIVE: I drove SMITH to the station where he was booked by Jailer JONES.

PASSIVE: During booking a marijuana cigarette was found in SMITH's shirt pocket.

ACTIVE: While booking, Jailer Jones found a marijuana cigarette in SMITH's shirt pocket.

Use the Right Words

You should write in plain English, not in police talk. Most people don't drive "vehicles," they drive cars, trucks, vans, buses, motorcycles and mopeds. They don't "respond," or "contact" or "observe." They drive, talk, and see. You should write things in a plain, simple style, just the way you talk. When discussing a traffic stop, you should write:

> "I turned on my red lights and SMITH stopped his car."

> NOT

> "I activated my emergency lighting equipment and initiated a traffic stop on the suspect vehicle driven by SMITH."

When discussing your contact with the drivers, you should write:

> "I told SMITH he ran a red light. When he answered me, I could smell beer on his breath."

NOT

> "I informed the suspect of the nature of the violation I had observed, and at that time detected a strong odor of an alcoholic beverage on or about his breath or person."

Ever since Sgt. Joe Friday graced the television screen on *Dragnet*, officers have been describing marijuana as "a green leafy substance with the odor and appearance of marijuana." Can't say it's marijuana, they thought, if we haven't proven it's marijuana. That always seemed silly to me. I know what marijuana looks like, and I know what it smells like. Based on my knowledge, I arrested a person because I was sure it was marijuana. Why not just write in the report that "I found a one ounce bag of marijuana."?

If those same officers found a half-filled bottle of beer, would they describe it as "a clear glass container filled with an amber, carbonaceous fluid with the odor and appearance of beer?" Of course not, because you know what beer looks like and smells like (Good Lord, you might even know what it tastes like!) and can testify as a reasonable and prudent man that it was beer. If it walks like a duck and talks like a duck, for the purposes of your report, it's a duck. Write it that way.

Avoid Abbreviations

Most people are familiar with some of the most common acronyms for agencies (i.e., the F.B.I., C.I.A. and the D.E.A.). Police officers often use a lot of others such as: B.A. (blood alcohol), D.L. (Drivers License), P.A.B. (Police Administration Building), I.R.C. (Inmate Reception Center ["Jail"]) and others.

I recently went over a traffic accident report that read, "P-1 was NB #3 LN I-110, attempted Ave. 64 OFF/R at an est. spd. of 80 mph, TC'd at the e.c.l. approx. 87 ft. S. of the JCT w/ Arroyo." (Translation: "Party #1 was northbound #3 lane of the Pasadena Freeway, attempted to exit at the Avenue 64 offramp at an estimated speed of 80 miles per hour, had a traffic collision at the east curbline approximately 87 feet south of the junction with Arroyo.") All of these are official, approved abbreviations found in the Highway Patrol's Collision Manual, but I really don't think that the average jury is going to be able to figure out what the officer was trying to say.

Using abbreviations can trim down your reports and make them faster to write, but unless the abbreviation is one that could be understood by the average layman, leave it out of your reports.

Disposition

Usually the last part of the report tells the reader what work still needs to be done to complete the investigation and bring the case to trial. In some cases, nothing further is needed, and your disposition should reflect that. In some, your disposition will simply reflect where the report will be routed. In others, a great deal of work needs to be done. If you know exactly what needs to be done, give the reader a hint. A disposition may be: "To Detective Bureau for review. Filing delayed pending 1) possible fingerprint identification from crime lab on knife, 2) identification of blood type on knife, and 3) return of blood alcohol results on suspect Matthew RONNEE."

Often you complete all the investigation that will ever be done in the field at the time the report is taken. Some typical dispositions might include (and you might combine several of these dispositions):

"Crime unfounded, no further action."

"Investigation complete."

"Courtesy report - Mail copy to the Smallville P.D."

"To Detective Bureau for follow-up."

"To District Attorney for complaint action."

"To District Attorney for felony filing."

"Non-Detention Petition requested - To Juvenile D.A."

"Counseled and released."

"No further action required."

"For documentation only."

A Final Check

Upon completion, you should reread every report for the following:

1) Elements of the offense. If you don't know them for sure, look them up in the appropriate book and ask your sergeant. The district attorney has to reject any case you present to him that doesn't contain the elements of the crime.

2) Potential circumstances that might bring penalty enhancements. In addition to the basic elements of any crime, there are many other factors that can make the penalty more severe. These include crime at night, in residences, those involving racial or religious hatred, suspects on parole, suspects with prior convictions (such as the "Three Strikes - You're Out" bills in several states), crimes against police officers, crimes with sexual motives, and the use of particular weapons.

3) Probable cause for stops, contacts, detentions and arrests, searches and seizures. In previous chapters, we discussed how you develop probable cause. When it comes to the report, it's vital that you document everything you used to develop that probable cause. I've seen more cases lost before they ever got to trial by motions to suppress evidence from the defense challenging probable cause.

4) Be specific. Instead of ambiguous statements like, "Suspect was in a high crime area," state exactly what has taken place, i.e., "The suspect was seen on the same block in which 14 auto burglaries and 37 auto thefts have been reported in the last six months." If you arrest the suspect for auto theft, you suddenly have a lot stronger case than if you just said he was in a high crime area.

5) Need for *Miranda* advisements and waivers. Any time you have a *Mirandized* statement you need to document the exact circumstances under which that advisement was given and the waiver of rights was received. Say exactly what you said and exactly how the suspect acknowledged what you said.

6) Statements made by the suspect. Other than under *Miranda*, suspects often make statements. Some are admissions; some are alibis. Always use the suspect's exact words when he admits or denies a crime. It gives investigators a lot more facts to work with in proving what happened and gives the attorneys a lot more material to build his case. Try to avoid summarizing statements like, "JONES admitted the robbery." Be specific with statements like, "JONES told me he never intended to hurt the victim, he simply grabbed the purse as hard as he could and the victim fell to the ground,"or quote his exact words.

The *Mirandized* statement only applies to the admissibility of a statement in court. Let the attorneys argue as to whether the statement can come before a jury. If the suspect tells you something "off the record" or in support of some lie, write exactly what he tells you. A ridiculous and easily disproved alibi may serve to convict the suspect just as well as a confession.

7) Statements made by witnesses. Here a lack of detail and exact quotations may be to your benefit. In court, you cannot testify to what someone else told you; that's hearsay. A statement from a witness has to come from the original source, so that witness is going to be subpoenaed to testify at the trial. (There are certain exceptions, such as "dying declarations" where the witness dies, and when you "impeach" a witness - attacking him with his own words. These exceptions are rarely encountered, and you shouldn't worry too much about them.) You can't predict exactly what that witness might say a year or two later, but you could guess that it won't be identical to what he says today. Rather than create an opportunity for the defense attorney to claim your witness made a "prior inconsistent statement" (which the average defense attorney will make seem like a big lie), just paraphrase what the witness said.

8) Last of all, check your spelling and grammar. You can be sure that your sergeant will, and attorneys have a lot of fun with your errors in court. A typical line of questioning on the witness stand establishes that you wrote the report and moves on to the questions, "When you wrote this report, was it the truth as you knew

it? Was it accurate in every way possible? Did you make any mistakes when you wrote this report?"

Answering that last question is a loaded one because everybody makes mistakes. If you deny making mistakes, the attorney will gleefully point out every error of grammar and spelling to you on the witness stand, and then ask the jury that if you made so many mistakes in the writing of the report, what mistakes of fact might also be present? If you admit to making mistakes, he can use that against you too.

The best defense for you is to carefully write and then proofread your reports. If you have the luxury of writing on a computer, get a good spelling checker and use it. If you type or hand write your reports, get a dictionary or an electronic spelling checker. Use them every time for every questionable word, and then if you are asked if you made any mistakes look him right in the eye and say, "None that I am aware of."

One last, repetitive reminder. Every report you write is a reflection on you. It represents the quality of your work, your professionalism, and your integrity. Take pride in your work and make every report the best possible product you can.

DISCUSSION QUESTIONS

1) Why do you think most states require persons reporting their cars as stolen to sign the police report?

2) Some agencies allow their officers to dictate reports. How would your organization of a report differ if you were going to dictate it?

3) How do patrol officers in your jurisdiction collect evidence? Is it a patrol responsibility or is there a specialized Crime Scene Investigation unit to perform that function?

4) Taking a police report is generally a "ministerial duty," and police are not required to take reports. By law, what reports are police in your state required to take?

5) Why do you think specific crimes are mandated by law to be reported?

6) Why do you think guns are required to be unloaded before sending to a crime lab?

7) What is the penalty in your state for deliberately falsifying a police report?

Seattle police detective John Barnes was recently in court on a robbery case. There were two suspects in the case but only one had been apprehended. During the middle of the trial the defense came up with a mysterious witness that would prove the defendant innocent. In fact, he was right outside the courtroom.

A recess was called and everyone left the court, including the victim, who promptly identified the mystery witness as the second suspect, whom Barnes promptly arrested.

COURTROOM PROCEDURES

LEARNING GOALS: After studying this chapter the student will be able to:

- Name the participants in a trial.

- Define subpoena.

- List the stages of a criminal trial.

- Describe how a patrol officer prepares to testify at a trial.

- Explain the patrol officer's role in a trial.

- List some techniques for testifying.

- Explain how a witness should deal with the jury.

- List the types of questions you can expect to face.

- Describe the future trends for courts.

COURTROOM BASICS

If you're an active patrol officer in a busy area, you are going to be spending a lot of time in various courts. Up to this point, you have considered the person you arrested a "suspect." Now that you go to court, that person is considered a "defendant." The case will wind its way through the judicial system, following a formal script with specific steps. The better you know the script and the cast, the better you will represent your department and yourself in trials.

Throughout the court process, be patient, and be prepared to wait. Courts work on their own unique timetable, and the judges and attorneys have many other activities going on behind the scenes. Many courts are only open for six hours a day, and the judge may only be on the bench for an hour or two.

A very typical day for an officer in court in my area is as follows:

8:30 a.m.— Arrive at court (subpoena states 8:45 a.m.), but find the doors locked.

9:00 a.m.— Bailiff unlocks doors and lets you and the public inside.

9:30 a.m.— Judge arrives on bench, calls calendar. Most cases are either disposed of on the spot (bench warrant issued, dismissed, continued, trailed, etc.) or placed on "second call." Judge then leaves.

10:30 a.m.— "Second Call" - Judge arrives, calls calendar. More cases are disposed of with plea bargains, continuances, etc. Your case is declared "ready," but there is some other matter that comes first.

11:45 a.m.— Judge announces they are breaking for lunch, orders all witnesses to return at 1:45 p.m.

1:45 p.m.— You arrive at court, find the doors locked.

2:00 p.m.— Bailiff unlocks doors, lets you in.

2:30 p.m.— Judge arrives, calls calendar. More cases are disposed of. When finished, the judge calls your case. Prosecution calls their first witness, the victim. Defense makes a motion to exclude all witnesses. You go sit in the hall.

4:00 p.m.— You get called into the court to testify, spend five minutes on the stand and are finished. One of the attorneys asks the judge for permission to recall you as a witness if needed. You get sent out into the hall again.

5:00 p.m.— Judge adjourns for the day, the D.A. comes out and says, "Oh, are you still here? We didn't need you after all. You can go home now."

Don't get the impression that the day was a total waste of time, it wasn't. Many cases and matters were handled by the court. The fact of the matter is that most of the participants (including you) have little personal interest in the matters at hand — it's just a job. They often have little regard for the efficient use of your time — you're just another witness in one of many, many cases. All of those witnesses wish they could get out of there, just like you, and each has told a sad story to the attorneys as to why their case should be handled first. Get used to the fact that your priorities are different than the court's, and that your concept of efficient case handling is far different than the other participants.

Your job is not over until you testify.

Preliminary Hearing

In felony cases, the initial complaint is charged in the municipal court, which also holds the arraignment, followed within ten court days by a preliminary trial. A *preliminary trial* is basically a judicial screening process for felonies in which the prosecution has to demonstrate to a judge that they have sufficient cause to believe the defendant committed the crime.

Both the defendant and his attorney are present at the preliminary trial. You must approach this hearing seriously because the rest of your case depends on this one hearing. Prepare for it just as intently as you would for the trial. You have a great personal stake in what happens.

Your testimony on "direct examination" is the easy part. Expect the prosecuting D.D.A. to lead you through your report, establishing all the facts required to tie the defendant to the crime. When you get to cross-examination by the defense attorney, things will heat up for you. The defense attorney has a different agenda: he's not really attacking your reasonable cause and there won't be any "affirmative defense" (testimony by the defendant, witnesses, evidence, etc.); he's laying the groundwork for his defense during the next trial.

The defense attorney will ask you many questions to tire you out and anger you. Everything you say will be transcribed and recorded for eternity by the court reporter. By pressing you hard, the defense attorney hopes that he can get you to lie, exaggerate, contradict yourself, make assumptions, give additional information that isn't in the report, and volunteer information and opinions, all to use against you later at trial.

Expect to be cross-examined at length. I've had preliminary trials that took several days and been on the stand for several hours at a time. It's a boring and sometimes exhausting experience. You prepare for it by being completely familiar with your report and by sticking to what you know.

Once all the testimony and cross-examination is over the prosecutor will recap his case and tell the judge why he thinks the defendant is guilty. When he's done, the defense attorney will have his shot at the judge. If the case was weak or confusing in any way, he will probably make a motion to dismiss, based on the prosecution failing to prove the case. If that is denied, he will give all his reasons to the judge as to why there is reasonable doubt about his client's involvement in the crime.

If the deputy district attorney is successful, the defendant will be "held to answer" or "bound over" and scheduled for trial in Superior Court. If unsuccessful, the case will be dismissed. If the defendant is charged with both misdemeanors and felonies, the offenses can be "joined" and tried together in Superior Court. (Cases can also be initiated in Superior Court by a county Grand Jury, but the average patrol officer will rarely ever deal with that situation).

Pretrial Interviews

In the vast majority of cases in which I have appeared, the prosecuting attorney wanted to talk to me before the case. You can't influence all the political, financial and procedural considerations of the court and the district attorney's office, so try to just be professional, cooperate fully with your assigned deputy district attorney, and do your job.

The defense attorney may also want to talk to you. Don't treat him like the enemy; he isn't. He's just another professional trying to do his job. Treat him professionally. The defense attorney has the right to talk to you (and to all witnesses who will testify in the trial), that's part of the *discovery* process that guarantees the defense access to every bit of evidence that might be used against them, but you also have the right to decline to speak with him if you choose. You can also select the time, place, and who will be there at the interview.

The most common tactic of defense attorneys is to engage you in small talk. They'll sit down and ask you a question on a minor point, or ask your opinion. "Kind of a petty case, don't you think, Officer? How did you spot this guy, anyway? I bet you make a lot of more important arrests, right?" I've always gotten along pretty well with defense attorneys by not discussing the case directly. If they want small talk, you can talk about the weather, baseball, or that latest episode of *America's Funniest Home Videos*, but not their client and the case at hand.

On the other hand, if you are approached by a defense attorney (or sometimes by an investigator hired by the defense attorney) you can tell him you will be happy to be interviewed at any time and place designated by the prosecutor, and ask him to contact the prosecutor to make those arrangements.

PREPARATION

Most police officers who make lousy witnesses in court just haven't taken the time to prepare themselves. I've seen officers come to court on traffic citations where they haven't bothered to read the ticket and not move when the judge calls the defendant. That's sloppy work. You should always be familiar with all of the documents related to your case.

The amount of preparation you do for any case will depend on the seriousness of the case. For a traffic citation, probably just reading the ticket again will be sufficient (although I usually go drive the area again, just to refresh my memory on the position of signs, lights, lane markings, etc.). On a murder case, you may spend weeks of preparation, carefully reviewing every document and re-examining every piece of evidence.

Police Reports: The primary document is your police report. Read it, and reread it, until you are familiar with all of the basic events and facts that will matter in court. You would want to know the day, the date, and the times. You don't have to memorize license plates, birth dates, or exact quotes. That would sound phony in court. You should, however, be familiar enough with your report that if one of the attorneys asked you *exactly* what the suspect said, you could say, "I don't remember exactly, but I wrote it in my report." If the attorney requests, you can then look it up in your report, find it easily, and still sound professional and thorough.

Court Transcripts: You may have testified earlier at a preliminary trial or hearing. If so, the D.A. may have a written transcript of that trial. It's a great idea to read that over, as well as the report, to refresh your memory about details and questions that might come up at the trial. This will help prevent you from contradicting yourself and keep the defense from "beating you up" with your prior testimony if you don't answer in exactly the same way at the next trial. Of course, if you find you answered something incorrectly in the transcript, bring it up with the D.A. handling the case. This will allow him to ask you about it and "rehabilitate" you, clearing up the mistake before the defense attorney can make a "big deal" about it in front of the jury.

D.A. Interview: I've previously mentioned the advantage in meeting with the D.A. before testifying. Discussing the facts and evidence that he intends to question you about in trial helps both of you. You should ask him what questions you can anticipate from the defense. If the D.A. is willing to spend the time to interview you, make sure you take advantage of the opportunity. This means you have to get to court early enough to give the D.A. some time, accommodate his schedule, and cooperate with any reasonable request.

Return to the Scene: In many cases, there is no need to return to the scene of the crime, however, in others it will be extremely useful to refresh your memory before you go to court. If your activity took place at night, take a look at the scene in daylight. Retrace your steps from a foot pursuit or vehicle chase, and take another look at windows, doors, and other access points. If a defense attorney can convince a jury that you are mistaken about something so basic as the scene of the crime, he can argue that you are mistaken about the facts, identification of the defendant, and interpretation of the evidence.

Bring the Evidence: It sounds dumb, but a lot of officers show up in court without critical evidence (i.e., test results, photographs, weapons [always check them in with the bailiff, judges get paranoid about having guns in court] and narcotics [always leaving the drugs sealed if and until you are asked to open the envelope in court]).

In many agencies, getting the evidence will be a simple matter of going to the evidence room, filling in a log book, and then taking the evidence. In a more formalized, bureaucratic department, you may have to fill out a request several days in advance, appear at the appropriate time at the evidence room, and sign for receipt of the evidence from some property technician. It's your responsibility to keep possession of the evidence until you return it to the evidence room, or until it is entered into evidence by the court.

Once you get the evidence, examine it. Make sure it's the same evidence you remember. Attorneys typically will ask you what you expect to find before you look in an evidence envelope. This is a favorite trick of the defense in rock cocaine cases, since they know the appearance of the evidence may be changed by the lab in testing. You sent them one big rock, but they broke the rock in half to take a sample. You tell the defense attorney you expect to find one large rock of cocaine, but when you open it you find three. He'll tell the jury you obviously mixed up the evidence. Know what the evidence looks like, and how and where you marked it for identification. The typical introduction of the evidence into the trial starts with the D.A. showing the evidence to the judge. For example:

> "Your Honor, I am holding a Taurus .38 caliber revolver, with the serial number removed. May it be marked People's exhibit #1 for identification?" The D.A. will then bring the evidence to you.
>
> "Officer, I'm showing you a Taurus revolver that has been previously marked as People's exhibit #1. Do you recognize this revolver?" You should reply with a simple, "Yes" (or "No" if you've never seen it before).
>
> "Officer, how do you recognize this revolver?" You would answer appropriately, based on your knowledge of the evidence, perhaps something like, "It has the evidence tag I completed attached to the trigger guard, and it has my initials in marking pen on the butt."
>
> "Officer, where did you obtain this weapon?" Again, just say where you got it: "I removed it from the front waistband of Mr. Smith on April 19, 1994."
>
> "Your honor, People move to admit exhibit #1 into evidence."

Sometimes, you will be asked to create evidence in court. The D.A. will ask you to draw a map or diagram of a route or crime scene, mark it with your initials, and then explain it to the jury. You shouldn't talk while drawing, wait until you are finished and then answer any questions from the attorneys. As you indicate things on your drawing, the attorney will usually ask you to mark them with numbers or letters to clarify for the record those things that you might be pointing to. On completion, the map or drawing will also be "offered" as evidence in the trial.

Refreshing Your Memory

Always bring your report with you to court. In a really busy patrol area, you may be writing dozens of reports each week. There is no way you can remember all of the details of every report. At some point, one of the attorneys will ask you some detail that both you and he know are

Use your time waiting to testify wisely by reviewing your report.

in the report, but a detail that you cannot remember. At that point, one of two things will happen. Either the attorney will suggest looking at the report to "refresh your memory," or you should ask permission, "I don't remember that information, may I refer to the report?"

Just be aware that there is a slight hazard in doing so. In some trials, the prosecutor may not want the jury to read the report, and may not have introduced it into evidence. If you bring a report to the witness stand, it can be "discovered." The defense can then introduce the report into evidence and ask you about anything at all in the report.

Impartiality

When you go into court, it's critically important to remember that you are there as an impartial witness, unbiased, dedicated to telling the truth no matter what the outcome of the trial might be. You aren't there to represent the prosecution, to help the prosecutor win his case, or to tear apart the defense; you are there to represent *the truth*.

Don't worry about the verdict, and don't try to anticipate the outcome of your testimony. On the stand, you need to treat the D.A., and the defense attorney alike, in a respectful, friendly, relaxed, non-confrontational manner. Don't try to help out the prosecution any more than the defense. Just answer the questions, and ask for clarification if you don't understand something. Don't volunteer information for the prosecution, and don't evade questions from the defense.

If you treat the defense attorney like something you'd like to scrape off your shoe, the jury will quickly recognize your dislike and begin to question your motives. That can hurt the case more than anything you might say if you were entirely open and honest.

Demeanor

Part of your demeanor is to remain absolutely professional in the face of insult and attack. Some defense attorneys deliberately try to get police officers angry on the witness stand, and many are highly skilled in doing so. They may attack you personally and professionally, painting a picture of you as untrained, uneducated, out-of-policy, and out of control.

Such attorneys are obnoxious and offensive for a specific purpose — to make your testimony personal rather than professional, to engage you in a battle of wits, to make you angry enough to cloud your thinking, disturb the flow of your testimony, and perhaps result in some spontaneous, angry comment that will help his case by making you appear to be an angry, spontaneous cop. If you react by becoming sarcastic, irritable, or insulting, you'll just lower yourself to his level. By understanding this defense tactic for what it is and keeping your testimony cool and professional in spite of such attack, you will be even more credible before the jury.

Dress for Success

When you go to court, you need to dress in a professional manner and in strict accordance with your department policy. Dress in a manner that tells the court that the case is important to you. Our department specifies either a uniform or a coat and tie. I've seen some officers comply with the letter of the policy by wearing a sports jacket and tie over their Levis. That's not a professional image. Since I'm a patrol officer, and what I do usually takes place in uniform, I like to testify in uniform. That lets the judge and jury see me like the defendant saw me, as a uniformed patrol officer.

When I worked in plain clothes at the time of the arrest, I prefer to wear plain clothes to court. Some officers show up in court in Levis, a "cop" T-shirt, Sam Brown and a raid jacket. That sends a clear message to the jury that you simply don't think the case is important and are a person who will do the absolute minimum necessary to get a job done. I prefer to look like one of the attorneys and wear a nice, conservative, pin-striped suit, or a sports jacket and slacks. I want the judge and jury to see someone who is professional in everything he does.

Professional also means not wearing sunglasses, wild prints, goofy ties (I've seen an officer wear a Three Stooges tie to court), gaudy jewelry, fraternity pins, obvious weapons, earrings on males, excessive makeup, or outrageous fashions. Wear conservative business attire, and you'll be more credible in court.

Officers in the Hall

As an officer testifying in court, you will find you spend a lot of time in the hallway. It's a wasteland of defendants conferring with their attorneys, jurors waiting for their trials to begin, and witnesses waiting to testify. Most officers try to make the best of it by having a good time with other officers, shooting the bull, telling a few good stories, and having a few laughs.

Unfortunately, many times the jurors on your case are sitting in the same hallway. They may assume that you are laughing about their case, and if they see you clowning around they may make the assumption that you are a clown. When they see you talking with other officers, they may well assume you are discussing that case causing the jurors to doubt your honesty. Just treat the hallway as part of the courtroom, and maintain the same professional standards as if you were in front of the jury. Who knows, that might be just the case.

CREDIBILITY

When you go into court, you need to be confident (not cocky) and professional in everything you do. You don't want to do anything in court that will make a judge or jury question your honesty in any way.

One of the things you will do is to promise to tell the truth. When you are called as a witness, you will either approach the clerk or mount the witness stand, face the clerk, raise your right hand and take the oath. There is a great variation from state to state, but most of them sound something like this:

> Do you, and each of you, solemnly swear or affirm
> that the testimony you are about to give in the matter
> now pending before this court is the truth, the whole
> truth, and nothing but the truth, so help you God?

You should stand during the oath with your head up and your shoulders back, essentially at attention. When the clerk is finished, you should answer in a clear voice, "Yes," or "I do." Then have a seat, adjust the microphone if necessary, and get ready for your testimony.

TECHNIQUES OF TESTIFYING

Testifying is not an easy, natural thing. I've testified many times over the years, and I still get nervous. It's important that you try to look as natural as possible. Show your interest, and pay attention to what people are saying. Don't lounge on the stand, sit up straight and be alert. Don't be cocky or sarcastic, but don't be afraid to be yourself. A sense of humor is fine (you can laugh at yourself), but don't make jokes on the stand. The court is not a comedy club.

Don't worry if you can't quite figure out what the attorneys are doing or where a particular line of questioning is headed. Sometimes the attorneys don't know either. There is a wide range of competency in the court, and some attorneys just aren't very organized. Others may simply be on a fishing trip, stirring up the testimony in the hopes of coming up with something good.

As a witness, you can only testify to facts you know of your own personal knowledge. You can't testify about what other people saw or did or thought. You can't testify about what you don't know, and usually you can't testify about your conclusions ("Objection! Calls for a conclusion on the part of the witness") or your opinions. That means you testify to what you saw, heard, or smelled.

Sometimes you'll need to illustrate your testimony.

You will testify about virtually every action you took during the course of the case. Most times, you had a good, valid, legal reason for doing what you did. When asked about it in court, explain it in a calm rational manner. The defense attorney will ask you questions that will make you and the jury think you did something wrong. If you get flustered and defensive, the jury will begin to think something *is* wrong.

As you sit on the witness stand, try to be relaxed, but don't slouch. Pay close attention to what is going on, and fold your hands in your lap if you need to.

You and the Jury

Some attorneys don't like you to look at the jury. They feel that a police officer will make them uncomfortable. I like to look at the jury, usually right after I sit down. After all, they are the audience that this entire show is directed toward. They should be the focal point of the courtroom. Scan the jury and get a feel for what type of people are there and how they are feeling. Jurors often get abused by the system; they get frustrated and angry. If the jurors look interested, you can probably testify in a little greater detail. If they're frustrated and angry, try to keep answers as short and simple as possible.

Once the attorneys start asking questions, you should direct most of your attention to them. You will notice that competent prosecutors often move around to position themselves in front of the jury, so your attention can be focused on them. Defense attorneys will manipulate you as well, standing on the opposite side of the court from the jury to direct your attention away from them. Remember that the jury is your audience, so if the question requires a lengthy answer, look to the jury as you answer.

Off the stand, bear in mind that the jurors can be anywhere. They could be sitting beside you in the hall, using the next stall in the bathroom, or eating at the next table in the cafeteria. Assume that the jury could be anywhere and behave appropriately. If the judge has ordered you not to discuss your testimony with other witnesses, stay away from any other witnesses. In general, stay away from the jury.

This doesn't mean that you have to avoid the jurors or act in an uncivilized manner. If you both come to a door, open the door politely. If a juror greets you, return his "Hello" or "Good Morning." But if a juror comments on anything related to the case or the trial, tell them politely but firmly that you cannot talk with them until the trial is over. Then let the prosecutor know exactly what conversation took place.

English

In the previous chapter on reports, we've discussed how important it is to write in a natural style. The same holds true for your testimony in court. Imagine the confusion you would create for a jury full of housewives when an attorney asks, "What did you tell the defendant to do?" and you answer, "I directed him to exit his vehicle." What does that mean? Did you tell him something, or did you gesture? Did you want him to get out of the car or did you want him to drive his car to a freeway offramp? Your answer should be clear and direct, "I told him to step out of his car."

When you're talking about the defendant, you should generally refer to him by his last name. "I told Mr. Smith to drop the gun," not "I told Fred (or "the defendant," "the suspect," or "the perpetrator") to drop the gun." That will also make your testimony consistent with the use of the last name throughout the report.

Pretend you're talking to your old aunt when you testify, and get rid of any police jargon, formal language, and profanity. (The expression "swearing like a trooper" refers to cavalrymen in the U.S. Army, not to State Troopers. It is not acceptable for a member of any law enforcement agency. Anytime you're in court, you should watch your #&#%*@!! mouth.) Just tell your story in plain English. Testify the way you talk, and don't worry about using contractions, idioms, or proper grammar and diction. Using police terminology, slang, or formal language will simply create communication barriers between you, the judge, and the jury. Speak in plain language, using the simplest, most direct language possible.

Objections

As you testify, any one of the attorneys may object to either the question or the answer. There is a formal procedure where the attorney says, "Objection!" and then states his reasons. As soon as you hear an attorney make an objection, you should stop and wait for the judge to make a decision. (If they don't like the interruption and want to get the answer into the record, some officers try to answer quickly before the attorney can explain. In this case, the judge will "strike" or remove your answer from the court record, so don't even bother with this tactic. It just makes you look dumb.)

Typical objections might be:

"Calls for a conclusion on the part of the witness,"

"Lack of foundation,"

" Irrelevant,"

"Argumentative," or

" Hearsay."

The judge will then allow the opposing attorney to be heard as to why the question or answer should be allowed. Then the judge makes a decision, which can be *sustained* (meaning he agrees and won't allow the question), *over-ruled* (meaning he disagrees with the objection and will allow the question), or a conditional answer "Over-ruled, but limited for purposes of probable cause in the preliminary hearing only." Once he rules on the objection, the judge will usually give an instruction, either, "You may ask your next question" to the attorney, or "The witness will answer the question" to you.

Sometimes the attorneys will argue about the objection for a considerable amount of time, quoting case law and law journal opinions. Sometimes courts break for lunch while the judge considers the objection. By the time they finish, you may not remember the question (sometimes they don't either). If you can't remember the question, just ask to have it repeated.

Volunteering Information

Your job as a witness is to answer the question and then stop. If the question can be answered with a "yes" or a "no," do so. Answer the question completely, but simply, and then stop. If the D.A. wants more detail, he'll ask you for it. If you volunteer information, you are just giving the defense more ammunition to use in tearing away at the prosecution's case.

On the other hand, it is perfectly correct for you to request to explain an answer if an explanation is necessary to prevent misunderstanding. I once testified in a case where I had identified four suspects from several hundred feet away. Answering "yes" and "no" questions from the D.A., I never had the opportunity to tell the court I was using binoculars. The defense attorney asked if I could identify faces at that distance. My answers could have been:

A) "No" (meaning — "not without binoculars"),

B) "Yes" (meaning — "certainly, when I use binoculars"), or

C) "Yes, but to avoid misunderstanding I should explain."

I answered "C," and the judge told me to go ahead and explain. I could then tell the court that I was using binoculars at the time I made the identification, that I always carry and often use my binoculars, and find I can easily identify people at several hundred feet by doing so.

Times and Distances

Times and distances can be important in a trial. They can make the difference between lawful and unlawful detentions, arrests, consents, searches, etc. They have a direct bearing on the accuracy of your report. They are very subjective. Perceptions may easily be altered by stress and the conditions at the time and thus, very easy to attack in court.

When it comes to time, don't just guess. In advance, check your dispatch radio logs so you know exactly how long it took to get to a call, detain a suspect, place him under arrest, take him to the station, and process and release him. Have those numbers handy in case you are asked. If asked about some time period that isn't recorded, tell the court your reasoning as you calculate it. If asked, "How long was it from the time you arrested Mr. Smith until he took the breath test?", you might answer, "Once I arrested him, I put him in my car and then called a tow truck. That usually takes about twenty minutes. Then I drove him to jail, about another five minutes, and we completed the preliminary search and booking paperwork, that usually takes about ten minutes, so I would say it was at least thirty-five minutes."

You should handle distances in a similar manner. If you're talking about a vehicle pursuit, drive it again and take note of the mileage. For shorter distances, measure when at all possible. Some attorneys like to play a game by having you estimate distances in the court room. I already know (by measurement) exactly how far it is from the witness stand to the first row of seats and the back wall in our local courts, so making an "estimate" in court is a little easier. If you don't know a distance, say so. Say, "I didn't measure it at the time, but the distance was about the same as from you to me (or between you and the bailiff, the flag pole, the rear door, or whatever is a similar distance)."

If you don't know the exact measurements, you can always approximate and qualify your answer as an approximation. The same is true for colors, ages, height, weight, temperatures, etc.

The Report on Trial

At some point in most trials, it seems like the report itself is on trial. Typically, the defense attorney asks:

"Did you write a report on this case?"

"Did you make any mistakes in writing this report?"

"Does this report contain all of the important facts?"

"Isn't the purpose of the report to document all the important facts about a crime?"

"You just testified to details that were not in the report. Why? Did you make a mistake, were you covering up the truth when you wrote the report, or are you lying now?"

Certainly, you will testify to different details in court than are written in the report. You can't write down every detail. Your report has only the important facts you used to establish that the defendant committed the crime. You can't judge how important the things you left out are until someone asks you at trial.

If you face this kind of questioning, you should answer that the report was accurate, factual and complete at the time, and your testimony is accurate, factual, and complete now. You simply can't report every conceivable detail in every report you take and you can't know the importance of any given detail when you write the report. If you made a mistake or omitted some important information that comes out at trial, simply admit you made a mistake. Everybody makes mistakes, but only a fool tries to cover up in court.

Questions

One thing that defense attorneys tend to do is ask questions, a lot of questions, sometimes confusing, sometimes seemingly stupid. They are all part of an overall effort to damage your testimony and reduce your effectiveness. If you show yourself easily confused by a rapidly changing, rapid-fire set of circumstances in court, wouldn't it be reasonable for the jury to assume that you were simply confused with the rapidly changing, rapid-fire set of circumstances in the field?

If you get a good D.A., he may run interference for you on some questions by making a timely objection. Always give the D.A. a few seconds before answering, so he has a chance to object before you blurt out the answer. Be prepared for some of these typical types of questions from the defense:

Surprise Questions: Occasionally an attorney will drop a question on you that takes you totally by surprise, something you forgot, something you missed, something that bears directly on your character or credibility. As an example, I had a case involving a black defendant in which the defense attorney suddenly asked, "Officer, you don't like niggers, do you?" There was a storm of protest from the prosecutor, and the judge made the attorney rephrase the question to, "Are you prejudiced against African Americans?" The original question was done purely to shock me and get me mad, and to make the jury think that those were my thoughts.

It was probably a stupid question on his part, and I think it hurt his standing in front of the jury. It really didn't bother me, and I didn't try to make a big deal out of it. I just answered, "I don't think I'm prejudiced against anyone based solely on their race." Just bear in mind that the only thing that really matters in court is the truth. Facts don't hurt a case, they simply exist to be interpreted by the judge and jury. If new facts surprise you, just keep calm, try not to look shocked, and answer the question truthfully.

Offensive Questions: Some defense attorneys can be incredibly hostile (actually, some prosecutors also share this trait). It's a specific technique designed to disrupt your testimony. Be professional, and simply answer the question as frankly as possible. Never get angry or argue with an attorney in court. Bear in mind that you are both professionals and simply doing your jobs to the best of your ability. If the D.A. realizes that the defense attorney is trying to start an argument, the prosecutor may object to the question as argumentative.

Confusing Questions: I can't count the number of times that an attorney has asked me such a lengthy, confusing, compound question, that I had no idea at all what he was asking. Court trials are complicated things, and some attorneys don't think well on their feet. If you can't figure out what the attorney is asking, don't guess, just say, "I don't understand your question." Usually the attorney will rephrase the question or explain what he meant.

Compound Questions: A compound question is one in which the attorney is really asking more than one question at a time. Sometimes you can clarify what the attorney is asking and answer the separate parts of the question in a manner that makes sense. If you can't, ask the attorney what part of the question he wants you to answer first.

Fast Questions: There's an old tongue-twister type of gag in which you ask someone to spell "S-T-O-P" ten times as fast as they can (try it, it's tougher than you might think), and then ask them "What do you do when you come to a green light?" The vast majority of people will say "Stop!", because the spelling task has prepared them for that response.

Rapid-fire questioning is just another technique used by defense attorneys. It's an effort to establish a rhythm of quick answers in the hopes of disturbing your composure. Your testimony is not part of a race so don't try to keep up with an attorney that acts like he's on methamphetamines and engages you in this type of questioning. Pause to consider the question and take your time in answering.

Friendly Questions: One defense technique is to get chummy with the witnesses, pretending to be a friend. He may ask if he can call you by your first name, suggest you call him by his first name, tell a few little jokes to get you laughing or do anything to get you to act in a social and unprofessional manner. It's okay to be human and smile at the defense's jokes, but don't lower yourself to his level.

Repeated Questions: If a defense attorney doesn't like your answer to a particular question, he may ask it again and again throughout the cross-examination. It could be exactly the same question, or it could be rephrased. The defense attorney is hoping for a slightly different (or completely different) answer so he can show that you contradicted your own testimony. If the D.A. catches what he's asking, he'll object ("Asked and answered" is the common form of the objection). If he doesn't, you can always call attention to the repeated question by responding, "I think you asked me that question earlier."

Repeated Answers: If you've ever seen the old films of congressional hearings in which Senator McCarthy was asking famous actors about their affiliations with the Communist Party, you know the most damning answer of all was to stand on one's Fifth Amendment rights and refuse to answer. McCarthy certainly knew that and used it to his advantage, forcing them to invoke their rights time and time again. Defense attorneys use a similar tactic by asking you a whole series of questions about which you know nothing. They hope to hear you answer time and time again with "I don't know," or "I don't remember." If you say it enough times, it can erode your credibility, just like McCarthy did in those hearings.

To avoid this image, take the time to carefully consider each question posed by the defense, and then give an appropriate response to that individual question. You might answer, "I didn't make any notation of that at the time," "I'm unaware of that," "No one mentioned that when I interviewed them," etc.

Ignorance: Some of the best answers you can give in any trial include: "I don't know," "I can't remember," and "I didn't see or hear that." Some officers seem compelled to come up with an answer for every question they are asked in court. A smart defense attorney will just keep asking questions about more and more unlikely subjects and make the officer look like an idiot.

If you don't know the answer to a question, just say so. It takes an honest person to admit ignorance, and telling the judge and jury that you don't know something will only add to your credibility.

Summaries: A favorite tactic of defense attorneys is the **summary**, a paraphrasing and condensation of your previous testimony. He'll begin with something like, "You've previously testified to the fact that..." and then paraphrase what you said. Make sure what he says accurately represents what you testified to because it is very easy for him to subtly change the meaning or importance of what you said.

In a burglary trial, I testified that I saw the defendant carrying a rolled-up, orange, terrycloth towel under his arm. He hid the towel, I found it, and it contained jewelry from a burglary. During cross-examination, the defense attorney made a major point over my identifying it as a towel. "Since it was rolled up, it could have been anything," he said. "Could it have been a robe?" "Could it have been a shirt?" "Could it have been a seat cover?" And then he summarized, "Since you testified you didn't know it was a towel, it could have been anything made of cloth, couldn't it?" My answer was, "No, it could have been any rolled-up, orange, terrycloth, towel-like material, but that was the only similar object anywhere near the defendant, and that object was a towel."

Case Discussion

Most defense attorneys will ask, "Did you talk to anyone else about your testimony?" The clear implication is that it would be bad to do so because your discussion of potential testimony would mean the D.A. coached you, or you were meeting with other officers to eliminate any possible contradictions. The fact is there is nothing wrong with discussing the facts of the case and your potential testimony with everyone involved. On the other hand, the D.A. shouldn't tell you *how* to testify (although many D.A.'s will tell you exactly that, to the point of saying, "If they ask you that, I want you to say this.")

Whether the answer is "yes" or "no," just say the truth. The answer may well be, "Yes, since I was writing the report, I discussed this case and everyone's testimony with every witness and officer at the scene, as well as the sergeant that approved the arrest, the lieutenant that approved the report, the detectives that did the follow up investigation, the deputy D.A. that filed the case, and the prosecutor handling the case today. We didn't talk about how I was going to testify, we talked about all of the facts of the case."

COURTS OF THE FUTURE

To anyone looking at the future of our court system, a number of things should be immediately obvious. First, everyone seems to recognize that the system is not ideal, and some changes are desirable. Second, there is a general feeling that we are too light on crime. Every politician in the last few years seems to be campaigning on issues of getting tough on crime, and efforts to raise taxes to build new prisons are still being passed. Third, virtually every form of government in the United States whether federal, state, or local, is facing budget problems where there is simply not enough money or resources to fulfill their missions in the way they have in the past.

Any observer of the court system can tell you that the American justice system is not efficient. One could argue that the summary execution of people in dictatorships is far more efficient, but obviously somewhat less protective of the rights of the accused than we are. Our system is so fiercely protective of the innocent that any changes in the court system are likely to keep most Constitutional safeguards in place. The use of video equipment is beginning to be established in the courts for the first time and will probably continue to grow. You can expect that any procedure that can be done with fewer resources, while still protecting rights, is going to be implemented in the next decade. Some of the things you could expect to see include:

Decriminalization of most traffic offenses: In many states, parking violations have become a strictly civil, administrative procedure, that never enter the courtroom. The issuing police agency handles the entire process by providing their own hearing officer and appeal process, and using civil procedures to collect the fines when necessary. In some states in New England, the same type of administrative procedure is used for speeding violations documented by photo-radar. In essence, the car receives the ticket, and the registered owner is responsible for the fine regardless of who was driving. In the next decade, I would expect every infraction, and many misdemeanors, to be handled in the same manner.

Downsized Juries: Juries are an expensive factor in major criminal trials. The selection and protection of a jury in a major case may take months and create incredible expenses for a small jurisdiction. Yet nowhere in the Constitution is it specified that a jury has to be twelve persons, that the jury has to be made up of an even number, or that the jury has to be present in the courtroom. The jury of the future might be smaller, perhaps six people, and they may be at remote locations far from the courtroom. Jurors could even be separated, each in some location alone, watching by video, deliberating the case by teleconference, and voting by video.

Longer Court Hours: Obviously, most courts are used only forty hours a week. With the courts overcrowded, it would be far cheaper to appoint more judges and hire more personnel and staff the same courtrooms for longer hours and weekends. The consequence could be that officers would have to appear on subpoenas at odd hours as well.

Trial by Declaration: In many states, traffic offenses are heard with no testimony from the officer. Instead, the court receives a written declaration from the officer describing what happened and uses that instead of direct testimony. This concept could easily expand to other criminal cases, and declarations (or depositions) may be done by video.

User fees: Today, it seems there are fees for everything. Some agencies charge up to eighty-five dollars for a copy of a traffic accident report, fifty dollars for a vehicle release form, up to a thousand dollars for the emergency response of police and firefighters to a drunk driver. Expect this concept to enter the court, perhaps with the salaries for officers going to court coming out of the D.A.'s budget, and with the loser in a criminal court trial (and any subsequent appeal) being billed for the costs of running those courts.

Video Arraignments: At present, most suspects are housed in a jail and then shipped to court for their arraignments. Expect video appearances, with the prisoner never leaving the jail, to be the norm in the future. Video trials may follow shortly.

Video Transcripts: Obviously, composing written transcripts on every trial is an expensive and time consuming process. Appeal courts in the future might look at a videotape of the entire trial, and thus be able to review not only the words, but the gestures, behaviors, and expressions in determining the propriety of any court decision.

DISCUSSION QUESTIONS

1) Does your state have a "Victim's Bill of Rights?" If so, what does that legislation contain?

2) Should plea-bargaining be eliminated from our court system? Why or why not?

3) Does the existing system of trial give too great an advantage to either the prosecutor or the defense?

4) What changes would you suggest to our current trial procedures?

5) Do you think the current standard of twelve jurors should be changed to something larger or smaller?

6) Is the current system of jury selection fair to all participants in a trial? Why or why not?

7) Do you think the losing party in a criminal trial should pay for the legal costs of the winning party?

8) Most police officers receive overtime for their court testimony. Do you think that affects their testimony in any way?

Four white men in Nashville, NC, were charged with shooting a black man and starting some fires, apparently solely for the purpose of provoking blacks to riot so that, during the ensuing melee, the four whites would themselves be able to loot some local stores.

CIVIL DISTURBANCES AND OTHER DISASTERS

LEARNING GOALS: After studying this chapter the student will be able to:

- Define the patrol officer's function in an emergency.

- List the duties of a "first responder."

- Name the considerations in setting up a command post.

- Explain mutual aid and how it is invoked.

- List the special precautions and actions a patrol officer should take in:

  — a civil unrest incident.

  — a bombing incident.

  — a hazardous materials incident.

  — a natural disaster.

  — a transportation incident involving a train, aircraft, or common carrier.

  — a major fire.

DEALING WITH DISASTER

All across America, people like to compare their cities to the towns painted by Norman Rockwell, and they like to talk about their police department like *Andy of Mayberry*. Everywhere I've gone I've heard the citizens, and the leaders of different communities, say again and again, "It can't happen here."

The fact is that it can happen here, and, given enough time, it will happen in your city too. During my career I've responded to incredible disasters that people just didn't think could happen in our city: multiple homicides, major earthquakes, floods, landslides, fires, bombings, strikes and hazardous materials incidents, and the greatest riots in U.S. history. In each of these incidents, we responded and dealt with the disaster with a minimum of personnel, equipment, supplies and planning. We got by, and we coped with the incident.

Time after time it has been proven that regardless of the plans made by management, it is you, the patrol officer (the "first responder"), that lays all the groundwork for a successful operation. What you do in those first critical minutes can save lives.

Fortunately, your reaction as a patrol officer to any disaster can be learned, and each disaster, no matter how different, requires you to perform many similar duties and functions. Just like a domestic disturbance call, each disaster shares many common characteristics, yet each is entirely unique. And like domestic disturbance calls, each disaster can threaten your survival.

Mental Preparation

You begin preparing for disasters by looking around your city and using your imagination. When I looked around my city to see what the dangers were, the potential for disaster seemed everywhere. Our city lies directly atop an active earthquake fault, and the last major earthquake damaged eighteen hundred structures in our city. Certainly, another major earthquake was a very real possibility.

Over a quarter of my city is covered in brushy hillsides with narrow, winding streets and marginal water pressure. Given the right wind conditions, my city could easily lose several hundred homes and encounter countless casualties.

Train tracks run from one side of my city to the other. I used to wonder what dangerous things might be contained in the seemingly endless freight trains and pondered on how I would respond to a derailment of an Amtrak passenger train. Now that railroad line has been purchased by the Metropolitan Transit Authority and will soon carry light rail passenger cars through our city at six minute intervals. The potential for disaster seems even bigger. How might I handle a crash between two of these passenger cars or a collision at an intersection with a semi-truck?

Looking into the sky, my city sits right under one of the busiest air corridors in the country. Commercial aircraft sometimes fly so low that I can make out the airline from the paint patterns. Not a shift goes by that the windows aren't rattled by helicopters from the military, law enforcement, and commercial enterprises. Private aircraft sometimes fly low enough to read their FAA numbers. It's only a matter of time before something falls out of the sky on my city. How could I and the other three officers on my shift cope with a disaster of that magnitude?

The streets aren't safe from disaster either. There's a freeway crossing my city, and semi-trucks and charter buses tear up the pavement of the main streets of my town every day. Who is to say what they all carry?

Almost twenty years ago, a large amount of my time in the police academy was spent learning riot formations and tactics. Ten years ago, I would have thought the potential for civil unrest was pretty unlikely, but the last few years have shown that the potential for riots is a very real and frightening possibility.

As with so many other aspects of law enforcement, your preparation for handling any disaster begins in your head. You need to begin thinking now about what disasters you could face as a patrol officer and begin thinking about how you would survive, respond to, and handle each.

Equipment

Your department will probably issue you the equipment they feel is appropriate to fulfill your patrol duties. In my department, that equipment has recently included riot gear: military Kevlar helmets, flak vests, gas masks, disposable handcuffs, and extra ammunition. Staying within department policies, you may want to carry some

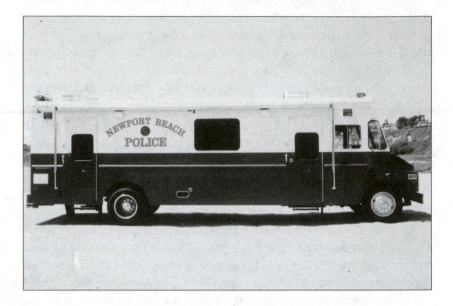

Typical mobile command center with interior view below.

additional equipment to ensure your survival capabilities in any kind of disaster. For instance, we know that in a major earthquake, flood, or hurricane; it may take several days for emergency assistance to get into your area. Could you care for your own needs for a few days? You might consider some basics: food, water, bedding, and toilet paper.

You need to constantly evaluate the risks you face and act accordingly. In my area, I don't have to worry about extreme cold weather, however, we do get fierce "Santa Ana" winds, so I carry goggles to protect my eyes. Because of the reality of earthquakes in my part of the world, I always carry my helmet, heavy leather gloves, and a couple of flashlights for rescue work. Recognizing the fact that our one paramedic unit may be overwhelmed in a city of twenty-five thousand people, I carry a lot of heavy bandages to control major wounds and a resuscitation bag to help with CPR.

If blizzards are a real potential in your area, you need to carry the necessary items to keep warm and continue functioning if you should become cut off from the rest of the world. If you live in a desert community, you may need to carry extra water and various types of survival gear. People living along the major river valleys of the Midwest face almost annual flooding and might want to carry flotation gear or rescue lines. Those who live on the southern coasts may face hurricanes, and those who live in Oklahoma and Kansas face tornadoes. Wherever you live, you have to evaluate the disasters you face. You have to make the decisions as to how you are going to react, survive, and fulfill your duties to your community, and then regardless of the equipment issued by the agency, you have to make sure you are prepared to fulfill those duties to the best of your ability.

Mutual Aid

Few law enforcement agencies have all the resources required to cope with any disaster that might occur. As a result, they all depend on *mutual aid*, the concept of borrowing officers, equipment, and supplies from other agencies. Mutual aid can be day-to-day, local, regional, or statewide. As a patrol officer, you really don't much care where help is coming from (or where *you* might be sent to help). During the Rodney King riots, I saw police officers from all over the state, including Highway Patrol officers, National Guard units and federal officers. Anyone with a badge and a gun was welcome to help out.

As a patrol officer, you will not be the one to request mutual aid. That request should come from your chief or at least the watch commander. When that person requests mutual aid, he will need to brief the agencies that are going to help and give them some estimate of the number of officers needed to assist, the equipment the responding officers should bring, and the location where they should stage. That is information that you, as a patrol officer on the scene, are probably best qualified to supply. Your primary responsibility in a mutual aid situation is to let your superiors know what you think your department will need to deal with this particular disaster and this unique situation.

Situation Assessment

One of your first responsibilities at the scene of an emergency is to figure out exactly what you have and communicate that to your supervisors. This evaluation is called a *situation estimate*. This basic intelligence information will be conveyed through the dispatch to whoever is making the decisions and acting on your information. Your initial situation estimate should include:

1) the type of emergency,

2) the exact location of the emergency,

3) the type of structures and/or vehicles involved in the emergency,

4) the exact size of the area involved and affected by the emergency,

5) the number of additional officers you think will be required to handle the emergency,

6) a suitable location for the Field Command Post,

7) a suitable location for a staging area,

8) safe, suitable, and convenient access routes for emergency vehicles and responding personnel,

9) any additional assistance you think might be required (ambulances, fire personnel, highway maintenance, public utilities,

Red Cross, National Highway Safety Transportation Board, etc.)

10) the number and type of casualties (your best estimate of those affected, evacuated, injured, and killed).

When you call dispatch with this information, you should have an organized, complete report. This avoids having the watch commander have to play "Twenty Questions" with you through the dispatcher and will expedite getting the assistance your community needs into the area.

Taking Action

Once you have assessed the situation and communicated with your watch commander through dispatch, you can direct your attention to control measures to actually deal with the disaster. As a patrol officer, your primary responsibilities include:

1) protecting life,

2) maintaining order in the community,

3) conducting traffic control,

4) protecting critical facilities from further damage,

5) controlling access to the involved area,

6) establishing communication, and

7) coordinating the response of other emergency personnel.

Once again, your first actions may well determine the success of all the operations that follow. What you do in the first few minutes are critical to resolving or "mitigating" the disaster. You need to understand your agency's policies and procedures, balance those with your knowledge of the area and field operations, and approach every incident positively, professionally, and properly. By positively, that means you should be sure of the outcome, sure of your abilities to do your duties, and sure of your agency's ability to ultimately deal with the disaster in an effective, comprehensive manner.

Setting Up a Command Post

Often one of the responsibilities of the first officers to arrive on the scene of a disaster is to establish a command post. It's important to select a suitable location. Typical places that might make a good command post site include: schools, parks, parking lots, closed roadways, and other government facilities. Some of the considerations you should make in choosing a command post site would be:

- strategic location close (but not dangerously close) to the disaster site;

- easy access to responding personnel and equipment;

- defensibility against snipers, mobs, bombs, etc.;

- sufficient space to assemble, stage, and organize responding personnel and equipment;

- availability of restroom facilities;

- availability of phones;

- access to electricity;

- available lighting;

- access to water (for fire fighting equipment, washing, and drinking);

- access to gas and other vehicle maintenance facilities;

- availability of a suitable helicopter landing area;

- structures for personnel briefing, rest, meals, and protection from the weather;

- storage facilities;

- suitable facilities to use as a temporary jail; and

- suitable facilities to use for a temporary morgue.

Once a site has been selected, you need to notify dispatch of the location, designate the routes you feel are appropriate for responding assistance and personnel.

Command Responsibility

At any given incident, there may be a huge number of personnel arriving from many different agencies and various emergency services. You might have fire departments, state officials, national guard units, politicians, and volunteer organizations. A major question might be, "Who's in charge?" Until that question is answered, it will be very difficult to deal with the emergency in an effective manner.

The responsibility for commanding any given incident starts with you as the first officer on the scene and can then shift once the nature of the event is determined and additional personnel arrive. A field supervisor, station commander, or staff officer arriving *may* assume command from you, but there must be a clear shift of the authority. Since you were assigned to the call, the incident is your responsibility until you are relieved. In other words, the sergeant or captain that arrives should tell you, "I'll take over now." The mere presence of a higher ranking officer doesn't mean they have assumed command. They may just want to observe or advise you, and let you handle the incident.

There can only be one incident commander. For most events that involve some sort of crime, the law enforcement agency will be in charge. For most events that involve natural disasters and forces of nature, the fire department (Chief, Battalion Chief, or some other member of the command staff) will assume command. Certain types of man-made incidents such as nuclear contamination or hazardous materials might involve other agencies, and the command structure might vary depending on the pre-existing plans in your area.

The incident commander only has jurisdiction over events in the field and at the scene of the disaster. In turn, he may be reporting to some higher command authority back at the station, either a watch commander, chief, or just a designated "officer in charge" (OIC). Generally the person back at the station monitors the radio traffic and dispatch operations, maintains records, assigns and coordinates personnel responding to the station, assists with liaison with other departments and agencies, and helps coordinate logistics and intelligence for use in the field. Depending on the size and scope of the disaster, there may be:

1) an Operations OIC (to formulate and execute the operational plans),

2) a Personnel OIC (to receive officers, account and assign for officers, track their assignments, and provide for their relief),

3) a Logistics OIC (to request, receive, and issue all assigned vehicles and other equipment, to provide for the security of the command post, and to command the field jail operations),

4) a Planning and Intelligence OIC (to gather, record, and evaluate information, arrests, and results; and to handle the media either himself or through an assigned "Public Information Officer" [PIO] or "Press Liaison Officer"),

5) a Communications OIC (to coordinate dispatch operations, to receive and record assignments, and to assign frequencies and radio equipment), and perhaps

6) other people designated as "Command Staff."

Disaster Areas

If the disaster is of sufficient magnitude, poses a threat to the public, or if crowds or onlookers are interfering with your operations or investigations, you may want to close the area to the public. Every state gives that authority to peace officers (and sometimes other emergency personnel).

You, as a patrol officer, can close your command post and the area around almost any disaster, including even a traffic accident. You have to mark the area physically, or with appropriate personnel, and you can arrest anyone, except a member of the press, who enters that area.

Basically, the only time you can keep the media out of a disaster area or any other area of police operation is if it is also a crime scene or if their presence would somehow interfere with the rescue efforts of emergency personnel. If the media wants to walk into danger and kill themselves getting the story, they are free to do so, and you don't have the legal authority to stop them.

In the first part of this chapter, we dealt with some generic instructions that can apply to almost any disaster. In the following pages are some much more specific comments, descriptions, and checklists for some common types of incidents. Each of these plans and approaches are intended to be highly flexible, and you should modify them for the incident you face.

CROWDS AND RIOTS

Historically, there have been many riots in the United States (although certainly there are many examples of civil unrest throughout the rest of the world that rival our worst riots). In the summer of 1966, there were riots in more than fifty cities including: Watts, Chicago, Newark, New Haven, Tampa, and Detroit. Since that time, there have been major riots in countless other cities. It is apparent that no place is immune. A riot is usually the culmination of a long process of social unrest, and you can see a pattern of growing hostility and aggression toward the police, often fueled by biased coverage by the local media. The triggering incident is often a relatively minor event, a simple arrest or confrontation that goes all to hell and turns into a major incident with a hostile crowd growing and attempting to engage the police. Often, the police initially withdraw to avoid further confrontation, appearing

You'll be called out on civil disturbances like this protest.

helpless and leaving the crowd to vent their fury on others. Vandalism, looting, arson and death can follow, at which point law enforcement engages in a massive action to contain the violence and destruction.

You can't control the nature, values, and social trends of your community; only your individual contacts with that community. Acting individually, you might be able to do many things to mitigate a riot and reduce damage, but as a patrol officer, you will likely be committed to the front lines as a nameless, faceless trooper in uniform. That pretty much defines your role, and largely eliminates your ability to use your community policing contacts to calm the situation.

Every officer on the front lines needs to have some basic equipment: a helmet (a Kevlar ballistic helmet is best, but even a general duty patrol helmet will prevent many injuries), a face mask, a ballistic vest, a baton, disposable handcuffs, and a gas mask if any of the agencies involved plan to use gas. However, all these things tend to mask your identity. The very people you talked with the previous day will not see you as an individual, but as just another officer in the line facing them. This total depersonalization makes each side more likely to hurt the other. Much of the power of the mob comes from the anonymity of the individuals. Do you think the persons who beat Reginald Denny would have been so bold had they known that officers watching the television coverage would know them by name? I have to think not.

The initial police response to any civil disturbance will usually consist of immediate action to protect lives and property. It is critically important that every officer exercise restraint, putting on a show of unified force, but not engaging the crowd directly, either physically or verbally. You should observe the crowd and their actions, and make some estimate of their potential for violence. You should take the time to try to identify the leaders and those committing violent and destructive acts. And then you simply have to wait until you have the personnel and equipment you need to engage and control that crowd.

When you do take action, it should be a coordinated effort, establishing a command post and then directing a flow of officers into the area in sufficient numbers to achieve your goals. If you have to retreat, you are only going to fuel the riot further.

Establishing a Perimeter

In the 1992 Los Angeles riots, which were so well documented on television, the destruction spread rapidly from "flash point" to "flash point." You could speculate that establishing a perimeter might have contained the violence to that area, preventing both the spread of the core group of rioters and any influx of additional persons into the riot. The perimeter would have to be wide enough that the officers in the line wouldn't be fighting for their lives. Once established, a large perimeter can then be pulled in as you reclaim the streets and control the situation.

Setting up a perimeter around a large incident requires a huge commitment of manpower, an almost impossible task for most agencies. In the real world of limited law enforcement resources, you may not establish a perimeter until the National Guard arrives on the scene in numbers. By then, as in Los Angeles, the riot may have grown far too large to ever contain.

Talking to the Crowd

Once the crowd is contained, your first step is to try to talk them into leaving without any further violence or destruction. Using a public address system or bullhorn, you need to communicate to the crowd, telling them that their assembly is illegal and that they must disperse immediately. Avoid making ultimatums; that tends to push rioters into action as the deadline approaches. You should also avoid telling the rioters specifically what you intend to do; it only gives them time to plan.

In some states, your warning will have to follow specific legal wording, something like, "I am Officer John Smith, a police officer of the Smallville Police Department. I hereby declare this to be an unlawful assembly and, in the name of the People of the State of California, command all those assembled at Park Avenue and Central Street to immediately disperse. If you do not do so, you will be arrested." Once the warning is given, you have to give them time to comply, leaving the area by escape routes you have left open for the purpose.

You should also use every community resource and leader at your disposal to help establish a dialogue that can resolve the incident peacefully. On the other hand, if the violence and destruction continue, it's time to use force in dispersing the rioters and arresting those responsible.

Arrest and Dispersal

As a patrol officer, you will have to depend on your supervisors to give you direction as to who to arrest and how. There are several basic strategies — one of *decapitation* (arresting the leaders and agitators) and one of *mass arrest* (simply arresting everyone present at the riot). As a patrol officer on the line, you won't be able to control the tactics, only your individual actions.

When you and your squad engage rioters, it is critically important to stay with your group in formation. Certainly, there is a great temptation to chase down the little jerk who throws a rock or an obscenity in your direction, but the integrity of the group of officers is dependent on a unified show of force in order to turn the tide of the riot. Stay with your squad, protect yourself, and follow your supervisor's commands and instructions as precisely as possible. Generally, there will be a "point" team making arrests, grabbing the targeted rioters, handcuffing them, and passing them back through your squad to a protected area.

Tactically, either using your formation or assisted by tear gas and other non-lethal weapons, you will disperse the crowd, driving them into pre-designated, heavily-monitored escape routes that will spread the crowd into controlled areas, dissipating the force of the riot.

One thing that most of the reports and studies have concluded is that the best way to control a riot is to prevent it in the first place. You do that by effective community policing, establishing an excellent working relationship with the citizens you serve, and preparing as a department and as individuals for any potential disaster. Your riot prevention begins with conscientious community policing everyday on your beat.

The Webster Commission Report

Following the disastrous riots occurring after the verdicts in the Rodney King trial in April of 1992, the "Webster Commission" published an extensive and often critical report on the Los Angeles

Police Department. Without commenting on the politics of the report, they offered some real insight into disaster preparation. Quoted are some of their recommendations below (found on page 180 in the report), which illustrate the type of preparation we've already discussed. These are some recommendations that could certainly be adopted and applied by any law enforcement agency. Specifically, the Webster Commission recommended:

> The Department's mechanisms of tactical alert and mobilization during emergencies should be stream-, lined and made more specific.
>
> Concepts of command and control for emergency response should be simplified. Consideration should be given to reducing or even eliminating requirements for the use of a duplicate command structure and Field Command Posts.
>
> Some method must be found to establish and maintain communications during emergencies from the field to headquarters, between LAPD field units, and between LAPD and non-LAPD units.
>
> Attention must be given to logistical support during emergencies, such as transportation, equipment, food, and the like.
>
> Specific plans must be developed for use of mutual aid resources, including what assignments to make to mutual aid resources, what command and control to use and how to operate with them.
>
> Strategies and tactics for civil disorder response should be reviewed in light of recent experience in Los Angeles and elsewhere. Particular attention should be given to development of coordinated department-wide approaches for use in a city-wide emergency, such as improved initial response capability, rapid containment, and an arrest strategy that is fully coordinated with all other agencies that must be involved.
>
> A triage scheme should be developed for the 9-1-1 response system that permits the Department to reduce and restore service according to pre-selected priorities as needed in the event of an emergency.

The Commission's recommendations should sound familiar because they echo some of the basic concepts of disaster preparation. Do the recommendations apply to your community? If so, where will the money come from to implement the recommendations? This seems to be the ultimate question of the day.

TERRORISM AND BOMBS

From the days of the Black Panthers and the Weatherman Underground to the World Trade Center, to the Marine Barracks in Beirut, patrol officers, like you, have been in the forefront of domestic terrorism. There are literally hundreds of active terrorist groups in the United States today, some more political or criminal than others, and most incredibly dangerous to you.

Terrorists employ bombing as one of the preferred methods of spreading terror. Bombs can range from a simple plastic cola bottle filled with nails and dry ice to hugely powerful car bombs. They may use military grade plastic explosives or crudely made pipe bombs. With the breakup of the Warsaw Pact countries, it is probably only a matter of time before some terrorist group acquires a nuclear device. Whatever the group, and whatever the bomb, the principles for handling any bomb remain the same.

Immediate Considerations

Remember, no suspected bomb is safe. Don't move it, don't touch it.

- Control radio traffic. Transmitting on a radio or cellular phone may detonate the bomb. There should be no radio transmissions within ¼ to ½ mile of your location.

- Immediately evacuate all persons in the area to a safe distance. The minimum safe distance is 300 feet if under cover, but for a bomb out of doors, you may evacuate for 2000 feet.

- Relay as much information to your supervisors as possible. If there was a threat, what time was the call received? What was the time of the detonation, or when was the detonation expected? Where exactly is the bomb located? What type of structures, materials, and other hazards are near the bomb? What or who is the specific target of the bomb?

If it looks like a bomb, treat it like a bomb — get away and evacuate.

Notifications

You need to determine what additional personnel, superiors, and special units such as the detective bureau or Arson and Explosives Unit you think you need at the scene.

Generally, there will be a formal "Bomb squad" to assist you (on a smaller department, they will probably be from the county or state, but you may also receive assistance from the F.B.I. or the Bureau of Alcohol, Tobacco and Firearms). If you have a device that is clearly military in nature such as: artillery shells, mortar rounds, mines, ammunition, bombs, rockets, grenades, etc., a special "Explosives, Ordinance & Demolition" (EOD) team will probably be sent by the military. You will generally have to have your commanding officer request one of these units.

You should always have the fire department respond to the area of any bomb call. If the device has not yet detonated, they can respond "Code-2" (no lights or siren) and they should stand by at a safe distance, ready to respond if needed. Paramedics should respond and stand by in a similar manner.

Search

When a bomb threat has been received and the detonation time has not been given, or when the deadline gives you sufficient time, you may search a building or area in an attempt to locate the device.

Your search has to be visual (you don't want to move anything that might trigger the bomb) and systematic. It's always best to bring someone familiar with that location since they can tell you what appears out of the ordinary. While searching you can't use your radio and have to continue to prohibit radio transmissions within ¼ to ½ mile of the threatened site.

Much of the damage and injury from a bomb comes from having the blast contained within a structure. You can reduce this force by leaving doors and windows open in the structure as you search.

Everyone searching should receive instructions not to touch, move, or attempt to disarm any suspected item. If they find something, they should isolate the items and keep all personnel away from the suspected item until the bomb experts arrive to handle it. If time permits, and you have the equipment and personnel, a wall of sandbags can be used to direct the blast in a safe or less damaging direction.

Before entering a building or area, you need to establish evacuation procedures. These procedures should coordinate with the company management and the fire department commander. Although you can close and evacuate a building or area, it's a touchy decision with great potential liability. Imagine closing down a major automobile manufacturing plant while you search the entire plant for a threatened bomb. You have no way of knowing if the bomb threat comes from a disgruntled worker looking for a longer lunch break, a union scare tactic designed to cost the company money, or a terrorist seeking to kill people. Millions of dollars could be lost by a relatively minor delay. You shouldn't make that decision alone unless a device has actually been located. Instead, the management of the company is going to have to determine if they believe the threat is credible, and then they should make the decision to evacuate.

Tactical Considerations After a Detonation

When an explosion has already taken place, you have many additional considerations. You need to take rapid action to rescue victims and prevent their further injury. You need to avoid having the scene contaminated and evidence destroyed by both curious onlookers and rescue personnel, and you need to prevent further damage and injury from fires, broken glass, and unstable buildings. Some of the actions you should consider include:

- Establishing a safe perimeter and sealing off the location. No one should be allowed into the area unless they have specific responsibilities at the scene. Evidence and injured persons can be spread over a huge area (the evidence from the Pan Am bombing over Scotland covered hundreds of square miles, an admittedly extreme example, but something you should consider). You should do your best to preserve all the physical evidence at the scene.

- All other persons should be evacuated from the immediate area. This will protect them from the danger at the scene and protect them from the possibility of additional bombs left by the suspect. You should also be aware that sometimes secondary bombs are left specifically to kill emergency personnel.

- Control traffic in the area to keep the curious out of the area and expedite the flow of emergency vehicles into the area.

- Request fire and medical assistance as needed. If you have many injured persons, you are going to have to designate a "triage" area, a place where the paramedics can sort out the dead, dying, seriously injured and the minor injuries. You will also want to notify local hospitals if they can expect large numbers of injured persons.

- Turn off the utilities (gas, power, water) to the location for the safety of everyone in the area.

LABOR DISPUTES AND STRIKES

Labor disputes can be a real challenge to the patrol officer. You have a duty to be completely neutral, treating both labor and management fairly and professionally regardless of your personal feelings or any stake you have in the outcome. A labor dispute or a strike can be as simple a matter as a few picketers in front of a location, or it could develop into a full scale riot involving hundreds of people. Some disputes are resolved peacefully, others result in violence, vandalism, and murder.

Your primary task as a patrol officer is to keep the peace, protecting lives and properties. Without taking sides, it's important to meet with representatives of both sides of any action before any incidents occur. You should be polite, but firm and fair in explaining the laws on picketing. Depending on the jurisdiction, picketers may be required to keep moving, to maintain a certain distance between picketers, and to avoid blocking sidewalks, driveways and streets. Even if you lack any specific laws regarding picketing, every individual has the right to exercise freedom of movement. If a person demands to enter or exit from property where he has lawful business, you should ensure his right to do so.

Begin by identifying who is in charge of each faction — the strike leader and the management representative. It will help if you can videotape or record your meeting in order to avoid any charges of impartiality in the future. Explain right up front that you expect both sides to behave in a lawful manner, that you will deal with any violations of law, and that you will hold them responsible for the acts of those they supervise. If you warn someone the first time, make sure you arrest them the second time. If you just keep warning, it becomes an empty threat and shows your position is weak. If you come across in a manner that convinces them of your ability to carry out appropriate law enforcement actions, you may preclude any real violence in the strike action on your beat.

If you do make an arrest or warning, make sure you explain to both the management and union representatives what action you took and why. Open communication will help stop rumors and prevent either side from getting unduly agitated. If you have a person you have identified as a specific troublemaker, let their representatives know that you feel he has been creating problems and should be removed to prevent any further problems. Oftentimes they will cooperate and remove that person.

Every action you take has to be neutral. You should not park on the company property and should avoid parking with the strikers. Do not take food or drink from either side, don't use the company bathrooms, and don't allow either side any special privileges. You can be courteous and friendly, but never indebted to either side.

Last of all, you must be patient. You have little control over the course or outcome of negotiations in a strike. All you can do is enforce the law, deal with violence if it occurs, and do your best to protect people, their rights, and their property.

UNNATURAL DISASTERS — PLANES, TRAINS, AND AUTOMOBILES

Sometimes disasters are purely man-made. Many of them involve transportation — aircraft crashes, train derailments, semi-truck crashes and bus plunges. They may involve hundreds of casualties and affect a huge area. Many such images come to mind: the Amtrak derailment with the locomotives burning in the river, the crippled airliner crashing in flames in a Sioux City cornfield, the scattered debris of a Boeing 747 over Scotland, or the runaway bus full of children in Palm Springs. All represent a nightmare for emergency services and an overwhelming task for the first officers on the scene. Once again, the burden for getting the rescue and recovery headed in the right direction lies with the patrol officer.

Some years ago when a commercial passenger jet collided with a small aircraft and crashed into a residential neighborhood, a nearby camera crew captured one of the first patrol officers arriving on the scene. He drove onto a block in which almost every home was burning, a block covered in body parts and debris. Over a hundred people were dead. Obviously, there was a lot of work to be done in initiating a massive response, evaluating the situation, relaying information to dispatch, and coordinating other units to where they could do the most good. Instead of evaluating that scene and initiating a response, that patrol officer grabbed a garden hose and started fighting a fire at the nearest home. By doing so, he committed himself to an action that was largely pointless and ineffective in terms of dealing with the overall situation.

There is an old axiom that says, *"When you're up to your ass in alligators, it's hard to remember that your objective is to drain the swamp."* That's exactly what you have to do as a patrol officer responding to one of these types of emergencies. The objective is to save as many lives and as much property as possible, and the best way to do that is to initiate and coordinate the appropriate response as soon as possible. You, as the first responder, are critically important to initiating that response. Once again your preliminary assessment is invaluable in saving lives and property.

Situation Assessment

Upon your arrival at the scene of a transportation accident, you need to make an estimate of the situation and relay that information to your communications center. Some of the information you should try to obtain would include:

1) The exact location of the accident and the size of the involved area. With aircraft accidents, the location may have to be determined by matching topography to map coordinates. On highways, you may use mileposts, and on rail accidents, you may locate the accident by the grade crossings.

2) The exact type and occupancy of structures involved, if any.

3) The type of vehicle(s) involved. If an aircraft is involved, try to determine if it is military or civilian, passenger or cargo, helicopter or jet, private or commercial, the size and class of aircraft, the size and number of engines, and any identification numbers that are obvious. When a train is involved you should try to determine the type (passenger or freight), the number of cars, any numbers off the engines, and the freight manifest or a passenger list. For motor vehicles such as trucks and buses, you would again get as much information about the vehicle, license plates, companies, I.D. numbers, cargo and occupants. It sounds like such information might be irrelevant to the emergency response, but it is not. Think of the different

considerations your might make on a bus accident, if you knew the occupants were all senior citizens from Portugal. Might your response be slightly different than a bus accident involving local school children?

4) You should make a preliminary estimate of the number of injuries and deaths. You may need a lot of ambulances from miles around, or a lot of coroners with body bags, or something in between. The sooner you can get out accurate information, the sooner the appropriate assistance will arrive.

5) You should relay your best estimate as to the additional assistance needed to handle the incident. At the scene of a bus accident, you may need only a few additional police units for traffic control, but dozens of ambulances. At the scene of an air crash, you may need only a few ambulances, but dozens of police officers to help search for debris and control a huge perimeter. Let communications know your best estimate of your needs.

As the first person on the scene, you know the situation better than anyone else. Pick a suitable location for a command post and designate staging areas. You should also advise the best available routes in and out of the scene.

Special Considerations

When responding to an aircraft crash, approach with the wind to your rear whenever possible, and avoid approaching on the same path as the aircraft. Avoid breathing any smoke or fumes (toxic and perhaps deadly materials may be burning). Be aware of the potential for fire and explosions. All vehicles have fuel and batteries. Military vehicles and aircraft may contain weapons and ammunition. Aircraft may also contain ejection seats and survival flares. Because of these dangers, the perimeter should be wide enough to protect the public (2,000 feet is appropriate on aircraft crashes), and no smoking or flares should be allowed at the site.

Once you deal with the immediate crisis, you need to establish security at the crash site. You should also provide traffic control, crowd control, and perimeter control, thus keeping all unauthorized persons away from the scene.

Crash Site Management

Once the immediate threat to public safety is resolved, you need to maintain the scene until the appropriate investigators can arrive and take over. As a patrol officer, you will not be responsible for conducting the investigation (although you might have to write some sort of preliminary incident report). Your responsibility will be to provide support for those conducting the investigation, usually personnel from the National Transportation Safety Board, the Federal Aviation Administration, the military, or some other state or federal agency. In the meantime, you can help their investigation by identifying all of the witnesses (many could leave before the national team arrives) and by gathering some of the basic information. For example:

a) time of crash;

b) location of witnesses at the time of the crash;

c) weather at the time of the crash;

d) direction of travel or flight;

e) actions, fires, defects, or explosions prior to the crash;

f) location of objects falling from aircraft or vehicles prior to crash;

g) impact angle and position of survivors;

h) anything removed from the scene and by whom;

i) location of survivors and evidence (deceased and injured victims may be widely diaplaced by impact);

j) protect all crash debris, but do not disturb the wreckage or the evidence.

HAZARDOUS MATERIALS

Closely related to the transportation industry are hazardous materials (i.e., cargo, by-products, or waste). Over the last decade, the definition of hazardous materials has expanded to what some consider to be extremes. There was a time when the fire department would routinely respond to traffic accidents and "wash down" the area using a hose to spray all the glass, gas, oil and debris into the gutter. Now the gasoline and oil are hazardous materials that must be picked up with absorbent materials and removed from the scene, and even the discharge from a motorhome's septic tank is handled as a "HazMat incident."

Hazardous materials are in every jurisdiction, and, as a patrol officer, you may respond to a number of such calls each month. One of the most common HazMat incidents you will encounter involves accidents with semi-trailers.

Semi-trailers transport everything from pool supplies to gasoline through cities everyday. They usually will have a prominent square placard with symbols and numbers on them, the "U.N." number that identifies the load (the most common one you see is 1203 for petroleum products such as gasoline. However, it could just as easily be 3039, which, of course, is 4-dimethylamino-6-[2-dimethylaminoethoxy] toluene-2-diazonium zinc chloride).

Any vehicle transporting hazardous materials is required to have the shipping papers located in the cab of the tractor within easy reach of the driver. On demand, the driver should show you these papers, but at the scene of an accident, you should never endanger yourself in an attempt to secure these documents. When approaching the scene of any accident involving any cargo, you should keep in mind these critical points:

1) Approach the incident cautiously and from an upwind (and upgrade) direction if possible. Resist the urge to rush in, you may become another casualty. You won't be able to help anyone until you know what *you* are facing.

2) Avoid inhalation of fumes, smoke and vapors, even if there are no hazardous materials known to be involved. Do not assume

that gases or vapors are harmless simply because they are odorless.

3) Keep your dispatcher advised of everything you do throughout the incident. This will make you easier to rescue if you become a victim and could prevent other personnel from endangering themselves or from duplicating your efforts.

4) Once you arrive, try to identify the hazards from as far away as possible. Never endanger yourself or others by trying to get to documents to identify the product. (Watch how fire department personnel respond to such incidents, they often stop a block away in their breathing apparatus and study the scene with binoculars. You should carry binoculars as well, it's worth the effort.)

5) Don't attempt to conduct rescues unless you are fully trained and properly equipped with a HazMat suit and breathing gear. If you go in after somebody and are overcome, you have simply added to the problem for other rescuers.

You can identify the hazards present by examining placards, container labels, shipping papers, and interviewing reliable persons. Evaluate all your sources, and then follow the procedures *exactly*. Agencies such as the state Office of Emergency Services, CHEMTREC (a private industry organization), or the National Response Center, can provide you with invaluable, detailed information for handling any material.

In every hazardous materials incident, you should secure the scene as soon as possible. Without entering the immediate hazard area, do what you can to isolate the area and assure the safety of people and the environment. Move and keep people away from the scene and the perimeter, and deny entrance to anyone who is not directly involved in the incident. Allow enough room to get emergency vehicles in and out of the scene.

When you set up a command post, you should also set up a decontamination area. This area will allow contaminated personnel to remain isolated from non-contaminated personnel, provide a place for them to remove all their clothing and equipment and wash-down their bodies, a secure area to place clothing and equipment in sealed containers, and an area for medical treatment.

Get the professional help you need. No agency is prepared to deal with every hazardous materials incident they encounter. Advise dispatch to notify responsible agencies, and call for assistance from fully trained and equipped experts. When the local fire department arrives, they should take command of the incident, and you should do your best to assist them.

NATURAL DISASTERS —
HURRICANES, EARTHQUAKES, FLOODS, TORNADOES

Natural disasters can occur with little or no warning, and can cut a huge path of destruction through your community. They are somewhat different in nature than other disasters because every area of the city may be equally affected. If the scope of the damage is quite large, getting assistance to you and the people in your community may be considerably slower. As a patrol officer in the field, you're in charge in your beat, perhaps with no supervisors, command staff, or assistance for a long period of time.

As with all disasters, your first responsibility is to figure out what you're dealing with. What is the scope of the problem in your beat? What will it take to deal with it? Think of the patrol officers out in the streets during the 1994 Northridge earthquake. The damage was unimaginable — collapsed buildings, houses, bridges, and freeways; huge fires; broken gas and water mains; streets blocked by debris and damage; dozens of deaths and thousands of injuries. Where do you start?

You have to begin with an evaluation, quickly touring and surveying your beat in order to coordinate response efforts and expedite rescues and recovery in your community. Your primary duty is to *evaluate the situation and report*. The temptation is to dig in and help people, but if you stop to engage in a rescue, that evaluation process is delayed and many, many people may suffer.

Damage Survey

One of the most important things to evaluate and survey are those facilities representing a high risk to the community or providing essential public services. Grab your clipboard, and start making detailed notes. Your initial survey should include the status of facilities essential to your community, including:

Emergency facilities: police station, fire stations, armories, and hospitals.

Transportation centers: Airports, docks, railways.

Road network: bridges, tunnels, elevated freeways, overpasses and underpasses.

Water supply: Dams, reservoirs, aqueducts, water tanks, and pumping facilities.

High-density locations: Schools, large corporations, high-rise buildings, hotels, retirement homes, apartment buildings.

Hazardous locations: Refineries, radioactive storage facilities, chemical storage areas, sewage treatment plants.

Utilities: Telephone offices and facilities, gas distribution stations, electrical relay stations, high-voltage power lines.

Detailed Survey

Once you've completed this preliminary survey and reported it to communications, you can begin a more detailed survey. Again, you should take careful notes. Those notes may be the basis for rescue efforts in your beat. Some of the things you should record include:

1) Locations of injured persons.

2) Locations of bodies.

3) The operation (or lack of operation) of telephone, water, gas, electricity, sewers, public transportation, and other systems serving the residents of your area.

4) Suitable locations for evacuation centers, helicopter landing zones, and command posts.

5) Locations known to contain chemicals, flammable substances, explosives, or radiation.

6) Collapsed or damaged locations requiring heavy equipment to conduct searches and rescues.

Disaster Operations

Once all the surveys have been completed, you have adequate information to determine where to direct the resources coming to aid your community. You can now begin the actual process of rescue and recovery. Some of the activities a patrol officer may be involved in might include:

1) search and rescue;

2) maintaining perimeter control to keep unauthorized people and vehicles out of the involved area;

3) conducting traffic control to expedite emergency equipment and personnel;

4) assisting in evacuation, establishing evacuations centers, and directing people to them; and

5) establishing a command post and/or staging areas.

FIRES AND ARSON

As a patrol officer, you will respond on many fire calls. Often the patrol officer actually discovers a fire. Lives depend on you entering a burning area or location to evacuate, search, and rescue persons. You will handle burning cars, trucks, trains, buildings, and brush. Each kind of fire has very specific dangers, something that firefighters spend months at an academy and years of experience in learning. You can't hope to know all that they know, so let's stick to a few basics. Primary dangers are: burning to death, smoke inhalation, firestorms, backdrafts and flashovers.

In any major fire disaster, you will carry out all of your first responder duties including establishing a command post and advising dispatch of your assessment of the situation. Unless the fire is contained in a single structure, you should also include the direction of the fire and the wind conditions, and describe the type of the area (business, residential, hillside, wooded, etc.).

Another of your considerations is arson. If you have any indication that the fire is suspicious in origin, you and/or the fire department (depending on who is responsible in your jurisdiction) will be carrying out a criminal investigation at the same time. You will need to try to preserve evidence at the source of the fire, and be aware that the suspect may very well be in the area, often watching the fire or actively assisting in fighting the fire. Just try to identify and record those persons present at your arrival, and detain anyone who appears obviously involved in starting the fire.

The vast majority of officers are poorly equipped to handle any sort of fire call. You won't carry any type of breathing apparatus that would allow you to breathe in smoky conditions (a gas mask will filter the soot, but not the poisonous gases that cause you to pass out and die). You won't carry heavy gloves that would allow you to handle hot objects without burning your hands. Your uniform and equipment make you a good candidate to be a human candle. (Most of us have polyester blend uniforms [made from petroleum!], and wear teargas and ammunition on our belts.) If you expose yourself to direct flame, you may well see your uniform ignite. Obviously, you have to avoid any contact with flames.

Bear in mind that flames can spread rapidly. On car fires, it is not unusual for the tires to explode, shooting burning chunks of rubber in every direction. Batteries can explode as the acid boils and forms hydrogen gas, and burning gasoline can flow and spread down the street. In an industrial setting, burning liquids can flow much faster than you can run.

You also have to worry about radiant heat. Some fires can be so intense that nearby objects burst into flame from the heat produced. I worked a major fire in a large hardware store where there was so much radiant heat that it melted down the lightbars and windshield seals on nearby fire trucks, and turned traffic control cones into little puddles of molten plastic. That same type of heat could cause your hair or uniform to burst into flame. Since heat rises, if you find yourself exposed, stay as low as possible and keep behind cover.

Smoke Inhalation

While the prospect of being burned may sound grim and dangerous, the greatest threat in a fire is from "smoke inhalation." Most smoke from any fire is toxic. In addition to the gases that can deprive your body of oxygen (carbon monoxide, etc.), vehicles and buildings are full of things that are genuinely poisonous. In addition to cargo and fuel, vehicles are full of plastic, rubber, and paint which produce toxins and carcinogenic products when they burn. Breathing these can kill you or lead to cancers that will eventually kill you.

Smoke inhalation can be absolutely deadly. Your lungs fill with gases other than oxygen or fill with solids such as soot and ash that reduce the function of your lungs to the point you die. Heat may sear and burn your lungs, esophagus, nasal passages and mouth so they swell up and close. In any case, suffocation and death are the results.

When you approach any fire scene, you should try to do so upwind, keeping the smoke away from your area of operations if possible. If you find yourself enveloped in smoke, get low and stay right on the ground. A gas mask will filter some of the solids, but is of little help with the poisonous gasses and lack of oxygen. The only safe way to operate in smoke is in a Self-contained Breathing Apparatus (SCBA) such as those worn by firefighters.

Firestorms

Firestorms occur when the fire is so big that it feeds and perpetuates itself. The intense heat creates a thermal updraft that sucks in more oxygen at the bottom, fanning the fire ever larger and consuming all the oxygen and fuel at the center. If you happen to be at the center of a firestorm, you're dead. If the firestorm is being driven by high winds, you may not be able to outrun it.

Firestorm conditions are often seen in forest and brush fires, but can also occur during large urban fires such as the huge arson fires of the Los Angeles riots. During a tragic fire in Oakland, California, an officer was killed on a residential hillside street while trying to drive some residents to safety. It's speculated that when the oxygen level dropped, his car died, and when it dropped further, he died. In the Malibu fires, there were a number of instances where firefighters lost their trucks and suffered serious burns in similar incidents. Patrol officers have to be aware of the tremendous risks presented by firestorms and try to temper their efforts within a fire area by the need for survival. If you see an approaching firestorm, you need to get out of the way, preferably by moving perpendicular to the path of the storm.

Flashovers and Backdrafts

A *flashover* is a fire phenomena that takes place inside of a burning structure. It is the critical point in a fire where there is so much heat built up that the upper portions of a room or building spontaneously burst into flame. It is primarily a heat phenomena. The heat of the fire rises. Once it reaches the combustion temperature of the materials in the room (curtains, books, shelving, bedding, wall paper, etc.), they ignite throughout the room (and sometimes adjacent rooms). This produces a situation that firefighters refer to as "a critical point for life safety and fire control."

I once had to drag a struggling store owner away from the cash register of his liquor store where the roof was fully involved in flames. He was gathering up cash and expensive liquors. We were no more than ten feet outside the door when there was a tremendous flash and a pulse of radiant heat. Looking back in the store, the entire store was a mass of flames from one end to the other. (The store owner later sued the department for the money he left behind in the store. That's gratitude!) The survivors of flashovers often report a sudden stillness in the room, sometimes followed by a loud hissing noise as the hot gases ignite. If you notice that stillness, you need to get low and get out fast; it could already be too late.

DISASTER PLANNING

Like so many other things in law enforcement, the key player in any disaster is the patrol officer. A properly prepared and trained officer can make the difference between success and disaster. You have to prepare physically, logistically (supplies and equipment) and mentally to deal with disaster.

Some agencies go to extremes, planning out every potential disaster scenario in exquisite detail, compiling manuals, and conducting training exercises. Others take the ostrich approach — burying their heads in the sand and telling themselves "Disaster just can't happen here." As a patrol officer, you probably won't have much affect on how your agency plans for disasters, but you should take a harsh, realistic view of what your agency has planned for and take appropriate measures to ensure your survival.

We know that a major earthquake is almost a certainty in the Los Angeles basin. One nearby department has prepared elaborately with enough shelter, bedding, generators, food and water to care for all of their personnel *and their families* for two full weeks. My own agency has made no preparations at all. After a major earthquake, the only food and drink in our station will be the contents of the candy and soft-drink machines in the officer lunch room.

Community Effort

Even if your agency has no disaster planning, you may be able to develop a local plan within your beat. Disaster planning should be a community effort. One of the main criticisms of the LAPD from the Webster Commission was that they didn't involve other agencies in their planning process. LAPD did have extensive plans and manuals to deal with riots, but apparently did a poor job at the command level of coordinating with the rest of the city and other agencies.

If you are practicing community policing, all of your community should have an opportunity to contribute to the process of disaster planning. It's their lives and property at stake as well. Your community has incredible resources. Tap into your businessmen and community leaders, and you may find you have sources for food and water, bedding, temporary housing, generators, construction equipment, medical supplies, search dogs, and perhaps even helicopters. People want to help you do your job in protecting them. Give them the opportunity.

Once you've developed a plan for coping with disasters, spread it around. The members of the community may have invaluable insight as to why something may or may not work, or may have ways of adding to the plan in significant ways. Your job is to listen, and give the people in your area the best opportunity for surviving and coping with disaster.

DISCUSSION QUESTIONS

1) In order, what disasters do you think are most likely to occur in your city or area?

2) What equipment and supplies do you personally carry in your car for disasters? What equipment and supplies do you have in your home?

3) In your jurisdiction, what agency would have command of a hazardous materials incident? Does that make sense to you?

4) What locations containing hazardous materials are close enough to your home or class to endanger you in a disaster?

5) What agency in your state is responsible for coping with disasters?

6) Much disaster relief is provided by private, volunteer organizations such as the Red Cross and Salvation Army. Do you think the government should be providing those functions instead?

7) Does your city, county, or jurisdiction have a disaster coordinator? If so, what are the coordinator's specific duties?

8) When a jurisdiction receives mutual aid in a disaster, do you think that jurisdiction (and the taxpayers within) should pay for those costs, or should they be equally shared by all taxpayers?

9) There are currently books available that describe how to make bombs from various common materials. Do you think the government should control their publication, and if so, how?

10) Who in government do you think should be responsible for disaster planning — agency officials (police and fire chiefs), politicians (mayors and city councils), or someone else?

Omaha Police Sergeant Steve Novotmy was glad he wasn't assigned to bike patrol. Recently, Novotmy was driving his police car when the car was attacked by a Rottweiler-Labrador dog. The dog left a 24-inch scratch and saliva on the side of the car. The dog's owner said the dog wasn't at fault since his paws never left the curb. Omaha Police Accident Investigator Bud Chase disagrees. "That doesn't matter," said Chase, "his mouth was in the street."

OFFICER SURVIVAL

LEARNING GOALS: After studying this chapter the student will be able to:

- List the major risks that police officers face.

- Name three causes of stress.

- Explain how you can deal with stress.

- List the diseases that represent the greatest threat to police officers.

- Explain how you can reduce the risk of disease.

- Explain why suicide is such an occupational problem.

- Profile a police officer killer.

- Describe three general principles of officer survival.

- Describe the National Law Enforcement Officers' Memorial Fund.

BASICS OF OFFICER SURVIVAL

What is officer survival? Ask most law enforcement officers, and they'll tell you all about the latest secret ninja-assassin techniques they just learned at commando college. To them that's officer survival — a matter of successfully avoiding death in the field at the hands of a criminal opponent. It's a viewpoint that tends to be locked in on the present. Unfortunately, this is an extremely limited view of the threats facing all officers. Officers murdered at the hands of others amount to just slightly more than two percent of all the officers that die each year.

A far more comprehensive approach should be taken to officer survival. Survival is your insurance for the future. When you think about officer survival, you should be looking well ahead into your future. When you first start your career, it's difficult to look much beyond probation, but the reality is you have to start planning your retirement very early in your career. Officer survival is the achievement of your lifetime goals — *completing* a satisfying career in law enforcement, and, ultimately, retiring to go on and enjoy life in good mental and physical health.

You face tremendous odds against living to enjoy your retirement. Sure, there are a lot of bad guys out there willing to kill police officers, but despite all the televisions shows, death at the hands of some criminal is statistically rare compared to other forms of death. You are more likely to kill yourself with your own gun than to be killed by a criminal. You are far more likely to die in an on-duty traffic accident. You are even more likely to die from a heart attack, stroke, or other cardiovascular disease. Unfortunately, there's a very good chance you will be injured during your career. While roughly 150 officers are killed each year in the line of duty, more than 50,000 are assaulted and 22,000 are injured.

Police officers usually have an unhealthy, unrested, stress-filled life-style designed to self-destruct the human body. I read once that the average career police officer dies at age fifty-six. While I don't know if that is still accurate, it should be enough to scare you. If you're interested in survival, you need to be tactically sound in the field and adopt a healthy, happy, tactically sound life-style as well.

The five big killers of police officers are:

1) Stress

2) Disease

3) Suicide

4) Accidents

5) Assault

We'll deal with each of these topics in order.

SURVIVING STRESS

Stress is right at the top of the list as the number one killer of law enforcement officers. Stress leads to many of the injuries and, in some cases, deaths attributed to other causes. Mental stress leads to officers who are preoccupied and cannot concentrate. Stress can cause fatigue and interfere with sleep, leading to accidents and mistakes. Stress can make an officer retire at an early age, low pension, and with high blood pressure. Stress can drive an officer to suicide unless he learns how to deal with it, and the physical effects of stress can lead to behaviors that destroy the body.

Causes of Stress

What causes stress for police officers? There are five main sources of stress for police officers:

1) the occupation,

2) the department,

3) the community,

4) your family, and

5) yourself.

There is nothing that can eliminate stress from your career. The pressures that produce stress in policing will always be present. What you must learn to do is to *deal* with stress — learning to adapt your life-style to accommodate and neutralize the inevitable stress of police work. To cope with stress, you have to understand stress, its effects on your body, and how you can channel stress into more productive activities.

Stress Warning Signs

Change of personality

Change in personal appearance

Excessive sick leave

Calling in sick during a shift

Calling in sick after days off

Increase in citizen complaints

Rapid mood changes

Sleep disorders

Frequent accidents

Taking unnecessary risks

Excessive use of alcohol or other drugs

Obsession with the job

Depression

Use of excessive violence

The above are indicators of the onset of a stress disorder. They are intended to be viewed collectively since several signs tend to surface within the same general time frame.

Stress from the Occupation

There are certain stresses inherent in police work anywhere you go. How they affect you will depend largely on your mental outlook and ability to adapt. The primary stressors are discussed below.

Life-style: Most people in America enjoy certain "normal" life-styles. They work during the day, they have weekends off, they have vacations during the summer, they don't carry guns, and people rarely try to kill them. When you become a law enforcement officer, you pretty much kiss that life-style good-bye.

The last time I regularly had weekends off was over 13 years ago. My department has a mandatory shift rotation policy, so at least three times a year I adjust my life and my family's life to work graveyard shifts and try to sleep during the day. Vacation sign-ups are based on seniority and overlapping vacations on the same shift are not allowed, so I've taken vacations at odd times (hey, the crowds at beach resorts are usually smaller when it's raining). I usually carry a gun with me, and wear clothing to conceal that gun, and I probably approach an ATM machine a little differently than "normal" people do.

Law enforcement requires a very different life-style. You need to recognize those differences and accept them. You need to make it plain to those you become involved with that this is your life-style. You need to reconcile the fact that you may never relax the same way in a bar, never look at a freeway traffic pattern the same way, never socialize at a party in the same manner as others.

Ambition: Some officers are content to go through their entire career as a patrol officer, never advancing, never aspiring to advance, and never taking a promotional examination. That's great if that's you! Officers like that probably feel very little stress in this area. Others seem driven to advance through the ranks, feeling like a failure if they do poorly on promotional exams, wallowing in stress and self-pity if they fail to meet their self-imposed deadlines for promotion and pay increases.

The reality of law enforcement is that you have little or no control over your own advancement. You can probably improve your chances with an outstanding record, a ton of recommendations, attending as many training schools and earning a couple of college degrees, but you have **no control**, whatsoever, over the process. You would like to think that you are competing fairly with other officers on a "level playing field," but that is not reality.

Law enforcement promotions are rarely decided purely on merit. Administrators tend to tailor the process to meet what they think the department needs and to meet **their** image of what the department should look like. If your chief is under pressure to increase the number of minorities in command positions, you may find that women and minorities have a seemingly unfair advantage. If the local ACLU is demanding community policing, you may see the next sergeant's slot go to the guy that's been handling Neighborhood Watch or D.A.R.E. If your captain is a veteran, you may see veterans in your department enjoy faster promotion. Regardless of what is taking place, and regardless of how fair you perceive the process, you have to understand that you probably cannot control it or change it. Once you accept this as fact, the stress of promotion should ease. If you can't accept it, find another job or find another department.

In a small agency, promotions may be few and far between. You may literally have to wait for someone to retire before you even have a chance at promotion. Again, recognize the reality, and don't have unrealistic expectations. I've seen excellent patrol officers become total basket cases as promotions approach, cramming like a college freshman before final exams. Time for another reality check. Either you have the experience, education, training and common sense or you don't. There is a lot you can do from the beginning to prepare yourself for promotion. There is very little you can do in a few days or weeks. If you find yourself cramming for a promotional exam, there's a good chance you aren't ready for a promotion. Step back, write it off as a good experience, and start preparing now for the *next* opportunity.

Responsibility: Some officers really feel a burden, every minute of every day. They feel responsible for protecting other people, and blame themselves when the people on their beat get hurt. They feel the weight of the world on their shoulders and an overwhelming sense of responsibility. They become convinced that they are vital to the department, and drive themselves to be there every minute. These are the guys that won't call in sick unless they are actually missing a limb; these types always carry a beeper and make sure the dispatcher knows the number. These are the same officers that pop into the department every day of their vacation "just to check on their mailboxes."

Time for another reality check. In most cities, the distribution of on-duty patrol officers to citizens is greater than one to five thousand. You can't possibly protect every one of those persons, but what you can say at the end of every day is that you did the best job you could, and that the persons on your beat are better off than if you hadn't come to work that day.

You also can't get too carried away with your own sense of importance. Your agency probably existed and managed to function well, long before you were hired and will likely continue to exist long after you retire. They manage to perform police functions on other shifts, on your days off, and when you take vacation. Yes, you are an important, vital part of your department's operations. But indispensable? Not a chance!

Another source of stress for police officers is the stress of being "on-duty" 24 hours per day. Another reality check — you are not on duty 24 hours per day. Yes, certain classes of police officers do have the authority of a police officer even when off-duty. However, very few agencies demand their officers take any action when off-duty. The fact that you have peace officer powers means that you carry a gun and take action if you choose. It doesn't mean you *have* to take action. The department doesn't pay you 24 hours per day. Learn to enjoy yourself off-duty, while still maintaining alertness, and if you find yourself in a situation where you see a crime occur, be a professional, well-armed witness, help other people if you can, but don't get killed in the process.

Cynicism: Patrol officers are some of the world's greatest cynics. They deal with the dark side of human nature day in and day out. They spend their whole day talking to criminals and upset people victimized by criminals. The citizens they stop are outraged that officer's think they're criminals. They see death, injury, and the absolute scum of the earth almost every day. If you're like a lot of patrol officers just starting in the profession, you'll spend much of your time off-duty with other cops with an equally jaded view of life. After a while, it's easy to dismiss the entire human race as a lost cause.

Fortunately, that's not reality. The vast majority of people are good, decent, hard-working people. Most respect the job you do, depend on your protection, and will support your efforts in the community.

Look for the good in your community and balance it against the bad. I remember bailing out of my unit in a shabby neighborhood at the end of a pursuit, and coming back about thirty minutes later expecting to find it stripped. Instead, I found the unit locked up with a young man sitting on the hood. "I just wanted to make sure nobody messed with your car, Officer," he told me. There's a lady in my city that brings cakes by the station every couple of weeks. There's twenty businessmen that pitched in donations to help equip a van for the

Explorer Scouts and dozens of others that contribute to an annual Safety Fair in a local park. There are hundreds of citizens that donate thousands of dollars to our police association fund-raiser every year, allowing us to support Little League, AYSO, Boy Scouts, and a dozen other charities. My town and yours are full of wonderful people. Do yourself a favor and get to know them!

Get to know people by meeting and talking to them on duty and by expanding your social horizons beyond your group of law enforcement buddies. Get involved with the good people in your city. Join a service club (Lions, Kiwanis, Optimists, Rotary, etc.), join a church, or volunteer as a coach, tutor, or scout leader. You'll meet some "normal" people and restore perspective to your life.

Disgust: Some of law enforcement is absolutely revolting. You will see (and smell, and taste) things that will make you vomit. One writer referred to this as "dirty work," and indeed it is! You will handle dead, rotting corpses, invalids covered in feces, and drunks covered in vomit. You will deal with dead animals in the street and street people whose body odors could evacuate the Super Bowl.

You will also see and hear disgusting things that will burn themselves in your memory forever. I well remember a seven-year-old whose father punished him by having an older brother hold the boy while the father drove a pickup truck over his legs. I remember a clergyman covered in blood from a neck wound, and the naked young man with him describing a bizarre story of sex and chicken sacrifices. I still remember the taste of garlic in my mouth after giving CPR (in the days before we had masks) to a hanging victim. And I remember the dead baby left for a couple of years in a young girl's closet. Incredible, disgusting images. Each had an impact on me, every one creating stress at some level.

The only way to deal with this type of stress is to talk it out. Don't let it become a monkey on your back. Vent your feelings with your fellow officers or your supervisors, with an understanding spouse, with some close friends, or your priest or rabbi.

Terror: Police work can be exciting, stimulating, and absolutely terrifying. I *still* feel the stress and excitement when I think about a shooting that took place over ten years ago. It's all right to be afraid, and a perfectly natural response to feel a surge of adrenalin when the alert tones sound, when shots are fired, and when you go into pursuit. It's your body's way of getting ready for action, of protecting you from injury and limiting potential damage. However, it can have a ruinous effect on your body when you experience that response day after day. You can't control the response, but you can control the way you recover.

When you experience a really frightening incident, you need to take the time to relax again. Take deep breaths to clear your mind and get your breathing under control. Get out of the car and walk a little bit, and it helps to talk it out by meeting with other officers in a relaxed setting. Talk about what happened, and how it affected you.

Be aware that adrenalin has a tremendous effect on your body, and the more intense the experience, the greater the effect. You'll relive experiences such as fights, shootings, pursuits and accidents again and again in your mind. Oftentimes, just the memory will be enough to create another adrenalin rush. A major incident can upset you in ways you don't even realize — making you impatient, short-tempered, and fatigued by interfering with your normal sleep. After such incidents, a good exercise session or a long run can help you burn off adrenalin and relax once you get home.

Mourning: As anyone who has ever attended a funeral for a peace officer can tell, law enforcement really mourn their dead. Police officers die from heart attacks, freak accidents, traffic collisions, cancer, and murder. We get almost daily teletypes about the death of police officers. Sometimes they are strangers — sometimes they are friends.

Some officers seem relatively unaffected by the death of another officer, to them it just means it's time to put the black band back on their badges. Some officers are saddened, and it's perfectly normal to shed some tears and grieve over the death of another officer. Some officers are truly devastated, so overwhelmed by the death of a police officer that they can no longer function. It's easy for us to relate to most line-of-duty deaths; you put yourself in their shoes and try to imagine what they could have done differently and speculate on what you might have done in their situation.

Most police officer deaths are preventable — the result of some errors, misjudgment, or just bad luck on the part of the officer who died. You have to accept the fact that law enforcement is a dangerous, sometimes deadly profession. Your life and the life of every other officer in the street is at risk. Learn from the mistakes of others, resolve not to repeat them, and you will increase your chances of surviving into retirement.

Stress from the Department

In one carefully controlled survey, researchers found that officers handled the stress of patrol relatively well. The stress that really tore up the officers were the stresses within the department (i.e., dealing with the bureaucracy, administration, Internal Affairs, personnel, and supervisors). This type of stress is relatively common in most work environments, but it tends to be exaggerated within law enforcement due to our restrictive policies and paramilitary structure.

Lack of Control: One source of stress is the total lack of control over many of the things that will affect you. You can't control who the department hires or why. You can't control who receives promotions, special assignments, training, discipline, or commendations. You have no control over the budget, the tax dollars going into the budget, or your department's purchasing process. Oftentimes the decisions of the politicians and administrators won't make any sense to you. You see what appears to be tremendous wastes of money, resources and time, and you are powerless to make any changes.

You have no control over your cases. You make what you think is a great arrest and follow it up with a great report. Then you find out that the detectives dropped the ball on a follow up, the D.A. filed it as a misdemeanor instead of a felony, the judge ruled against admitting some key piece of evidence, or the jury acquitted for some bizarre reason. You don't control the court, or the supreme court, or the legislators making unenforceable laws.

Those officers that feel stress over such events tend to take such events personally. It's almost an insult to them if the department doesn't buy new cars on schedule. These officers aren't taking responsibility for their own lives and actions and are losing touch with reality.

Over the years, you'll drive brand new patrol cars, and drive cars just one step away from the salvage yard. Some years the department's fleet will be in great shape, and some years it will be terrible. Learn not to worry about it, because you have no control over the state of the cars and shouldn't spend any time or emotions worrying about them. Your job is to patrol your beat in a safe and responsible manner. If you're driving a car with more than 100,000 miles on it, it's up to you to be smart enough to recognize that car's limitations. If there's not enough cars to go around, you might have to double up. If there's not enough officers to go around, you might have to cover another beat, and you better be smart enough not to get in over your head because back-up could be a long way away. Learn to concern yourself with the things *you* have control over, and don't let the things you can't control bother you.

Lack of Closure: We all need validation in our lives, the knowledge that our efforts have value and purpose. We would like to know what happens to the people we deal with. If you write a good report, it's nice to know whether the D.A. rejected or filed the case. When we arrest a bad guy, it's great to hear that he ended up going to prison. When we counsel some juvenile, it's great to hear that something positive happened ("Yes, ladies and gentlemen, thank you for electing me as your senator. As you all know, I owe it all to Officer Fred Smith.").

The reality is that most of the time, you never know what happened. Your case, your evidence, and the body you arrested, all go their separate ways to the detectives, the D.A., the crime lab, and the jail; and you never hear what happens. Some officers tend to get frustrated as a result. If this lack of closure causes you stress, *you* need to address it, because the system will rarely provide you with any feedback.

Take satisfaction in simply doing **your part** of the job to the best of your abilities. Be confident in your abilities and in the quality of your work and arrests, so if some other part of the system lets the bad guy walk away unpunished, it really doesn't bother you. If you find this lack of any follow- up causes you stress, make friends with the detectives and check up on your cases. Get permission to pull some of your case files from a few months ago and see what happened to the suspects. In the meantime, learn to give yourself feedback, take pride in your own arrests and work. Chances are that self-generated feedback is about the only feedback you're going to see.

Lack of Recognition: Virtually every operation of a law enforcement agency is focused on pursuing and apprehending bad guys. As a result of this focus, police administrators and supervisors are almost universally rotten at recognizing good work on your part. Added to the fact that you probably work for a big, cumbersome bureaucracy, chances are that the vast majority of the really good things you do will go unnoticed and without comment. Of course, when you screw up just a little bit, you'll hear about from everybody in the organization — from the guys in the locker room, to the sergeant at briefing, and all the way to the Chief's office.

Having unreasonable expectations of recognition from the organization just creates stress. Since you know that logic and merit seem to have little to do with administrative decision making, just assume the worst and accept the following as reality.

1) Your best reports will go unnoticed and unread.

2) The last person to whom you really gave a break will come into your sergeant to file a complaint.

3) Evaluations usually focus on the negative aspects of your performance.

4) The laziest, least deserving officer you know will probably get the next promotion.

5) Someone with absolutely no interest in the topic will probably get the training class you desperately need and really want.

6) Someone less deserving than you will get the "Officer of the Year" award, meritorious service award, or whatever.

7) Your regularly scheduled "merit" raise will be late (usually because someone just forgot or misplaced the paperwork).

The point is not to set your expectations too high. This isn't a perfect world, and sometimes things won't go your way. Accept it, and continue to be the professional you are and the community deserves.

Lack of Training: Most cadets are pretty impressed by their academy training, but once you get out into the streets, you'll find out exactly how little training you actually received. Most of the training you get in the academy is required by your state's laws. No more, no less! Like this book, no academy can take the time to teach you all of the specific techniques you will need in the few months they are given. All they can hope to do is teach you the basic principles and hope you can build on those yourself.

Once you get out of the academy, you'll go through a period of field training. Given the tight finances of every agency in the country, there is a very real drive to keep field training as short as possible. Field training in a small rural agency may be one week; in a large agency it's six months. My department has a 12-week program, which can be extended as needed. Whatever length your training is, you will find it too short. Without question, every trainee would benefit from longer training, but there comes a point where the agency says, "That's good enough, time to learn on your own."

Once you're through with field training, you'll find yourself in an even more frustrating situation. There are hundreds of classes every year on a huge variety of subjects. You'll see flyers and advertisements for classes and seminars, and you'll find your agency has little or no inclination to send you to any of them.

In most states, a certain amount of "advanced officer" training is mandated by law. This requirement can often be satisfied by sending you back to the academy for "legal update" classes. About the only other classes most agencies will send an officer to are those related to a new assignment: motor school for motorcycle officers, special schools for those promoted to F.T.O., sergeant, or detective, S.W.A.T. and gang schools for those assigned to special units, etc. If you, as a patrol officer, want to attend that great Las Vegas seminar on officer survival or the week-long class in blood spatter analysis offered only in Miami, you will generally have to do so on your own. That means arranging for the time off by getting other officers to cover for you or by burning precious vacation time, paying all your own fees and expenses. Worth the money? Certainly, but you have to pick and choose carefully, select only those classes that will do you the most good.

In addition to such formal classes, most agencies provide informal "roll call" training, usually five or ten minutes of instruction provided by the shift sergeant at the start of watch, sometimes done in person, sometimes by using the VCR. The problem with this type of training is that the sergeant may or may not be qualified to teach, and may or may not be interested in the subject. This can result in you being "taught" by a sergeant who can't teach anything, doesn't care, and is completely ignorant of the topic.

Some officers get really stressed out over a lack of training. I've heard the complaints a thousand times: "How can the department ask me to do (*insert the task of your choice*) when they haven't trained me to do that? What about the liability? What happens if I get hurt?" The fact is that the department expects you to be flexible and use common sense and the law in everything you do. Use your brain, shut up, and do the best you can in any assignment you are given.

In my department, I was sent to various schools two or three times per year. I enjoyed the training but felt it didn't meet my needs. Instead of crying about it, I got busy, took a lot of schools on my own, and went back to college until I got a master's degree. I bought a lot of books and tapes and spent the time to learn from them. If you feel your training is inadequate, don't get too stressed out, it's your own fault. Take some personal responsibility and get educated.

Lack of Equipment: A lot of agencies have poor equipment, especially when it comes to their cars. It's largely a result of the equipment being the one area of the budget that the administration can really control. Salaries and benefits are usually mandated by a contract, and the number of police officer positions is usually so politically sensitive that no chief in his right mind (*don't even think it!*) would ever propose cutting officers unless mandated to do so. But cars are a major budget item, and one that can be delayed into another budget year when things really get tight.

The same is true with your weapons and radios. It would be nice if your agency could purchase new, top of the line equipment. However, the reality is that your agency is likely to purchase the cheapest, satisfactory equipment from the supplier that offers the lowest price.

Again, some officers feel an incredible amount of stress from having "substandard" equipment. "What if you were driving in a pursuit and the wheel fell off?" they might ask. Well, then you might die, and it would be your own fault for driving so fast when you knew your car was unsafe.

You should know your capabilities and the capabilities of your equipment. If you have a car that you don't think is safe above 55 miles per hour, don't drive faster than 55 miles per hour. If you have a car that doesn't have operating lights and siren, don't respond Code-3 on any calls. If you are going into an area where you know your crappy radio can't "get out" to dispatch, tell the dispatcher where you are going and when you expect to get back into contact *before* you get into that area. Use your brain and take some personal responsibility for your equipment. It's your life! Don't lose it by stressing out over things you have no control over, or by depending on equipment you shouldn't.

Corruption: It seems that almost everyday, there are tales of law enforcement corruption — officers committing burglaries, selling drugs out of their patrol cars, arrested for rape, or indicted for stealing money from drug dealers. This is major corruption, obvious to all. When officers are this corrupt, it can cast suspicion and stress on all of us.

It can also cause major stress for an officer, especially when the corruption is within his own department. Think of the stress you would feel if you suspected or knew that other members of your squad were violating the law themselves. Who could you trust? What if your supervisor or even your chief were engaged in such activity? Who could you tell, and how could you stay out of it?

Right now, a sheriff in a small county in California is under indictment for gambling away drug seizure funds. Think of the stress created on those members of the department assisting the attorney general in the investigation. How would you deal with that stress?

If you want to avoid being corrupt yourself, there is only one course of action. Each and every time you see something corrupt, you need to tell the person involved that you see it, you believe it to be wrong, that you won't tolerate it in your presence, won't be involved in it, and will report it up the chain of command the next time you see it. Then you need to follow up, and report it each and every time. It will be tough to do, but you'll sleep better at night.

Policies: As a police officer, your actions are controlled by both the law and by department policy. Some law enforcement agencies have volumes of policy that detail everything from how and when to change your flashlight bulb to the correct way of removing staples. Others have very small manuals that leave a lot of discretion to the officers. Regardless, almost every agency will have policies on shooting, use of force, and pursuit driving.

Sometimes department policies can be far more restrictive than the law, and this can create stress and frustration for the officers. Imagine seeing a criminal fleeing past in a vehicle, knowing that your agency's policy won't allow you to chase him, but knowing that the agency in the next jurisdiction could and would chase him.

If you find you cannot work under existing policies, you really only have two choices: change the policy or change to a different agency. Changing policy is not easy. You would have to thoroughly research the law and similar policies in other agencies, write a new policy, support and justify the change in a logical manner (without getting personal or offending the authors of the original policy) and then submit it as a suggestion up the chain of command. In some agencies this might work, in others you probably don't have a chance. In either case, doing the work might make you feel better.

Bureaucracy: When you signed up to work for a law enforcement agency, you went to work for the government. Frequently that means working for a bureaucracy. Bureaucracies are often slow, ponderous, incompetent, and highly compartmentalized. Think about a "bureau" in the sense of furniture, a big dresser with a lot of drawers. If you're looking for socks and open the wrong drawer, you won't find any. That's what our agencies are like. If you need some equipment and go to personnel, you won't find it. If you have a pay problem and send a memo to the Records Bureau, don't expect action. It's a bureaucracy, and half the problem is finding the right drawer.

Now some agencies work a lot better than this, and the bureaucracy is smaller and more efficient. Just don't count on it. In most agencies, things run slowly. Pay raises and evaluations are long overdue, policy changes run a few months behind changes in law, and the new cars arrive about a month after the old ones are auctioned off (don't get too hopeful, because the equipment for those new cars won't be ordered until the new cars arrive). Dealing with this bureaucracy can be frustrating and stressful.

There's two things you can do to reduce this stress. The first is to learn everything you can about your bureaucracy. Learn what each of the bureaus do, who is in charge, and who is responsible for what functions. Learn the policies and procedures, so if you file for reimbursement for that Big Mac you bought to feed a prisoner, you know what form to use, who to direct it to, and how soon you should receive a response.

Last of all, you should recognize that when things don't happen or when the department does something wrong, it probably isn't done out of any ill feelings toward you. It is just done because it's a bureaucracy, and they're not very efficient at doing anything. It's a rule that is so important I've engraved it on my clipboard: "*Never attribute anything to malice that you can explain as incompetency.*"

Supervisors: When you're assigned to patrol, you will find yourself working for a wide variety of supervisors. You will find them under a variety of titles: Sergeant, Senior Deputy, Agent, Lieutenant,

Corporal, Senior Officer, Master Patrolman, etc. You will see supervisors who are brand new and grizzled veterans who made sergeant before you were born. They will cover the range of human attributes — kind and mean, ignorant and educated, intelligent and stupid, concerned and apathetic, loyal and traitorous, liberal and conservative, petty and fair.

There's an old saying that "*You can always tell a sergeant, but you can't tell him much.*" That's true for you as a patrol officer. You generally can't pick your supervisors (although sometimes you can pick your shift). You didn't train the supervisor, and you didn't promote him. You're stuck with him. But there's a secret method of working with supervisors you don't like — simply do your best, and make him look good.

Since he supervises you, you make him look good when you do a great job. If you make an excellent arrest, he's going to tell his boss, "Hey, my shift just made a great arrest." If you produce great stats, his shift will have great stats. If you consistently do good work, he'll have that much less to criticize and that much more to praise you about. You don't have to make friends with your supervisor, indeed, that might not be possible. But you do have to work for him, and the best way to reduce stress and keep yourself happy is to do the best job you can every single day. Do it for yourself!

Headhunters: In every department, there is somebody in charge of investigating the police officers that work there. Since that person investigates the affairs and activities of those *inside* the department, the function is usually called "Internal Affairs," and the actual investigation is called an "I.A." In a small department, the person responsible is often the detective or the detective supervisor. In a large department, there may be a separate "Internal Affairs Division" ("I.A.D.") or investigators assigned to a "Civilian Review Board" ("C.R.B.").

You may be investigated by other agencies as well. The public defender employs investigators who sometimes want to prove you did something wrong in making an arrest. The district attorney will also investigate complaints of police misconduct, as will the attorney general's office and the F.B.I.

Generally, you shouldn't feel any stress from these investigators unless you really did something wrong. Then you need to worry. Some agencies go out of their way to solicit complaints (the Los Angeles Sheriff's Department has a "1-800" number on a bumper sticker on their patrol cars), while others carefully screen and investigate *before* accepting a complaint.

Chances are you *will* be unjustly accused of wrongdoing in your career. Your best protection is a sparkling performance record and full cooperation with the department. Make it plain to the investigators that you have done nothing wrong and expect to be fully vindicated, talk to your union or association to make sure you are legally protected (they may provide you with an attorney or other representative), and cooperate fully in the investigation.

Stress from the Community

Some of the stress that police officers feel is generated by the community we serve. You bust your butt day and night to serve the community, and, instead of being appreciated, you hear some citizen make it all seem pointless with some ridiculous statement. I sat in a public forum after nearly being killed by a drunk driver who hit my patrol car head on and listened to a member of a citizen's "watchdog" group complain that the police department wasn't taking good care of our cars. After passing on raises for three years, I heard a newly elected city council member attack our benefits. "If you want to run with the big dogs, you got to get off the porch!" he told us. What he got was fifty angry, stressed out cops who can't understand why he was attacking the people that protected him. The very community you serve, its lawmakers, courts, media, and community groups can cause you more stress than all the criminals combined.

Laws: Politicians enact laws that they think will make them popular (and re-elected) by the public. The fact that the law may be unworkable, unenforceable, ridiculous and unconstitutional is not important.

Frequently the city codes you are charged with enforcing reflect particular concerns that matter only to a very few people. In one major metropolitan city, the mayor's sister ran a florist's shop and vendors "illegally" selling flowers on street corners became a major priority with one unit assigned solely to that function. My city has laws forbidding gasoline-powered leaf blowers, knives over two inches in length, drying garlic out of doors, using gasoline-powered skateboards on equestrian trails, and selling *True Detective* magazines to minors.

When we're out looking for burglars and rapists, these laws seem silly, but, obviously, they are important to someone who pays your salary.

Just remember, you get paid exactly the same whether you're arresting someone for murder or citing some gardener for using a gasoline-powered leaf blower. Your job is to follow instructions and to enforce the law. Those laws were voted in by the people (or their elected representatives), and if everyone agreed the laws were silly they would vote to change those laws. Since they haven't, you must do your job, as instructed, to the best of your ability, and don't get stressed out over laws somebody else wrote.

Court: As a patrol officer, you deal with the reality of the streets. When you respond to a drive-by shooting, you're the one holding a bandage against a wound and listening to the weeping of family members. When you arrest a suspect, you're the one that has to wrestle him to the ground and listen to his vile language as he curses you, your ancestors, and your entire profession. When you arrest a drunk, you deal with the filth and the odor of feces and vomit.

When you get into court, reality stops. It's a clean and antiseptic world where the suspects are all bathed and groomed and dressed in their Sunday best. Odors aren't allowed in court, wounds are usually healed, memories are faded, and color photos are often excluded because the sight of blood in living color might be too prejudicial for the jury to handle.

Prosecutors just don't seem to care and are often unfamiliar with the case they're questioning you about, Defense attorneys turn every cross-examination into a personal attack. Judges appear to fall asleep on the bench (no doubt tired from a late night meeting at the ACLU), and juries often defy all common sense. Stir in a system of parole and probation guaranteed to *keep* the most dangerous criminals on the street for the greatest amount of time, and you have a genuine source of stress for officers.

If that weren't enough, the entire scheduling of the court is inconvenient. The court system works banker's hours, usually nine to five on weekdays with holidays off. You may work those same days and hours when you finally have fifty years on the job and reach the rank of Junior Assistant Undersheriff, but, until then, every court appearance takes a chunk out of your days off, vacation, kid's birthday, or your sleep time.

Just to keep your sanity, you have to disassociate yourself from the entire court system. It just exists in a separate reality with no relationship to your job performance whatsoever. Go to court and do the best you can every time, and recognize the fact that what happens to your case once you're done testifying has nothing to do with common sense or logic.

Court decisions used to bother me. I used to wait out in the hall, or, when allowed, in the back of the court to see how *my* case would come out. Then I realized it wasn't my case. "It's The People of the State of California versus Joe Blow." As far as the court was concerned, I'm just another witness giving evidence in another case. I learned to testify and then walk out the door, satisfied that I've done my best. Learn to do the same, and you'll remove another source of stress.

Media: Your local media (radio, television, newspapers) is in the business of selling papers. Police stories are big sellers. Just look at the top TV shows or the top ten Hollywood movies, and you can see how fascinated our society is with law enforcement. The media likes to think that they always publish the truth, verified through multiple sources, but many times they seem to get police stories all wrong. Why?

Much of it is our own fault. The media encounters someone complaining about police brutality or other improper conduct. "I got beat up by the police," says a bruised and bandaged suspect. Then someone else steps forward, perhaps a friend or neighbor. "I saw it too," he says, "they beat him up for no reason at all." Now the media has a story, verified by a witness. They come to the police station and ask for our side of it, and the official Public Information Officer says, "No comment."

There may be no comment for a number of reasons. These could include:

a) An investigation is under way, and any comment could hurt that investigation.

b) It has become a personnel issue, and we legally can't comment on personnel matters.

c) The suspect was a juvenile, and we can't comment on juvenile matters.

d) No charges have been filed yet, and we can't allege a crime until we file charges on the suspect.

e) There is a lawsuit pending, and the city attorney has instructed us not to comment.

f) Your chief just doesn't like the media.

With no comment from the law enforcement agency, what do you expect the media to report? When you work with the media, be courteous and give them as much information as possible. If department policies don't allow you to comment on a matter, tell the media that and tell them why. "I'm sorry, I can't comment on those charges of brutality since the case is still under investigation, and the D.A. has not made a decision about filing charges yet. I will get back to you as soon as that situation changes." That's the type of statement that can be published, demonstrate that there might be another side to the story, and keep every officer's stress level a few notches lower.

Activists: Every community has its "activists" — people who try to affect the local law enforcement agency by becoming involved. They all have their own agenda. The American Civil Liberties Union (ACLU) is one obvious group of activists, but other groups might include: the National Association for the Advancement of Colored People (NAACP), Mothers Against Drunk Driving (MADD), the Taxpayer's Alliance, the Sierra Club, Greenpeace, People for the Ethical Treatment of Animals (PETA), or the League of Women Voters. Some groups cause officers a lot of stress.

These groups may feel that you and your department aren't doing something right — from brutality and racism, to a failure to arrest enough drunk drivers, to not running your animal control program correctly. They will hold press conferences, conduct picketing, and perhaps file lawsuits. Believe it or not, police in Azusa, California were accused of "excessive force" when they shot and killed a 350 pound bear heading into a residential neighborhood after trying to trap and tranquilize it unsuccessfully for hours. Excessive force? How else do you stop a bear?

As with most things, the only protection you have for your peace of mind is to consistently obey the law and follow department policy (a good insurance policy through your union helps as well). These groups are rarely attacking you, as an individual (although you may be the person named). They are seeking broad changes in government and society. They want to change laws, policies, and attitudes. If you conduct yourself in a legal and ethical manner, there will be little for them to pursue and they'll move on to other issues and incidents.

Stress from Your Family

As if all the other stresses of law enforcement weren't enough, many officers get a lot of stress from their own families. Law enforcement is "hell" on relationships of all types. You work bizarre days and hours. It takes some very considerate, understanding, loving people to put up with your schedule.

Spouses: Everyone knows that the divorce rate is high in law enforcement. It's not just a matter of schedules, it's a matter of emotions too. You will ride an emotional roller coaster, sometimes coming home elated or excited, and sometimes depressed or afraid. Sometimes you'll want to share your feelings; sometimes you'll want to be alone. It's next to impossible for a spouse to read your state of mind and accommodate your every mood.

You have to understand that your spouse has fears and feelings as well. Your spouse may be afraid every time you walk out the door, and the stories you share may just frighten him or her further. Sometimes your spouse may want to hear your stories, other times he or she may not want to talk about your work at all. Resentments can build, with a feeling that the other spouse is carrying an unfair burden for raising the family, and suspicions can be raised about coming home late or working with a partner of the opposite sex.

The only solution is good communication. Each spouse has to clearly communicate what he/she wants to share and talk about, and each must understand what the job is all about. Involve your spouse with the department, let him/her meet the people you work with, and if possible, set him/her up on a ride-along so he/she can see a little bit of what you really do for a living. It might establish the foundation for a much better relationship.

Children: Your job can also be confusing for your kids. There will be many days when you get up after they've gone to bed, and arrive home to go to bed while they're still in school. You won't be there for some of those Little League games and Scout hikes.

Other kids may see their parents every night at dinner; your kids may not see you at dinner for months. It can be hard for them to understand that daddy or mommy works at night and sleeps in the day, and hard to adjust to the fact that other parents don't carry guns with them all the time.

As with your spouse, you need to be open and honest with your kids. My kids grew up around the police station, and feel perfectly at home in a patrol car. They accept that as the natural course of things in our family. My kids know what I do and see me in uniform on a regular basis. In the middle of the week, my wife and kids often meet me for dinner and think it's great good fun when daddy gets a "hot call" and goes tearing out of the restaurant with the lights and siren.

You also have to learn to stop being a cop when you walk in through the door. It would probably not enhance family relations if you threw every guy coming to date your daughter against the wall and frisked them. Learn to relax and enjoy your family.

Parents: Screwed up relationships work in both directions, and the stress on families won't spare your parents either. It can be especially tough if you still live at home with your folks. Once you become a police officer, you fall out of their social patterns, miss meals with them, come and go at all hours of the day and night, and suddenly have many things you cannot share with your folks.

Some will be flatly opposed to you working as a police officer, will never understand why you want to be a cop, and will always feel that you've wasted yourself. I think it still mystifies my folks why I chose this profession, but they've been supportive and proud. Still, my dad asks me when I am going to get a "real job," and my mom has yet to figure out my duty schedule. Again, communication is the key to good relationships. Instead of letting resentment build, do your best to explain. If you can't get along with your folks, get out! You've got your own life, and your own income so find your own place to live and relax.

Stress from Yourself

Particularly for the new patrol officer, one of the greatest sources of stress is your own mind. You are constantly measuring yourself against some standard and driving for acceptance and respect. Every police supervisor hopes for personnel who are motivated, but when you push too far it can become unhealthy and a threat to officer survival.

Always bear in mind that since these particular stresses come from within, unlike every other source of stress we've discussed, these are totally in your control.

Ambition: As we discussed earlier, ambition becomes a problem in two ways, first, when you become too focused on peer approval and, second, when you become too focused on promotion. Peer approval and acceptance is part of a natural process when you enter an organization. The other patrol officers will be watching you and evaluating you on a daily basis — seeing if you measure up to their standards, pull your own weight, and can be trusted with their lives.

This becomes a problem when *you* feel you aren't measuring up and work harder at being accepted than you do at being a good patrol officer. It can become downright dangerous if you feel you have to prove your bravery. I once read a phrase in an officer survival text that said, "*This ain't the movies and you ain't John Wayne.*" I liked it enough I put it on my clipboard so I would see it every day. Just focus on doing a good job, doing your best on every call and every case. Peer acceptance will come when others see that you are doing your best.

Similarly, you can't be too focused on being promoted. Sure, it's a healthy and natural desire to go up through the ranks, but it is a process that is largely beyond your control. Prepare yourself with the best education, experience, and training you can get, and don't worry about when you will get promoted. If you're good and the process is fair, you will probably get promoted. On the other hand, if you're not so good or the process is unfair, you will *still* probably get promoted, but it will take a lot longer. Hang in there and do your best, and don't let the promotional process affect your life.

Integrity: Much of a patrol officer's duties constitute a test of integrity. A patrol officer will be tempted by it all: abuse of power, relationships, money, sex, and political influence. For some officers, this creates enormous stress. They seem to constantly wrestle with moral issues. "Can I date that gorgeous girl I just took a burglary report from?" "Can I buy that car I just ran?" "Should I make a bet on that horse the bookie told me about?" "If I accept that leather jacket, is it really a gratuity?"

If you're going to survive in this profession, you have to have a strong moral center. You have to know from the first day that your integrity will never be for sale, and you have to be convinced that there is no right way to do the wrong thing. If you're asking yourself the question, there's a good chance it's wrong for you, and you shouldn't do it. Save yourself the stress — and don't.

***Blame*:** Some officers seem to blame themselves for everything, or at least to accept the blame for others. People will try and dump incredible guilt on you. *You* are going to cost them their license if you give them a ticket. *You* are going to cost them their marriage if you report this crime. *You* are going to be responsible for an increase in their insurance rate, for getting them evicted, for costing them their job, for publicly humiliating them.

If that weren't enough guilt, some officers are always "what-ifing" themselves. "What if I had been there a little quicker?" "What if I had given better CPR?" "What if I had patrolled that street?" The fact is that life goes on whether you are there or not. Most of the time, you are not there when people are hurt or victimized. Sure, things might have turned out differently if you were right on the spot, but you have a couple of thousand people you patrol and you can't be everywhere at once.

You are not to blame for what happens to those you arrest or cite. They are. They are the ones who violated the law, and they are the ones who will suffer the consequences. You don't send people to prison, the judge does. You don't cost them their license, their poor driving does. It's a matter of personal responsibility. You are not responsible for what happens in the lives of those you take law enforcement action against; the criminals are. Take responsibility for your own life and lower your stress level another notch.

Dealing with Stress

So now we've cataloged dozens of sources of stress, the number one killer of police officers. All these problems and not one solution, only vague generalities. That's because there is no magic cure, no perfect solution for dealing with stress. Stress is highly individual, and you must take the actions that work the best for you. Here are some general actions you should take to help keep the levels of stress as low as possible:

1) Get proper rest. Make sure you have a place where you can sleep and not be disturbed, and take the time out of your schedule to get enough sleep every day.

2) Learn to relax. Take up a sport or a hobby, and get away from law enforcement in your off-duty hours.

3) Exercise regularly. You will look and feel better, function better, and burn off a lot of frustration and stress.

4) Talk out your stress. Discuss incidents and problems with your peers or supervisors, learn to communicate your feelings to your family, talk to your friends or your priest, but get it off your chest.

5) If you still can't handle it, talk to a professional. Your department may provide you with peer counseling, psychologists or psychiatrists who may see you in confidence without ever telling the department. They may be able to help you through your toughest times.

6) Last of all, get another job. For some, law enforcement is simply too stressful to handle. If it's costing you your health and potentially your life, get out while you can and take up some other career.

SURVIVING DISEASE

Every year about 150 law enforcement officers are killed in the line of duty. That's just a fraction of the estimated 2,050 who die each year of cardiovascular disease — heart attack, stroke, high blood pressure, rheumatic heart disease, and other related problems. On the average, a police officer dies 15 percent sooner than his civilian counterpart. What a shame to spend your life protecting others and only get to live 85 percent of a normal lifespan!

Many of these deaths could have been prevented with a few basic changes in life-style. If you knew that a particular activity such as serving narcotics warrants carried a high risk of death or injury, you'd take all sorts of special precautions, obtain specialized training and use special equipment. Here are some of the high risk factors associated with cardiovascular disease. Consider the special precautions, training, and equipment you might use to reduce *these* factors.

Blood Pressure

About 10 percent of the U.S. population suffers from high blood pressure, and many of them don't know it. There are often no symptoms. The only way to know is to have your blood pressure checked regularly. Start now. See your doctor, or simply have it checked regularly by your local paramedics. Your blood pressure is of critical importance to you staying alive.

Left untreated, high blood pressure can kill you one organ at a time. High blood pressure is a factor in heart attacks, strokes, and kidney failure; it can damage your nervous system as well.

Doctors know a lot about high blood pressure. They know that most cases can be controlled with proper diet and medication, and they know that one of the major factors that can elevate your blood pressure is stress. Consciously working to keep your stress at a minimum may add years to your life.

Diet

There's a lot of Americans who are overweight, at least 25 percent by most calculations. If you're significantly overweight, you have twice the chance of having a heart attack as someone who is not. Getting fat is a problem. We tend to eat what we can, when we can. Since we're often in a hurry, we eat far too much fast food. When it's late at night, sometimes the only thing open is the doughnut shop, which is hardly the healthiest of meals.

If you want to live a little longer, you can reduce your chance of cardiovascular disease by simply lowering your intake of sugars, saturated fat, and cholesterol. If you want a comprehensive diet, you need to see a professional (i.e., a doctor, nutritionist, or dietitian), and you always want to talk to your doctor before making any substantial changes in your diet.

There's no big mystery to eating a healthy, balanced diet. We get inundated with healthy dietary information almost daily. If you're too fat and not eating healthy, do something to change it. At your particular age, physical condition, and activity level, you may have very special requirements. See your doctor and get a diet tailored to your needs. If you need help, join Overeaters Anonymous, Weight Watchers, or

This kind of stop is awfully tempting but should be avoided.

Jenny Craig. If dieting sounds boring, you should take a look at the inside of a coffin. *That's* boring.

Tobacco

If you're a patrol officer, we assume you have some reasonable degree of intelligence. It doesn't take a rocket scientist to tell you that tobacco kills people. Tobacco in just about any form will shorten your life. If you smoke anything (i.e., cigar, cigarette, or pipe), you will face atherosclerosis, heart attacks, lung cancer, throat cancer, and a 70 percent higher death rate than your non-smoking peers. If you chew tobacco, you can look forward to cancer of the lips, tongue, and throat, not to mention some of the most disgusting teeth this side of Jurassic Park.

Most agencies recognize that a smoker is a rotten health risk. In many law enforcement agencies there is a non-smoker's preference, meaning that if there are two equally qualified candidates for the job, a non-smoker gets it over a smoker. Our buildings are becoming non-smoking areas, and many agencies have policies forbidding smoking or chewing on duty at any time. Insurance companies give non-smoker discounts because a smoker is at greater risk for disease and accidents.

If you don't smoke or chew, don't start. Don't even think about it. If you do smoke or chew, stop. Stop today before you peel another minute off your lifespan. Again, if you think you need help, talk to your doctor. If you have insurance, they may pay for a program to help you because it's a great investment on their part. If you smoke, stopping will extend your life more than any other thing you could do.

Exercise

Hand-in-hand with diet is exercise, another absolutely essential ingredient in your survival. Take a look at any jail or prison in the country, and you will see exercise programs. The bad guys that may try to kill you work out for *hours* every day. They get huge and strong, and probably put in far more hours on weight training than you could ever afford to.

Exercise is absolutely essential, not just so you can have half a chance at wrestling with some parolee, but just so you can stay alive. If you don't use your body, it will atrophy, leaving you weaker and weaker and more susceptible to disease and injury.

You don't have to become a regular at Gold's Gym to get into shape. What you do need is a mix of aerobic exercise to keep your heart and lungs in shape, calisthenics to build agility and flexibility, and weight-lifting to build your strength. Plan on thirty minutes to an hour per session, and plan on working out at least three to four times per week.

Most law enforcement agencies have some sort of weight room usually equipped with treadmills, exercise bikes, rowing machines, and creaky old weight machines. You can't just walk in and expect to have an instant program, it takes a plan. Get together with some sort of professional, either a trainer or a doctor, and put together an exercise program you can keep up for life. If you don't have access to any other professional, a few paid trips to the local YMCA or a health club can put you on the right track.

To have a successful, workable plan of exercise, you have to make it a part of your daily work routine. When you come to work, you probably do some routine tasks (i.e., check the mailbox, check and clean your weapon, shine up the leather gear, and put on the uniform). You take a certain amount of care with your appearance, and you take a certain amount of time to prepare for your shift. Make the lifetime commitment today to give the same care and time to your personal appearance and make sure that your body is dependable and capable.

SURVIVING SUICIDE

Ever considered suicide? Lots of law enforcement officers have, and according to some sources, at least two hundred a year kill themselves. A peace officer is 83 percent more likely to commit suicide than your average citizen, and, as a police officer, you are more likely to die by your own hand than at the hands of a criminal. Ninety percent of the time the officer committing suicide uses his own duty weapon to do the job.

There is nothing special about officers who kill themselves. Most are patrolmen, ages 30 to 45, most married and described as quiet, reliable, good cops. They kill themselves for the usual reasons — to inflict guilt and punishment on the spouses, children, enemies and friends they blame for their problems and to escape from a life they just don't want to deal with and can't figure out how to change.

In *The Officer Survival Manual*, Devallis Rutledge gives warning signs of impending suicide that you should look for in yourself and your fellow officers. They are:

Threatening Suicide: Take it seriously whenever anyone makes any statements like "I'd like to shoot myself," or "I don't think I'll be around here much longer." That's a person that needs immediate help.

Attempting Suicide: Unfortunately, most cops have seen enough suicides that they know how to do it successfully. There aren't too many survivors to help.

Depression: Ten percent of the population suffers from depression, and that means that ten percent of all cops probably suffer from the same. Some of the telltale symptoms are:

Sleep disturbances, especially early awakening

Loss of appetite and abnormal weight loss

Frequent indigestion or constipation

Loss of interest in normal sexual activity

Loss of interest in work, family, and hobbies

Lack of ability to concentrate

Lethargy — no drive to get anything done

Nervousness, anxiety, and sudden crying for no reason

Lack of communication with friends and family

Withdrawal from life and social isolation

Personality and Behavior Changes: Day in and day out you see the same officers. You get to know them, and you know their moods and habits. You should pay particular attention when any of your fellow officers exhibits sudden and extreme changes in behavior such as changes that seem foolish and totally out of character. You should be aware of sudden changes in:

Mood or demeanor

Sexual habits, or sudden promiscuity

Drinking or drug usage

Recklessness and impulsiveness

Work habits, absenteeism, use of sick days, or tardiness

Final Arrangements:

Sudden interest in making out a will

Revision and organization of life insurance policies

Purchase of a burial plot or similar arrangements

Making farewell phone calls or letters

Giving away valuable personal possessions

Making unusual cash gifts

Converting assets to cash to pay off mortgages

Setting up trust funds for children

If you are thinking about suicide or recognize some of these warning signs in yourself or those you work with, you need help. The first thing you need to do is to identify the problem. Then you need to enlist help to change your situation.

There are an incredible variety of resources that can help save your life. Assuming they aren't the problem that is causing you stress, you can turn to your spouse, your children, your friends, your co-workers, your chief or sheriff, a marriage counselor, a family counselor, a minister, a family doctor, a mental health clinic, a crisis intervention center, a psychologist, a psychiatrist, a neurologist, or a social worker. If you want to be totally anonymous, there are hundreds of suicide prevention centers and hotlines that are just a phone call away.

Nothing will change unless you take action, and killing yourself is no solution. *Make changes, get help*.

SURVIVING ACCIDENTS

Every year, about two hundred police officers are killed in the line of duty in traffic accidents, and over two thousand are seriously injured. Many other officers are injured or killed in accidents involving training, firearms, falling to their death, being struck by batons, breaking bones, dislocating joints, twisting ankles, or suffering burns or gunshot wounds. Almost every one of these accidents is preventable; most you read about, and they seem just plain stupid.

Traffic Accidents

Traffic accidents are probably your greatest risk. While you are certainly better trained and experienced than the average motorist, you have a much larger exposure to accidents. The average motorist doesn't spend up to twelve hours per day behind the wheel, isn't trying to operate a radio and computer keyboard while driving, isn't driving on emergency runs and pursuits, and isn't constantly walking and standing in traffic.

While you might assume that you were most likely to be killed during a pursuit or Code-3 run, statistics indicate that as much as 90 percent of all patrol car accidents happen during routine driving. Driving skills and dangers have been thoroughly covered in previous chapters, but here's a recap of the special risks you face as a patrol officer:

Fatigue: A lack of sleep is a chronic condition for many patrol officers. You need to recognize when you're tired and take appropriate actions to wake up: stopping, getting some exercise, getting some coffee, talking to your partners, whatever it takes to get the blood flowing and the brain working again.

Distraction: This is another specialty of patrol officers who are trying to do two things at once. Learn to operate the radio, siren control, and basic functions on your computer without taking your eyes off the road. If you've got something on your mind that's really bothering you, stop and talk it out with someone else, and try to resolve some course of action before you crash and burn.

Assumed Right-of-Way: Most drivers are extremely polite and careful around a patrol car. You can get away with tailgating and cutting people off, and most drivers won't even make an obscene gesture. You get into trouble when you take this courtesy for granted, assuming that other cars will yield to you in a patrol car even though you don't have the legal right of way.

Weather: Many patrol officers get into the bad habit of driving too fast and aggressively under normal conditions. When visibility and traction are reduced by bad weather, they still tend to drive too fast and aggressively. The predictable result is a lot of wrecked patrol cars. Good tires and ABS brakes are a poor substitute for good judgment and common sense.

Safety Belts and Shoulder Harnesses: In many states, police officers are exempt from the safety belt laws. Unfortunately, you are not exempt from the laws of physics, which state that if the car stops suddenly and you aren't safety belted, you get to play "Kiss the Windshield." There is no excuse for not wearing a safety belt. Utilize every safety device available, every time.

Pedestrian Hazards: Whenever you have to be out on the roadway for a traffic stop, traffic control, or an accident investigation, use common sense. Work in an area protected from traffic by your unit or by barricades, be as visible as possible to traffic (using your flashlight, reflective vest, or white gloves), and always look at traffic before you move anywhere on the roadway.

Firearms Accidents

Every year, police officers die in training accidents. Most of these involve firearms, used in role-playing exercises of some kind which are designed to simulate "real world" situations. Police officers die in simulated car stops, SWAT incidents, and when learning gun takeaways. Often both the victims and the shooters are highly-trained veteran officers.

Role-playing is great, it's an effective tool, but it has to be conducted under strict supervision. Live-fire exercise must follow the traditional rules of the range. All muzzles must be pointed downrange at all times, you fire only on command, you never aim a loaded weapon at anyone. That's great for target training, but since we try to prepare for the real world, we also conduct role playing exercises with the real weapons we use.

When you are going to do any training using any weapons, you have to follow a few simple rules.

1) You must be totally isolated from the public. Your training area has to be in a location where nobody can wander into the middle of the exercise, where no mistakes can be made because someone doesn't know it's just an exercise.

2) Someone has to supervise. Call him a range officer, safety officer, training officer or whatever, there has to be someone with the authority to watch without participating, to impose rules without being questioned, and to stop things immediately if needed.

3) Every gun is unloaded and every magazine, speed loader, and stray bullet surrendered to the supervisor. The supervisor checks every weapon, as does the owner of the weapon and every other person involved in the exercise. Only when everyone agrees that all guns are unloaded does the exercise proceed.

4) If you or anyone has bad feelings about the exercise, or any reservations at all about participating, assume that something is really wrong and stop right there. We train to survive, but it is equally important to survive training.

SURVIVING ASSAULT

I'm not an expert in officer survival. I don't live and breath tactics. As you have read in previous chapters on arrest and control, I am not a big believer in trying to learn specific techniques for dealing with specific actions of suspects. There have been many excellent books and magazine articles on officer survival written in the last two decades. Some of the better ones that come to mind include *The Deadly Routine* by Jack Morris, *Officer Down, Code 3* by Pierce Brooks, *The Officer Survival Manual* by Devallis Rutledge, *Street Survival: Tactics for Armed Encounters* by Ronald Adams, Thomas McTernan, and Charles Remsberg, *Street Work: the Way to Police Officer Safety and Survival* by Steve Albrecht, *The Tactical Edge: Surviving High-Risk Patrol* by Charles Remsberg, and *Total Survival* by Ed Nowicki. Every one of these books is worth reading, they will stimulate your mind, get you thinking in terms of survival, and teach you invaluable tactics that could save your life.

In addition to these texts on officer survival, there are literally hundreds of videos and books on specific aspects of officer survival. There are entire books on handcuffing, high-risk entry, traffic stops, police dogs, prisoner transportation, batons, biker gangs, edged weapons, prisoners on PCP, vehicle searches, bombs, prisoner psychology, raids, and snipers. Everything you read has something to offer.

I can't hope to cover in a chapter, or even in a single book, all of the tactics, rules, principles and information offered in these texts. What I can do is to offer a few concepts to head you in the right direction. Like many patrol officers, I am a generalist, and I believe that what you really need to learn to survive in law enforcement are the general principles of survival.

ANALYSIS OF OFFICER DEATHS

In any patrol call you are assigned to handle, there is a certain level of danger that you expect. Some tasks you automatically assume are more dangerous (such as when serving a narcotics search warrant), and you use different tactics and equipment to deal with that higher threat. Often our assumptions are wrong, as the most routine situations rapidly escalate into a situation in which you are assaulted. It is absolutely impossible to predict which incident will kill you (one officer was recently killed on a barking dog complaint), but it might be useful to look at what type of call officers were handling when they were assaulted and killed. The F.B.I's 1993 statistics are:

TYPES OF CALLS RESULTING IN DEATH

The investigation of suspicious persons or circumstances led to the murders of 28% of the officers killed in 1993 and was the source call resulting in nine percent of the assaults.

Narcotics investigations led to the murder of 15% of the officers.

Fourteen percent of the murders, and 21% of the assaults stemmed from "attempting miscellaneous arrests."

Disturbance calls including: family quarrels, domestic disturbances, barking dogs, and man with a gun calls, led to nine percent of the murders and a whopping 31% of the assaults on police officers.

Robberies in progress, or the pursuit of robbery suspects led to the deaths of nine percent of the officers and only one percent of the assaults on officers.

Traffic stops and vehicle pursuits were the source of eight percent of the officer murders and 10% of the officer assaults.

Six percent of the officers killed were murdered by ambush, entrapped and killed by suspects who premeditated the murder.

Handling a burglary in progress call, or actually pursuing burglary suspects resulted in the murders of four percent of the officers, and accounted for two percent of the assaults.

The transportation, handling, and custody of prisoners led to the deaths of three percent of the officers killed, and accounted for 11% of those assaulted.

Handling mentally deranged persons led to the deaths of one percent of the officers killed in 1993 and two percent of the those assaulted.

"Other miscellaneous activities" resulted in no officer murders, but accounted for 11% of the assaults.

Could it happen to you? The officers killed each year range from chief to patrol officers, from rookies on their first day to veterans approaching retirement. Here's what the average police officer murdered in the United States looks like:

OFFICER PROFILES

The average officer murdered was a white male, age 34, married, and high school educated.

Those killed had an average of eight years experience.

Eighty percent of the officers were assigned to vehicle patrol and were in uniform. Seventy percent were working a one-man unit.

Most were described as good natured, well-liked, friendly, and conservative in their use of force. Most were competent and received good evaluations, although a number of them showed a decrease in performance in the months prior to their deaths.

TIME AND LOCATION

Fifty-eight percent of the officers were killed at night, 15% in the early morning, and the remaining 27% during daylight.

Forty-nine percent of the officers murdered were killed in the South.

Most of the officers died during arrest and crime in progress calls, usually on streets and highways and parking lots, and usually within five miles of the suspect's residence.

PROFILES OF POLICE KILLERS

Trying to figure out who might try and kill you is just as hard as trying to figure out what call might be dangerous. The vast majority of the population would never even think of killing a police officer, but there is that small minority of criminals that would kill you in a heartbeat and then spit on your bleeding corpse. Police officers have been killed by women and children, by forgers and shoplifters, and by people in wheelchairs. The F.B.I. did a comprehensive study of police killers and found the following profile:

POLICE KILLERS
Sex..................... 96% male; 4% female
Age..................... 26 years average
Race.................... 60% white, 40% other
Height.................. 5 feet, 9 inches
Marital Status.......... 54% single, 32% divorced, 12% married, 2% separated
Education............... 60% high school, 6% college

So, the average person who tries to kill an officer is sort of an average looking white guy. On the other hand, the killers shared some interesting characteristics:

A majority of the offenders were identified as having some personality disorder (it seems kind of obvious that murdering police officers would be considered "antisocial").

The majority had criminal histories, and half either murdered or tried to murder someone before killing the officer.

Three-quarters of the killers said they were engaged in some type of drug or alcohol activity when they killed the officer.

Seventy-four percent said they regularly carried a handgun and most started doing so at age 18. Thirty-four percent carried the gun on their persons, 20 percent concealed the guns under their seats, and 12 percent on the seat of the vehicle.

Half of the killers said there was nothing the victims could have done to prevent their deaths after the initial confrontation.

TECHNIQUES FOR SURVIVAL

If you've read the previous 14 chapters, you already have acquired many specific tactics for officer survival. More importantly, you have some concept of things that can increase your chances of survival and mistakes that can kill you. Those concepts are the things that will keep you alive in the field. I could describe tactic after tactic, but each field situation is unique and different and requires a change of tactics to respond appropriately and safely. You have to adapt these general principles using common sense and logic. Here are a few of the general principles we've already covered throughout the text.

Fatal Mistakes

I've seen this same list in dozens of publications and books, the first being Pierce Brooks excellent *Officer Down - Code 3* (although this same list of mistakes could well have been written by Wyatt Earp, for all I know). Here are the ten fatal errors that have repeatedly killed experienced police officers:

1) INATTENTION: Failing to keep your mind on your job or preoccupation with personal problems into the field.

2) TOMBSTONE COURAGE: No one doubts your courage, but there are few situations where you should try and make a dangerous arrest, or approach a dangerous call, without assistance. Wait for backup.

3) FATIGUE: Police work requires constant vigilance and alertness. Falling asleep can kill you, and being asleep endangers you, your partners, and the public.

4) POOR POSITION: Never let anyone you are stopping or questioning maneuver you into a position of advantage. Never let a suspect approach your car; you approach him. Remember there is no such thing as a *routine* call or traffic stop.

5) IGNORING DANGER SIGNS: Recognize unusual activity, strange cars, warnings and hunches. Know your area and its people, and watch for anything that is out of place.

6) NOT WATCHING THE SUSPECT'S HANDS: It's the hands that will kill you. Is the suspect reaching for a weapon or getting ready to strike you? Keep you eyes on his hands and protect yourself.

7) RELAXING TOO SOON: Observe each situation as if it will kill you, never assuming it's another false alarm or routine call. Your life, and your partner's life, are at risk on every call.

8) IMPROPER HANDCUFFING: Properly handcuff *every* prisoner behind the back, palms outward, double-locked. Never transport a prisoner without handcuffs..

9) IMPROPER SEARCHING: There are many places to hide weapons. Criminals often carry a number of weapons and are able and prepared to use them against you. Do you search every person you take custody of? Do you keep searching after you've found one weapon?

10) DIRTY WEAPON: Is your weapon clean? Do you know it will fire? How about the ammunition? When did you last fire? Your life may depend on this weapon. Keep up your shooting skills, and maintain your ability to fire accurately.

General Concepts of Survival

With the ten fatal errors in mind, there are a few key concepts of survival we can review in the same manner. These are the flip side of the fatal errors, call them "keys for survival."

1) ALWAYS WEAR BODY ARMOR: Roughly 75 percent of all police officers killed in the line of duty were not wearing body armor. Fifty-six percent of those officers were killed by wounds to the torso, the one place well covered by a vest. With the light weight, flexibility, and economy of modern vests, there is no excuse for not wearing a vest. Comfort should not be the issue... vests are considerably more comfortable than bullet wounds, and you get to take the vest off at E.O.W.

2) ALWAYS USE COVER: Cover means a solid object that will stop bullets like an engine block, telephone pole, or brick wall. Concealment hides you but doesn't stop bullets. If a criminal can guess where you're hiding, he can shoot through concealment, but not through cover.

3) KEEP CONTROL OF YOUR WEAPON: Your duty weapon should be carried in the best holster money can buy, a holster

designed for that specific gun. Never lose or give up control of your gun. Learn how to protect your gun in the holster and how to retain it in your hand, and practice weapon retention techniques regularly.

4) WAIT FOR BACKUP: Never go in against known odds. Unless someone is being killed, and you have a reasonable plan and a good chance at rescue, always wait for superior numbers and firepower. Be patient and wait for backup every time.

5) HAVE A PLAN: You should have a good idea of what you are going to do on every call. Talk it over with your partner before you ever get to the call. Ask yourself the "what if" questions and be mentally prepared for any possibility.

6) COMMUNICATE: Talk to your partner and other responding officers prior to your arrival and while you're at the scene. Let everyone know your plan and your position. Never get out of the patrol car without the dispatcher knowing what you're doing, what the license plate is, and where you are.

7) ALWAYS SEARCH: Make a commitment to thoroughly search every suspect you detain or take custody of, no matter how many times he has been searched by others. If you find a weapon, keep searching for more. If you're searching a building or vehicle, keep searching as thoroughly as possible until you'd bet your life the suspect is not there.

8) ALWAYS CONTROL YOUR PRISONER: Avoid one-on-one confrontations, always use superior numbers of officers and superior levels of force. Handcuff every single prisoner without fail, behind their back, palms apart, double-locked.

9) MOVE SMARTLY: When you have to leave cover, make yourself a difficult target. Make rapid, unpredictable movements. If you have a long incident, change positions when safe to do so.

10) DUCK: Your profile is great for photographs, otherwise keep your head down. Approximately forty percent of all officers murdered are killed by wounds to the head. Present the

smallest possible target. Look around, not over, and observe from both low and high positions.

11) ALWAYS CARRY A BACKUP WEAPON: Fifteen percent of all officers murdered are killed with their own weapon. Have a backup of sufficient caliber to incapacitate the suspect. Carry it in a concealed but readily accessible position. Practice with it as if your life depended on it.

12) BE SURVIVAL MINDED: Think survival every minute of every shift. Be confident of your abilities, be determined that no matter what happens, no matter how badly you are hurt, you will fight back with all your resources and keep fighting until you win. Give yourself the resources of physical fitness, mental preparation, a solid education, and an ethical foundation. Know for a certainty that you will always survive and come back home.

OFF-DUTY ENCOUNTERS

One last topic for officer survival is that of off-duty encounters. Most officers have thought a little bit about what they would do if they suddenly found themselves off duty and in the middle of an armed robbery. The cop in us says we'd just stand our ground like Dirty Harry and kill all the bad guys. The reality is that you'd better prepare yourself right now to make some tough decisions about off-duty law enforcement actions. There are some basic questions you need to ask yourself to survive an off-duty encounter. Only if you can answer "yes" to each question should you take any law enforcement action.

What is the threat? Do you know how many suspects are involved, exactly where each is, and what weapons they have? Are you sure what is going down? Is this a confrontation between drug dealers or between dealers and undercover police? Be sure before you act!

Will my actions be legal? Not all patrol officers enjoy the powers of a peace officer off-duty. If you have to take action, including arresting and possibly killing the suspect, will your actions be within the laws of your jurisdiction?

Will my actions be within policy? Some agencies have policies that require an officer to take action off-duty, some agencies discourage off-duty action, others may forbid it. What does your policy manual say? Failure to follow policy might allow an injured suspect to sue you. If you have to take action, will you be violating department policy, or will you be in compliance?

Can I avoid detection if I don't act? Unless lives are in immediate danger, you are often better off simply being a good witness. On the other hand, if you're wearing your department T-shirt and baseball cap, or if the suspects are collecting everyone's wallet, there's a good chance you'll be identified as a cop. Many bad guys think the only good cop is a dead cop, so if you think you cannot avoid detection as a police officer you may be forced into action.

Am I properly armed and equipped to take action? Knowing what the threat is, do you have a weapon that gives you a realistic chance? Are you going up against machine guns with your trusty 2-inch? Are you trying to engage four suspects with five shots, or do you have reloads? If they submit to arrest, what are your going to do with them? Do you have handcuffs, or some other plan to contain them when help arrives?

Am I in proper physical shape to take action? Are you fully alert and physically fit or sick, fatigued, medicated, drunk, or disabled? Is there anything that is clouding your judgment or affecting your perception?

Do I have a tactical advantage? Are they alert to my actions or distracted elsewhere so I can surprise them? Am I outnumbered and outgunned? Do I have any concealment or cover?

Can I avoid being shot when the police arrive? Will the arriving officers recognize me, or am I in a foreign jurisdiction? Do I have my badge and I.D.? Is there anyway I can get a description of myself to responding units before they arrive?

If you have taken the time to think, plan, and prepare yourself for the possibility of being caught up in an armed robbery, assault, murder, or other incident, you will either take or not take action based on sound reasoning and common sense. If you can't answer each of the above questions with a resounding "yes," you should simply blend into the scene, utilize your expert skills as an observer, and be a professional witness and a survivor.

THE NATIONAL LAW ENFORCEMENT OFFICERS' MEMORIAL

In Washington D.C. there is a beautiful memorial to all the officers who did not survive, who were killed in the line of duty. The concept is similar to the Vietnam Veteran's Memorial, featuring a wide courtyard surrounded by a marble wall engraved with the names of the thousands of officers who have given their lives to public service. Visit it if you get the chance, it's a beautiful, moving place, one that brings tears to the eyes of most law enforcement officers.

The memorial is funded primarily by tax-deductible donations. You can send your donation to:

National Law Enforcement Officers Memorial Fund
1360 Beverly Road, Suite 305
McLean, VA 22101

May your name never be added to those on the wall.

DISCUSSION QUESTIONS

1) What could law enforcement agencies do as organizations to reduce the stress on their police officers?

2) List three causes of stress and explain how you would attempt to alleviate them.

3) Do you think "community activists" serve a valid function? What are their positive contributions?

4) What more could be done to promote physical fitness of police officers?

5) Do you think that an officer who attempts suicide should ever be returned to patrol duty?

6) It has often been said that handling domestic disputes is one of the most dangerous calls to handle. What could be done to make them safer?

7) Do you think that law enforcement agencies should encourage or discourage the off-duty involvement of their officers in crimes they observe?

The New York Post reported in June that Manhattan gang leaders were selling drug dealers exclusive sales rights to certain street corners in Harlem for as much as $1 million.

* * *

The Palm Springs Jail announced a new public service in July. Non-violent offenders can make reservations to serve their time in a tranquil area of the jail, out of the vicinity of traditional felons and midemeanants, for a fee of as little as $500, depending on the crime.

* * *

Schenectady, NY, jail inmate Jose Rivera Martinez, 33, filed a $750,000 lawsuit in February against the county jail, alleging that he was permanently disfigured in 1990 by the warts he received from eating jail-issue hot dogs, to which he said he was allergic.

THE FUTURE OF LAW ENFORCEMENT

LEARNING GOALS: After studying this chapter the student will be able to:

- Predict how the economy will affect the future of law enforcement.

- Explain the role grants will play in patrol operations.

- Theorize what changes and trends can be expected in the law.

- Analyze the trends in current court decisions, and explain how they could affect the future.

- Anticipate how prisoners will be treated differently in the future.

- Name the major changes that will occur in patrol.

- Identify the major emphasis of law enforcement agencies in the future.

- Estimate what kind of weapons patrol officers might use in the future.

- Compare and contrast the patrol car of the future to current models. Describe how they will compare to civilian vehicles.

- Describe how reports and investigations will be conducted in the future.

FUTURE TRENDS

Most of you who are reading this book are just entering patrol duty and can anticipate 20 to 30 years in law enforcement. The future holds incredible technical innovation and the potential for major societal changes. Gazing into the crystal ball, we can predict a lot of things that might happen based on the technology in place today. The changes in society are anyone's guess, and the chapter that follows is *my* best guess.

It appears that we may be seeing a conservative swing in society on a number of issues, in particular crime and punishment. With conservative interpretation of the laws, there has often been a lessening of individual freedom and lower expectations of privacy. Perhaps that's the price that must be paid for a "safer society."

A safer society seems to be the theme of the nineties, the basic platform of almost every politician. The call for safety brings a mixed bag of liberal and conservative notions, with the same people calling for both complete gun control and greater use of the death penalty. Tougher jail sentences and a new "three strikes" bill illustrate the desire of the public for an increased anti-crime stance.

There also seems to be a trend toward demanding more financial responsibility from government. With a slow economy, and a reluctant tax base, that means that great technological advances will be unavailable to most of us in law enforcement unless short-term cost savings can be clearly demonstrated. Expect police administrators to become real penny-pinchers, trying to squeeze the most service out of limited budgets, with efficiency being the key. That means there's great room for innovative concepts in the next decades, but a greater risk of failure for those who employ them. When you look at the future of law enforcement in this country, the driving force for every innovation is going to be money.

MONEY

As a nation, we have committed a great deal of our monetary resources to social programs: Social Security, Medicare, food stamps, housing, veterans, to name a few. The federal government is taking more and more of a bite from the average taxpayer and returning less money to the individual states. In return, many states are taking more and more money from counties and municipalities. Across the nation, law enforcement budgets are taking the hit, with lay-offs the most common result.

Social Security and similar programs are entitlements where funding is reserved and essentially guaranteed. I believe we might well see public safety receive similar entitlements — guaranteed dollar amounts (probably at levels below today's budgets) regardless of the financial condition of the local economies. This will force cuts elsewhere during times of crisis but also prevent windfalls to law enforcement during times of plenty.

Budgets

The resulting law enforcement budgets are going to be lean, providing a minimum of service and personnel. New technology will be out of the reach of many agencies unless there are clear and immediate cost savings to be realized. The number of personnel will be fixed, despite population growth, and the resulting tight job market will put law enforcement jobs at a premium, greatly reducing turnover of personnel.

Expect police administrators to cut corners wherever possible, leaving personnel positions vacant, scrutinizing overtime, actively promoting any revenue producing programs, pushing expenses onto employees, stretching patrol cars for many extra miles, reducing training to the minimum required by law, and deferring capital expenditures (building programs, major equipment purchases) for as long as possible.

Grants

With a shift of funds away from local government, expect the state and federal governments to offer "assistance" in the form of grants. It is important to understand that grants always have some strings attached: their purpose is to advance the agenda of those agencies offering the grants. When the National Highway Transportation Administration offers grants to assist in enforcing maximum speed limits on the nation's highways, it does so because it believes the 55 mile per hour speed limit is a valid premise in reducing traffic deaths and injuries. It doesn't matter if you disagree, or if there is no statistical basis for that belief in your area, the federal government uses the financial incentive to advance *their* beliefs.

The result of grant requirements is that outside agencies will have increased control over what your agency does. Your community will have less control over setting the priorities of your agency.

User Fees

"User Fees" are a hot topic in government — the notion that those who use a specific service are those who should pay for it. In law enforcement, there are many common user fees: drunk drivers often pay for the cost of officers and equipment responding to the emergency they create, people whose cars are impounded pay an administrative fee to have their vehicle released, applicants pay for fingerprint processing, violators pay to have corrections certified on vehicle violations, trustees pay for the cost of their incarceration, probationers pay for the cost of their programs, and insurance companies pay outrageous amounts for a copy of accident reports.

Many critics of user fees feel this represents an unfair double taxation — a taxpayer pays for all of the operations of a police department, then is billed again when he uses their services. Regardless, almost every agency charges these fees, and the number of services subject to user fees seems to expand almost daily. In the future, user fees will either be eliminated or controlled by laws. It may be only a matter of time before *everything* a patrol officer does gets billed to the user (i.e., charging every patrol call according to some rate schedule).

CRIME

Voters and politicians seem to be following up on campaign promises to get tough on crime. "Three strikes, you're out" and similar laws are establishing tough mandatory penalties for a variety of violent crimes.

Computers will represent another area of expanding crime law. This year, New York enacted one of the most sophisticated and severe laws in the growing area of computer tampering. Fines range up to $50,000 for those who alter or destroy computer data. It will take computer literate, sophisticated officers to enforce such laws.

Drugs

This country has spent a fortune in the "war on drugs," with little affect on either usage or supply. We have seen an evolution in the last two decades, where the possession of marijuana has gone from being a major felony to a mere infraction punishable by a negligible fine.

There is a strong movement among many knowledgeable people, including some top judges and law enforcement administrators (vehemently opposed by equally qualified people), to decriminalize the entire spectrum of drugs. It would still be against the law to be drunk in public, but the possession, use and sale of almost every drug would be decriminalized, regulated, and probably taxed. If this were to happen (and it is almost sure to happen within at least one state in the next decade), it could bring about a tremendous shift in the priorities and programs of law enforcement agencies.

Gun Control

Despite the best efforts of the National Rifle Association, the Second Amendment privileges of gun ownership are facing more and more restrictions. Initially there were bans on assault weapons, and the scope of forbidden guns seems to be growing daily. New restrictions came in under the "Brady Bill," placing far more restrictions on the personal possession of handguns. If the trend continues, gun ownership by private citizens may virtually cease. As stocks of civilian guns and ammunition dwindle, you can anticipate that higher prices will be charged to the limited law enforcement market.

Violence

America seems to be an ever more violent society. Violence is a dominant theme in music and entertainment, and random murder has become so commonplace that the term "drive-by shooting" has taken on a trivial, meaningless aspect. Human life seems to be valued less than ever before. Stories on murders are often buried deep in newspapers and rank far behind weather and sports in the television news broadcasts.

Our politicians have attempted to address this situation with stiffer penalties for most crimes and mandatory sentences for violent, multiple-felony offenders. As penalties become more certain, there may be a corollary increase in the willingness of criminals to eliminate witnesses to avoid the severe penalties.

Terrorism

According to research, trend analysis, and expert opinions, the next decade will see terrorist activity increase inside America. Terrorists will exploit sentiment against the military, spread their influence among emerging youth groups, and expand into new geographical regions. Special interest groups (i.e., environmentalists, pro-life) will engage in sabotage, bombings, and violent demonstrations, and the drug trade will increasingly use street gangs to dominate territories and prevent interference from law enforcement.

Death Penalty

Since 1989, there has been an almost exponential growth in carrying out the death penalty. Executions have become so common that they no longer command the great media attention they once did. The number of crimes mandating the death penalty have been expanded, and most of the constitutional limitations on the death penalty have been met by those states using it. As prison populations continue to grow, you can expect to see more and more prisoners on death row. With the conservative swing of the court system, the appeal process, averaging almost 17 years today, may well be shortened considerably. In the 1990s you can expect more executions than ever before.

COURTS

Primarily as a result of the war on drugs, there has been a steady, conservative swing to case decisions in the Supreme Court, setting the precedent for lower courts. Where once *Miranda* was inviolable, now there are certain exceptions. Most of the stringent case law on search and seizure are being tempered with common sense exceptions in the public interest. There is an ever-so-mild trend toward justice, with the idea of sustaining the conviction of clearly guilty defendants even though the police made a "harmless error." Certain types of searches without warrants have been allowed.

There seems to be a trend toward reducing prisoner "rights" (to cable TV, exercise, libraries, etc.). On the other hand, the courts have generally continued to support and even expand the rights of uncharged defendants, placing more limitations on the length of time and the conditions under which a defendant can be held prior to a judicial determination of probable cause.

Meanwhile, all of the traditional paperwork of the court is being reduced to electronic media. Traffic citations now have bar codes at the bottom for easier processing. Drug offenders are screened for probation with a computer-based program in twenty-six states — a program whose evaluations are advertised as 98% accurate. Trial transcripts, case law and penal codes are all being scanned, digitized, and stored on either optical or magnetic media.

Citations

Already the trend in traffic citations is to make the matter an administrative process rather than a criminal one. The days of a face-to-face confrontation between an officer and defendant are almost gone. In its place is a written deposition from the officer. In some jurisdictions, citizens ready to plead to traffic citations can insert their credit cards into a machine similar to an automatic teller, view a computer likeness of the ticket, and then plead guilty and pay the fine on the spot.

Video Arraignments

Today in Los Angeles, a pilot project uses state-of-the-art audio and video equipment to link jail facilities with the courtroom for "face-to-face" arraignments. This eliminates expensive transportation and security arrangements when arraigning felony defendants. This system reduced transportation runs by 38% and saved the county $300,000 the first year. With those demonstrated savings, expect similar programs to be adopted throughout the country.

Video Deposition

With personnel costs being a major factor in the budget of any agency and court overtime soaring out of sight, patrol officers may soon testify via video deposition at criminal trials. Both prosecution and defense attorneys could question an officer during his duty shift, record the questioning, and then present the tape in court as evidence. Perhaps some day the jury themselves will watch trials by video, rendering electronic verdicts from some remote location.

Electronic Transcripts

Court reporters now use computer-aided transcription, where the recording keypad is linked to a computer that translates the keystrokes into text. Experts predict that within a decade, voice recognition computer systems will have evolved to the point where they can accurately track and separate all of the conversations in a courtroom, perhaps replacing the court reporter altogether.

JAILS

America's jails are a growth industry. Jail and prison populations have reached an all time high. This is largely a result of mandatory sentences and strict enforcement of drug laws. Crime is a young person's activity, with the number of people engaged in crime dropping dramatically after age 25. As America's population grows older, a trend well documented by census figures, you can expect a corresponding decrease in the number of persons committing crimes. The predictable response will be to keep the jails filled by penalizing those involved in crime with longer and longer jail terms.

Design

In the jail of the future a prisoner and a guard will rarely ever occupy the same space. Modern jails are designed with wall-to-wall video monitoring, computer controlled tracking systems, and electrically controlled doors. In a modern lock-down facility, such as California's Pelican Bay, prisoners leave their cell only a few hours each day and travel a path of electronically operated doors to the exercise area. Such high-security prisons have virtually eliminated assaults against employees and other prisoners and are universally hated and feared by inmates in the federal system.

Prisoner Rights

There is a popular feeling among voters that prisoners live in some sort of health club. Indeed, California's 1968 Prisoners' Bill of Rights allows prisoners to watch violent movies, receive pornography through the mail, refuse to bathe, and lift weights. That law has been attacked with increasing political strength, coupled with demands that officials remove all weight-lifting equipment from jails. The trend appears to be towards more restrictive limits on prison behavior, a limiting of rights, and the removal of all or most of the weight lifting equipment.

Privatization

Increasingly, governments are turning to private corporations to run prisons and local jails and to provide local and interstate transportation of prisoners. Private industry can provide lower costs, since they rarely have the expensive employee benefits (i.e, health care, retirement, and wages) that government provides its public safety employees. Many of these operations are highly successful and well established.

In 1993, the town of Sussex Borough, New Jersey actually replaced its police force with private security guards, reducing the police budget by two-thirds. The project was shut down in less than two months by a court order sought by the attorney general. However, the objections seemed to have a distinctive "pro union" flavor to them. Although the project was deemed a failure, New Jersey officials continue to be contacted by municipal officials from around the country and throughout Europe. It is an idea that may become popular and could be modified to the point where private security officers provide all but a few key law enforcement services in the community.

PATROL OFFICERS

Patrol officers have come full-circle in law enforcement. Once the patrol officer was the core of the organization, and any assignment to detectives, motors, or other specialties carried a bonus of extra money. Now the LAPD is actively negotiating for a patrol bonus — extra salary for those officers who agree to work patrol. It seems the patrol officer is becoming a valuable commodity.

This is because patrolling has become a key aspect, a specialty of its own, requiring ever more knowledge and experience and the focus of community policing efforts. With the commitment of almost every police department to community policing concepts, the prestige, value, and authority of patrol officers has risen dramatically and will probably continue to rise.

Civilianization

The vast majority of a patrol officer's duties do not require a highly trained person with a gun. A majority of reports are simply exercises in documentation with no suspect to arrest anticipated and no danger to the report writer.

To reduce costs, many agencies have turned to civilian employees to perform tasks traditionally done by patrol officers. Non-sworn civilians handle a variety of duties in many agencies including: dispatch, laboratory work, custodial duties, parking control, and some patrol work under the title of "Police Assistant" or "Community Service Officer." These employees handle "cold" reports, low-level crimes, parking citations and vehicle impounds. As governments turn to such employees for budgetary reasons, you can anticipate fewer patrol jobs, the specialization of a patrol officer's job, and that the position of police assistant or its equivalent will effectively become the entry level position for those seeking to become a police officer.

Since police assistants shouldn't become involved in actual arrests, you may well see far lower standards required than those demanded of police officers, particularly with regard to the standards of physical fitness. Under the Americans with Disabilities Act (ADA), handicapped persons could well be hired for such positions, and it would then be difficult for officials to exclude them as potential candidates for police officer positions. Eventually, job standards would have to be based purely on actual job performance for that individual agency.

Education

As the job of patrol officer becomes more specialized and technical, you may expect to see higher educational standards imposed on entry-level police officers. Four or more year degrees and more academically challenging academies could become the norm.

Training

Walk through any video arcade in America and you can see the future of law enforcement training. Used in training commercial pilots and the military, lasers, holograms, and compact discs can create infinitely varied training scenarios, simulating everything from shoot-don't-shoot situations to pursuits and domestic disputes with incredible realism. The cost benefits and total safety offered may make video based training the dominant method for law enforcement in the 1990s.

Age

As part of a trend often called "the graying of America," the average age of many police forces has been rising. During the 1970s, the average age in police departments was approximately 27. Today, averages are around 39. Older officers are valuable, they tend to make up in wisdom what they may have lost in physical agility, but as they approach retirement, there will be a higher demand for entry level officers (because of tight budgets, retirements are exceeding the number of new hires in many departments), and a real premium placed on the remaining officers with experience. Those veteran officers remaining will be prime candidates for promotion within the agency.

Physical Fitness

A minority of agencies in the United States have mandatory physical fitness programs; most agencies try to avoid the issue. If an agency establishes a medical screening program and determines that 10% of the patrol force has high blood pressure that might interfere with their ability to perform their duties, could they afford to reduce their patrol presence by that 10%? If not, could you assume the liability of allowing them to return to patrol?

As a result, agencies are beginning to institute programs designed to maintain fitness and prevent problems. As the work force ages, you can expect more agencies to take a greater interest in health maintenance programs and more agencies to offer financial incentives to the officers who meet their standards.

LAW ENFORCEMENT AGENCIES

While the trend of law enforcement agencies for decades has been to provide more and more social services, in these years of tight budgetary dollars and rising crime rates, you can expect to see service cuts and a re-emphasis on fighting crime. Overwhelmed by the volume of crimes, many major agencies no longer respond to non-injury traffic accidents, have eliminated crossing guards, have victims of non-violent minor offenses complete their own reports by mail, and laugh at requests to assist citizens locked out of their houses or reports of barking dogs.

Some administrators see their mandate as fighting crime with all their resources, but this can be contrary to good community policing if the community expects additional services and doesn't understand their elimination. Nevertheless, given the absolutely grim financial shape of many local governments, service cuts will be the reality of the next decade in almost every law enforcement agency.

Community Policing

Community policing is obviously the hot topic of the '90s, implemented by almost every agency in one form or another, and a frequent demand of community activists. Expect police administrators to incorporate community policing into every aspect of the department, but with a primary emphasis on crime reduction and public safety.

A typical application of this type was in Reno, Nevada, where traffic officers met with residents and worked with city agencies to resolve local traffic problems. Through their program, the accident rate declined, the number of traffic citations dropped 50%, and the workload on the police department was reduced by diminishing or eliminating neighborhood traffic problems.

In Tacoma, Washington, citizens were assisted by police in organizing themselves into groups to seek solutions to gang activity. They formed a partnership of 92 organizations and neighborhoods fighting substance abuse and successfully closed down more than 250 drug-dealing locations.

With these types of programs, you are going to see more control exercised over law enforcement by the community itself, and less control over specific programs, procedures, and budgets by police administrators.

Consolidation

I'm sure that at one time there was some sort of specific formula that police administrators used for determining the personnel needs of law enforcement agencies. Something like, given a hundred police officers, you would require 10 clerks, 15 dispatchers, eight cadets and two administrators to support them. With the introduction of Computer Assisted Dispatching (CAD) and Automated Records Management (ARMS) that ratio has changed significantly. Because of computers and technology, that same number of support personnel might support five hundred or a thousand officers.

The predictable result is consolidation, eliminating "surplus" personnel from the organization by combining a number of agencies' similar functions under one roof. The dominant trend is toward regional dispatch centers, a single location handling the 9-1-1 operations and dispatching for every law enforcement agency and fire department in the area, oftentimes organized into a geographical "region." Similarly, regional databases are being established, integrating all of the records of the agencies in the region into a single database controlled by a regional systems manager.

This sharing of resources is not limited to just dispatch or records. Where once only sheriff's departments provided contract law enforcement services to incorporated municipalities, there is a growing trend toward contracting with other municipal departments and to the formation of regional "super" police agencies. These agencies work when "win-win" situations are created, where the contracting agency gets the benefits of cheaper law enforcement and the contractor gets the benefits of operating a larger agency. This provides greater flexibility and specialization than would be possible if they were limited to policing their own jurisdiction.

Privatization of Functions

Whenever there is a dollar to be saved, local governments have been turning to private enterprise to perform certain functions. Once purely government functions like: street sweeping, park maintenance, computer processing, trash collection, code enforcement, building permits, and even fire protection were successfully contracted out by government bodies. Increasingly, private enterprise has been offering law enforcement functions as well.

In addition to jail operation, entrepreneurs are offering to handle data processing, parking control, traffic control, helicopter patrol, canines, bomb responses, background investigations, drug testing, laboratory analysis, training, and even automated speed enforcement. If the price is right, budget-minded administrators are going to bite. The result may mean fewer specialized assignments for patrol officers, and a further reduction in police personnel and functions outside of the central function of patrol.

EQUIPMENT

The future of law enforcement equipment can accurately be predicted from the space program and military research. "Spin-off" technology has given us an incredible variety of products, from ballistic fibers to laser sights, from advanced communications to fiber optic surveillance equipment. The advanced technology available to law enforcement today is limited only by the budget.

Ballistic Protection

Ballistic protection once meant a bulky, stiff vest. Today, ballistic fibers are built into much lighter, more flexible garments of every variety including: raincoats, gloves, helmets, vests, and raid jackets. Lexan and similar clear plastics are made into ballistic clipboards, helmet visors, shields, and even patrol car windows.

As the material has gotten cheaper, stronger and lighter, it has more and more applications. The coverage offered by vests now includes side protection and groin protectors. If technology continues to advance, ballistic coveralls and uniforms are a very real possibility.

Non-Lethal Weapons

The future looks bright for non-lethal weapons, many of which are being developed through research by the Department of Energy and the National Institute of Justice. (The Department of Energy became involved because they developed a lot of this stuff as part of the security for nuclear weapons systems.)

Sticky foams are one potential weapon. These may be fired from a large "gun," from as far as 35-feet away and act like contact cement, sticking the suspect to the floor or to whatever he touches. Rigid foams also have potential as instant structural barriers, capable of freezing a suspect in place or blocking up doors or windows.

Already O.C. ("Pepper") spray has become the most popular form of non-lethal chemical weapon. It is now available in an incredible variety of delivery systems, from grenades used in riot control to a spray that uses a "shotgun blast" stream and a foamy base that makes the spray stick to a suspect. You can expect to see a much wider variety of chemical weapons become available to patrol officers in the future.

Chemical weapons may move beyond irritants such as teargas into the realm of drugs. One possibility is the synthetic narcotic Alfentenil. A quick spray can drop a suspect in his tracks but, unfortunately, tends to depress the central nervous system and slow respiration to unacceptable levels.

Lofentanyl is another possibility, incapacitating a suspect for up to two minutes, but delivery is a problem. One potential delivery system would be a dart gun to inject the drug, and proposals have been made to incorporate such a weapon into both batons and flashlights. Another possibility is a paintball gun which could splatter a suspect with a combination of a drug and DMSO, which would be immediately absorbed through the skin. The main drawback would appear to be public opinion. We readily accept doctors prescribing medicine in a patient's best interests, but that's a far step from having police officers inject drugs into suspects against their will.

"Dazzler" light and laser weapons are also being studied. They use brilliant pulses of light to distract, disorient, and control violent suspects and, potentially, even crowds. The concept has been proven with "flash bang" grenades currently in use by SWAT teams.

One non-lethal weapon already in use is the Taser (believe it or not, an acronym for "Thomas A. Swift's Electric Rifle"), a device that shoots a pair of barbs into a suspect's clothing to deliver an electric charge, immobilizing the suspect over 85 percent of the time. These and similar devices will probably become a readily available, common tool carried by patrol officers.

Another approach is the magnetophosphene gun, currently under development at the Oak Ridge National Laboratory in Tennessee, a weapon that delivers a pulse of energy from a range of up to 60-feet and can even deliver a concussion like a blow through a wall. The pulse of energy disorients a suspect and makes him "see stars." A thermal gun under development uses electromagnetic radiation to raise a suspect's body temperature, resulting in almost 100 percent incapacitation. The Army experimented with focused chamber devices a number of years ago, using blank ammunition or an explosive mixture of gas to create a focused shock wave that could blow in windows or knock a man to the ground from considerable distances.

Lethal Weapons

Recognizing that about one out of every four police officers is killed by his own weapon, more than 15 years ago, engineers first developed a "smart" gun that would only fire in the officer's hand.

Those first guns depended on a heavy magnetic ring to trip a safety device in the gun. There were obvious disadvantages: you had to have a ring on each hand, another officer could not fire your weapon either, the modifications were expensive, and if your grip wasn't just right (say, due to being shot), the gun wouldn't fire in your hand either. New technology might allow tiny little inserts in a ring to be recognized by the gun, or an actual port scanner in the trigger guard could read and recognize an officer's particular fingerprints.

Technology available today can put a laser sighting device on any weapon and within the frame of some handguns. Lasers can provide pinpoint shooting accuracy under ideal conditions, and leather manufacturers are now offering a variety of duty holster configurations to handle weapons with laser mounts.

Personal Video

Video cameras have shrunk to tiny sizes, so small that a camera can now be attached to the helmet or uniform of a patrol officer, feeding video of the officer and suspect back to a command post or to a recorder for future use in court. Audio bugs are available today, built into baseball caps, belly packs, cigarette packs and even Walkman-styled personal stereos. These units are so small that they are virtually undetectable, and they offer the ability to continuously monitor and protect a police officer during his shift.

Personal Tracking

The incredible miniaturization possible through advanced silicone chips has created a wristwatch that can relay an officers location, pulse, and blood pressure to a command post. This would allow dispatchers to follow an officer in foot pursuit, and send assistance immediately if the officer was injured.

INFORMATION

Information technology has "exploded." We live in a time when words like "information revolution" and "information superhighway" are being taken for granted. With these new systems, we are going to be able to track criminals better than ever before. It will be a rare event to have a criminal slip through the cracks of the criminal justice system.

Criminal histories from every computer system will be available to you in the station, and in your car, and perhaps in the palm of your hand. Identities will be instantly verified by scanning a single finger or thumb in an optical port on your citation computer or mounted in your car. Interactive computers will read the fingerprint and then produce previous booking photographs and additional information (scars, tattoos, addresses, etc.) for further verification.

Crime Analysis

The state of the art in many departments is a pin map. Patrol officers are expected to look at the colored pins identifying different crimes on a map of the city, and then try to predict the best places to patrol. New software uses complex, automated data analysis to identify clusters of criminal activity in a community, preventing and solving crimes. A pilot program in Illinois helps police departments plan crime prevention and interdiction efforts by determining when and where a particular crime is likely to occur.

Database Systems

At present, most agencies use computers to analyze information from investigations. Increasingly, those involved with narcotics investigations are linking into networks, allowing them to share information from multiple investigations in diverse agencies, exposing associations between people, property, and evidence. I would expect this concept to expand to the point where every criminal investigation from every law enforcement agency will ultimately be entered into some common database. Ultimately, the report you enter as a patrol officer may provide leads from common factors with reports from anywhere in the nation.

THE PATROL CAR

The patrol car you drive in the next few years is going to turn into an interactive electronic suite. Cellular phones are becoming standard equipment, allowing officers access to people without radios, and allowing more private conversation with dispatchers and supervisors. The video camera and recorder has become state of the art, with tiny cameras mounted out of sight just below the windshield, and armored VCRs mounted in the trunk. Computers and sophisticated radios allow for advanced confidential communications abilities and report writing that can be instantly transmitted to others.

Mobile Data Terminals

At the present, mobile data terminals (MDT's) are used primarily in very large agencies with sophisticated dispatching operations. As the technology improves, you can expect to see MDT's in every patrol car, linking every officer directly into local and national computer systems.

Heads Up Displays

The inside of patrol cars is getting flooded with data, and looking down at the screen of an MDT to get information on a call, read the comments, and write a report can be a major and dangerous distraction. The answer is the Heads Up Display (HUD) which uses the same technology used by military fighter pilots to project the information on a screen directly in front of the driver. HUDs in use today cannot only project the computer screen, but also show the speed display of a radar unit and the patrol car's own speedometer.

License Plate Scanners

A camera, scanner, and optical character recognition software already exist today that allow a unit mounted at the side of the road to read and recognize 60% of the license plates that pass by. The system could then alert officers at a checkpoint or tollbooth ahead that a stolen car or wanted person was headed in their directions. The system works today, but so overloads the state license plate system that it can't be used. As the software improves, and hardware allows for greater data flows, such systems may see widespread use at every intersection, precisely tracking the movement of stolen cars.

Researchers foresee the time when a tiny version of the camera and scanner can be mounted on the front of a patrol car, allowing the patrol car to scan every plate in sight, and notifying the officer of the location and direction of any wanted license plate.

Lasers

In the field of speed detection, lasers have made huge inroads into the radar market, with more than 2,000 units in operation in over 40 states. Lasers appear to give better target identification than radar and are less easily detected (although the consumer market has been flooded with laser detectors). Costs for laser speed measurement units have dropped dramatically while the quality has improved, and lasers will probably be the standard for the next decade.

Blood Alcohol Analysis

Blood alcohol analysis machines are already being mounted in the trunks of patrol cars and will only get smaller and more accurate with the passage of time. Passive alcohol systems which measure the blood alcohol on the breath of a person have been reduced to the size of a candy bar and are fairly accurate. The sensors are being reduced in size, and could ultimately be mounted on your cuff or the entire unit reduced to the size of a pencil.

Tracking Devices

The Automatic Vehicle Location System is made up of individual vehicle tracking units and a control center in dispatch. The in-vehicle unit provides tracking information such as speed, direction, and status. The control center is a computerized mapping and monitoring station that allows dispatchers and supervisors to view all patrols cars at the same time and displays a single map of your jurisdiction. The system includes the use of two-way radio, cellular networks, and satellite communications. With this system, the dispatcher can identify and locate any patrol unit within 20 feet of its true location. To help guide the patrol officer, the system includes mobile data terminals, mappings systems, dead reckoning devices, and alarms systems with various sensors, panic buttons, and vehicle sirens.

Prisoner Control

While front seat safety air bags that deploy on impact are now state of the art on all patrol cars, the wave of the future is in the back seat. The current state of the art is a fiberglass unit that replaces the entire back seat. This has recesses for the prisoner's hands behind his back, safety restraints, and offers easy cleaning and no place to hide contraband.

A new system has a large air bag designed to subdue violent prisoners in the back seat of the patrol car. Activated by the officer, a fan or compressor would inflate a large, heavy bag that would slowly pin any out-of-control prisoner to the back seat of the patrol car.

Look for a video camera watching the prisoner as well. The image could be recorded as part of the report (documenting the prisoner's condition, sobriety, and the fact that he was not abused), could record any conversations between prisoners, and could be transmitted live to the station so the prisoner could also be monitored by supervisors and dispatchers.

CIVILIAN VEHICLES

Automotive technology has made tremendous leaps in just the last few years. Cars are incredibly comfortable, quiet, and fast. Many sports cars, and a few unlikely looking sedans, will do over 150 miles per hour, far faster than most patrol cars. With the widespread use of ABS brakes, these cars could be just about impossible to follow in a traditional pursuit. Police are going to have to develop new policies, tactics, and technologies to stop the cars of tomorrow.

Disabling Devices

One concept that appears could actually reach production is a vehicle disabling system. This would allow police to electronically disable another vehicle from the patrol car, which could virtually eliminate many pursuits and make felony stops and traffic stops more safe.

Tracking Devices

Two devices are currently on the market that allow law enforcement to electronically locate stolen vehicles. One system uses satellites, the other radio repeater towers, and both appear to work well with high recovery rates. Given the success of these systems, you may well see them incorporated into vehicles at the time of manufacture with a minimal cost in comparison to the $600 or so for aftermarket installations.

Security Systems

Today almost every car on the market is available with an optional alarm system from the manufacturer, and many cars have them as part of the standard equipment. With the incorporation of computers into the alarm systems, and silicon chips integrated into the keys, the theft of new cars will become increasingly difficult. Those stealing them will be sophisticated criminals, difficult to detect, difficult to catch, and probably unafraid of police. Tomorrow's car thief may be a far greater threat to the average patrol officer than the thief of today.

REPORT WRITING

The report writing style of the future will be in "plain" English — reports written just like you speak. That's because, in the future, you may well simply dictate your first draft to a computer, thus allowing you, your supervisor, or investigators to clean up and edit the report before you sign and file it. The medium of reports tomorrow is electronic, on tape and optical disc.

Citations

The citation book of tomorrow will be a far cry from the leather book with a pad of citations we are all familiar with. Technology in use today has reduced the process to a citation book sized computer and printer. You key in specific information on a tiny keypad and input driver's license information and vehicle registrations with a single swipe of an identification card with a magnetic stripe. The computer prints out the violator's copy on the spot, and the department's "copies" are downloaded automatically at the end of the day into the department's computer. A future improvement will be the addition of a single digit port scanner and optical window in which the violator will place his thumb or forefinger for electronic fingerprint identification of his identity.

Computers

Computers are changing faster than monthly magazines can keep pace. Since word processing is a relatively simple task for most computers, even the most basic of computers can be used for writing reports and producing other law enforcement documents. Once reduced to a report, it's an easy matter for appropriate programming to extract data and compile statistics for the department.

Computers have shrunk from towers, to desktops, to laptops, to palmpads. A palm-sized unit can incorporate a keyboard, or may feature a touch sensitive screen allowing you to fill in computer generated forms, and even sketch crime scenes and accident diagrams. When you return to the station, you can communicate with the department's database and printers with an infrared link and never connect a cable.

Software isn't limited to reports, either. Today's library of software includes: accident reconstruction, field interview database, case law, Identikits, computer mug shots, case management, and crime scene sketch. The software of tomorrow is virtually unlimited.

Dictation

Currently, voice recognition technology exists that can turn what you say into printed words. The technology is limited, however. The most sophisticated system has only a 60,000 word vocabulary, must be "trained" for each user, and the speaker has to pause after every word. Dictating a police report in this manner would be difficult. Experts estimate that a "what you say is what you get" system that is fully functional, reliable, and economical is only a decade away. When that occurs, the emphasis in law enforcement skills may shift from the ability to write, to the ability to organize and narrate stories.

INVESTIGATIONS

Tomorrow's patrol officer may be armed with a fascinating variety of tools to conduct field investigations. Hand held type vacuums may be able to sweep a surface for particles of a suspect's hair or skin flakes, providing identifying genetic material for DNA analysis.

A video camera, miniaturized and with almost unlimited recording capacity, will become the standard means of recording a crime scene. This will provide a visual record for a judge and jury, putting them right at the location as you search and discover evidence.

TOMORROW

The technological future of law enforcement is brighter than it has ever been. We're at the forefront of many kinds of technology, living in an information revolution, driving a pursuit equipped vehicle on the information superhighway. It should be fun!

Some aspects of law and the economy may appear pretty bleak, but the future for patrol officers will be promising. There has always been a need for patrol officers, and there always will be a need for patrol officers. The greed and stupidity of criminals throughout our society are the best job insurance we could have. Enjoy tomorrow, and enjoy a career patrolling your community.

DISCUSSION QUESTIONS

1) Do you think your local law enforcement agency's budget is funded appropriately? Why or why not?

2) Do you think user fees are fitting, or do they really represent improper double taxation?

3) Do you support decriminalization for drug offenses? Why or why not?

4) What effect will terrorism have on patrol operations in your community in the future?

5) Do you think gun control works?

6) Do you think prisoners should be allowed access to weight lifting equipment in prison? What limitations would you place on their use?

7) Do you think it is appropriate for officers in the field to have complete access to criminal histories of suspects, or is it a violation of the suspect's privacy?

8) Do you think continuous video monitoring of a patrol officer is appropriate, or is *that* a violation of the officers' and suspects' privacy?

9) Should a handicapped person be considered for a patrol officer position? Why or why not?

10) Should the government place a limit on the maximum speed a car can be designed to go?

INDEX

America's Most Popular
Practical Police Books